The Best of
THE
PACIFIC
COAST

ALSO BY GERALD W. OLMSTED

The Morrow Guide to Backcountry Europe
Fielding's Lewis and Clark Trail

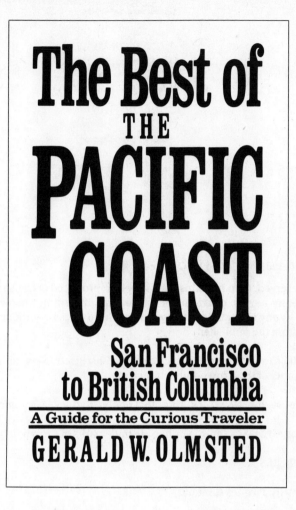

The Best of
THE
PACIFIC COAST

San Francisco to British Columbia

A Guide for the Curious Traveler

GERALD W. OLMSTED

Crown Trade Paperbacks
New York

꙳꙳꙳꙳꙳꙳꙳꙳꙳꙳

*To the memory of
Franklin Osburn Olmsted,
who had a great curiosity
about this world*

꙳꙳꙳꙳꙳꙳꙳꙳꙳꙳

Published by Crown Publishers, Inc., 201 East 50th Street, New York, New York 10022. Member of the Crown Publishing Group.

Random House, Inc. New York, Toronto, London, Sydney, Auckland

CROWN TRADE PAPERBACKS and colophon are trademarks of Crown Publishers, Inc.

Printed in the U.S.A.

Cartography by Jacques Chazaud

Library of Congress Cataloging-in-Publication Data
Olmsted, Gerald W.
    The best of the Pacific coast: San Francisco to British Columbia/
  by Gerald W. Olmsted.
        Includes index.
        1. Northwest   Coast   of   North America—Description   and   travel—
Guidebooks.   I. Title.
F852.3.O46   1989
917.95'0443—dc19   88-18933
ISBN 0-517-57159-5

10   9   8   7   6   5

CONTENTS

INTRODUCTION

The bear went over the mountain,
The bear went over the mountain,
The bear went over the mountain,
To see what he could see.

Winnie the Pooh's inquisitiveness got him nothing but a bee-stung nose, and according to the old song, the bear found only "the other side of the mountain." Yet it is exactly this gift or curiosity that makes travel so much fun. What's around the next bend, over the next hill? What does the country look, feel, and smell like, and why? What geologic events shaped the earth, and how did the climate change it? Has the land been tamed or exploited, and if so, how? Who lives there now, what do they do, and what's on their minds? What is their history and their folk-lore; what is unique about their life-style, the food they eat, and the way they play? And where can I play? In these pages I've tried to provide some answers to these questions, but, more important, I have tried to pique your curiosity in the hope that you'll discover for yourself the hidden charms of this lovely coast.

Fortunately (or unfortunately, depending on your circum-stances) having a curious mind impels you to slow down, to look for the small things that collectively define the nature of a coun-try. The Chinese have a saying, "You can't see a flower from a galloping horse," and so it is with a trip along the Northwestern Pacific Coast. To discover its charms requires that you allow plenty of time to travel the rural highways, back roads, and country lanes, to poke into nooks and crannies, and to keep an observant mind open for the unexpected: a sudden burst of sunlight on a cresting wave, the cast of a shadow on a rocky cliff, the spout of a whale, the skittering of a deer, or the screech of an eagle. To understand this country is to paddle a canoe, fish alongside a local, tour a mill, attend a concert, or buy a work of art from the person who made it. It is to visit an Indian reservation, have breakfast at the farm town coffee shop with all the pickups parked out front, or enjoy a drink at the saloon where the loggers go after a day in the woods. And it is to visit the museum in the onetime home of the richest man in town and chat with the docent or to pace the deck of a ferry with a fellow who is doing nothing more exciting than going home to his place in the country. To know this coast is to examine the bugs in a rain forest and to capture the magic of the green flash of a Pacific sunset.

The thousand-odd miles of Northwestern Pacific Coast are laced with fishing villages, mill towns, Indian reservations, logging camps, and farming communities. There are lighthouses to explore, tide pools to examine, whales to watch, boats to sail on, waves to ride, trails to walk, glaciers to climb, fish to catch, and beaches to comb. Best of all, there are few parking meters and fewer traffic lights and, in some places, hardly even a road. If you share my premise that most cities in North America are pretty much alike, you'll agree that it is the upcountry where you must look to find the uniqueness of an area, and that is exactly the kind of place we are going to explore. Yet much of this trip is through resort country with golf, swimming, tennis, scuba diving, water skiing, even cricket and croquet. But we will also visit some ghost towns and, just to find the exception that proves the rule, explore one of the West Coast's most cosmopolitan cities.

We'll find cozy B&Bs and country inns and dine in excellent restaurants, sample the finest wines the world has to offer, and, in one instance, capture the sybaritic life of a first-class resort thirty miles from the nearest road. You don't have to be the outdoors type to enjoy this adventure, but you'll probably be one when you finish, for although humans have done much to make this trip easy and comfortable, it is, in the end, seeing the spectacle of what nature created along this magnificent coast that is the raison d'être for making the journey.

SOME NOTES ABOUT FOOD AND LODGING

DINING

Only the more unique restaurants are listed, grouped according to price (dinner for two including wine and tip): ● Inexpensive (less than $30), ●● Moderate (less than $60), and ●●● Expensive. Excellent food (especially salmon and red snapper) is available all along the route. Most restaurants are "fully licensed," to use the Canadian term, meaning beer, wine, and cocktails are served.

LODGING

Lodging is listed according to price (room for two during high season): ✔ Inexpensive (less than $40), ✔✔ Moderate (less than $85), ✔✔✔ Expensive, and ✔✔✔✔ Luxury (more than $150). Listings are approximate only. Variations in individual rooms, seasonal discounts, and the inclusion of cooking facilities often make rooms cost more or less than indicated. Ordinary motels are listed only for stopovers where more interesting accommodations are generally not available. Only those B&Bs having more than four rooms are listed. People of all ages are welcome at youth hostels (bring your own sheet/blanket). Condo resorts (where you rent someone's apartment) are becoming quite popular. Many require multinight bookings. Vacation rentals, where a local real estate firm rents out homes in the area (bring your own sheets), are also becoming more common but are not included here because they appeal mainly to vacationers, not travelers.

Reservations are recommended during July and August and

on other weekends when the weather is nice, especially at the following places: Mendicino, California; northern Oregon coastal communities; Olympic National Park, Washington; Port Townsend, Washington; La Conner, Washington; the San Juan Islands, Washington; and the Gulf Islands, British Columbia. It is always best to make reservations at the fancier hotels and out-of-the-way fishing resorts.

CAMPING

Only state and federal campgrounds are listed. There are also a few county parks and hundreds of private RV parks along the route.

National Park Service   No reservations accepted.

Parks Canada   No reservations accepted.

National Forest Service   No reservations accepted.

Provincial Parks   No reservations accepted.

California State Parks   Reservations (with deposit) can be made for most campgrounds through a firm called Mistix: P.O. Box 85705, San Diego, California 92138. Allow ten days. Phone reservations charged to Visa and MasterCard accepted: (800) 446-7275. Many campgrounds have hookups and showers. Some parks offer "Enroute Camping," where day-use parking lots are opened for overnight RV use. Sites must be vacated during the day. Parks along our route offering this service are Van Damme, Westport-Union Landing, Benbow Lake, Humboldt Lagoons, and Humboldt Redwoods.

Oregon State Parks   Mail reservations (with deposit) accepted for camping between Memorial Day and Labor Day at Sunset Bay near Coos Bay, Beachside, Beverly Beach and South Beach near Newport, Devil's Lake at Lincoln City, Cape Lookout near Tillamook, and Fort Stevens near Astoria. Write to the address listed in text. All others are first-come, first-served. Most campgrounds (except walk-in) have hookups and showers.

Washington State Parks   Mail reservations (with deposit) accepted for camping between Memorial Day and Labor Day at Fort Canby near Long Beach, Fort Flagler and Fort Worden near Port Townsend, and Moran on Orcas Island. Write at least fourteen days in advance to the address listed in text. All other campgrounds are first-come, first-served. About half the campgrounds have hookups and showers.

PART ONE

The California Coast

MARVELOUS WEST MARIN

The Parklands Next Door

The **Golden Gate** marks the southern boundary of what I call the Northwestern Pacific Coast, that part of the edge of the North American continent where the Spanish influence was almost nil. This waterway is the verge between two climates that separate two distinct cultures. Mediterranean best describes the land to the south. The grass is yellow, and shrubs have small resinous leaves to withstand the summer drought. It is farming and ranching country, the kind of place the Spaniards knew something about. By contrast, forests dominate the land to the north, nurtured by winter rains and the fog that hangs around much of the year. The sea too is colder, a place where the fur-trapping Russians, and the Scots and English who followed, knew they would find seal and sea otter. There is little mystery, therefore, why it happened that Catherine the Great's hunters worked their way south along the Pacific Coast, stopping at Bodega Bay, barely forty-five miles north of here, and the Spanish *vaqueros* and the *padres* who followed them came up from the south, building their northernmost mission at Sonoma, a village at roughly the same latitude. The Golden Gate, it seems, is more than a spectacularly beautiful waterway. It marks the line where each culture had simply come to the end of the kind of place in which it felt comfortable living.

This is not to say that Spain never had an influence north of the Golden Gate. We'll encounter numerous places bearing names given by early Spanish navigators. But due to a combina-

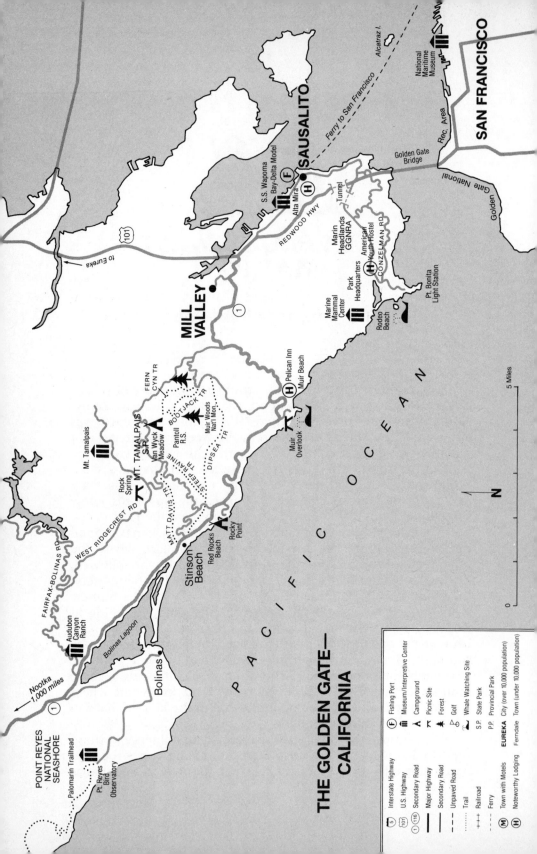

THE GOLDEN GATE— CALIFORNIA

SAN FRANCISCO

National Maritime Museum

Alcatraz I.

Ferry to San Francisco

Rec. Area

Golden Gate Bridge

Golden Gate National

SAUSALITO

Ⓕ S.S. Wapoma
Bay-Delta Model
Ⓗ Alta Mira

REDWOOD HWY

Tunnel

Marin Headlands GGNRA

American Youth Hostel Ⓗ

CONZELMAN RD

Park Headquarters

to Eureka

101

MILL VALLEY

1

Marine Mammal Center

Rodeo Beach

Pt. Bonita Light Station

FERN CYN TR

Pelican Inn Ⓗ
Muir Beach

BOOTJACK TR

Muir Woods Nat'l Mon.

Pantoll R.S.

Mt. Tamalpais

MT. TAMALPAIS S.P.

Van Wyck Meadow

Rock Spring

DIPSEA TR

STEEP RAVINE TR

Muir Overlook

Rocky Point

WEST RIDGECREST RD

MATT DAVIS TR.

FAIRFAX-BOLINAS RD

Red Rocks Beach

Stinson Beach

Audubon Canyon Ranch

Bolinas Lagoon

Bolinas

Noolka 1,000 miles

1

POINT REYES NATIONAL SEASHORE

Palomarin Trailhead

Pt. Reyes Bird Observatory

PACIFIC OCEAN

N

5 Miles
0

Ⓕ Fishing Port
🏛 Museum/Interpretive Center
⌂ Campground
☂ Picnic Site
🌲 Forest
⛳ Golf
      Whale Watching Site
S.P. State Park
P.P. Provincial Park
EUREKA City (over 10,000 population)
Ferndale Town (under 10,000 population)

⑤ Interstate Highway
⑩① ⑪⑥ U.S. Highway
      Secondary Road
      Major Highway
      Secondary Road
      Unpaved Road
      Trail
++++ Railroad
      Ferry
Ⓜ Town with Motels
Ⓗ Noteworthy Lodging

tion of timidity, excessive secrecy (like today's patent laws, the rules of European colonization required an explorer to publish his claims to make them "legal"), and a lack of resolve by the throne, Spain lost her chance to dominate the Northwestern Pacific Coast. Ironically, this abandonment was formalized by the Nootka Convention of 1790—and Nootka is our final destination on this odyssey. I chose that harbor because, without your own boat, it is the northernmost and westernmost place you can get to on this coast. (Even Alaska's coastal towns are located away from the Pacific Ocean.) But there is another reason, too. San Francisco was the first harbor to be frequented by Europeans on this shore, tracing its beginnings to Juan Bautista de Anza's founding of the presidio in 1776. Barely eighteen months later, Captain James Cook dropped anchor in Nootka and thus a dot was imprinted on the maps of the day, a dot that delineated the principal rendezvous for European navigators exploring what we now call the Pacific Rim. A third of a century would elapse before a single other European/American settlement made its appearance along the thousand-mile coastline that separates the two harbors.

The words "Golden Gate" suggest romance and adventure. In 1846 John Charles Frémont gave this strait its name. He thought of it as an analogy to Turkey's Golden Horn with as many riches pouring in from the Orient as they did during Byzantine times in Constantinople. He was only slightly wrong. The thousands of ships that sailed in through the gate a couple of years later were laden not with gold, but gold seekers. The gold itself went the other way, much of it to New York to finance the Civil War.

Frémont knew more about this country than an earlier pathfinder, a navigator named Garciá Rodriguez Ordóñez de Montalvo, who sailed along the southern part of this coast in 1510. In his log, he wrote

> Know ye that on the right hand of the Indies there is an island called California, very near the Terrestrial Paradise and inhabited by black women without a single man among them and living in the manner of the Amazons. . . . Their island was the strongest in all the world, with its steep cliffs and rocky shores. On the whole island, there was no metal but gold.

On our adventure we will meet no Amazons, and the gold is gone, but we will see a terrestrial paradise and a country that does indeed have steep cliffs and rocky shores. And although geographers will disagree, many sociologists think Montalvo was right about one thing. Culturally, at least, California is indeed an island.

I felt it would be proper to start this journey on foot, something you can do too by parking at the San Francisco anchorage of the Golden Gate Bridge. But normally the experience is a bit flawed because the pedestrian walkway is only inches away from noisy, fuming cars, buses, and trucks; even though the view is spectacular, the din and the smell makes it hard to get into a proper mood for such a symbolic gesture. So I showed up at dawn on Memorial Day, 1987. It was the bridge's fiftieth birthday; the directors had reluctantly decided to bar vehicles from the span for two hours, figuring that if the two hours began at six A.M., almost no one would show up. They were wrong. San Franciscans, it seems, feel about their bridge the way New Yorkers do about the Statue of Liberty and Parisians about the Eiffel Tower. By the time my party got to midspan, we were joined by three hundred thousand others who had an equal love for this grand structure. What started out to be a bridge "walk" became a bridge "stand." It took two hours to inch our way back to shore.

So I returned later to admire designer Joseph Strauss's sculptured masterpiece with its orange-red towers, which provide a warming contrast to the fog that almost always seems to dance between the slender cables that support the roadway. "The bridge to nowhere," the locals call it on days when fog envelops the entire structure. But on a more or less clear day, the View Point parking lot is filled to capacity; hundreds of people have deserted their cars to walk out on the bridge and capture one of the truly grand vistas in the world. Marigolds, Shasta daisies, Mariposa lilies, and rhododendrons grace gardens along the pathway leading to the pedestrian sidewalk. It's a fine place to look back on "The City" and its neighbor, the infamous Alcatraz Island, looming murkily in the east. The sense of excitement and adventure is strong, for at your back is urbanity, the home of five million people, yet just across this handsome bridge begin the rural highways, back roads, and country lanes that will lead to the beauty spots of the Northwestern Pacific Coast. The bridge seems to be a catapult, cocked and ready to launch you into a world of rurality and loveliness.

GOLDEN GATE NATIONAL RECREATION AREA

Before you've even crossed the bridge, you've left most of the Bay Area's urbanity behind. You're in a narrow strip of parkland, part of the national recreation area that boasts hiking and biking paths, picnic tables, and belvederes galore, stretching almost from downtown San Francisco to the sand dunes of the Pacific shore. GGNRA, as most people call it, is administered by the National Park Service and includes much of the Marin Headlands that you see across the strait. Nowhere in the world is there so much open space so close to a major city. Indeed, on the route this book lays out, you'll be in the midst of lands administered by either the federal government or the state of California for the next fifty miles. Up ahead lie a hundred hiking, riding, and bicycling trails; unpaved and free from public motor vehicle use, they make a four-hundred-mile pathway through an incredibly scenic and, many believe, magical land. So don't plan to travel too far, this first day on your trip. There's much to see in the parklands next door.

MARIN HEADLANDS • (Two-hour side trip)

Just across the bridge, a hundred yards beyond the Marin-side Vista Point parking lot, is a sign that states simply "Redwood Highway." Years ago, the powers-that-be endowed U.S. Highway 101 with that name, even though it is a two-hundred-mile drive along this road before you see your first great stand of virgin redwoods. Fortunately, we won't have to go that far. But first, pause to look back on "The City" from the Marin Headlands. At the Alexander Road exit duck back under the freeway and head up the steep Conzelman Road that climbs the northern precipice of the Golden Gate. This is the former location of the army's Forts Baker, Barry, and Cronkhite. Crumbling concrete gun emplacements and Nike sites line the road—built at great expense, their guns and missiles were never fired in anger. One beneficial fallout of the arms race is that these weapons became hopelessly outdated, and the land is now open for us to enjoy. The wind is blowing hard; it always does here, for you're standing in the throat of San Francisco's air-conditioning system. The Pacific breezes, cooled by deeply swelling ocean currents, come racing in toward the interior valleys, pausing long enough here to give the City its wet, gray summer days, before scudding off to cool the vineyards of Napa and Sonoma.

The summit where one of the batteries was located has been renamed Hawk Hill because this is one of the three best places in the country (the others are in Pennsylvania and New Jersey) to watch raptors (birds of prey). Ornithologist Alan Fish was quoted in the local newspaper as saying that the eagles, hawks, and vultures don't really like to cross open water, so they hang around here getting up nerve to fly across the Golden Gate. Birders have counted nineteen different species and claim to have seen three thousand raptors in a single day.

Beyond the bunkers is fabled **Point Bonita Lighthouse,** a squat tower atop an isolated rock marking the northern entrance to the harbor. In the early days, the army, fearful of the menace to navigation posed by this rocky shore, sent out a soldier with a cannon with instructions to fire it every few minutes when the fog came in. He ran out of gunpowder in a day and a half. A lighthouse equipped with a foghorn proved to be a better idea. It's open to the public, but only on weekend afternoons. "As soon as we get some money, we'll keep it open all the time," says park ranger Steve Holder. "We think it will become one of the biggest tourist attractions around." He's no doubt right, for it's hard to imagine a more spectacular seascape. The half-mile trail leads down a sheer bluff, plunges into a tunnel, and then soars out over the foaming surf on a rickety-looking suspension bridge that terminates abruptly at the diminutive white-painted tower. The original 1855 light was two hundred feet above the ocean—a mistake, it turned out, because the often low-lying fog left the light in clear skies, while below, ships were groping about, unable to find their way.

Around the bend is the **Marin Headlands Park Head-quarters,** which includes an interpretive center near the half-mile-long Rodeo Beach (you pronounce it "ro-DEE-o" here; we're not in Beverly Hills). Nearby is the **California Marine Mammal Center,** where the public is invited to watch stranded or orphaned seals, sea lions, and otters being nursed back to health.

Some lovely trails, but no roads, follow the wild rugged California coast north of Rodeo Beach. So to return to U.S. 101, drive through the quaint old army tunnel that bores under Wolf-back Ridge. It's a one-way road, so you may have to wait five or six minutes for the green light to signal that the oncoming traffic has cleared.

Sausalito • Population: 7,100

Nestled in a cove just east of Highway 101 is the once sleepy village of Sausalito, the West Coast's answer to Marblehead, Massachusetts. Taking the ferry from San Francisco (boats leave from the Market Street Ferry Building and Fisherman's Wharf) is a delightful way to come here, but most people drive. "The biggest industry in town is parking fines," says architect Audrey Emmons, a longtime resident. "Even our mayor [the onetime 'Madam' Sally Stanford] couldn't keep old rowdy saloons from being replaced by T-shirt shops and chic boutiques. The place is getting ruined—it's going uphill," she says with a genuine look of mourning for a lost paradise. Yet a stroll along the miles of piers—they're not fenced off here like so many yacht harbors these days—provides a close-up view of some of the finest sailing vessels in the world.

North of town, along Bridgeway Boulevard, is the old Marinships, the shipyard where thousands of Liberty and Victory ships were built during World War II. One old building houses the mammoth **San Francisco Bay-Delta Model,** a project built by the Army Corps of Engineers to study the tidal action of the bay. Here, in a replica the size of four football fields, you can

DOG HOLE SHIPS OF THE REDWOOD COAST

More than 250 of these ships were built between 1882 and 1923, launched at shipyards in San Francisco Bay, Eureka, Portland, and Puget Sound. Their names form an itinerary for the trip we are taking: Gualala, Point Arena, Greenwood, Albion, Navarro, Mendocino, Caspar, Noyo, Fort Bragg, Westport. Mariners called them steam schooners, though they seldom unfurled their canvas, a holdover from an earlier time when little engines were fitted into coastal sailing packets. These wooden ships were small, averaging less than one thousand tons. They had to be, for as author Jack McNairn put it in *Ships of the Redwood Coast:*

You just don't go puttering around through breakers and into windswept dog-holes on the Mendocino shore in a liner or a 10,000-ton freighter—for much the same reason that you avoid driving an automobile through the revolving front door of the Palace Hotel.

The ruggedness of the Coast Range prevented the easy construction of roads and railways, so this fleet provided the only practical communication for most of the Northwestern Pacific Coast. Foodstuffs and machinery were taken north; lumber, tanbark, shingles, and railroad ties were brought south. If you ran a mill in Mendocino and wanted to visit your banker in San Francisco, you took the boat. That's why the *Wapoma* looks rather odd—she has cabins for forty-five passengers. She was built by Charles R. McCormick, a mogul in the shipping industry who went on to form one of the largest firms in the Pacific trade.

To be master of one of these vessels required skills of an extraordinary nature. Legend has it that during a heavy squall in Eureka Bay, Captain Oscar "Rain-Water" Johnson navigated his ship a block and a half up C Street before he realized his mistake, then calmly ran full astern and backed out into the harbor again.

watch the tides ebb and flow just as in real life, except that you have to wait only fifteen minutes to see a cycle.

Resting sadly but safely atop a barge out in front is a ship of special interest to us. The **Steam Schooner *Wapoma*,** built in 1915, is the last survivor of a fleet of diminutive boats that once plied the northern California coast, calling at tiny ports to pick up passengers and cargo, mainly redwood (see Dog Hole Ships of the Redwood Coast, page 9). Although you can't go aboard this wooden-hulled beauty, you can get a sense of what these hybrid sail/steam ships looked like. *Wapoma* is part of the splendid collection of ships at the **National Maritime Museum** in San Francisco, but she's deteriorating so rapidly that the National Park Service hauled her out of the water and now has its hands full just trying to keep the vessel from becoming nothing but rust and dust. Volunteers are assisting in the project, so with luck she'll float again.

FOOD AND LODGING   Sausalito, California 94965

✔✔✔ **Alta Mira Hotel**   Generations of the more affluent San Franciscans have enjoyed brunch on the deck of this fine old pink-stuccoed hotel on a hill overlooking the harbor. Bulkley Avenue. (415) 332-1350.

✔✔ **Sausalito Hotel**   14 Victorian rooms in a refurbished old Spanish-colonial-style building next to the ferry terminal. 16 El Portal. (415) 332-4155.

✔ **Fort Barry Hostel**   American Youth Hostel Association. Located in a former army officers quarters building. 941 Fort Barry. (415) 331-2777.

●●● **Ondine's**   Lavish restaurant overlooking the harbor. (415) 332-0791.

●● **Scoma's**   Sausalito's branch of a longtime favorite San Francisco fish restaurant. (415) 332-9551.

MUIR WOODS NATIONAL MONUMENT

California Highway 1, dubbed "Shoreline Highway," branches off from U.S. 101 just north of Sausalito. After a couple of miles you begin climbing, and the road becomes narrow and twisty. This is exactly the kind of country road we'll be following (though there are some escape routes back to the interstate) all the way to Vancouver Island. After passing a few outlying residential tracts you suddenly find that you've left city life behind

EAST VS. WEST: MARIN COUNTY STYLE

In a way Marin County, the butt of countless jokes, comes by its yuppie reputation quite naturally. It has the image of being the land of hot tubs and peacock feathers, Porsches and BMWs—the place where you're just not with it if you don't have a cellular phone in your car. In Marin it's a mark of status to be seeing a shrink. It's not surprising that this is so; the county itself is a bit schizophrenic. Many would argue that there are in fact two counties: East Marin and West Marin. East Marin, where all the people live, probably deserves its upscale, affluent image, but it is also the home of many environmentally sensitive people who didn't want to see their county become one vast sprawling suburban wasteland—another San Fernando Valley.

Fortunately, the ridges and gullies that fan out from the dominant landform, Mount Tamalpais, present a formidable barrier to auto transportation into West Marin, and furthermore, most of the land on the other side of the mountain is held in public ownership. Yet much of what's left is privately owned dairying country. All that would have been necessary to replace those milk barns with houses and condos was to take the wiggles out of the roads. It was not to be. West Marinites like their rural atmosphere, and with the help of caring people from both sides of the mountain, multiacre land use ordinances were passed and roadway improvements discouraged. Without a radical change in policy, the western part of the county will remain pretty much as it is now. And the now is pretty nice.

(see East vs. West: Marin County Style, above). On this sojourn you won't see another traffic signal until you reach Fort Bragg, 160 miles up the coast, and less than one hundred miles of our road is four-lane, all the way to Nootka. Near the top of the ridge, turn off Highway 1 at the sign directing you to Muir Woods. Watch out for tour buses—they take up a lot of the road, and an awful lot of them come this way.

The national monument, named for the California poet and naturalist John Muir, is the Times Square of the tree-looking crowd; well over a million people a year come here. A ranger speculated that of all the people in the world who have actually seen a redwood tree, 80 percent have seen them only in this park. Yet the canyon where these *Sequoia sempervirens* live is lovely, and a half-hour stroll among these giants is a sobering experience. There's a nearby gift shop and snack bar that seems out of place in this serene forest, so a better idea is to take a picnic lunch and walk on through Muir Woods National Monument (where picnicking is not allowed) and up the hill to the Mount Tamalpais State Park. The area is laced with hiking trails. A fine map titled "A Rambler's Guide to the Trails of Mt. Tamalpais and the Marin Headlands" is available at Muir Woods Ranger Station. Modesty prevents me from naming the publisher. A nice two-hour walk is to climb up the Bootjack Trail to Van Wyck Meadow ("Population: 3 Stellar Jays," reads the professionally painted sign), turn right on the Troop 80 Trail, and then follow Gravity Car Grade and Fern Canyon trails back to Muir Woods. The path winds through a tan oak and madrone forest, climbs past a waterfall where ladybugs congregate by the millions, skirts around some serpentine outcroppings, and then meanders through a young redwood forest. On this walk, you'll get a sense of why so many Bay Area people have such special feelings about the area surrounding Mt. Tamalpais. Allow a couple of hours for the trek.

Muir Beach • Population: 150

You rejoin State Highway 1 at the lower end of Redwood Canyon, about three miles southwest of Muir Woods. A jog left brings you to Muir Beach, an often fog-shrouded cove in July and August, but a popular spot in the spring and fall when the weather is more apt to be sunny.

Highway 1 twists its way up to **Muir Overlook,** where on a clear day you're rewarded with a fine view of the Farallon Islands and the entrance to the Golden Gate. It's a bit whimsical to imagine, but years ago the sea below you was awash with potatoes, the cargo of a coastal packet that foundered here early in this century. Potato Patch Shoals, as it has been called ever since, is arguably the Bay Area's best salmon fishing waters. Shoreline Highway snakes along the cliffs, ducking in and out of lateral canyons, so what looks to be a ten-minute drive on a map turns out to take twenty. A mile before the resort town of Stinson Beach, a steep trail leads down to **Red Rocks,** a cove where most people shun the use of swimsuits and opt instead for an all-over tan.

Stinson Beach • Population: 650

This oldtime resort town is a bit schizophrenic; there's an old section with shingle-wall summer houses on tiny lots and a long stretch of strand graced with large, expensive beach homes. The road leading to the latter is private, but you can walk along the beach if you like. GGNRA operates a large beach here, which is mobbed on sunny days but at other times is quite serene. If the fog pays an unexpected visit, browse in one of the art galleries or have a drink at the Sand Dollar. If you're in a walking mood, hike up the side of Mt. Tamalpais on the Matt Davis Trail and return by the redwood-forested Steep Ravine Trail. The round trip takes about three hours.

Stinson Beach is the destination of the famed Dipsea Race, one of the oldest long-distance footraces in the country. For seventy-five years, as many as one thousand runners (nonparticipants give them less flattering names like "crazies") run up a 671-step flight of stairs out of Mill Valley's canyon-bottom location, struggle over Windy Gap, careen down Suicide Hill, chug up Dynamite and Cardiac hills, and coast down Swoop Hollow, only to find themselves having to cope with Insult Hill before finally staggering into this seaside community.

The strand at Stinson Beach protects shallow **Bolinas Lagoon** from the rages of a sometimes stormy Pacific. In the 1960s, conservationists and local citizens beat back a plan to dredge the bay and convert it into a yacht harbor, complete with rows of slips, motels, restaurants, and turning basins. The result is that the mud flats and tidal waters are still home to western grebes, arctic loons, pintail ducks, and numerous nonmigrating birds. This too is the sometime home of the colorful monarch butterfly, which migrates here in the early spring.

FOOD AND LODGING   Stinson Beach, California, 94970

✔✔ **Pelican Inn**   7-room B&B and restaurant with beer and wine in a publike atmosphere. Muir Beach, 94965. (415) 383-6000.

✔ **Steep Ravine**   12 primitive state park cottages.

✔ **Pantoll Campground**   18 walk-in campsites.

● **Sand Dollar**   Bar and cafe. (415) 868-0434.

MOUNT TAMALPAIS STATE PARK • (One-hour side trip)

Instead of proceeding directly up the coast, turn east at Stinson Beach and take the narrow road that climbs up a steep ravine to Pantoll Ranger Station, nestled in a dense forest only forty minutes from San Francisco's Montgomery Street. When I asked ranger Dave Gould who camps here, he replied, "Well, if you want to work at this ranger station in the summer, it's helpful to speak German." The Northern European culture, of course, places great emphasis on the outdoors, and those who come to visit this area must be quite astonished to find what they call a "nature park" this close to a major city.

America's Most Scenic Country Road. That's the opinion of the media people who make car commercials for TV—those who, with great wisdom, have discovered the ideal place to show off their Mercedes Benzes, Z cars, and BMWs. More auto-promotion film has been shot along the stretch of road north of Pantoll than anywhere else in the country. Drive up the hill to a parking area called Rock Spring and turn left on West Ridgecrest Road. The next five miles are absolutely spectacular, especially when the fog bank starts rolling in and the setting sun lends a golden tinge to the clouds below. Pause at one of several turnouts set in grassy meadows. Daredevil hang-gliders love these spots; if the thermals are right, they can soar for an hour before landing on the beach one thousand feet below. Behind you are second-growth redwood forests sheltering thousands of deer, a few mountain cats, an occasional coyote, and some pesky feral pigs. The latter are creating quite a controversy. It seems these descendents of once domestic porcines are rooting up the ground, presumably wrecking the watershed. Rangers want to erect a fence to keep them out of the parklands. Nature lovers are incensed.

Turn left when you reach Fairfax-Bolinas Road and return to sea level at the northern end of Bolinas Lagoon. Detour a quarter of a mile south along Highway 1 and look toward the east, where you'll see a lovely old white clapboard New England–style farmhouse nestled in a wooded draw. This is the headquarters of the **Audubon Canyon Ranch,** which was set aside to preserve a nearby heronry. During the nesting season, February to mid-July, the ranch is open to visitors who enjoy the walk up a short trail to a spot that looks directly out over the nesting trees of the great blue heron and the snowy egret. Observing the nuptial rituals and feeding habits of these giant birds is a memorable experience. The ranch has an extensive nature interpretive center and a fine bookstore, and there are always people around who can help you identify the hundreds of species of birds that frequent the area.

Bolinas • Population: 800

There is no sign along Highway 1 directing you to the nearby town of Bolinas. For years, no sooner had the highway department put one up than the locals tore it down. So persistent were their efforts that the charade became the topic of a front-page

Wall Street Journal article, and a local cartoonist did a hilarious strip showing the mayor of San Francisco, who wanted to declare Bolinas a sister city, being turned away by a barricaded army at the entrance to town. The locals, many of whom are of the counterculture genre, say they don't want tourists to come to their sleepy little former fishing village. Yet many of us do; we come to stroll its one-block main street, to wander along the shore of the lagoon, and to enjoy the tiny beach around the point. Bolinas, incidentally, is an Indian word of uncertain meaning. Contrary to popular belief, it does not refer to the baleen species of whale.

FOOD AND LODGING   Bolinas, California 94924

- **Wild Rose Cafe**   Home-style food in an old Victorian home. (415) 868-9969.

- **Smiley's Schooner Saloon**   Local hangout. (415) 868-1311.

The bluffs along the ocean west of town are gentle, but the waves at times are anything but. Just offshore is the sinister Duxbury Reef, site of numerous shipwrecks including the steamer *Lewis,* which foundered here in 1853. Fortunately all four hundred of her passengers were saved. Mesa Road leads northward, passing the **Point Reyes Bird Observatory,** the only full-time ornithological research station in the United States. Exhibits are open to the public during the spring and summer. A little farther along is the Palomarin trailhead at the southern boundary of the Point Reyes National Seashore, a place we'll visit next.

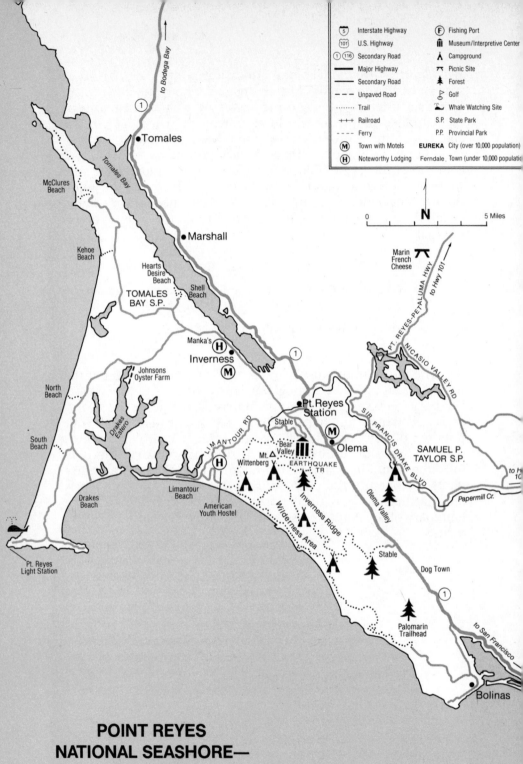

POINT REYES
NATIONAL SEASHORE—
CALIFORNIA

N

0   5 Miles

to Bodega Bay

Tomales

McClures Beach

Tomales Bay

Marshall

Kehoe Beach

Hearts Desire Beach

Shell Beach

TOMALES BAY S.P.

Manka's

Inverness

Johnsons Oyster Farm

North Beach

Drakes Estero

South Beach

Pt. Reyes Station

Stable

Bear Valley

Mt. Wittenberg

EARTHQUAKE TR

Olema

Limantour Beach

American Youth Hostel

Inverness Ridge

Wilderness Area

Drakes Beach

Pt. Reyes Light Station

Stable

Dog Town

Palomarin Trailhead

Marin French Cheese

PT. REYES-PETALUMA HWY

to Hwy 101

NICASIO VALLEY RD

SIR FRANCIS DRAKE BLVD

SAMUEL P. TAYLOR S.P.

Olema Valley

Papermill Cr.

to H 10

to San Francisco

Bolinas

LIMANTOUR RD

2

POINT REYES NATIONAL SEASHORE

The Bay Area's Wilderness

North of Bolinas the California coast makes a hook out into the Pacific—a sort of a miniature mirror image of Cape Cod. Punta de los Reyes was the name given to the point by the Spanish navigator Sebastián Vizcaíno, who passed by here on Epiphany in 1603, the day of the Three Holy Kings. Nowadays, most people say "Point Rays"; only purists and a few of us curmudgeons use the Spanish pronunciation "ray-es." The peninsula was originally part of a Mexican land grant that came upon hard times. The resourceful sheriff of Marin County repossessed the property for unpaid taxes and promptly sold it—not once but three times. He got rich and managed to stay out of his own jail, but the lawyer who sorted out the mess was the ultimate winner. As payment, he got the whole fifty thousand acres. The idea for a seashore park emerged in the mid-1930s, but it was not until 1962 that enabling legislation was passed by Congress and signed into law by John F. Kennedy. It was expected to cost $13 million, but by the time the last tracts were purchased, the price had soared to $56 million—"a cost overrun worthy of an aircraft carrier," as author John Hart put it in his book *Wilderness Next Door*.

OLEMA VALLEY

The infamous San Andreas Fault comes back on shore at Bolinas and heads north, creating the ten-mile-long Olema Valley and the fifteen-mile Tomales Bay. Highway 1 wends its way up this rift zone, bisecting two distinct geologic areas. The heavily wooded land to the west along Inverness Ridge is lurching north at a rate of several inches a year, so say the geologists. Northern Californians don't like to think about it, but at one time, that land was in Los Angeles. The soil is decomposed granite, quite unlike the Franciscan sedimentary rocks found on the other side of the road, and some of the vegetation is unique to the area. This is the home of the lovely bishop pine, a conifer that forms an umbrella shape rather than the traditional tall conical form of most pines. The species is named after St. Louis, bishop of Toulouse, the same fellow who gave San Luis Obispo its name. The world's largest is located along Inverness Ridge. Lincoln Fairley, an old-timer in the area, calls it the "Arch Bishop."

Botanists have also found the largest sargent cypress on the ridge to the east of the highway. Not to be outdone, Fred Sandrock, a fellow who cares more about that side of the road, has christened it "Master Sargent." One tree that people have divided opinions about is the ubiquitous eucalyptus, which grows like a weed in the Olema Valley. Imported from Australia, it has no natural enemies—so far. The National Park Service wanted to start eradicating a stand near Dog Town, but a howl of protest put that plan on hold. Recently, however, there have been reports of an invasion of a new insect in southern California that has been attacking eucalyptus. Some environmentalists, those who would like to rid this parkland of all exotic species, have been accused of hatching a sinister plot to import the bug.

Olema is a curious valley. One stream flows south, another north, but since the land has shifted so much, their headwaters have moved past each other. For some distance they run parallel, each competing for the same raindrops.

Shortcut Access to Point Reyes

Readers wishing direct access to the Point Reyes peninsula should drive north on U.S. Highway 101 to the Sir Frances Drake Boulevard exit and follow that road to the town of Olema. Along the way you pass through **Samuel P. Taylor State Park,** a lovely redwood grove, long a favorite of San Franciscans who used to come here on a narrow-gauge railroad. The drive from the Golden Gate Bridge to the two-building hamlet of *Olema* takes about an hour.

POINT REYES NATIONAL SEASHORE

Turn west off Shoreline Highway at Olema and drive a couple of miles to **Bear Valley Visitors Center.** Though there is almost no development on the peninsula, the National Park Service estimates that 3.5 million people come to enjoy this area each year. An old barnlike building has exhibits displaying the flora, fauna, and geology of the area and a bit of its history. Nearby is a replica of a **Miwok Indian Village,** but elsewhere there is little to show for man's presence save for a couple of stables, a lighthouse, and a number of dairy ranches. Most people come to walk or ride horseback or just to be out in the country for a day or so.

It is unlikely that anyone who was here on June 6, 1906, ever forgot it, for early in the morning, the land to the west leaped northward a full fifteen feet in a few cataclysmic seconds. In their book *Bonanza Inn,* Oscar Lewis and Carroll Hall described a bit of what people later saw:

> The cypress tress and the rose garden had moved away from the front of the house and now stood in front of the barn. The clump of raspberry bushes had slid down from the north and occupied the space vacated by the roses. The eucalyptus trees had marched to a position opposite the barn, and in the process one had shifted from the foot of the line to the head.

To get a sense of these events, stroll along the half-mile-long **Earthquake Trail.** Crazily positioned fence posts, relics from a famous photograph of the time, have been reset in the ground so you can see exactly how far the earth moved that fateful day. You're left to speculate whether it's true or not that Bessie, a grazing cow, was astride the fault when the earth opened, swallowed her up, and then closed again, leaving only her tail to mark the spot where the dastardly deed took place.

The park headquarters is along a flank of Inverness Ridge, an area so densely wooded with moss-encrusted bishop pine, Douglas fir, California bay laurel, and madrone, you might think you're in a rain forest. A nice day hike to see this microenvironment is to walk out through Bear Valley, turn right on the Old Pine Trail, then follow the Sky Trail to Mt. Wittenberg and return to the park headquarters via the Horse Trail. The walk, which alternates between forest and meadow, takes about four hours.

Most of the land west of Inverness Ridge is designated the **Point Reyes Wilderness Area,** meaning that no vehicles of any kind are allowed, not even bicycles. This is backpacking country. The National Park Service has constructed four campsites (permit required) that can be reached only by trail. Two nearby stables rent saddle horses or will arrange to pack your dunnage into one of the camps.

Beyond Inverness Ridge, the park takes on an entirely different character. It's a rolling, fog-shrouded, almost treeless country reminiscent of the Scottish Highlands. This is the home of the exotic, almost pure white European fallow deer and the recently reintroduced spotted tule elk. Take the road to **Limantour Beach,** which branches off about two miles north of the park headquarters and leads to a long, wave-swept strand. A walk up the beach leads to Limantour Estero, a Spanish word that means lagoon or estuary. It is one of the few wetlands in the state that is not managed in some way or another.

FOOD AND LODGING   Olema, California 94950

✔✔✔ **Reyes Seashore Lodge**   New 21-room lodge, with library, sitting room, breakfast. P.O. Box 39. (415) 663-9000.

✔ **Point Reyes Hostel**   Dormitory rooms near Limantour Beach. (415) 663-8811.

✔ **Samuel P. Taylor State Park**   65 campsites.

● **Jerry's Farm House Restaurant**   A local hangout. (415) 663-1264.

POINT REYES PENINSULA • (Half-day side trip)

Sir Frances Drake Boulevard, which we have been following since Olema, skirts along the west side of Tomales Bay. Five miles north of the park headquarters is a delightful resort town.

Inverness • Population: 800

Before the turn of the century, some professors from the University of California got together to establish a summer community nestled in the wooded lee of the nearby ridge. They looked across the bay at the treeless, mist-shrouded hills and thought of Scotland. Streets are named Dundee, Argyle, Cameron, and Balmoral; St. Columba's Church is almost as pretty as its namesake on the island of Iona. Even the quietly modest yacht club chose the "Flying Scot" for its sailboat racing fleet.

Though the names may be Scottish, the food is decidedly Czechoslovakian. Manka's, many believe, has the best food in West Marin (and some cozy rustic cottages, too), and Vladimir, Manka's son-in-law, serves meals only slightly less fancy. For lunch, however, the locals don't go to restaurants. They stock up at Johnson's Oyster Farm before heading out to the beaches for a barbecue. You might want to do the same. The oysters are grown on wires, suspended from wooden frames built in the tidal waters of nearby Drakes Estero.

The southern reaches of Tomales Bay are popular for sailing, and the saltwater here is the warmest you'll find on this trip. Inverness Ridge acts as a fog barrier, so the swimming beaches often enjoy sunshine while the ocean sands are shrouded in dense, swirling fog. **Tomales Bay State Park** includes Shell Beach, a quarter-mile walk from a side road, and Heart's Desire Beach, where picnic tables and barbecue pits are surrounded by a magnificent bishop pine forest. In town, the Shaker Workshop West sells traditional Pennsylvania-type furniture and artifacts, and across the street is the **Jack Mason Museum,** a treasure trove of local lore.

FOOD AND LODGING   Inverness, California 94937

✔✔✔ **Blackthorn Inn**   5-unit B&B. P.O. Box 712. (415) 663-8621.

✔✔ **Golden Hinde Inn**   Motel units on Tomales Bay. Boat launching. Restaurant and bar. 12938 Sir Francis Drake Boulevard. (415) 669-1389.

✔✔ **Inverness Valley Inn**   10 cottages. Tennis. P.O. Box 629. (415) 669-7250.

✔✔ **Ten Inverness Way**   4-unit B&B. P.O. Box 63. (415) 669-1640.

●●● **Manka's Inverness Lodge**   First-class dining in a farmhouse atmosphere. 9 rooms and cottages. 30 Callender Way. (415) 669-1034.

●● **Vladimir's**   Restaurant and bar. (415) 669-1021.

Beyond the town of Inverness, the county road goes over a low divide and drops into the treeless moors of the northern half of the national seashore. Much of the Bay Area's milk comes from the cows you see all about, beasts who share their pastoral home with hikers. In *The Legend of Devil's Point*, author Bret Harte claims that Sir Francis Drake stashed some of his loot near here. Harte's description of the land is hardly flattering:

A more weird and desolate-looking spot could not have been selected for [its] theatre. High hills . . . enfladed with dark *cañadas*, cast their gaunt shadows on the tide . . . sea fog [comes] with soft step in noiseless marches down the hillside, tenderly soothing the wind-buffetted face of the cliff until sea and sky [are] hid together.

[He] chose this spot to conceal quantities of ill-gotten booty taken from neutral bottoms, and had protected his hiding place by the orthodox means of hellish incantations and diabolical agencies. On moonlight nights a shadowy ship was sometimes seen when fogs encompassed sea and shore . . . the creaking of a windlass, or the monotonous chant of sailors, came faint and far, and full of magic suggestions.

Buried treasure isn't the only mystery surrounding Drake's visit (see Nova Albion: "A Convenient and Fit Harborough," below).

The county road ends near **Pt. Reyes Lighthouse,** which, since it juts out so far into the ocean, is the best place to watch the gray whales during their winter swim to Mexico. On a clear, not too windy weekend, so many Bay Area people come to watch these migrating monsters that the National Park Service now provides shuttle bus service from an overflow parking lot a mile away. The lighthouse, located at the bottom of a long flight of stairs, is popular in its own right. Its three-ton Fresnel (the "s" is silent) lens was manufactured in Paris, shipped around Cape Horn in a windjammer, and hauled out to this windswept hogback in an oxcart. There are a number of beaches along the ocean.

Pt. Reyes Station • Population: 1,000

Around the turn of the century, when people took more time to visit the countryside, the narrow-gauge North Pacific Coast Railroad tunneled under the mountains separating East and West Marin, snaked its way down Papermill Creek, and emerged to

~~~~~~

NOVA ALBION: "A CONVENIENT AND FIT HARBOROUGH"

In 1579 the soon-to-be-knighted Francis Drake had been at sea for nearly two years, searching for the legendary Strait of Anian and engaging in a little freebooting when the occasion presented itself. It is a bit ironic, but it was silver, not gold, that caused Drake to put the helm of the *Golden Hinde* over and strike for a friendly shore. Luck had brought him in contact with the Spanish galleon *Cacafuego,* carrying 1,300 bars of silver and fourteen chests of coin. The booty was almost too much for his little vessel; her seams began to bulge. Drake promptly began searching for "a convenient and fit harborough." That much we know. He found a harbor, but where?

His log describes how he put in under the lee of some chalk bluffs, similar to those along the English Channel at Dover. Ancient Europeans had called England "Albion," meaning white hills, so Drake named his landing site Nova Albion. But there are also chalk bluffs near Point Arena seventy-five miles north. He spoke of meeting Indians, though, which scholars think were the Miwoks, so he must have landed somewhere in Marin County. He also wrote about finding eggs on a nearby island, certainly one of the Faralones, as there are no other offshore islands anywhere near this latitude. All of this suggests the captain landed near the beach that bears his name.

But a map, published ten years after his voyage, depicts "Portus Nova Albions" at a site tantalizingly similar to a place on the Marin shores *inside* the Golden Gate. Did the great navigator find the grandest harbor on the Pacific? In 1936 a plate was found on the bay-side mud flats of Marin. Could it be real? Francis Fletcher, the chaplain of the *Golden Hinde,* wrote: "Our generall caused to be set up a monument of our being there . . . namely a plate of brasse fast nailed to a greate and firme post. . . ." A careful cleaning of the newly found object revealed these words:

Bee It Knowne Vnto All Men By These Presents
Ivne 17 1579
By The Grace Of God And In The Name of Herr
Maiesty Queen Elizabeth Of England And Herr
Successors Forever I Take Possesson Of This
Kingdome Whose King And People Freely Resigne
Their Right And Title In The Whole Land Vnto Herr
Maiesties Keepeing Now Named By Me And To Bee
Knowne Vnto All Men As Nova Albion
Francis Drake

So the mystery was solved. Or was it? Skeptics pointed out that the object could have been moved to the bayshore site by anyone, an Indian, a beachcomber, or someone who wanted to prove that Drake came inside San Francisco Bay. Alas, most historians think the plate is a fake, though it does occupy an exalted place in the University of California's Bancroft Library. So where is Drake's true landing site? After four hundred years the jury is still out. Maybe someday we will know. It is a startling thought, but it was nearly two hundred years after Drake's voyage that the next man of European stock set foot upon these western shores.

follow the shores of Tomales Bay as it struggled toward the resorts of the Russian River. A station along the line gave this town its name. Though you're only an hour and a half from San Francisco, the place can best be described as a cow town, though the residents are not the pointy-boots, ten-gallon-hat type of cowboy. People here just like horses, and a visored cap, a dirty pair of blue jeans, and barnyard-smeared Nikes will do just fine, thank you. They shop at Toby's Feed Barn and down a beer or six at the Western or at the 2 Ball Saloon and eat at the Station House down the street.

The midsummer parade features the Las Galinas Valley Sanitary District Non-Marching Band (they ride on a flatbed truck) and two or three hundred people on horseback. Incredibly, the clock over the volunteer firehouse blares out a "moo" at lunchtime. Members of a summer stock theater looked out over the barnyards toward the long, narrow Tomales Bay and decided they would call themselves the Hot Tomales. The town is justly proud of its weekly newspaper, the *Pt. Reyes Light,* which won a Pulitzer Prize for its investigative reporting of the pseudoreligious sect Synanon. But nowadays people get more fun from reading the gossip found in the "Sheriff's Log" column. Editor David Mitchell cites a few of his favorites:

- A man reported he dispersed a pair of prowlers in his backyard by hurling avocado pits at them.
- Someone used a screwdriver to break into a resident's house and dismantle the doorbell.
- Officers saw a man in his car who had been bobbing for clams in the lagoon.
- A Tomales woman claims her breast has been hooked up to an automatic milking machine.

FOOD AND LODGING   Pt. Reyes Station, California 94956

✔✔ **Holly Tree Inn**   B&B. P.O. Box 642. (415) 663-1554.

●● **Station House**   Restaurant. (415) 663-1515.

CHEESE COUNTRY • (One-hour side trip)

Those who know about such things make the seemingly outrageous claim that since the climate just inland from Point Reyes Station is much like Normandy's, the dairies here produce as good a quality of Camembert as in France. To judge for yourself, turn right just north of town and follow the Petaluma highway seven miles to the Marin French Cheese Co. They have been making Camembert and Schloss cheeses here for 125 years, and I would agree with the experts: they have finally gotten the hang of it. The hundreds of bicyclers and those out for a pleasant afternoon drive who picnic by the pond out front apparently agree, too. The cheese is delightful, especially when enjoyed with a bottle of zinfandel, another French product that Californians have learned how to make.

Shoreline Highway hugs the eastern shore of Tomales Bay, in spots following the old right-of-way of the long-vanished railroad. Anglers fish for herring, rock cod, flounder, and halibut, which are taken from small craft launched from the several boat ramps surrounding the tiny town of **Marshall.** Near the north end of Tomales Bay, the highway turns inland following a bayou for a few miles. The pilings from an old railroad trestle stand mute in the lapping water. The pride of the village of Tomales is Diekmann's General Store, an old oiled-wood-floor establishment that might well be a set for a 1920s movie. You're in Sonoma county now, a lovely area we will explore in the next chapter.

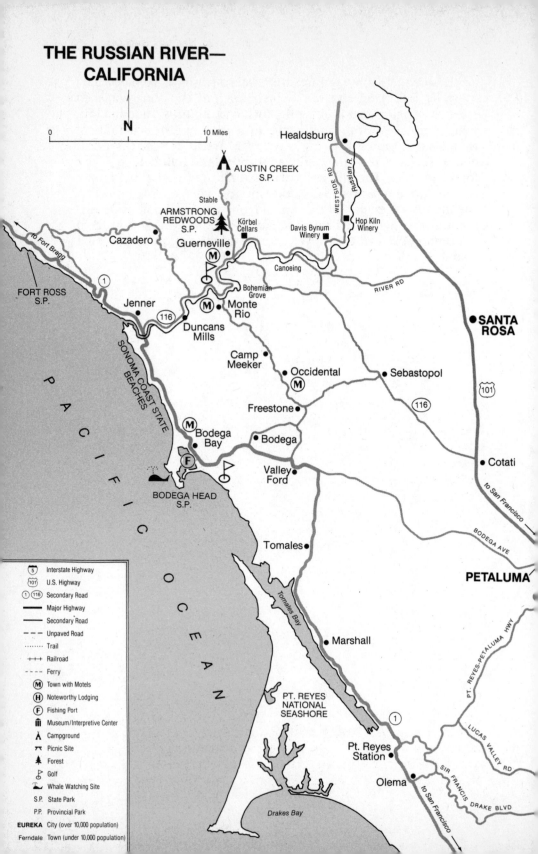

THE RUSSIAN RIVER—
CALIFORNIA

N

0   10 Miles

Healdsburg

to Fort Bragg

AUSTIN CREEK
S.P.

Stable
ARMSTRONG
REDWOODS
S.P.

Körbel
Cellars

Davis Bynum
Winery

Hop Kiln
Winery

WESTSIDE RD

Russian R.

Cazadero

Guerneville

M

Canoeing

FORT ROSS
S.P.

Jenner

116

Bohemian
Grove

Monte
Rio

M

RIVER RD

SANTA
ROSA

Duncans
Mills

Camp
Meeker

Occidental

Sebastopol

M

SONOMA COAST STATE BEACHES

Freestone

116

PACIFIC

M

Bodega
Bay

Bodega

101

F

Valley
Ford

Cotati

BODEGA HEAD
S.P.

BODEGA AVE

Tomales

PETALUMA

OCEAN

Tomales Bay

Marshall

PT. REYES-PETALUMA HWY

5	Interstate Highway
101	U.S. Highway
1 116	Secondary Road
	Major Highway
	Secondary Road
	Unpaved Road
	Trail
+++	Railroad
- - -	Ferry
M	Town with Motels
H	Noteworthy Lodging
F	Fishing Port
🏛	Museum/Interpretive Center
⋏	Campground
⋈	Picnic Site
🌲	Forest
⛳	Golf
⚓	Whale Watching Site
S.P.	State Park
P.P.	Provincial Park
EUREKA	City (over 10,000 population)
Ferndale	Town (under 10,000 population)

PT. REYES
NATIONAL
SEASHORE

Pt. Reyes
Station

LUCAS VALLEY RD

Olema

to San Francisco

SIR FRANCIS DRAKE BLVD

Drakes Bay

3

RUSSIAN RIVER RESORTS AND VINEYARDS

"A Goodly Country and Fruitful Soyle"

North of Point Reyes, the country between the ocean and the interior valleys takes on a more sylvan character. The Coast Range lowers considerably for the next thirty miles, the hills are grassy rather than forested, and the area is punctuated with eucalyptus-studded dairy farms and livestock ranches nestled in gentle swales. Reverend Francis Fletcher, chaplain of *Golden Hinde,* wrote of this area "a goodly country and fruitful soyle, stored with many blessings fit for the use of man." Romanian-born New York artist Christo thought this was "goodly country," too, for he chose these undulating slopes for his celebrated sculpture *Running Fence.* After examining several other sites, he settled on the Marin/Sonoma hills because they seemed to represent "a typically American culture." *New Republic* critic Marina Vaizey wrote:

> The sculpture itself is simply a beautiful and amazing thing. Running Fence in some uncanny way is not only a piece of sculpture . . . but itself sculpts the land, and is in turn sculpted by the wind and the light.

The fence, completed in 1976, consisted of two thousand shimmering white woven nylon panels, each eighteen feet high, which were strung from wires attached to steel poles. Twenty-four miles long, it sinuated over the landscape from San Francisco Bay to the Pacific, crossing Highway 1 just south of the Sonoma

County line. It was torn down after a couple of months, much to the relief of the farmers over whose land it meandered. Yet it left its legacy. For those of us who saw it, the fence served as a reminder of the beauty of this land, of its gentleness, and of how someday this place will probably succumb to the developers' onslaught.

Shortcut Access to the Russian River Resorts

Readers wanting a direct, more or less high-speed access to this country should follow the Highway 101 freeway north to Petaluma. Take the Washington Street exit and follow the signs to Bodega Bay. You join our northward trek at Valley Ford, about an hour's drive from the Golden Gate Bridge.

Valley Ford • Population: 126

Dairyman's Bank built a handsome building here in 1893. It's now a branch of the Bank of America. A grocery store with a gas pump outside and restaurant round out the town's commercial enterprises. The countryside hereabouts is one of the premier bicycling areas in northern California. Numerous little country lanes, almost car free, meander over the rolling hills, passing farm driveways marked by the name of the rancher printed under the logo: "California Cooperative Creamery" or "Polled Hereford Association." You're now in Sonoma County, second only to Napa in the fame of its vineyards, which we will visit. But first, continue north on Shoreline Highway to the coastal community of Bodega Bay.

FOOD AND LODGING   Valley Ford, California 95472

✔✔ **Green Apple Inn**   4-room B&B. 520 Bohemian Highway. (707) 874-2526.

●● **Dinucci's**   Italian restaurant and bar. (707) 876-3260.

Bodega Bay • Population: 300

The Spanish never settled along the northern California coast, but they did leave their mark on the early maps. The noted explorer Juan Pérez anchored his schooner *Sonora* here in 1775 and named the bay after one of his officers, Juan Francisco de la Bodega y Quadra. Quadra's name will crop up many times in the course of this journey. Here, Pérez found only Miwok Indians. The Russians, looking for a place to grow grain to supply their starving sealers in Sitka, Alaska, dropped anchor here in 1809. They didn't stay, but the venture led to the establishment of Fort Ross three years later.

Though it was slow to take off, Bodega Bay is now fast becoming a popular fishing resort. The booming inland cities of Petaluma and Santa Rosa are less than an hour away by good two-lane roads. In the summer, the temperature is often above a hundred degrees in the inland while at the same time it is in the sixties along the coast, so it's no wonder that so many people come over for dinner or Sunday brunch at places like The Tides and Lucas. The Tides is part of a large fishing, charter boat, fish market complex that has been serving excellent, moderately priced meals for years. Lucas is a bit more "*nuevo* California" with urethane-finished oak tables, spindle-back chairs, and a cocktail lounge where stem glasses are stored upside down above the bar.

The bay was dredged in the 1940s, making this the largest harbor between San Francisco and Eureka. San Franciscans don't like to admit it, but the Bolinas fleet is now larger than the one at the fabled Fisherman's Wharf. Party boats take scores of fishermen out onto the continental shelf for salmon fishing beginning in May and bottom fishing year round. On days when the wind is not too high, they also offer voyages to watch the two whale migrations: southbound between November and January and northbound in March and April. The county has built a new harbor and launching ramp called Spud Point Marina. The name comes from the fact that in earlier times, this was potato country; farmers grew a legume called "Bodega reds." Bodega was not exactly the wisest place to build a town. The soil is sedimentary deposits laid down directly atop a fracture zone—a combination sure to cause havoc the next time the San Andreas decides to act up. An electric utility started construction of a nuclear power plant out on Bodega Head, just northwest of the village, now only a large hole in the ground; more thoughtful souls scratched their heads and said, "Whoops!" **Bodega Head** is now a park, owned by the state. Like the Point Reyes peninsula, it is a scrap of what geologists call the "Salinian block," the granitic landmass that has been drifting northward for the last twenty million years.

The ten-mile stretch of coast between Bodega Bay and the mouth of the Russian River is dotted with coves and strands known collectively as **Sonoma Coast State Beaches.** The shoreline is lovely, but a caution is in order. These are not swimming beaches; the water is too cold, and "sneaker waves" can come in any time of the year. A spot at Duncan's Landing is called Death Rock for good reason. Surf fishing, beachcombing, and picnicking are popular activities.

FOOD AND LODGING   Bodega Bay, California 94923

✔✔✔   **Bodega Bay Lodge**   78-unit motel near golf course. Coast Highway 1. (707) 875-3525.

✔✔✔   **Bodega Coast Inn**   21 rooms overlooking the bay. 521 Coast Highway 1. (800) 346-6999.

✔✔✔   **Inn at the Tides**   88-unit motel on bluff above the fishing port. Restaurant and bar. P.O. Box 640. (707) 875-2751.

✔✔   **Sea Horse Guest Ranch**   6-room B&B; trail rides. P.O. Box 277. (707) 875-2721.

✔   **Sonoma Beach State Park**   Wright's Beach, 30 campsites; Bodega Dunes, 98 campsites.

●●   **Lucas Wharf Restaurant**   Bar. 599 Highway 1. (707) 875-3522.

RUSSIAN RIVER RESORTS/SONOMA WINE COUNTRY • (All-day side loop)

We will be visiting a lot of beaches and fishing villages on this odyssey, so you might want to take an alternate to the coast route. Instead of continuing on Highway 1, three miles west of Valley Ford turn right on the county road to **Bodega** (not to be confused with Bodega Bay). In 1962 Alfred Hitchcock chose this village for the location of his celebrated film *The Birds*. That was the biggest thing to happen thereabouts since 1839, when James Dawson and Edwin McIntosh got into their little tiff. Jim and Ed were partners; they shared the house they had built on a Mexican land grant; but, as in many such arrangements, they had a falling-out. Unable to agree on who got what, they appealed to General Vallejo, who gave the land to McIntosh. Angry at the decision, Dawson sawed the house in two and ox-carted his half away—the history books, alas, don't say to where. Pride of the hamlet is the white-steepled, New England–looking St. Teresa Catholic Church and the two-story Potter School, which for a time housed a nice restaurant but now stands quiet and sullen. The nearby hamlet of Freestone marks the northern limit of the rolling hill country. Up ahead looms the forested mountains of the Russian River country.

Occidental • Population: 800

Four miles north along Bohemian Highway is the remarkable town of Occidental. The railroad arrived here in 1877, whereupon one J. W. Noble built a hotel that he called Summit House because this was the highest point on the line. The town is nestled in a little valley, surrounded by redwoods, clinging to rugged mountainsides. Many who live here would call this a magical land; perhaps it is the place Montalvo, that fanciful fellow who named California, had in mind when he wrote

In this island called California, with the great roughness of the land . . . are many griffins the like of which are not found in any other part of the world. In the season when the griffins give birth to their young, these women . . . go out to snare the little griffins, taking them to their caves where they raise them. And . . . they feed them the men taken as prisoners and the males to which they have given birth. All this is done with such skill that the griffins become thoroughly accustomed to them and do them no harm.

Occidental is famous for its food, but not of the man-child variety. The indoor boccie ball court suggests that this town is Italian. Sunday nights find all three restaurants packed to the rafters with folks who come from as far away as San Francisco to enjoy a family-style meal out in the country. It's little wonder that people call this place "calorie gulch." The coming of the railroad brought the loggers, so most of the trees you see are second and even third growth. There used to be the stump of a redwood near here that was twenty-three feet in diameter (seventy feet around). Old-timers say that a fellow (derogatorily called a "bolt cutter") worked on that tree for two solid years, hacking out six hundred thousand shingles.

FOOD AND LODGING   Occidental, California 95465

- ●● **Fiore's**   Italian restaurant, bar, motel. 3657 Main. (707) 874-2865.

- ●● **Negri's**   Italian restaurant, bar. 24-unit motel. P.O. Box 84. (707) 874-3623.

- ●● **Union Hotel**   Italian restaurant, bar, motel. P.O. Box 427. (707) 874-3662.

RUSSIAN RIVER GORGE

North of Occidental, the Bohemian Highway passes the summer-home community of Camp Meeker and drops into the Russian River resort area. The colonists at Fort Ross named the river Slavianka, meaning "Little Beauty," an apt choice. It's a strange river in a way, though. It doesn't go the way it's supposed to. The headwaters are in the sunny climes of central Mendocino County, and for much of its seventy-five-mile run to the sea, it nurtures some of the finest vineyards in the world. Then, instead of heading toward San Francisco Bay as the topography suggests it should, the river (for reasons only plate tectologists seem to understand) makes an abrupt right turn, heads for the coastal range, and forces its way through twenty-five miles of terribly rugged mountains, struggling mightily to reach the sea.

Lumbermen were the first to recognize the value of the Russian River gorge. To get the timber out they built two rail-roads: the narrow-gauge road we have been following from the south and a broad-gauge line that came downstream from the east. By the 1910s, most of the timber was cut (the main town in the area was called Stumpsville), but it became apparent that people would just like to vacation here. Resorts, many of them quite stylish, sprung up around the stumps of fallen giants. It's not surprising when you consider the climate. The coast is fog-bound; ten miles inland it is clear. Sunlight heats the river, whose currents bring clear warm swimming water to the redwoods. The Russian River became one of the premier destination resorts in the west. There have been good times and bad times ever since.

The good times were when people could board a ferry in San Francisco, transfer to a train at Sausalito, and arrive here 4½ hours later. A 1912 picture shows a crowd waiting for the train. Gentlemen, wearing three-piece suits and sporting panama hats, are chatting with ladies attired in long white dresses and carrying parasols. The scene has a relaxed yet surprisingly formal appearance. But over the years, fires and floods have taken their toll. In 1923 a fire, said to have started in a moonshine still, spread from Guerneville to the sea. The last train to San Francisco departed in 1935. This narrow gorge is simply not wide enough to accommodate all the runoff from winter rains; over the years the river has risen as much as thirty feet above its banks. People were discouraged from building substantial structures. Today, unhealed scars mark the flood of 1986.

For the wealthy, at least, times have always been good at the nearby **Bohemian Grove.** For one hundred years, powerful men of the world have gathered there for the annual summer encampment. The Bohemian Club, headquartered in San Francisco, was originally for artists and musicians who enjoyed putting on shows and concerts. To help pay the bills they started recruiting from corporate ranks, but keeping to tradition, they still require their less artistic members to sing in the chorus, carry a spear, or help out backstage. The two-thousand-acre "grove" of virgin redwoods provides the setting for their annual "Hi Jinks," a play performed in an outdoor theater. For a week during the summer, chief executives of the largest corporations in the world mingle with presidents and princes, kings and sultans, as they celebrate what they describe as "the cremation of care." The event has been called "the greatest men's party on earth (also the title of a book about the club)." The have-nots who live nearby have a different view. They feel that the moguls should nurture care and caring, not cremate it, and the San Francisco lesbian community has taken swipes at the encampment, too. Taking over a couple of nearby gay resorts, they stage a "Midsummer Dyke's Dream," which they call "the greatest women's party on earth."

Bohemians of a different sort began coming to the Russian River area in the 1950s. The hippie movement was in full swing; the cheaply built homes along the river were just what the flower children were looking for. Then in the 1970s the San Francisco gay community discovered the charms of the area. But that life-style is becoming less concentrated, and the Russian River is now going through yet another transformation. Barbara Hoffmann, manager of the local Chamber of Commerce, estimates that ten years ago 30 percent of the houses were occupied full-time, with 70 percent for vacation use only. Now that ratio has been reversed. Retirees are moving in, and many are commuting to the electronic factories near Santa Rosa. Others, like Khysie Horn, moved here simply because they wanted to escape from city life. Seven years ago she opened the Quicksilver Mine Co., which sells only local products: wine, fabrics, art, and books. She feels a bit tied down, she says, but being your own boss and living in such a lovely spot provides the compensation. Some who live here have a sense of humor—John Schubert, for example. His business card, which lists a post office box but no phone number, reads as follows:

> Russian River historian, anthropologist, archivist, writer, speaker, researcher, instructor, tracker of tall tales, dealer in past events. Custodian of: regional relics, printed matter, memorabilia, artifacts, dust, important junk, and trash. All donations accepted.

Monte Rio • Population: 900

The Bohemian Highway joins the river at Monte Rio, the smaller of the two towns in the gorge. This is more or less the center of the steelhead fishing part of the river. The canyon is dotted with legendary holes with names like Freezeout Riffle, Lone Pine Pool, Duncan Hole, Alligator Snag, Watson's Log, Brown's Pool, and Austin Creek Riffle. The fishing has changed in the last few years, the result of the construction of Warm Springs Dam, which created Lake Sonoma seventy miles upstream. The river flow is controlled now; fishermen say that's not too good, but a large hatchery at Healdsburg supplies the river with many more fish than are normally caught in a year. Canoeing has become popular in recent years, especially in the spring when the water is higher. The typical put-in place is Healdsburg, where trips as long as five days are possible. Numerous outfitters rent equipment.

The nearby hamlet of **Duncan Mills** has a complex of old buildings that has been turned into a shopping area with boutiques and arts and crafts shops.

FOOD AND LODGING Monte Rio, California 95462

✔✔ **The Village Inn** The Bing Crosby film *Holiday Inn* was shot here. The 25-room hotel has been refurbished. Restaurant and bar. P.O. Box 850. (707) 865-2304.

✔✔ **Northwood Lodge** 18-unit motel adjacent to a golf course. P.O. Box 188. (707) 865-2126.

•• **Blue Heron Inn** Restaurant in a funky old clapboard house in Duncan Mills. (707) 865-2269.

•• **Casanoma Lodge** *Berghütte* tucked back up in a side canyon has rooms above a German restaurant and bar. P.O. Box 37, Cazadero 95421. (707) 632-5255.

Guerneville • Population: 900

It's "Gurn-ville," you are politely advised if you pronounce it with the middle "e." George Guerne built a sawmill here in 1865. A few years later the tallest-known tree in the world was felled on nearby Fife Creek. The skyscraper, 367 feet 8 inches, was as tall as a thirty-story building. The town may not look like the Wild West, but it has had its share of derring-do over the years (see Black Bart: Highwayman, below). Guerneville is the hub of a resort area that has numerous funky cabins, several good motels, some trailer sites, and a couple of B&Bs.

BLACK BART: HIGHWAYMAN

The hastily convened sheriff's posse that rode out of Guerneville one summer day failed to catch their man, recovered no loot, and, furthermore, returned to the sleepy town with their dignity somewhat shattered. They had the misfortune of becoming the first of many who would try to capture the elusive highwayman Black Bart, "poet laureate of outlawry."

On August 3, 1877, the morning stage was bumping along the road from Fort Ross when a dapper man, dressed in a long linen coat and an eyehole-punctured flour sack over his head, stepped out of the shadows and brandished a double-barreled shotgun. "Throw down the box," he is reported to have said in a deep and hollow voice. What the posse later found was the strongbox, empty of the $300 in gold and in its place a note, written on the back of a waybill, signed "Black Bart, PO 8."

> I've labored long and hard for bread,
> For honor and for riches,
> But on my toes too long you've tred,
> You fine-haired sons of bitches

Black Bart went on to hold up twenty-eight stagecoaches in California. Always the money was replaced by scraps of doggerel:

> Here I lay me down to sleep
> To wait the coming morrow,
> Perhaps success, perhaps defeat
> And everlasting sorrow,
> Yet come what will, I'll try it once,
> My condition can't be worse,
> And if there's money in that box,
> 'Tis munney in my purse.

The robbery of a stage from Sonora proved to be his last. The box containing $4,800 was difficult to open; he cut his hand, and when surprised by another rider, he fled with the money but left the handkerchief he had used to succor the wound. William Pinkerton's detectives had their clue: a laundry mark reading "F.O.X. 7." The ninety-first laundry they checked recognized the mark as belonging to one Charles E. Bolton, a San Franciscan described as "a distinguished-looking gentleman who walked erect as a soldier and carried a gold-knobbed cane." Bolton was sentenced to seven years in San Quentin and released in five. When asked by a reporter if he planned to write any more poetry, Bart replied: "Young man, didn't you hear me say I would commit no more crimes?" From that day on he was no longer seen, but most historians pooh-pooh the story that he was "pensioned" by Wells, Fargo & Co. on the understanding that he would rob no more stages.

FOOD AND LODGING Guerneville, California 95446

✔✔✔ **Brookside Lodge** 26-unit motel. (707) 869-2470.

✔✔ **Highlands Resort** Gay and bisexual resort near Armstrong Redwoods. P.O. Box 346. (707) 869-0333.

✔✔ **The Estate** 11-unit B&B. 13555 Highway 116. (707) 869-3313.

✔✔ **Fife's** Gay bar and resort. P.O. Box 45. (707) 869-0656.

✔✔ **Radford House** 7 unit B&B. 10630 Wohler Road, Healdsburg 95448. (707) 887-9573.

✔✔ **Ridenhour Ranch House Inn** 7-unit B&B. 12850 River Road. (707) 887-1033.

✔ **Austin Creek State Recreation Area** 25 campsites. No trailers.

✔ **Camelot Resort** Motel. P.O. Box 467. (707) 869-2538.

●● **Burdan's Bar** Roadside tavern and restaurant. (707) 869-2615.

●● **Buck's Ranch** Restaurant and bar, dancing. (707) 869-0101.

ARMSTRONG REDWOODS STATE RESERVE/AUSTIN CREEK WILDERNESS

This grove of *Sequoia sempervirens* (see Three Kinds of Redwoods, page 37), located three miles north of Guerneville, has a more woodsy feel than Muir Woods, which we visited earlier, because there are far fewer visitors and thus fewer "Keep on the Trail" signs. A round (section of a fallen log) tells a bit about what went on in this land. The segment, about eight feet in diameter, has markers noting what happened at the exact time that some of the rings on the tree were formed. Some dates are

848	Tree germinates
1066	Battle of Hastings
1215	Magna Carta signed
1492	Columbus discovers America
1579	Sir Francis Drake lands on the California coast
1776	Declaration of Independence signed
1906	San Francisco earthquake
1978	Tree destroyed by vandals

A steep, twisty road leads back into **Austin Creek Wilderness Area,** where hiking trails lead out into the rugged country-

THREE KINDS OF REDWOODS

Paleobotanists (plant-fossil specialists) looked at their "history books," the rocks, and concluded that at one time three species of redwoods had inhabited this planet, and that they had been around for 160 million years and had onced covered much of the northern part of the world. The characteristic needle imprint was found in rocks as far away as northern China. But only two species managed to survive the glaciers that withdrew a million years ago, and they lived only in California and a tiny part of Oregon. Or so everyone thought.

The first written record we have of the tree is from the diary of Fray Juan Crespi, a Franciscan missionary traveling with the Portolá expedition in 1769. While marching along the Pajaro River, one hundred miles south of San Francisco, they sighted some giants, which they named *palo colorado,* meaning "red tree." Archibald Menzies, a botanist with Vancouver, noted seeing some in 1794, but it was another Englishman, A. B. Lambert, who gave us part of the name, *Taxodiaceae* (cypress) *sempervirens* (ever-living). As the science of dendrology became more precise, Hungarian botanist Stephen Endlicher recognized that the tree was not a cypress at all but something quite different. He chose the name of the noted Cherokee chief Sequoyah (who never got farther west than the Sonoran desert of New Mexico) but unaccountably latinized the name. When the Sierra redwood was identified as a cousin of the coast tree, it was also given the generic name *Sequoia,* but the specific adjective *gigantea* was added, meaning "gigantic." For reasons best known to botanists, the ending *dendron* (Greek for "tree") was also added, so if you want to be precise about the Sierra tree, say *Sequoiadendron giganteum.*

Both species have a similar wood color, but there are many differences. The Sierra tree's needles are smaller and more oval-shaped, and they propagate solely from seeds nestled in inch-long, purple, egg-shaped cones—seeds so tiny it takes one hundred thousand to make a pound. One tree can produce a million seeds, but they must have uncluttered ground and a modicum of sunlight to germinate. Though few survive, they take hold quickly for the life they are going to keep so long, and within a few years a sapling may grow to be six feet high. The coast tree can reproduce from seeds, too, but most start from sprouts growing from the stump of a mother tree. Look carefully in a second-growth forest. You'll see redwoods growing in a circle—the now rotted stump of a downed giant nurtured its progeny. Both species have bark containing an abundance of bug-resistant tannin, but the Sierra variety grows to a thickness of several feet, the coast tree less than one. Limbs on the *gigantea* are much larger; it looks like a stout warrior, whereas the coastal tree seems more like a tall, lithe princess.

But what of the third species? With a touch of the dramatic, botanists speculated that the tree had not existed since man himself existed. Imagine, then, the excitement that must have occurred in the scientific community when it was announced that forester Professor T. Wang had found what looked to be a redwood in the village of Mo-tao-chi in northern China. "Here was a fossil come to life in the unexplored interior of China," said University of California Professor Ralph Chaney. The tree proved to be only six hundred years old, but it was, in the words of botanist Alfred Powers, "but a generation of the uninterruptedly oldest race of trees whereof man has knowledge." Numerous other samples were subsequently found of the species named *Metasequoia,* or "dawn redwood." The limbs grow upward rather than downward, and it is deciduous. You can now see specimens at the Botanical Garden in Fort Bragg (Chapter 5), on the campus of Humboldt State University (Chapter 7), and at the Botanical Park in Ladysmith (Chapter 18). A noble tree.

---

side. A nearby pack station rents horses or will pack your dunnage into several remote campsites.

WINE COUNTRY

Sonoma County is justly proud of its world-famous wineries. Of the forty or more vineyards stretching out along the Russian River, we'll pause to visit three, chosen because they are quite different yet are open every day.

Three miles east of Guerneville on River Road is Korbel Champagne Cellars, one of the oldest wineries in California. Dug into the hillside above the river is the lovely stone cellar that has been converted into a combination museum and storage area. Artifacts from the old railroad days are commingled with examples of early wine-making apparatus and photographs of life in a quieter time. Daily tours of the winery provide an insight into the differences between making champagne and table wine. You learn which grape varieties go into the *cuvée,* the fermented, first-run wine, and how yeast and sugar are added to the bottle to begin the *tirage,* the second fermenting, which at this winery is done by the old in-the-bottle process called *méthode champenoise.* The operation of riddling, the daily turning of the bottles, is explained. Witnessing the elaborate disgorging technique used to get rid of the residual yeast gives an insight into why champagne is so expensive. The tour concludes, of course, in the tasting room, where you sample champagnes with various levels of *dosage,* or sugar content. Korbel makes eight varieties here (in ascending order of sweetness): Blanc de Blancs from Chardonnay grapes; Blanc de Noirs from Pinot Noir; Naturel, a champagne with no added sugar; Brut; Extra Dry; Sec; Rosé; and a Rouge.

The process is tightly controlled because, as guide Mike Swartz explained it, "Champagne in the bottle begins to deteriorate after a couple of years, so there is no sense in keeping it around. When you toast your twenty-fifth wedding anniversary you want to relive the memory, so we take great pains to produce an identical product year after year. What you drank then tasted exactly like what you can buy right now."

To view an entirely different type of operation, drive east on River Road a couple of miles and turn left on Westside Road. Continue on for about three miles to the driveway of the family-owned Davis Bynum Winery. Davis has been associated with wines for more than thirty-five years, first as a writer for the *San Francisco Chronicle* and then for the last twenty-five as wine maker *extraordinaire.* He got his start by making an upscale jug wine that had a picture of a red footprint on the label. Called Barefoot Bynum, it was so well received that he whimsically added the subtitle Château La Feet. Since then he has devoted his attention to premium and what the trade now calls super-premium wines. His operation typifies the changes that have occurred in the California table wine industry since the early 1970s. In these small, boutique wineries there is no attempt to be consistent year after year. The fun is to ask questions: "What new and exciting wine can I produce from the cards [meaning the grapes] that I have been dealt this year? What was the weather like, what grapes do I have, and when should I pick the fruit? How can I create something special—how long should I leave it in the oak, or should I use oak at all? Is the cabernet so strong I should tame it down with some merlot? We had a warm spell—should I wait and try for a late harvest, 15 percent alcohol zinfandel? That'll blow people's minds!" Davis must have answered some of these questions correctly; he's been winning gold medals year after year.k

Though there are a couple of picnic tables outside, the tasting room is not slick; Davis's staff assumes that you have been on a winery tour before. Instead, he offers a half-dozen samples of what he's been up to recently. Perhaps it is a Gewürztraminer, a Pinot Noir, or a Petite Sirah. If you buy the last, he'll caution you to "lay this down for a couple of years."

I asked Dave if he had spotted any trends in the last ten years. "I think people are shifting away from the Chablis-type dry wines to those with a bit more subtle, fruity taste like a sauvignon blanc and the flinty flavor of the Chardonnay," he said. "People don't want a lot of tannin but a more complex, mellow taste. And there is beginning to be a slight shift toward the reds, though it's too early to tell if this will continue. I'm finding that I like the reds better now, though."

Hop Kiln Winery makes very good wine here, as their seventy-five awards attest, but there is another reason to make the detour a couple of miles farther up Westside Road. The winery and tasting room are located in a restored 1905 hops-drying barn that is quite handsome, especially when framed by rows of newly leafed vines. If the light is right, you'll capture the quintessential photograph illustrating the beauty of California's famous wine country.

4

NORTH SONOMA AND SOUTH MENDOCINO COUNTIES

A Wild and Lonely Coast

We pick up our northward trail at the spot where the Russian River meets the Pacific. State Highway 1 snakes its way north for ninety miles before coming to a community that has more than a few hundred people. This lonely rockbound coast, however, is punctuated with some nice inns, resorts, and restaurants that we'll visit, and there are several alternative routes that beckon the adventuresome traveler away from the more well-traveled road.

Shortcut Access to the Sonoma Coast

Readers wanting to start their exploration of the California coast north of the Russian River should drive forty-six miles north on U.S. Highway 101 to the town of Cotati, where State Highway 116 branches off to Sebastopol, a pleasant farming community and longtime home of *Peanuts* cartoonist Charles Schulz. It is thirty-five miles from the Highway 101 turnoff to the little hamlet of Jenner, where we rejoin Highway 1. The trip from the Golden Gate Bridge takes about two hours.

Jenner • Population: 100

For five months of the year, starting in mid-February, many of the hundred thousand or so harbor seals that live in California's coastal waters migrate to the Russian River bar to give birth to their offspring. Cows suckle their pups on the sands of the spit

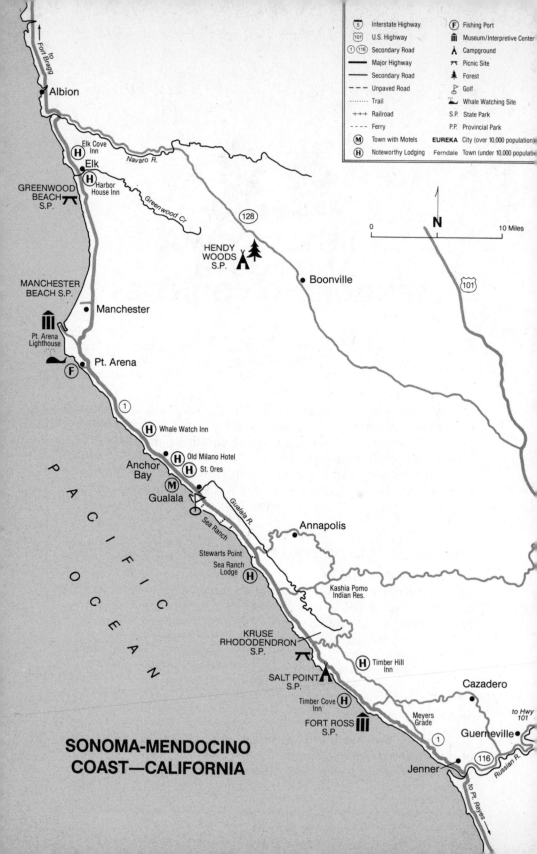

SONOMA-MENDOCINO
COAST—CALIFORNIA

that juts out toward the ocean. Believe it or not, a lot of people don't like seals. Fishermen say they feed on the steelhead and foul up their nets. Seals who were victims of gunshot wounds have washed up on the shore. Sightseers are probably a bigger danger, however. We like to get too close to these shy creatures. The pups are forced back into the water, thereby reducing their body temperature, so the experts say. "The sheriff's deputies can't help," Dian Hardy was quoted in the local newspaper as saying. "They're too busy collaring drunks and hauling tourists from dangerous perches on deadly rocks and crumbling oceanfront cliffs." So she and other volunteers formed a group called Stewards of the Slavianka (the Russian name for the river) to come out to the sands and warn people (and their dogs) away.

The little little coastal community of Jenner boasts some summer homes and a couple of restaurants, but little else—surprising, considering the beauty of the place. Highway 1 hugs the coast for a couple of miles, ducks inland for a bit, and then abruptly climbs a cliff high above the turbulent Pacific. The five-mile stretch between the Meyers Grade turnoff and Fort Ross is one of the most spectacular in California, rivaling the famous Big Sur road south of Monterey. You're eight hundred feet above the ocean looking straight down on an angry sea. If that's not enough to scare you, reflect on the fact that you are almost directly atop the San Andreas Fault. A more soothing thought, however, is that this is open grazing country and during spring and early summer, when the grass is green, you share the road with livestock who are not the least bit hurried to get out of your way.

FOOD AND LODGING   Jenner, California 95450

- ●● **Murphy's Jenner by the Sea**   Restaurant and B&B. Coast Highway 1. (707) 865-2377.

- ●● **River's End**   Restaurant and cabins. P.O. Box 32. (707) 865-2484.

FORT ROSS STATE HISTORIC PARK

Historians felt so strongly about the importance of this place (see The Russians Are Coming! The Russians Are Coming!, page 44) that the state of California spent lavishly on reconstructing the old fort that had, in this century, been almost obliterated by earthquake and fire. The site is lovely now that the highway has been rerouted away from the ruins. The massive stockade sits defiantly atop a grassy marine terrace a hundred feet above the sea. You wander through two blockhouses, the commandant's house, a barracks, and the double-steepled Orthodox Church, the

THE RUSSIANS ARE COMING!
THE RUSSIANS ARE COMING!

Ivan Alexander Kuskof, the fellow who built the place, named it Rossiya, "Little Russia." The Spanish, who hated its very existence, called it La Fuerte de los Rusos. The Californios (Mexican settlers) were probably the ones who corrupted it to Fort Ross.

The fort might have been a success, but its timing was wrong. The sea otter, whose pelts had brought so much wealth to Catherine the Great's Russian American Fur Company, was by 1812 fast becoming an endangered species. Nevertheless, the vessel *Chirkov* stood offshore one spring day and landed a party of twenty-five Russians and eighty Aleuts who started building a settlement encircled by a fourteen-foot-high, hewn-timbered stockade, complete with two-story blockhouses, gun slits, and all. Inside they constructed fifty-nine buildings, including a chapel, the commandant's house, barracks, two warehouses, a blacksmith shop, and a jail.

Three years before, the company had taken 1,400 otter skins from California waters—Czar Alexander I must have been pleased. By the time Fort Ross was established, however, there were a tiny number of otter left, so the colonists turned to farming, something about which these men, trained for the sea, knew almost nothing. Wheat began to rust in the damp climate; gophers and field mice damaged the row crops. Apples and pears did a little better, but fruit hardly made for a complete diet. So they turned to shipbuilding. The wood they chose was so ill suited that the ships began to rot.

It's hard to imagine why the Mexican government would view this feeble Russian invasion of North America as a threat, but it did. In 1823 Mission San Francisco Solano was rushed to completion in the village of Sonoma forty miles southeast. It marked the northernmost outpost of Spanish/Mexican influence in California. But General Mariano Guadalupe Vallejo, commandant at Sonoma, had his eye on the wrong enemy. To counter the Russian presence, he encouraged Americans to settle here—an unwise move, as it turned out.

By 1841 Czar Nicolas I decided to cut his losses. When the Hudson's Bay Company showed no interest, the last commandant, Alexander Rotchev, looked for a local buyer. Vallejo rejected his terms, but a peripatetic Swiss, John Sutter, came forward and bought the place lock, stock, and cannon for $30,000: $2,000 down and the balance in yearly installments (which were never paid). For that he got 1,700 head of cattle, 900 horses, mules, sheep, agricultural implements, and an arsenal of *French* weapons. Why French? The muskets, it was later discovered, had been dropped in the snow as Napoleon's army retreated from Moscow. Sutter carted everything that wasn't nailed down to his New Helvetia (Sacramento). The Russians retreated to Sitka, where they remained until 1867 when Secretary of State William Seward came forth and bought the future state of Alaska for a little over $7 million.

Meanwhile, in Sonoma, the gringos who had accepted Vallejo's hospitality turned on their host; their Bear Flag Revolt in 1846 led to the cessation of California to the United States and proved to be the swan song for the Mexican way of life in northern California.

---

visual symbol of the place. A first-class interpretive center houses exhibits describing not only the Russian presence here, but also that of the Pomos, who frequented the area when fishing for mussels, squid, and abalone.

One of the loveliest resorts along the wild Sonoma coast is Timber Cove Inn, located a few miles north of Fort Ross. The massive timbered lobby and bar is dominated by a man-size fireplace, and a cozy restaurant looks out over the surf. Outside is a handsome seventy-two-foot-high obelisk, a monument to peace carved by San Francisco's favorite sculptor, Beniamino Bufano. On a foggy day the children the statue depicts seem to be reaching toward Bufano's unseen but strongly felt heaven. **Salt Point State Park** has paths leading to lovely ocean vistas. Nearby is **Kruse Rhododendron Preserve,** a delightful place in May and June when the flowers are at their best. Some of these rhododendrons, which form an understory for Douglas fir and bishop pine, grow twenty feet high. A five-mile trail leads back to Salt Point.

FOOD AND LODGING

✔✔✔ **Timber Cove Inn**   21780 Highway 1, Jenner, California 95450. (707) 847-3231.

✔✔ **Salt Point Lodge**   Bar, restaurant, and motel units overlooking the Pacific. 23255 Highway 1, Jenner, California 95450. (707) 847-3234.

✔ **Salt Point State Park**   30 drive-in and 21 walk-in campsites.

MOUNTAIN COUNTRY BACK ROAD • (One-hour side trip)

Our objective, though, is to follow the road less traveled, so instead of heading north on the Shoreline Highway, take the little country lane that heads due east from Fort Ross. It is wise, however, to have a good map before starting this side loop, because the road inexplicably changes names a few times; there are a number of alternate routes, several of which lead back to the ocean; and nowhere are things very well signed. In spots the road is so narrow that you might have to back up to find a place where two cars can pass. (The uphill vehicle has the right-of-way on one-lane mountain roads.) In other places, however, there is no problem at all; uphill traffic goes around one side of a tree, downhill the other.

During much of the year the climate changes noticeably as you climb up the mountainside. Highway 1 may be fogbound when there's sun up above. Coastal grasses give way to redwoods and then to hilltop meadows. Once atop the ridge you encounter a view that is constantly changing, first out over the ocean and then toward the wild, almost roadless Sonoma interior. Is this the southern reaches of the notorious marijuana-growing country you've heard about? That's not the kind of question you ask of a local.

The rural sense is pervasive. Dirt lanes, muddy in winter, duck off into forests of madrone and California bay. A couple of cows and a dozen sheep share the road with a rattly old stake-bed truck; the white-bearded driver is hauling a brace of horses to who knows where. In the drier areas redwoods are replaced by an oak savanna; chartreuse-colored moss clings to gnarled trunks. The road meanders through grassy areas where weathered, speckled-gray grape-stake fences bend and twist, pointing every direction except the way the builder intended. In the spring, California poppy, lupine, and Indian paintbrush decorate the sunnier slopes. Redtail hawks and turkey vultures circle overhead. You pass a farmhouse with an ill-tended apple tree out front and an old lug tractor rusting away in a ditch. When I drove by, a woman with her hair tied in a bandanna stopped her hoeing, turned around, and eyed me carefully. Strangers are not a common sight along this road.

At the top of the ridge, turn left on Seaview Road. There are surprises here. The first is the elegant Timberhill Ranch, a group of shingle-sided buildings nestled among the trees. Is that a llama in the corral? Besides exotic beasts, there are an immense swimming pool and a number of tennis courts. The well-furnished lobby seems the ideal place to curl up with a good book. Hostess Barbara Farrell waxed lyrical about the food. "We had smoked trout salad for lunch today, and tonight we'll serve salmon bisque and roast duckling with orange sauce. And you should see our wine cellar!"

Farther down the road is a dilapidated farmhouse, not unusual hereabouts but made startling by the fact that the front yard is decorated with half a dozen giant modern pieces of steel sculpture. You pass the Me-Koy-Yo Indian Rancheria with its tiny school; here the road changes name to Hauser Ridge. It drops steeply into the Gualala River and then climbs again, inexplicably changing its name again, this time to the more colorful-sounding Tin Barn Road. Then comes an "only in California" kind of sight: a five-story-high Buddhist shrine with colorful kitelike flags fluttering all about. The nearby temple with its gold-colored roof sporting three tulip-shaped cupolas can be seen from five miles away.

Kashia Pomo Indian Rancheria, sadly, is strewn with junk automobiles. "A few years ago," a fellow at the Stewarts Point parking lot told me, "the Indians started charging a two-dollar toll for crossing their land. It was illegal, of course, but I paid them anyway. They seemed to need the money." There are a few old buildings here, but most of the residents live in house trailers. This is the junction with the road to **Stewarts Point,** which drops steeply down to the coast, meeting the Shoreline Highway at an old-fashioned general store.

FOOD AND LODGING

✔✔✔✔ **Timber Hill Inn**   10 secluded cottages overlooking the wild Sonoma interior. Tariff includes three meals a day. 35755 Hauser Bridge Road, Cazadero, California 95421. (707) 847-3258.

Sea Ranch • Population: 280

Highway 1 keeps about half a mile inland from the sea along the northernmost ten miles of the Sonoma coast. The in-between property is a large housing development called Sea Ranch, a project of Castle and Cooke, one of Honolulu's old "Big Five" sugar companies. Architecturally, the place is stunning; gray clapboard and shingle-sided houses snuggle between bunchgrass-covered dunes. Ice plant, not lawn, decorates the yards; cypress provide a bit of privacy without blocking too much of the view. A few critics, those who don't like contemporary architecture, have described the houses as "Bodega Bauhaus," or "mineshaft modern," but most people think they are perfect for this stark coast. Residents jog along private roads, comb the beach, and hike in the woods above the highway. It is an ideal second home or retirement community for the thousand or so families who have purchased lots here.

So why did Sea Ranch become such a cause célèbre? Simply

because many people didn't think it was fair to close ten miles of one of the prettiest sections of California's coastline. The developers quite naturally wanted to provide a safe environment for their residents. The best way to do this was to keep out the public, so roads were patrolled and those without an invitation were fined. Coastal access advocates were outraged—they took the developers to court. The battle raged for years, eventually reaching the Supreme Court. The outcome was a compromise—sort of. Sea Ranch has provided four access trails to the beach, one on the south end of the property, two in the middle, and one on the north adjacent to the public golf course. Since there is no place to park along the highway, parking lots (modest fee) were built at each trailhead. One lot has six stalls, one five, and one seven. So, except for the golfers and the strollers nearby, eighteen families at any given time can legally intrude on ten miles of beach. One can only guess what the cost in litigation fees per shoreline visitor turned out to be. Sea Ranch residents, however, needn't worry about the place being overrun by outsiders.

FOOD AND LODGING   Sea Ranch, California 95497

✔✔✔ **The Sea Ranch Lodge**   20 ocean-facing rooms above a large restaurant and bar. P.O. Box 44. (707) 785-2371.

Gualala • Population: 585

People disagree on the origin of the name of this lovely coastal river and the town at its mouth. Some say it is a Spanish rendering of Walhalla, the Teutonic abode of heroes fallen in battle. But others say it comes from an Indian phrase, *wha-la-la,* meaning "meeting of the waters." Whichever, it should be pronounced with a "W," not a "G," but it seldom is.

The village has an unpretentious feel. There seems to be more grocery and hardware stores than a place with this population could support, but there is a reason. The hills above town are sprinkled with home sites; retired people have moved into this country in recent years. For recreation they gather at the fifty-foot-long bar at the Gualala Hotel, a place built in 1903 and the last surviving building of a once bustling lumber community. You're likely to see men wearing mud-spattered boots and wide suspenders to hold up their jeans. Beer is the preferred drink. A sign in the tiny lobby reads "For rooms, see the bartender."

North of town, the coast takes on a ruggedness similar to the more famous Pebble Beach area. Monterey cypress hug the cliffs; little sunny meadows reach out toward the sea. An upscale country-inn community is beginning to develop here, spearheaded by the handsome new St. Orres. The building is a carpenter's delight with wood mullion windows, cut-glass door panes, and a dining room occupying a three-story-high atrium. When I asked the innkeeper what inspired the onion-dome architecture, she reminded me that Fort Ross was not far away, and that a Russian atmosphere was, therefore, quite proper. The food, though, might better be described as "California cuisine," and it is very good. By far the most expensive place to stay hereabouts is the Whale Watch Inn, which occupies a magnificent site on a cliff overlooking the surf. No children or pets are allowed; there is no TV, and smoking is not permitted in the rooms. It's a wonderful place to escape the modern world, especially in the winter when the waves are so spectacular.

FOOD AND LODGING   Gualala, California 95445

✔✔✔✔ **Whale Watch Inn**   18 luxury rooms. 35100 Highway 1. 884-3667.

✔✔✔ **St. Orres**   17-room European-style inn (bath down the hall) and some cozy cottages. P.O. Box 523. (707) 884-3303.

✔✔✔ **Old Milano Hotel**   8-room B&B in a restored 1905 building on a bluff with a magnificent view. Hot tub. 38300 Highway 1. (707) 884-3256.

✔✔✔ **North Coast Country Inn**   4-room board and batten-sided B&B. Hot tubs. 34591 South Highway 1. (707) 884-4537.

✔✔ **Gualala Country Inn**   14 modern rooms overlooking the ocean. P.O. Box 697. (707) 884-4343.

✔ **Gualala Hotel**   19-room hotel, bar and restaurant. P.O. Box 675. (707) 884-3441.

✔ **Gualala Point Regional Park**   26 campsites.

POINT ARENA • Population: 550

As you approach Point Arena, the seaboard takes on a different character. Instead of hugging rocky cliffs, Highway 1 traverses a half-mile-wide plain, occasionally ducking into the steep narrow canyon of a short coastal stream before emerging onto yet another mesa. These shelfs, called sea terraces, were once the ocean floor, uplifted one hundred thousand years ago by the continual jousting of the Pacific and American plates. Sea terraces will dominate the landscape all the way to Fort Bragg sixty miles up the highway. You are now back in dairying country.

There is nothing fancy or upscale about Point Arena. An

Italian restaurant, where the locals eat, is across the street from an old-timey, somewhat faded motel next door to the filling station and garage. There is a hint, though, that the character of the area is changing. A natural foods restaurant serves "better than authentic Mexican dishes, homemade pasta, and delicious vegetarian cuisine." In all my travels, I've never met a farmer or a rancher who cared a whit about *cuisine,* let alone the vegetarian variety.

This is the best spot in which to get an idea of the tremendous difficulties involved in trying to ship out timber from the Mendocino coast. Point Arena was, and still is, a port—of sorts (see Mendocino's Dog Hole ports, below). Recently the town fathers wanted to revive their linkage with the sea, so they turned to various public agencies for money. A marine railway, part of

MENDOCINO'S DOG HOLE PORTS

The Mendocino coast presented an uncomfortable challenge to American lumbermen. There were trees aplenty but no easy way to get them to market. The redwood forests were confined to a strip no more than a few dozen miles from a shoreline that happened to be particularly devoid of any reasonable harbor. The fact that few roads exist even today seems to prove there was no practical way of getting the logs out via an inland route. Yet Yankee ingenuity found a way.

Originally the Mendocino landing sites were called "outports," anchorages at the mouths of streams or in the lee of eroded headlands. Seasoned captains, looking at the reefs and exposed rocks, and struggling with undertows and treacherous riptides, named them "dog holes" because, as one said, "they offer barely enough room for a dog to turn around." At first, lighers (small flat-bottomed scows) were used, which could be loaded from makeshift piers and worked out to a ship lying offshore, where, amid the rising and falling swells, the cargo was somehow manhandled aboard. The work was dangerous and expensive. This gave impetus to the construction of the so-called apron or slide chute. Lumber ready for shipment was stored on a bluff. An A-frame was built on rocks out in the cove from which a ramp or slide was hung. If the weather wasn't too bad, a captain, his eye half on the coast and half on the potential profits of the cargo, crept gingerly into the "harbor" and warped his ship into a fixed position by means of lines attached to buoys and eyebolts (called "bollards") driven into nearby rocks. Lumber was slid down the ramp piece by piece to crewmen waiting on the deck. An iron gate slowed the logs down, and a second brake, called a "clapper," further reduced the speed to a point where the deckhands could grab the material on the fly and haul it below. It wasn't easy, especially when the ship took a roll and the chute was suddenly pitched up into the air. Most likely it was the clapperman's responsibility to see that the men were not impaled by the careening boards.

As the ships became larger they could no longer snuggle up close enough to the shore to utilize an apron chute, so mill owners devised what was called a wire or high line chute. A cable was strung from the bluff out over a moored ship and anchored to the mast (or in some cases the far shore). A system of sheaves and block and tackle allowed a platform loaded with lumber to be swung out over the vessel, where it was lowered onto the deck. Passengers, with some indignity, were loaded the same way. Initially gravity provided the power. A counterweight, connected to a second line, pulled the unladen platform back on shore. The additional weight of the next load of lumber (or people) hauled the counterweight back up the hillside. By the end of World War I, steam donkey engines had replaced the counterweight, but the basic high-wire system was used until the late 1930s.

---

an old Coast Guard station, was allowed to rot away. In its place a spanking-new steel pier was constructed, but not a run-of-the-mill, tie-up-your-boat-and-walk-ashore kind of pier. Built twenty feet above the raging surf (where it is presumably safe from winter storms), it projects four hundred feet out into the ocean swells. Launching from this height isn't easy. If the sea is not too rough, a swimming-raft-size float hinged to a long ramp is first lowered into the water by means of a block and tackle. Boats loaded on trailers are then driven onto the pier and swung out over the water using a giant crane. Boaters scamper down the steeply inclined, heaving ramp, hop aboard their bobbing craft, and quickly head out to calmer offshore water. The pier and its apparatus cost $2 million. "There is an ad in the paper for a harbor master," a fellow out walking his dog told me. "But look at the wind and those waves! You can't launch a boat in weather like this. These westerlies are what we get most of the time, and this pier only works when the wind is coming from the north. They don't need a harbor master. What they need is a night watchman!" Modern technology, it seems, has yet to tame the wild Mendocino coast.

Turn off Highway 1 a couple of miles north of town and take the narrow lane out to the **Point Arena Lighthouse.** In 1792 George Vancouver, a fellow we'll get acquainted with later on, named this grassy headlands Barra de Arena, meaning "sand bar." Many a ship has gone on the sands since that time, including ten that foundered during a single night, November 20, 1865. It's little wonder that the U.S. Light House Agency (forerunner to the Coast Guard) chose this spot for the most powerful light on the California coast. The original tower, constructed in 1870, was destroyed in the San Francisco earthquake, but fortunately the "first order" Fresnel lens survived. A docent told me why the tower is so high: "Long before Columbus proved it once and for all, mariners knew that the world was round—how else could you explain that when you watch a ship sailing out to sea, its hull disappears first, the mast last? The curving earth simply gets in the way of your line of sight." Here, the combination of a 115-foot tower and a four-million-candlepower beam results in a light that can be seen twenty miles out to sea and even farther if you happen to have crow's nest duty and your ship has a tall mast.

A museum, located in the old foghorn building, has a collection of photographs showing many of the wrecks that occurred nearby, and you can climb the 145 stairs to see the old light and its magnificent lens. Several of the keepers' homes are now available for vacation rental from the nonprofit organization that runs the lighthouse. If you are looking for solitude, this is the place.

The tiny town of **Manchester** once boasted a large creamery that no doubt employed a goodly crew. The invention of refrigerated trucks doomed the operation; raw milk now goes directly to the cities. Largest of the rivers in these parts is the Garcia, whose floodplain is the winter home to thousands of whistling swans, the only true American swan, also called the tundra swan. In March they migrate north to the Arctic circle, where they stay until November. The best place to observe these beauties, as well as other shore birds, is among the dunes and coastal ponds of **Manchester Beach State Park.**

FOOD AND LODGING   Point Arena, California 95468

- ✔ **Point Arena Lighthouse**   Cottages. P.O. Box 11. (707) 882-2777.

- ✔ **LaBou's Lodge**   40 old-fashioned motel rooms. 135 Main Street. (707) 882-2000.

- ✔ **Manchester Beach State Park**   41 primitive campsites.

- ● **Giannini's**   Italian restaurant and bar. (707) 882-2146.

A few miles north of here we take final leave of the San Andreas Fault. The rocks on the west side of the highway had their origin near Santa Barbara. In their book *Roadside Geology of Northern California*, authors David Alt and Donald Hyndman speculate that it might have taken ten to twenty million years to make this trek, and that if so, a San Francisco–size earthquake would have occurred every century or so. Since we're coming up on the centennial of that quake, perhaps it is best that we hurry on.

Elk • Population: 200

No elk have frequented this countryside in nearly one hundred years, but the name seems to have stuck, even though many a local insists the place should revert to its former name, Greenwood. They have a point—the old name is a famous one in western history. Caleb Greenwood was a trapper with Manuel Lisa and William Ashley in the 1820s and became one of the most famous of the mountain men. He was celibate until the age of sixty-one, then had five children by a half-blood woman whose mother had married a French-Canadian *voyageur*. Their sons were instrumental in founding this town. Caleb guided the first wagon train over the Sierra Nevada in 1844 and then, at the age of eighty-four, went off to help rescue the few survivors of the ill-fated Donner party.

In its heyday, when two or three boats a week anchored offshore, Elk was what historian Lee Benson, exercising a bit of understatement, calls "a town with nonpuritan values." It boasted half a dozen hotels and twice that many saloons. They weren't for tourists in those days. Loggers came in from the woods to collect their semiannual $500 paycheck, and they could hardly wait to spend it. Employees were paid by check, drawn on a San Francisco bank. Bartenders and innkeepers took 5 to 10 percent off the top for converting paper to cash and then took that right back in payment for watered-down whiskey and a flea-infested straw tick. In his book *Ships of the Redwood Coast*, Jack McNarin comments sadly:

> It is said, and with some authority, that only one payroll was ever sent to Greenwood in the early days, the same money being used over and over again.

The timber ran out in the 1930s, and the dog hole port hasn't seen a cargo ship since. Yet Greenwood Cove boasts some of the most interesting sea stacks on the entire Northwestern Pacific Coast. These hunks of former headland, with their secret caves eroded by unceasing waves, make tempting spots for exploration. Boats and kayaks can be rented in Elk.

FOOD AND LODGING   Elk, California, 95432

✔✔✔ **Harbor House Inn**   10-room B&B in a 1917 house built entirely of redwood. Tariff includes dinner. P.O. Box 369. (707) 877-3203.

✔✔✔ **Elk Cove Inn**   9-room B&B in the former guest house of the L. E. White Lumber Co. Restaurant serves German and French dinners for guests and others who call ahead. P.O. Box 367. (707) 877-3321.

✔✔ **Greenwood Lodge**   7-room B&B. P.O. Box 172. (707) 877-3422.

●● **Greenwood Pier Inn**   Restaurant and lodging. (707) 877-9997.

Elk marks the end of the lonely part of the Mendocino coast. At the Navarro River, a highway comes in from the interior, bringing most of the people who frequent the northern part of this seaside paradise.

5

MENDOCINO'S MAGICAL COAST

Country Inns and Farmhouse B&Bs

A scant forty miles separates the mouth of the Navarro River from the place where Highway 1 turns inland and ceases to be the Shoreline Highway. It is forty miles of arguably the most beautiful coastline in the United States—a land where rich folk come to play, a place where escapees from urbanity have retired to newly planted gardens, where logging still plays a boisterous role in the local economy, and where artists by the score gather to discuss their work and commiserate about the scant financial rewards of their chosen profession. For years this was backwater California. Whether it will become another visitor-dominated place like the Monterey peninsula no one knows, but its natural splendors make that a possibility, much to the chagrin of many who have spent their lives eking out a living in this idyllic countryside.

For most visitors, the Mendocino coast begins at the point where State Highway 129, threading its way down the Navarro River, finally meets the sea.

Shortcut Access to the Mendocino Coast

Seventy-five miles north of the Golden Gate Bridge, the "Redwood Highway," U.S. Highway 101, ceases to be a freeway and finally turns into a rural road. Before World War II, once you passed San Rafael you were out in the country, but now that doesn't occur until way north of Santa Rosa. Healdsburg, a pleasant town on the fringes of urbanity, is more or less at the

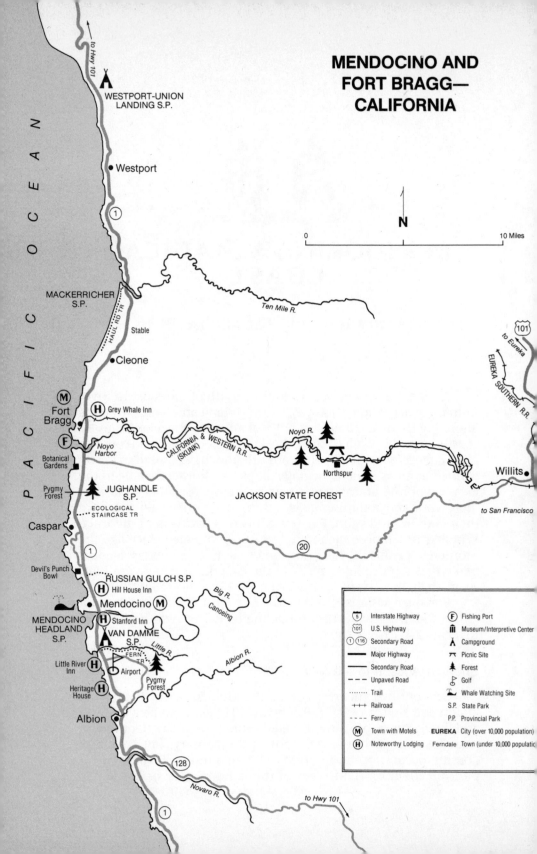

MENDOCINO AND FORT BRAGG— CALIFORNIA

PACIFIC OCEAN

to Hwy 101

WESTPORT-UNION
LANDING S.P.

● Westport

① 1

N

0   10 Miles

MACKERRICHER
S.P.

HAUL RD TR

Ten Mile R.

Stable

● Cleone

to Eureka

101

to Eureka

EUREKA SOUTHERN R.R.

Ⓜ
Fort
Bragg

Ⓗ Grey Whale Inn

Ⓕ

Noyo
Harbor

Botanical
Gardens

Pygmy
Forest

CALIFORNIA & WESTERN R.R.
(SKUNK)

Noyo R.

Northspur

Willits ●

JUGHANDLE
S.P.

ECOLOGICAL
STAIRCASE TR

JACKSON STATE FOREST

to San Francisco

Caspar ●

① 1

20

Devil's Punch
Bowl

RUSSIAN GULCH S.P.

Ⓗ Hill House Inn

● Mendocino Ⓜ

Big R.

Canoeing

Ⓗ Stanford Inn

MENDOCINO
HEADLAND
S.P.

Ⓐ

VAN DAMME
S.P.

Little R.

Albion R.

Little River
Inn Ⓗ

FERN
TR

Ⓐ Airport

Pygmy
Forest

Heritage
House Ⓗ

Albion ●

128

Novaro R.

to Hwy 101

① 1

center of Sonoma County's wine country. Beyond is Geyserville (where, curiously, there are no geysers), and then comes the tiny hamlet of Asti, named for the grape-growing region in northern Italy. Wineries to visit along this stretch of road include Souve-rain, Pedroncelli, Geyser Peak, and Italian Swiss Colony. If you're still fit to drive after all those tasting rooms, turn off the main road at Cloverdale and follow the two-lane State Highway 128 until it ends at its junction with the Shoreline Highway. It's a twisty-turny fifty-six-mile road, but much faster driving than the one we've been following. Yorkville, Boonville, and Philo are hamlets amid mountains and vineyards along the way. The latter two towns are situated in the newly emerging *appellation* Anderson Valley. The drive from San Francisco to the sea takes about three hours.

Albion/Little River • Population: 350

When I first drove up this coast in 1951, we booked a room in Fort Bragg's Piedmont Hotel, now with its top floor lopped off and just a restaurant. There was hardly any other place to stay. My next trip was in the mid-1960s. By then Fort Bragg had developed an extensive "motel row," but people then hardly considered staying in anything other than a standard highway "auto court." It wasn't until the early 1970s that things began to change, spurred on by the success of two nearby establishments, the Heritage House Inn and the Little River Inn. They were, it turned out, harbingers of a revolution in tourism on the Mendo-cino coast. The forty-mile stretch of road up ahead now boasts half a hundred country inns and B&Bs, and no longer is a room just a place to rest after taking in the scenery. The lodging itself, and the life-style it espouses, is the raison d'être on the Mendo-cino coast.

Our first encounter with this sybaritic life-style is at Heritage House Inn, nestled in a little cove that reputedly was used for rum-running during Prohibition. They say Baby Face Nelson hid out here when the G-men were on his track. In 1949 the Dennen family bought the old farm and turned the only surviving build-ing into a guest house. By the early seventies, the demand for rooms far exceeded what was available, so cottages were con-structed on the sloping, cypress-forested grounds. There are now sixty-nine of them, each of which has been given a name like Scott's Opera House, Barber Pole, and Salem. Guests enjoy a beautiful lounge with a walk-in-size fireplace and dine (coat and tie required) in a large, well-appointed restaurant. A cocktail bar looks out over the Pacific.

The village of Albion is the site of an immense truss bridge that lets you avoid a tortuous drive down to the river bottom and then up the other side. A small marina is located nearby. Author Barbara Dorr Mullen quotes one early traveler's description of this country:

> The piece of coast between Albion and the next place, Little River, seemed to me almost the finest I had seen. Such headlands, black and wooded, such purple seas, such vivid blaze of spray, such fjords and islets, a painter would be ravished by it.

Little River Inn too has prospered from America's changing vacation demands. Originally with only a few rooms above the bar and restaurant, it has grown to a fifty-unit establishment, one of the most popular on the coast. The white clapboard building, built in 1867, has rooms overlooking the ocean or the nine-hole golf course out back. Cottages and modern motel rooms are also available. The place boasts rather proudly: "No facilities for conventions, groups, or larger parties are available."

Nearby **Van Damme State Park** was the gift of a local gentleman who was born here, moved to San Francisco where he became a ferry boat mogul, and then returned here to live out his last years (he died in 1934). Day visitors can enjoy a walk along the old skid road that pushes its way up Fern Canyon. This stream, typical for this coast, isn't very long and therefore never had enough water to float timber down to the mills. Loggers tried building storage dams that were then dynamited in the hope that the resulting flood would wash the logs down to the sea. The practice was only marginally successful. **Fern Trail** is paved for most of its 2½-mile length and therefore provides a nice place to walk during the rainy season when other trails might be too muddy.

A few miles north is **Big River,** a jewel of a stream where no homes or resorts despoil the lushly forested shores. Tidewater extends inland for eight miles, ideal canoeing water. Canoers are a canny lot; most plan their day so they paddle upstream on a flooding tide and return on an ebb. Rentals are available at Big River Lodge.

FOOD AND LODGING   Albion/Little River, California 95456

✔✔✔✔ **Heritage House Inn**   Restaurant, lounge, rooms, and cabins. Tariff includes breakfast and dinner. Little River. (707) 937-5885.

✔✔✔✔ **The Stanford Inn by the Sea: Big River Lodge**
Lovely motellike establishment located on a bluff above

Big River. The 40 rooms, complete with TV, fireplaces, sofas, and four-poster beds, have balconies that face the ocean. P.O. Box 487, Mendocino 95460. (707) 937-5615.

✔✔✔ **Little River Inn** 52 rooms and cabins, restaurant and bar. Little River. (707) 937-5942.

✔✔✔ **Rachel's Inn** 5-room B&B. 8200 North Highway 1. (707) 937-0088.

✔✔ **Glendeven** 10-room B&B in an 1867 farmhouse. Little River. (707) 937-0083.

✔✔ **The Victorian Farmhouse** 6-room B&B built in 1877. P.O. Box 357. (707) 937-0697.

✔✔ **Fensalden Inn** 7-room B&B in a farmhouse located on a bluff half a mile east of the highway. Nice walking. P.O. Box 99, Albion 95410. (707) 937-4020.

✔ **Van Damme State Park** 74 campsites, 10 walk-/bike-in sites.

●● **Ledford House** Continental dining. (707) 937-0282.

Mendocino • Population: 950

It's been described as a New England village on the California coast, a picturebook town, a Left Bank, a Walden or Brook Farm, and a new Zion in the wilderness. No one accuses the place of being a tourist trap, but Mendocino the village and Mendocino the area seem to have two different personalities. In the village you'll find Pepperwood Potters and a camera shop called Visual Feast. Corners of the Mouth stocks natural foods and grains; The Body Experience, soap. Boutiques have names like The Great Put On, To Have and to Hold, Southern Exposure, and Rainsong. Compass Rose offers leather products; Local Motive sells gifts, as do The Cobweb and Personal Expressions. Hair Force advertises total hair control. Sky's No Limit is a kite shop, The Village Idiot rents videotapes. Haberdasheries include the Mendocino Tee Shirt Company and the Mendocino Hat Company, and there is the celebrated Mendocino Bakery plus the Mendocino Ice Cream Company, Mendocino Chocolate Company, and Mendocino Jams and Jellies.

In contrast, a look at a local handout paper, *Mendocino Country*, gives a different slant to the character of the area. Advertisers include Biofeedback Institute of Mendocino, Heartwood Healing Arts Institute (massage therapy/natural health counseling, transformational therapy, and clinical nutrition), Sweetwater Gardens (a hot tub and sauna spa), a firm that advertises "advanced massage training in polarity therapy," Triad Healing Center (co-creators' weekends include instruction in "Touching the Earth, Loving Ourselves"), and the Wellspring Renewal Center, which offers "spiritual retreats." The Apple Hill Orchard sells "organically grown fruit trees," and Frey Natural Wines features "organically grown grapes." Perhaps both were produced from plants distributed by the Abundant Life Seed Foundation and were helped along by products sold by the North American Organic Fertilizer Company or their competitor, the Carlbat Bat Guano Company.

My impression is that Mendocino today is what Carmel was forty years ago, a charming, somewhat unassuming place where people come to relax, to escape from the tyranny of the telephone, to discover (or rediscover) a life without television, to do some reading, browse through art galleries, and stroll a bit, to eat well, and to make new friends. In short, it's a return to a perceived turn-of-the-century life-style.

Mendocino, one of the oldest towns in California, was originally called Meiggsville, but perhaps because word filtered north from San Francisco about the founder's shenanigans (see Honest Henry Meiggs, page 61), the inhabitants opted for a more respectable name. The sawmill here closed in 1937. Somehow the town survived the 1906 quake, it never burned . . . and, miraculously, it also escaped the land speculators' greed—thanks to a combination of luck and hard work by a lot of people. Unlike in Caspar, the next mill town north, many houses in Mendocino were privately owned. When Caspar's mill closed, the company razed the buildings; it was cheaper than paying taxes on them. There were, to be sure, a loss of many homes in Mendocino, but most remained occupied during the big sleep between the closing of the mill and the time when an arts and tourist community began to flourish. Boise Cascade, a lumber company turned conglomerate that owned the headlands property, began to make noises about building a high-density resort on the former mill site. "The plans were gross," said longtime resident Ed O'Brien. "I think they hired the worst architect they could find just to scare us into doing something." Predictably, the community united against the project. The state of California stepped in and agreed to buy the property for a state park, but only if the townsfolk promised not to spoil the place next door. Thus was born the Mendocino Historical Review Board.

"We can't change the color of the paint on this building without their approval," the docent at the Ford House Museum fumed. "Those guys at the review board run this town."

"Not so," said board member Ed O'Brien, "but we have had an effect on this place. A fellow wanted to put a neon sign in his store. A lot of us traipsed over to the county seat in Ukiah. 'How big a sign?' one of the supervisors asked. 'Just a foot or so long,' was the reply. You know, that supervisor was about to approve the damn sign, and I was mad! So I jumped up and said, 'Whoa. The size doesn't make any difference; the ordinance says everything has to be made of the same materials used when the town was built. Neon signs didn't exist in those days.' So we got it stopped, and that set the tone for what followed."

HONEST HENRY MEIGGS

"Honest" Henry's sobriquet wasn't exactly like Lincoln's, nor was his life, but he left his imprimatur on the settling of the West. Harry didn't have much money, but he thought big. In 1852, when he ran out of trees to cut in the Berkeley hills, he loaded his sawmill machinery aboard the schooner *Ontario* and sailed for the redwood coast. It wasn't long before he employed over five hundred loggers in the nearby forests. But Mendocino, it seems, wasn't big enough, either. Only a place among San Francisco's nabobs would do, and real estate speculation would be his game—speculation focusing on the then undeveloped area north of Telegraph Hill now known as North Beach. He built Meiggs Wharf where the tourist-oriented Pier 39 now stands, and he gobbled up land as fast as a hardy handshake and a big smile could convince the citizenry to loan him money. Alas, the boom slowed down—his pyramiding scheme began to demand huge amounts of cash, and he found himself saddled with loans costing 1 percent per *day,* as the locals later found out. As a member of the board of aldermen, he did what every good San Francisco politician of the day was prone to do—he found a way to do some "creative financing." Warrants were his vehicle. "In the case of the warrants, as in that of scrip," say T. H. Watkins and R. R. Olmsted in their book *Mirror of the Dream,* "gold went into the city treasury and paper came out." Unfortunately, Honest Henry's paper was forged. One fine October day in 1854, he told his friends he was taking his family for a bay cruise aboard his lavishly outfitted bark *American.* Nightfall found the little ship far over the western horizon and the good folks of San Francisco $800,000 poorer.

Arriving in Santiago, Chile, Meiggs had to pawn his watch to survive, but within five months he became prosperous as a builder of railroads. His fame grew; the government of Peru practically commanded him to come north to help them build lines over the Andes, so he did. The great Don Enrique, as he came to be known, employed twenty thousand men to build the Central Railway of Peru, the highest in the world. His name is now a legend in the annals of railroading.

The second important event was the establishment of the Mendocino Arts Center, a project that owes its existence to the energies of Bill and Jennie Zacha. The center, built on the site of a burned-down mansion, lured internationally known visual artists, craftsmen, and performing artists. Cultural attractions brought the tourists, and thus Mendocino began its renaissance. That has been both good and bad. Suzanne Siskin told me that one of her friends, now in her seventies, has lost all her neighbors to the boutiques. Rents got so high they all moved out. "If I get into trouble after dark, there's no one around to call to for help," Suzanne quoted her as saying. Ed O'Brien talked about the ultimate irony of this change. "You know, when I got out of high school, most of my classmates had to leave because there were no jobs. Houses were vacant—you could buy one for the price of a Ford. Now it's different. See that car out there? A house now costs three or four times as much as that. So the young still move out. Oh, there are plenty of jobs, but they can't afford to live here." The car Ed was pointing to, incidentally, was a Rolls-Royce.

The Mendocino Land Trust has been active in preserving the place. The few new buildings here are done in good taste and show the owners' wise decisions not to skimp on the pocketbook. All this has made Mendocino a charming place. The town has three visual symbols: a white, ten-foot-high carved-wood statue, *Father Time and the Maiden,* which sits atop the former Masonic Hall; a dozen or so lattice-timbered towers, each topped with a redwood water tank; and the Presbyterian church, which looks like it might have been moved from Sturbridge, Massachusetts.

Main Street has two historical museums. The **Ford House,** one of the town's oldest, was purchased by the state and is now operated by volunteers working under the auspices of the Mendocino Area Parks Association. Photos showing logging operations adorn one room, paintings by local artists hang in another. Across the street is **The Kelley House Museum,** which is supported by the Mendocino County Heritage Network. The 1861 house is set in a garden with a pond where geese paddle around, much to the delight of the younger generation. Community activities of one sort or another seem to be staged all year long. There is a whale festival in March, a food and wine festival in May, a chili cookoff in July, and a mushroom festival and Oktoberfest in the fall. For children there is a ten-penny carnival on the Fourth of July and a sand castle building contest on Labor Day.

The **Mendocino Arts Council** is the center for cultural events in the area. The Helen Schoeni Theater hosts Sunday-afternoon concerts, a summer music festival, and a professional theater company that stages plays throughout the year. Twenty art galleries display the works of local artists. Indicative of the changing face of the town is the remodeling of the old Mendocino Hotel, a once seedy place that has been redone with period furniture in the lobby and brass bedsteads in the upstairs rooms. Though the hotel is expensive, most guests have to walk down the hall to the toilet and shower (a terry-cloth robe hangs in the closet of each room). A bar, large restaurant, and garden cafe make the public areas lively the year round. A new addition on the lot behind the hotel has modern rooms overlooking a handsome garden. One of the newest places to stay is the Hill House Inn, which overlooks a lovely cove. Designed to resemble a New England farmhouse, it boasts a fine restaurant, a bar, and, as if to thumb its nose at Little River Inn, conference facilities. But Mendocino's real charm lies in its B&Bs, the most visible of which is the gingerbread MacCallum House, a mansion that also has a restaurant and a bar. The funky Cafe Beaujolais, whose chef published a best-selling cookbook under that name, is only one of the many fine places to eat.

FOOD AND LODGING   Mendocino, California 95460

✔✔✔ **Blackberry Inn**   13-room B&B a bit out of town. 44951 Larkin Road. (707) 937-5281.

✔✔✔ **Mendocino Hotel and Garden Cottages**   51 rooms and cottages, restaurant and bar. P.O. Box 587. (707) 937-0511.

✔✔✔ **Hill House Inn**   44-room resort hotel, restaurant and bar. P.O. Box 625. (707) 937-0554.

✔✔✔ **MacCallum House**   21-room B&B, restaurant and bar. P.O. Box 206. (707) 937-0289.

✔✔ **Agate Cove Inn**   9 cottages and 2 rooms overlooking the sea. P.O. Box 1150. (707) 937-0551.

✔✔ **Ames Lodge**   7-unit B&B in a forest three miles east of town. P.O. Box 207. (707) 937-0811.

✔✔ **Bay Company Inn**   4-room B&B. P.O. Box 817. (707) 937-5266.

✔✔ **B.G. Ranch**   4-room B&B south of town. 9601 North Highway 1. (707) 937-5322.

✔✔ **Brewery Gulch Inn**   5-room B&B south of town. 9350 North Highway 1. (707) 937-4752.

✔✔ **Joshua Grindle Inn**   10-room B&B in an 1879 home. P.O. Box 647. (707) 937-4143.

✔✔ **Mendocino Village Inn**   14 rooms in a Queen Anne mansion. P.O. Box 626. (707) 937-0246.

✔✔ **Sea Gull Inn**   9-unit B&B. Continental breakfast served in your room. P.O. Box 317. (707) 937-5204.

✔✔ **Sea Rock Inn**   12 cottages and 4 luxury rooms, most overlooking the sea. P.O. Box 286. (707) 937-5517.

✔✔ **Sears House Inn**   9-room B&B. P.O. Box 844. (707) 937-4076.

✔✔ **Whitegate Inn**   6-room B&B in an 1880 home. P.O. Box 150. (707) 937-4892.

●● **Bandon's Whale Watch Restaurant**   Upstairs bar and restaurant overlooking the bay. (707) 937-4197.

●● **Cafe Beaujolais**   Celebrated California cuisine. Breakfast and lunch, dinner during the summer. (707) 937-5614.

●● **Papa Luigi's Wellspring Restorante**   Homemade pasta. (707) 937-4567.

●● **Sea Gull Inn & Cellar Bar**   Cozy restaurant. The bar is on the third floor. (707) 937-2100.

A lovely thirty-six-foot-high waterfall at the end of a 3½-mile trail is one attraction at **Russian Gulch State Park.** Other trails meander out over the headlands to the spectacular **Devil's Punch Bowl,** a caldron formed by the collapse of a two-hundred-foot-long sea cave.

The little dog hole port at the mouth of Russian Gulch hardly seems like a proper spot for a shipyard, but it was—for a short time. In 1866 Thomas Peterson built the three-masted schooner *Susan Merrill* at a reported cost of $18,000. Four hours after launching she went aground at Noyo, barely five miles north of here, a total loss. History does not record what Susan thought of the venture, but that spelled finis to shipbuilding at Russian Gulch.

Caspar, once one of the largest communities on this coast, is a virtual ghost town now. Some old pilings along the creek, rotting and awash at high tide, are all that remain of the Caspar Lumber Company mill. An extensive railroad used to haul out the logs, but much of the forest was isolated when a huge wooden trestle spanning Jughandle Creek became a pile of matchsticks in the 1906 earthquake. Railroad buffs will enjoy reading author

Ted Wurm's *Malets on the Mendocino Coast,* which describes the diminutive four-cylinder compound steam locomotives used on the line. One of the few surviving buildings from that era is the Caspar Inn, where country, rock, or folk music performances are given on weekends.

Less than a mile north of Caspar is **Jughandle State Reserve,** site of one of the most interesting hiking trails on the entire California coast. In less than three hours you can go back five hundred thousand years in time to see how the oceans shaped this magnificent countryside. The five-mile (round trip) trail dubbed **The Ecological Staircase** wends through four marine terraces, each one a hundred feet higher in elevation and one hundred thousand years older than the one below. You start on the same terrace we have been following throughout Mendocino County, where for one hundred thousand years windswept lowland firs, pines, and cypress (called *krummholz,* German for "bent wood") have combined with the grasses to create this scenic wonderland. The ocean below is laying down yet another terrace that, in its turn, will also be uplifted. After a mile or so of walking through stands of red alder, tanbark oak, and big leaf maple, you climb to the second terrace and suddenly you're in a mixed-conifer forest of bishop pine, grand fir, Sitka spruce, and western hemlock. At the third terrace the trail wends past giant Douglas fir and second- and third-growth redwoods with an understory of bold, rough sword fern, delicate five-fingered ferns, and the umbrella-leafed redwood sorrel.

The fifth terrace is the most interesting because hardpan has developed less than a foot below the surface, making it difficult for plant roots to grow deep into the soil. This is the **Pygmy Forest,** a land of stunted cypress and the Bolander pine that is unique to this area. A fifty-year-old tree may grow to no more than an inch in diameter and two to five feet in height. Other flora include rhododendron, manzanita, and huckleberry. You can drive to another pygmy forest south of here, part of Van Damme State Park. At Little River, go east three miles to the parking lot, a half mile past the airport. Interestingly, the only other pygmy forest we'll see is eight hundred miles north of here at the Pacific Rim National Park.

Fort Bragg • Population: 5,000

North of Jughandle Creek the Shoreline Highway barges across a thinly forested marine terrace interspersed with some nondescript commercial and residential buildings. You get the sense that you're about to leave the rural fairyland we have been driving through, and you are. But in some ways the country up ahead is a welcome relief because Fort Bragg is a real, honest-to-goodness workingman's town. Traffic signals, three of them, impede your progress—the first since leaving Sausalito. Don't fret. It's another 150 miles to the next one, and at least here there are no parking meters.

Fort Bragg is a mill town, the only one left on the Mendocino coast, and thus provides a hint of how things used to be in many of the ghost towns we have been visiting. It has led an on-again, off-again existence for 140 years, first as an Indian reservation (see An Ignoble Experiment: The Mendocino Indian Reservation, below), then for a brief time as an army fort, and twenty years later, as a lumber town, subject to all the ups and downs of that cyclical industry. The mill survived when others folded because the Union Lumber Company (now Georgia Pacific) invested in a forty-mile railroad that snaked its way over the mountains to connect with the outside world. It was twenty-six years abuilding and cost $1.7 million, but the tracks still exist and the trains now draw tourists who, in no small way, are a large part of Fort Bragg's economy.

AN IGNOBLE EXPERIMENT: THE MENDOCINO INDIAN RESERVATION

As thousands of gold seekers scrambled over the California countryside, they not surprisingly came into contact with Native Americans, often with disastrous consequences. The government's solution to the problem was simple: the Indians should be removed from white influence, "both for their own survival and for white progress." The twenty thousand or so Pomos, Bokagas, Ukiahs, Kianamaras, Masilla Coons, Wappas, and Labitaos who lived in the Mendocino area were to be rounded up and sent to a place of their own. The twenty-five thousand acres lying along the coast between Noyo and Ten Mile rivers were perfect, wrote Henry L. Ford, the agent who was sent out to establish a reservation.

I find the selection is admirably adapted for an Indian Reservation as there is no place [nearby] that is susceptible of settlement by the Whites; therefore no road would pass through the Reserve, and the Indians if kept thereon would be entirely isolated.

Heretofore the local tribes had spent little time along the coast; they preferred the warmer inland climes and so were "isolated" from the land where they had lived for centuries. It wasn't the first or the last time that the least desirable land (meaning where there was probably no gold) would be given to the natives. Franklin Pierce approved the establishment of the Mendocino Reservation on May 22, 1856.

The following summer Agent Ford was able to boast, "There were 3,450 Indians on the reservation," although he did admit that 1,500 were "absent with permission to visit former haunts to gather food," and that he had some difficulty with runaways. Also, "there were 8,075 'wild Indians' in the vicinity, many of which occasionally lived here."

Shunting the natives onto a reservation meant that someone had to pay for their upkeep. Agent Ford had a solution:

> There is about three thousand acres of as good wheat land as there is in the State and about six thousand acres of as good potatoe land as can be found anywhere. There is also four Rivers on the location which abound in fish which with the shell fish that abound on the Coast could be made to furnish at least one third of the Subsistence for all the Indians that can be induced to go to this Reserve.

What led Agent Ford to believe that his charges would become farmers is curious. With the exception of the Mandans in North Dakota, few northwestern tribes ever showed much inclination to grow crops.

Though there was no gold in the hills, there was something equally valuable—trees. Alex McPherson, a squatter, built a mill on the north bank of the Noyo River that quickly developed into a small white settlement that became a source of disease and disturbance within the reservation. Inland logging on the Noyo River caused silting, which had a deleterious effect on the salmon fishery. A report stated that some whites purposely allowed cattle and hogs to destroy Indian crops, thereby hoping for abandonment of the reservation. A settler, Samuel Watts, killed an Indian without provocation. The natives retaliated by killing Watts. Inland, things were worse. Whites were accused of stealing Indian children and selling them. The government's answer was to send in the army to keep the peace. In June of 1857 Lieutenant Horatio Gibson and a detachment of twenty soldiers from the Presidio of San Francisco arrived to establish a fort, naming it after Colonel Braxton Bragg, who had won fame in the Mexican War but later, as an officer of the Confederacy, was to suffer the onslaught of U.S. Grant's forces at Chattanooga.

The soldiers amused themselves in predictable ways. "Last Monday night was made hideous here by the drunken soldiers going to the Indian lodges for squaws," wrote one of the agents. The biggest engagement with the enemy apparently was in May of 1863, when a detachment of twenty men was ordered to "chastise" a band of Indians who had killed several head of cattle and two valuable horses. They surprised thirty or forty Indians, killing four and wounding three, "the latter so badly that I found it useless to bring them along," boasted the officer in command.

By 1858, a scant two years after its founding, a special agent sent out to assess the situation wrote:

> . . . lamentable failure where the reservations are simply government almshouses, where a considerable number of Indians are insufficiently fed and scantily clothed at an expense wholly disproportionate to the benefits conferred. The whole place has an effete, decayed look that is disheartening.

There were now only 750 left on the Mendocino Reservation. In 1861 Colonel Francis Lippitt mused:

> The Indians carried thither have all soon returned to the usual haunts, and these return worse than they went, having acquired the taste for beef and learned to covet many articles they were before ignorant of. If they could be all transported to the Tejon Reservation, or, still better, to one of the Santa Barbara Islands, they could never return hither again.

Though there would be no Elba for these tribes, the colonel was to get his wish. Two years later a government report stated:

> The buildings and improvements have been suffered to fall into decay, the adjacent country is occupied by whites, and many settlers have gone upon the reservations; and the result has been that they are almost entirely abandoned by the Indians, who prefer to gain a precarious living as best they may, rather than submit to those vexations and aggressions incident to so close a proximity to the whites.

In 1864 those who were left, the old, the weak, the diseased, were sent inland to the Round Valley Reservation.

The Civil War caused priorities to shift for the little garrison at Fort Bragg. The soldiers were sent to Utah to guard the Overland Mail Route. The reservation land was subsequently sold—for $1.25 an acre.

A quick drive through town on Highway 1 leaves you a bit disappointed, but there are little gems to be found if you stop to look. The old company store is one, located on Main Street. It is no longer owned by Georgia Pacific, and it sells only clothing now. But a look at the architecture gives a hint of the paternalism that used to exist in company towns like this. The floors are oiled wood, and elegant beams and trusses are made of redwood, and a mezzanine surrounds the huge salesroom. The cashier's office used to be above the front door. Salesclerks would stuff a customer's money into a little metal cup, attach it to a trolley, and send it zooming upstairs on high wires located throughout the store. Though no longer used, the contraptions are still here for all to see. The **Mendocino Arts Council** now operates a gallery on the mezzanine.

Another gem in Fort Bragg used to be the old-fashioned blue-and-white library (built by the lumber company, of course), which recently and tragically burned to the ground. Next to the ruined site is **The Guest House Museum**, operated by the City. The 1892 three-story Victorian mansion was the home of the founder of the Union Lumber Company and later became guest quarters for visiting dignitaries. Two old locomotives, a steam donkey, and high-wire blocks are set up outside. The **Fort Building**, the only surviving structure from the days of the reservation, is located a couple of blocks away.

When I saw a notice that the Mendocino Succulent Society meets on the first Tuesday of every month, I realized that Fort Bragg is also a place of gardens. The combination of weather and soil produces a prolific assortment of ornamentals. Four nurseries sell a hundred varieties of rhododendrons from large to small, as well as fuchsias, orchids, pelargoniums, begonias, and azaleas. Showplace of all this activity is the **Mendocino Botanical Gardens,** a fifty-acre tract of woodlands and headlands that include most of the local species of flora and some exotics as well. You walk through a tremendous bishop pine forest, and in the spring the flower display is dazzling. My favorite specimen, however, is the dawn redwood, planted from seeds brought from China.

Fort Bragg's main tourist attraction, however, is the **Skunk,** the affectionate name given the little yellow railcars (see Emil's Skunk, page 70) that trundle along the tracks of the old California Western Railroad and Navigation Company. "You can smell 'em, before you can see 'em," the locals complained when diesels replaced steam locomotives in 1925. Thus the name Skunk. During the summer, old-fashioned locomotive-pulled passengers cars are used to handle the crowds. Several flatcars, now fitted with benches, are open to the sky, making the ride almost as spectacular as Switzerland's Bernina Express. On occasion the company fires up an old steamer, appropriately dubbed the Super Skunk, and runs her out to Northspur, halfway to Willits.

The line is only forty miles long, but the tracks twist so much ("like a snake with a bellyache," wrote an old-timer) that the journey takes almost three hours. Over to Willits and back is an all-day adventure, so to accommodate those with less time, dur-

EMIL'S SKUNK

I rode the "Skunk" in the middle of February—a bright clear day. This forty-mile line, I discovered, is precious, especially in winter. The tracks cross the Noyo River a dozen times, and I could watch the salmon returning to their spawning grounds and their date with death. The sparseness of leaves provided little shelter for the numerous deer that paused to gaze at our little yellow railcar rambling through their home. It was cold, but the oil-fired furnace at the center of the fifty-year-old car provided a cheery accent to the day, and I mused that it might be even nicer if it was raining torrents. But this day fishermen were strung out along the right-of-way. Some had used the train to get here and would return the same way since roads are few and far between in these coastal mountains.

Loggers were out, too, rigging high leads to snake the redwood to staging areas on the ridge tops, using techniques perfected one hundred years ago. Surprisingly, a fresh-cut forest doesn't look as devastating as one might expect; the needles are still green and blend in with the damp ground. The narrow tracks that meander through the woods intrude little on this beauty. You can reach out the window and grab a sward fern if you choose. We slowed down so the conductor could snatch a mail sack hanging from a hook alongside the tracks, and later we stopped to unload merchandise at an un-attended platform located a few feet into the woods. A fellow with an infant slung in his backpack trotted up to the departing train, banged on the window, and passed in a letter to be posted in Fort Bragg. A teenage student stepped off the train, had his fare card punched, and gave his mother a hug. These incidents seemed to make one thing clear: this train is the sinew that holds the cultural fabric of this roadless community together.

In the middle of what seemed like nowhere, the train paused at a sign reading "Emil's Station" to pick up a passenger dressed in a corduroy sport coat and carrying a briefcase. He introduced himself: Emil Burkhardt. He was going to town to shop for groceries. A chemical engineer, trained in Germany, he and his wife had es-chewed the automobile, opting to live off the land. But he was perplexed. The Mendocino Coast Railway, which now operates this passenger service, had petitioned the Interstate Commerce Com-mission to abandon service during the winter. Twenty-five or thirty people were aboard my train, but Emil said there are sometimes less than five. "Why don't they advertise winter use? The fog-free weather is often better than in the summer, and the forest smells are over-powering." He thinks a partial closing would lead to an ultimate abandonment. "How could they make this into another ugly logging road?" So he asked me to write to the ICC. I did, of course.

ing the summer the company schedules a morning and an afternoon run from each end. They meet in the middle; passengers
who want to go clear through change trains. Those with a half
day to spend return on the train they went out on. On summer
Saturdays, the railroad operates an afternoon/evening Barbecue
Special. Passengers sip wine and listen to live music as they
trundle through the woods. A feast is set out on picnic tables in
the lovely forest at Northspur.

Most of Fort Bragg's shopping district is on Franklin Street,
one block east of Highway 1. The unpretentious stores are interspersed with pool halls and beer parlors where the mill hands
come to relax or blow off a little steam after work. The town has
its Victorians, too, but few have the fixed-up look of Mendocino's
homes. There is a hint of change, though. The Old Coast Hotel
and Restaurant (great creole food) has been refurbished and now
is a nice place to stay. So is the onetime company hospital that is
now The Grey Whale Inn. Colette Bailey, a consummate innkeeper, is active in the promotion of the B&B concept and dis-
penses all kinds of advice about what to see and do and where to
go for the perfect dinner.

Most tourists opt to have dinner a mile south of Fort Bragg at
Noyo Harbor, one of the more interesting fishing ports we'll see
on this sojourn. The entrance to this rock-ridged port is only two
hundred feet wide, a boiling caldron of wicked white water when
the tide is flooding and the wind is blowing hard. Heaving boats
struggle mightily against the angry swells, and their pilots seem to
be squinting through spindrift-lashed windows as they steer for
the calmer waters outside. Inbound transit isn't any easier, but
there's a payoff at the dock. Squid, rock cod, and a local delicacy,
red snapper, are taken, but salmon is the money catch along this
coast. "A guy can get $3.25 a pound at dockside," a fellow told
me. "One 'king' might fetch $100, and with a good boat and
crew, you can make $2,000 a day." Since they charge over $7.00
a pound for salmon steak in Berkeley, somebody besides the
fellow who braved that terrible harbor mouth is getting a piece of
the action. And he didn't have to face the fury of this so-called
pacific ocean to earn it.

Several Noyo firms operate "party boats" for sportfishers.
Snorklers dive for abalone during the season, but this delicacy, a
marine snail, is getting harder to find. Commercial harvesting is
now banned in California; the Department of Fish and Game is
trying to ensure an adequate food supply for the frolicsome sea
otter, which has taste buds as fine as we do. The "abs" you find in
restaurants now come from Mexico. The state is experimenting
with methods to improve the abalone's chances of survival, and

maybe someday hatcheries will be developed to increase the population.

FOOD AND LODGING　Fort Bragg, California 95437

✔✔ **Harbor Lite Lodge**　70-room motel overlooking Noyo Harbor. 120 North Harbor Drive. (707) 964-0221.

✔✔ **The Surry Inn**　New 53-room downtown motel. 888 South Main. (707) 964-4003.

✔✔ **Cap'n Capps' Country Inn**　4-unit B&B in an 1883 house east of Casper. 32980 Gibney Lane. (707) 964-1415.

✔✔ **Colonial Inn**　8-unit B&B. 533 East Fir Street. (707) 964-9979.

✔✔ **Grey Whale Inn**　14-room B&B. 615 North Main. (707) 964-0640.

✔✔ **Glass Beach B&B**　9-room B&B. 726 North Main. (707) 964-6774.

✔✔ **Old Coast Hotel**　16-room hotel and restaurant. Oak at Franklin. (707) 964-6443.

✔✔ **Orca Inn**　7 rooms and cottages north of town. 31502 North Highway 1. (707) 964-5585.

✔ **MacKerricher State Park**　143 campsites.

•• **Gardens Cafe**　Restaurant overlooking Mendocino Botanical Gardens. (707) 964-7474.

•• **Capt. Flynt's**　Restaurant and bar overlooking Noyo Harbor. (707) 964-9447.

•• **The Wharf**　Restaurant and bar overlooking Noyo Harbor. (707) 864-4283.

• **Piedmont Hotel**　Italian restaurant. (707) 964-2410.

The countryside becomes rural again just beyond Fort Bragg. The little village of **Cleone** is aptly named—it's a Greek word meaning "gracious and beautiful." Three miles north of Fort Bragg is the entrance to **MacKerricher State Park,** where rocky headlands have given way to sand dunes. A freshwater lagoon, formed by the dunes, is popular for swimming, fishing, and rowboating, and a two-mile nature trail skirts its perimeter. The Haul Road, once used for logging, stretches the full length of the park. Cars are allowed on the southern three miles, allowing easy access to the long, driftwood-littered beach. The northern section stretching to Ten Mile River is popular for bikers and joggers and horse riders who can rent mounts at a nearby stable.

Westport • Population: 100

Highway 1 becomes lonely again since the road has a fraction of the traffic it saw south of Fort Bragg. Beyond Ten Mile River the character of the land becomes more like what we saw north of Point Arena—the highway traverses a marine terrace for a few miles, then suddenly corkscrews down into a coastal stream before popping up again on the other side. It takes a half hour to drive the fifteen miles to the only coastal settlement we'll see for a while. In 1878 Westport had a 375-foot-long wharf, six sawmills, fourteen saloons, and a pea canning factory. The wharf was built by James T. Rodgers, a fellow from Eastport, Maine; thus the name Westport. The principal products were shingles, railroad ties, and tanbark, the latter shipped to the leather tanning works on San Francisco Bay. There is little here now except a post office, a grocery store, and an old hotel whose false-front architecture makes it look right out of a cowboy movie.

Highway 1 has been rerouted and straightened north of Westport, so for three or four miles the driving becomes easier. The old road has been converted into **Westport-Union Landing State Beach,** which has campsites overlooking the ocean. This treeless bluff has no windbreaks, so the park is primarily used by RVers. Beachcombing is a popular pastime, and during the spawning run, tiny surfsmelt are taken by fishermen using the same sort of A-frame dip net the Indians used two hundred years ago.

FOOD AND LODGING   Westport, California 95488

✔✔ **Cobweb Palace**   6-room hotel with bar and restaurant. P.O. Box 132. (707) 964-5588.

✔✔ **Dehaven Valley Farm**   Restaurant, rooms, and cottages overlooking the sea. 39247 North Highway 1. (707) 964-5252.

✔ **Westport-Union Landing State Beach**   130 campsites.

We have now come to the end of the Mendocino coast. Up ahead looms the massive bulk of Cape Vizcaino (Sebastián Vizcaíno explored these waters early in the seventeenth century), the southern rampart of California's "Lost Coast." The mountains come right down to the sea north of here, mountains so rugged that even now few roads penetrate the vast wilderness. This eighty-mile stretch of California is called "lost" for good reason. Almost no one knows about it, and fewer still have ever been here. We'll find a way, though.

PART TWO

The Redwood Empire

6

EEL RIVER VACATIONLAND

Avenue of the Giants

There has never been a tree that has quite captured man's fancy like the sequoia, not only because of its size and stately beauty, but because these living fossils represent a tenaciousness that is an inspiration to all who wander through their mountain home. California poet Edwin Markham expressed his feeling as well as anyone I have come across:

> These great trees belong to the silences and millenniums. They seem, indeed, to be forms of immortality, standing there among the transitory shapes of time.

We have visited two old-growth redwood forests before on this sojourn, Muir Woods in Marin County and Armstrong Redwoods in Sonoma County, but neither experience quite prepares you for what lies ahead. Thanks to the efforts of a lot of concerned people and organizations, U.S. Highway 101 is graced with grove after grove of giants, many crowding the pavement itself. Even people in a hurry, those who don't bother to get out of their cars, come away sensing that they have seen one of the truly great wonders of the world. We'll go those in a hurry one better, though, for we'll explore forests away from the noise of the highway, and we'll find spots where a visitor can loiter, quite alone, among a cast of thousands of the mightiest living things God chose to put on this earth.

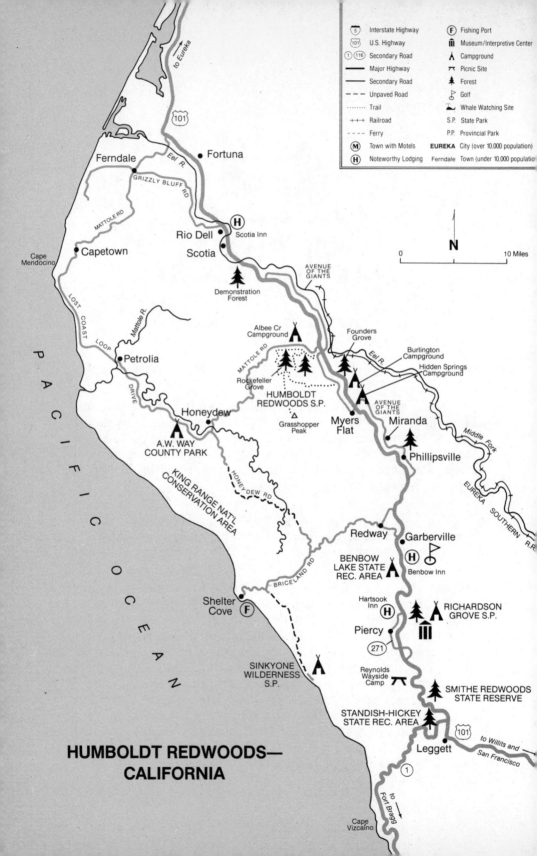

HUMBOLDT REDWOODS—
CALIFORNIA

Legend:

Symbol	Description
5	Interstate Highway
101	U.S. Highway
1 116	Secondary Road
——	Major Highway
——	Secondary Road
– – –	Unpaved Road
······	Trail
+++	Railroad
– – –	Ferry
M	Town with Motels
H	Noteworthy Lodging
F	Fishing Port
🏛	Museum/Interpretive Center
Ⲁ	Campground
⋔	Picnic Site
🌲	Forest
⛳	Golf
Whale	Whale Watching Site
S.P.	State Park
P.P.	Provincial Park
EUREKA	City (over 10,000 population)
Ferndale	Town (under 10,000 population)

N

0 · · · · · · · · · · 10 Miles

to Eureka

101

Ferndale

Fortuna

GRIZZLY BLUFF RD

Eel R.

MATTOLE RD

Rio Dell

H Scotia Inn

Scotia

Capetown

Cape
Mendocino

AVENUE
OF THE
GIANTS

Demonstration
Forest

LOST
COAST
LOOP

Mattole R.

Albee Cr
Campground

Founders
Grove

MATTOLE RD

Burlington
Campground

Hidden Springs
Campground

Rockefeller
Grove

Petrolia

DRIVE

HUMBOLDT
REDWOODS S.P.

Eel R.

Grasshopper
Peak

Myers
Flat

AVENUE
OF THE
GIANTS

Miranda

Middle Fork

Honeydew

A.W. WAY
COUNTY PARK

KING RANGE NAT'L
CONSERVATION
AREA

HONEYDEW RD

Phillipsville

EUREKA
SOUTHERN
R.R.

Redway

Garberville

BENBOW
LAKE STATE
REC. AREA

H
Benbow Inn

BRICELAND RD

Shelter
Cove F

Hartsook
Inn

H

RICHARDSON
GROVE S.P.

Piercy

271

🏛

SINKYONE
WILDERNESS
S.P.

Reynolds
Wayside
Camp

SMITHE REDWOODS
STATE RESERVE

STANDISH-HICKEY
STATE REC. AREA

101

to Willits and
San Francisco

Leggett

1

to
Fort Bragg

Cape
Vizcaino

P A C I F I C   O C E A N

Shortcut Access to the Eel River

We begin our redwood adventure at Leggett, the hamlet where State Highway 1 terminates at its junction with U.S. Highway 101. The obvious shortcut to this part of the world is to stay on Highway 101 all the way from San Francisco. The 180-mile journey from the Golden Gate Bridge takes nearly four hours, but there is reason to dally a bit. North of Cloverdale, the turnoff for Chapter 5, the Redwood Highway struggles through the steep gorge of the Russian River before reemerging into a broad valley.

Hopland • Population: 817

This quiet village is home to the lovely Fetzer Winery, which has a nice tasting room adjacent to a fine restaurant. For a more unique experience, however, pause at a firm you would perhaps expect to find at a place called Hopland, the Mendocino Brewing Company. This restaurant *mit biergarten* typifies how a small but growing number of entrepreneurs are catering to California's changing imbibing habits. Companies producing less than ten thousand barrels a year are called microbrewers. Mendocino Brewing's seven-hundred-barrel production certainly qualifies as micro, but the brews themselves are more properly called macro. Each of their four products has a big, strong, zesty flavor and packs considerably more wallop than your run-of-the-mill Bud or Coors. According to a brochure:

> "Peregrine Pale Ale is made with a pale malt and Cascade hops." Blue Heron Ale is similar, but "cluster bittering hops are added" to give it more zing. Red Tail Ale contains a "caramel malt" to give it a bit more body and a deep amber color. Those who like to down a potion the color and consistency of pine tar will enjoy the Black Hawk Stout, "made with a fully-roasted black malt, blended with pale and caramel malts and spiked with both cluster and Cascade hops."

Red Tail Ale, their most popular brew, is available in fifty-one-ounce magnum bottles, "the industry's only forty-two-pound six-pack," the barmaid chortled. When I visited the place, a couple left with $75 worth of beer in the trunk of their car. "We're from Munich," said the fellow. "It's almost as good as what we get at the Hofbrauhaus!" My view is that the Blue Heron Ale, the most German of these local brews, is in fact better than what I had at that famous German tavern.

Ukiah • Population: 12,000

Ukiah, the Mendocino County seat, has a remarkable museum considering the size of the town. **The Sun House,** a stately craftsman-style redwood bungalow built in 1911, was the home of Dr. John Hudson and his wife, Grace. The couple took a great interest in the Pomo Indians who lived nearby, he as an ethnologist, she as a portrait painter. The city recently constructed the **Grace Hudson Museum** on the property to house his collection of baskets and other Pomo artifacts, to display a few of her paintings, and to provide space for touring art shows. Ann Kelly-Holder, an art historian, told me that painters of the day criticized Grace Hudson for depicting a too romantic picture of the Pomos, but I felt that her portraits, with their large soulful eyes, seemed to capture a warmth among these people that others perhaps had failed to see. The grounds around the museum provide a fine place for a picnic. The recently constructed **Lake Mendocino,** located a few miles northeast of town, has another nice picnic area that includes a popular swimming beach.

Ukiah marks the northern limit of the so-called wine country and is the southern extremity of what might best be described as "lumber country." Wineries to visit include Cresta Blanca, Parducci, and Weibel, the latter famous for its Green Hungarian.

Willits • Population: 4,384

North of Ukiah, the Redwood Highway leaves the Russian River. After climbing the 1,900-foot Redwood Summit, you drop into a broad valley at the headwaters of the Eel, the river we will be following for most of this chapter. The town of Willits is a railroad junction, the eastern terminus of the famed Skunk trains. Full- and half-day trips leave from here during the summer (see Chapter 5). Another railroad, the Eureka Southern, heads north. In recent years tourist trains ran over these tracks, but at this writing the company is in receivership. That's a sad fact because the route goes away from Highway 101, following the middle fork of the Eel rather than the south fork. For thirty miles the tracks snake along the riverbank where no roads exist at all.

THE REDWOOD EMPIRE

Highway 101 meanders through some bucolic oak-savanna country, passes through the pleasant town of **Laytonville** (several cafes), and then begins to drop into the steep-sided canyon of the Eel.

We have finally reached the Redwood Empire. The little

hamlet of Leggett marks the southern limit of the north coast's redwood forests. A store and a motel with some rustic cabins cling to the riverbank. For the next seventy miles Highway 101 threads its way through the riverside home of the giant trees. All but ten miles of this is a four-lane divided highway, thanks or no thanks, depending on your point of view, to the efforts of the late Randolph Collier, a state legislator from Eureka, known as the "father of America's freeways." Controlled-access roads allow fast driving through this convoluted countryside, but in places they have had a noxious effect on exactly what conservationists have fought so hard to preserve (see Save the Redwoods League, below). When the highway engineers proposed barging straight through Richardson Grove, cutting a two-hundred-foot swath

SAVE THE REDWOODS LEAGUE

Two million acres of redwood forest graced the California landscape prior to the coming of the whites. By the turn of the century, two-thousand-year-old sequoias were being felled at an alarming rate, prompting a group called the Sempervirens Club to enlist the help of philanthropist Phoebe Apperson Hearst (William Randolph's mother) in their efforts to save at least a few of these giants for future generations to see and enjoy. Through their efforts, a forest twenty miles north of Santa Cruz was purchased and incorporated into Big Basin State Park, established in 1902. That set the stage for the founding of the Save the Redwoods League, which has, over the years, been instrumental in preserving 150,000 acres of virgin trees, 50,000 of which are in state parks, the balance in lands administered by the National Park Service. Over $40 million has been raised by the league so far. At today's timber and land prices, the property is worth fifty times that amount.

The league hired landscape architect Frederick Law Olmsted, Jr., to survey potential purchases. Their objective was to gain ownership of complete watersheds so that erosion could be controlled and wildlife habitat maintained. Firms like the Pacific Lumber Company agreed to delay timber harvesting until funds could be raised to purchase the land. The league hit on a fundraising scheme of dedicating individual forests to large donors, thus explaining why there are so many signs and plaques in the forest. The last large-scale additions were made in 1978, when President Carter signed the Redwood National Park Expansion Act, which also provided for rehabilitation of cutover lands.

through an old-growth forest, many Californians got up in arms. Governor Ronald Reagan's office denied that he ever said, "If you've seen one redwood, you've seen them all," but tree lovers are convinced he did. This particular freeway project got stopped, however, and even those in a hurry are obliged to slow down in a few spots. Not everyone has, judging from the scars on some of the roadside monarchs. But fortunately, much of the old road is still extant, so for forty of the sixty freeway miles you can duck off the fast road and explore this country at your leisure. Senator Collier's monument did have a predictable effect on how the lumber from Humboldt County's mills goes to market. It used to be shipped by train; now a surfeit of eighteen-wheelers compete for your share of the Redwood Highway.

The first of many state parks along Highway 101 is **Standish-Hickey State Recreation Area,** located a mile north of Leggett. Though most of the trees are second growth, a nice trail leads to an old beauty called the Captain Miles Standish Tree, named after the Pilgrim ancestor of the family that donated the land for the park. The trail passes a thirty-five-foot waterfall. Three miles farther downriver is **Smithe Redwoods State Reserve,** a nice place for a picnic or a swim in the Eel's warm water.

Around the bend is Confusion Hill, the first of a number of tourist attractions located along this highway. Any excuse at all will do for the establishment of a redwood gift shop; this one has some crazily constructed buildings that give the illusion that the laws of gravity are out of whack. A miniature railway takes children on a short ride through the woods. I guess it's best just to list these so-called attractions and get it over with, for though some may be fun for families with children, and shoppers will find others interesting, in my view they take a bit away from the inspiring solemnity of these forests. Anyway, you'll come upon the Chimney Tree and House in a Tree, a One Log House, the Shrine Drive-Thru Tree, the Eternal Tree: Hobbiton, U.S.A. (where the Hobbit lives, according to the brochure), the Immortal Tree, and the Grandfather Tree. Each has a shop selling artifacts made from redwood burls (the wartlike growths that append themselves to old trees). Burls are easy to carve into dishes and platters, and their twisty grain provides an interesting mottled-surface finish. Artisans sell redwood carvings of mountain goats, bears, gorillas, Indian chiefs (one feather or many), and pony-riding cowboys.

State Highway 271 is the designation assigned to the old road that, in spots, parallels the freeway. Your first access to this "slow road" is nine miles north of Leggett, where the two-lane biway ducks off to right, hugs a cliff on a sidehill viaduct, crosses under the freeway, and wanders through the tiny town of **Piercy.** A bit north of here you take final leave of Mendocino and enter the lumber kingdom of Humboldt County. The next major forest, **Richardson Grove State Park,** is one of the oldest and most widely used of all the redwood parks. Generations of California families have camped in this grove named after the twenty-fifth governor of the state, Friend W. Richardson. Children swim in the river and fish for small trout. This is the home of the playful river otter, on occasion nuzzling faces of curious-minded swimmers. Park rangers conduct campfire programs and lead nature hikes. The Fallen Giant is a famous old landmark located near an interpretive center where volunteers explain a bit about the redwood and its habitat. Just outside the park is a fixture of the redwood country, the well-loved Hartsook Inn, which has moderately priced cottages nestled in the woods and a large restaurant set in a fine 1930s building. Nearby **Benbow Lake State Recreation Area** is a nice place to have a sunny picnic or go canoeing on a placid reservoir.

Grande dame of the hostelries along the Eel River is the stately half-timbered, Tudor-style Benbow Inn. When I first stayed here in the early 1960s, the hotel had just reopened after a long hiatus brought on by World War II. The golf course, located just across the dirt airstrip, had been brought back to life, and although the hotel had a faded look and the gardens had pretty much gone to seed, you could sense the elegance the place must have displayed in its early days. Now the airstrip is gone, replaced by the freeway, but the grandeur has been brought back; the gardens have been replanted, and the rooms have been redone with antique furniture. A plaque certifies that this building is listed in the National Register of Historic Places. Wicker tables and chairs grace the red-tiled lanai near the entrance. Inside, the white, terra-cotta-ceilinged living room with its giant fireplace is furnished with thirty or forty chairs and sofas, a grandfather clock, and a bevy of tasseled lampshades. Four or five jigsaw puzzles are set about, waiting to be completed by guests seeking a more leisurely pace to life. The Windsor-chaired dining room (coat and tie required) reflects an older age, the dimly lit bar has an English pub–like atmosphere, and outside, the oak-shaded patio is a lovely place to while away an afternoon, sipping iced Chablis while reading a book. Of all the places we'll visit on this odyssey, Benbow is certainly one of the most gracious.

FOOD AND LODGING

✔✔✔ **Benbow Inn**   Country inn, restaurant and lounge. 445 Lake Benbow Drive, Garberville 95440. (707) 923-2124.

✔✔ **Hartsook Inn**   Restaurant and 62 cottages. Piercy 95467. (707) 247-3305.

✔ **Benbow Lake State Recreation Area**   75 campsites.

✔ **Richardson Grove State Park**   169 campsites.

✔ **Standish-Hickey State Park**   162 campsites.

Garberville/Redway • Population: 1,800

Garberville is the commercial center of southern Humboldt County and, deservedly or not, has the reputation of being the marijuana-growing capital of North America. When I wandered into a saloon for a midday beer, I spotted two bearded men having an earnest, businesslike conversation. When I sat down at the next stool, they abruptly moved out of earshot to a far corner of the room, where they continued their discussion standing up. Numerous law-enforcement agencies have joined together to promote the highly publicized CAMP operation (Campaign Against Marijuana Planting). Various techniques are used to spot illegal growers—including the use of low-flying airplanes, helicopters, and all-terrain vehicles.

Garberville has a wide-open, western feel. Among other attributes it boasts a fine newspaper, the *Redwood Record*. Though much of its economy depends on tourists, it doesn't seem touristy. The population is smaller than nearby Redway, but this is where everyone comes to shop, and half a dozen motels and several restaurants line the main drag. My favorite eatery is the Eel River Cafe, not so much for the food, but for the 1940s sign out front. Neon lights switch on and off, giving the illusion that the white-hatted chef, a frying pan in hand, is tossing a flapjack in the air.

FOOD AND LODGING   Garberville/Redway, California 95440

✔✔ **Humboldt House Inn**   55-room motel. 701 Redwood Drive. (707) 923-2771.

✔✔ **Brass Rail Inn**   17-unit motel and restaurant. P.O. Box 225, Redway 95560. (707) 923-3188.

✔ **Sherwood Forest Motel**   33-room motel. 814 Redwood Drive. (707) 923-2721.

✔ **Motel Garberville**   30-room motel and restaurant. 948 Redwood Drive. (707) 923-2422.

✔ **Motel Rancho**   22-room motel. 987 Redwood Drive. (707) 923-2451.

● **The Trees**   Restaurant. (707) 923-3837.

Phillipsville/Miranda • Population: 600

One of the prettiest drives in America, appropriately named the **Avenue of the Giants,** begins about eight miles north of Garberville. This is one spot where you're glad of the nearby freeway, because those in a hurry avoid the old road, so you don't have someone dogging your tail all the while. Thousand-year-old redwoods snuggle up to the pavement. The highway slithers about, not to avoid a steep embankment or find a better grade, but simply to dart around a tree the highway builders deemed too beautiful to destroy. Though much of the land here is in public ownership, there are a number of in-holdings where villages have sprung up. Phillipsville and Miranda are two nice little towns smack in the middle of the resort area, but another hamlet, Weott, suffered an inglorious fate during Christmas week in 1964 when the Eel flooded, and it no longer exists.

FOOD AND LODGING   Phillipsville/Miranda, California 95553

✔✔ **Miranda Gardens Resort**   Cottages and motel units. P.O. Box 186. (707) 943-3011.

✔✔ **Whispering Pines**   Resort motel. P.O. Box 246. (707) 943-3160.

● **Knight's Restaurant**   Meyers Flat. (707) 943-3411.

HUMBOLDT REDWOODS STATE PARK

Miranda marks the southern entrance to Humboldt Redwoods, largest of all the fine parks run by the state of California and bulwark of the southern Humboldt County redwood protection zone. An interpretive center is located at the park headquarters near Burlington Campground. Take the Meyers Flat exit if you're still on the freeway. The campsites here are almost always full in July and August but quite peaceful at other times of the year. Nearby is the Garden Club of America Grove, a nice place for a picnic. By far the most visited site is **Founder's Grove,** located near the confluence of the south and middle forks of the Eel. A self-guiding nature trail threads its way through this land of leviathans. Pay special attention to the Dyersville Giant, a noble tree, one of the largest of all the coast redwoods, and, because it is still growing, one that has a chance of becoming the tallest. A poet put it well when he wrote: "These trees tickle the feet of the angels."

A visit to the groves along the Avenue of the Giants, however, provides only a glimpse of the magnificence of this park. The main event, **Rockefeller Grove,** is tucked up in the side canyon of Bull Creek. Five miles of creekside bottomlands are filled with the most extensive stand of old-growth redwood to be found anywhere. At Founder's Grove, cross under the freeway and drive four miles up Bull Creek Road to the Big Trees parking area. A new sign reading *"Tall* Tree" points to a trail leading to a redwood where an older sign reads *"Tallest* Tree." It was the tallest-known tree when measured in 1957 (359.3 feet), but it isn't anymore (see The Tree World Hall of Fame, below). Another nearby tree isn't quite so lofty, but it is bigger, measuring out at 235,000 board feet. The forest is nicer here than at Founder's Grove, simply because of the absence of freeway noise. Dead silence seems appropriate for these sobering places.

THE TREE WORLD HALL OF FAME

Tallest, oldest, biggest—how do we compare these monarchs of the forest? Just measure them or count the rings is the obvious answer, but it's not that simple. Take the tallest, for example. Trees grow, of course, and two trees don't grow at the same rate. Moisture, sunlight, soil nutrients, and competition from nearby species all play a part in a tree's size. So the tallest today won't necessarily hold the record twenty years from now. Lightning or gale winds might knock the top off a champion or, worse still, topple the whole tree. So the botanists hedge their bets by adding the word "known" to their record-setting proclamations. Herewith are the current title holders.

Tallest: 367 feet, 8 inches.

These coast redwoods are far taller than their Sierra Nevada cousins, so the champion is among the *sempervirens* species. For years the tallest was thought to be the 359-foot Rockefeller Tree in Humboldt Redwood State Park. Then in 1963, while on an exploring trip for *National Geographic,* Dr. Paul Zahl found himself on a hillside overlooking an isolated grove along Prairie Creek, sixty miles north of Founder's Grove. That they were giants he had no doubt—tall enough to invest in a surveying crew that quickly confirmed his wildest dream. He had found the tallest tree in the world, the Mount Everest of all living things. This colossus is fully forty-five feet taller than the most lofty Douglas fir (322 feet) and soars seventy feet higher than the tallest Sierra redwood (291 feet). But things change, and the top of what became known as the Libby Tree died; now foresters think a new winner will soon have to be crowned, maybe even the Dyerville Giant.

Largest: 600,000 board feet.

The estimated board footage of a tree is the accepted

measurement for determining the world's largest living thing. A board foot is a slab of wood one foot wide, one foot long, and one inch thick. The winner is the General Sherman tree, a *gigantea* in Sequoia National Park in the Sierra. This corpulent conifer is thirty-two feet in diameter at chest level (100 feet around), soars 272 feet into the air, and contains two and a half times as much wood as the largest *sempervirens*. The largest coast redwood ever cut was one felled by the Union Lumber Company near Fort Bragg. It was 334 feet high, 21 feet 2 inches in diameter, contained 140,800 board feet, and was 1,728 years old. It's a sobering thought, but at today's retail prices, the tree would have been worth $300,000.

Oldest: 6,000 years.

No redwood can lay claim to being the oldest living thing in all the world. That honor goes to the scrawny little bristlecone pine, a grizzled Methuselah that lives in the rocky, windswept soil of the White Mountains of eastern California. Their 13,000-foot-high home has six months of frost and very little rain, so few other plants compete for the scarce nutrients found between the rocks. Bristlecones grow slowly, but at the same time they age slowly. They predate the Trojan War by two thousand years, whereas the Sierra redwoods are thought to be no older than four thousand years. These coastal trees are just whippersnappers, seedlings at the time of Christ.

For an even better sense of these woods, stay at nearby Albee Creek Campground. A number of trails fan out from here. The best half-day loop is to go down the canyon on one side of Bull Creek and return on the other. The walk takes about three hours. Five backpack campsites are located farther out in the woods. The Johnson Trail Camp, also called Tie Camp because railroad ties were milled here, is a nice staging area for climbing 3,379-foot Grasshopper Peak. Four cabins survive that can be used in inclement weather. Another easy half-day hike is to walk up the fire road to the Bull Creek Trail Camp.

Scotia—Company Town • Population: 950

For nearly seventy-five years they were a fixture in the northwestern woods. Company towns sprang up wherever there was timber to be cut and boards to be made. The Sierra Nevada boasted Standard, Pollock Pines, and Westwood, towns displaying great industry and decorum during the week but hell-bent for Christmas on Saturday night. The Cascade Range saw a few last a long time—McCloud, for instance—but others, like Tenant, became nothing but dust save for some recollections in the rapidly fading memory banks of a few of us who remember steam locomotives chugging through the woods. Caspar, Greenwood, and Westport along the California coast are no more. Some of the bigger mill towns life Fort Bragg and Samoa still exist, but they have long since become amalgamated with the normal goings-on of the world around them. Only three survivors—Port Gamble, Washington, Gilchrist, Oregon, and Scotia—can still rightfully carry the appellation "company town." Of the three, Scotia is by far the most interesting—the quintessential, paternalistic old logging camp/sawmill settlement where everyone who lives here does so at the beckoning of "The Company."

The Pacific Lumber Company, I learned from Dave Gality, who works there, owns everything. Each worker's house has been built from the same plans and painted an identical white with a color-coordinated trim. Yards are as tidy as in Grosse Pointe; I wondered if every lawn was mowed the same day. Unlike most Pacific Northwest towns, you see no house trailers or jalopies parked out back; tricycles are retrieved and stored on the porch along with the other paraphernalia of a young family. The company owns the hospital, the grocery store, the filling station, the handsome redwood-sided recreation hall (no longer used), and the town's only hotel (which, not surprisingly, has the only saloon). Even the electric utility is company-owned; power comes from burning mill refuse. Two white-steepled churches, looking as if they were designed by the same architect, grace the gently sloping streets. One is Catholic, the other Presbyterian. Though workers buy from independent merchants now, firms like Rexall Drug, Ben Franklin, and Coast to Coast, these in turn lease space in the old company-store building. The lines from Tennessee Ernie Ford's old song—"St. Peter, don't yah call me 'cause I can't go; I owe my soul to the company store"—may no longer be true in the literal sense, but I saw a sign in the cafe reading "Please settle up accounts on payday."

The wooded canyon sides crowd in around Scotia, allowing the piquant smell of fresh-sawed redwood to linger. Staying here is like living in a museum, but not the Colonial Williamsburg kind. Here, things just go on the way they always have, with no artsy historical pretense. No one wears a period dress, there is no gaslight nostalgia, and there is almost nothing to do after dark except cruise Main Street on Saturday night or watch TV beamed off the satellite. Yet it is a fascinating place to be.

Scotia Inn is the place to stay. The two-story redwood, carpenter-gothic lobby has been refurnished with comfortable sofas and a grand piano. The restaurant occupies one of the handsomest rooms in northern California, with frosted-glass chandeliers hanging from a redwood-paneled ceiling. A giant ornate coffee urn graces one wall. Ten upstairs rooms have been renovated with European silk wallpaper, and you no longer have to share a bathroom with the guest next door. Fittingly, the one room that has not been redone is the downstairs bar. The prewar art deco design is shabby now, but it somehow seems okay for this workingman's town. Mill hands come to relax after work. The conversation I overheard was hardly what I expected to hear in the north woods. A logger was lamenting about the sad state of his golf game.

The magnificent old bank building, constructed entirely of bark-clad redwood logs, is now a museum. A fading photograph shows fifty or more men, proudly standing on a single log. Another shows the mill, surrounded by hillsides quite devoid of trees—the same slopes you see outside that are now densely forested with second-growth redwood. "If these mountains were flattened out," one logger is reported to have complained, "they would cover all of the United States and half of Texas, too." But they weren't, so ingenious men had to find ways of getting out the timber. They built narrow-gauge railways with outrageous grades and employed geared-down steam locomotives. One, built in Erie, Pennsylvania, by Charlie Heisler, stands mutely outside. No fire has warmed her belly in thirty years. Nearby is another gigantic steam-driven yarder called a Washington Duplex Flyer, whose huge winches powered the cables used to snake the logs out of the canyons. A local fellow, John Dolbeer, invented its forebear, the donkey engine. "It wasn't big enough to have a horsepower," he chortled. In the 1880s, donkey-engine manufacture was the largest industry on the West Coast.

While studying a display of "high line" blocks, I listened to an old-timer tell a friend about how things used to be in these woods. Pointing to a diagram describing how garden-hose-size cables were threaded through twenty-inch diameter pulleys, he explained the function of the main line, the slack line, and the haul-back line and how the tail blocks, head-trip blocks, and the straw-line blocks could be moved about so that trees could be snatched up from the whole canyon with a single siting of the flyer. "The choker," He said, "had the most dangerous job because you never knew quite which way a twenty-ton log was going to go when it was snatched up by the donkey puncher." He reminisced about the problems he had as a high climber trying to top a "barber chair," a tree that was likely to split when the crown was lopped off. "You're sixty feet in the air, tied to the swaying tree with a leather belt. If that bugger cracks open, the belt could cut you in half. That's why we always sawed clear around through the sapwood first. Then the heart wouldn't split."

To get a sense of the woods, I drove a few miles south of town to visit what the Pacific Lumber Company calls a demonstration forest. A pleasant path leads through a stand of second-growth trees, redwoods and Douglas fir interspersed with California hazel, Pacific yew, evergreen huckleberry, and madrone with an understory of grand fern, sward fern, and vine maple. A brochure describes much of what you see and explains the rationale behind modern logging practices. The virtues of selective logging are explained, whereby thirty percent of the old growth is left standing to provide seed stock for new trees. The trail passes near a selectively logged forest, which certainly doesn't have the ugliness of the clear-cut land you see elsewhere. All is not well on the visual scene, however. PBS did a documentary about how the Pacific Lumber Company was recently taken over by a conglomerate and, in order to pay off the debt, started clear-cutting like everybody else.

Scotia's pièce de résistance is a tour of the mill. From 7:30 A.M. till 11:00 A.M., and from 1:00 P.M. to 3:30 P.M. on weekdays, you can watch one of the most interesting industrial operations around. After picking up a permit at the company headquarters, I drove to a special parking lot where signs direct the visitor along a self-guided tour. On a third-story footbridge I looked out over the thirty-acre mill pond. Surprise. No hobnailed boots here. The "pond monkey," pushing the logs around with a ten-foot pole, was wearing Reeboks and had on a life jacket. The bridge leads to the "barker," a barn-size machine that removes the six-inch-thick redwood bark by means of a high-pressure nozzle. I watched through a massive water-soaked window as bark shards came hurtling toward us like debris from a blast of TNT. A cord was dangling from a lever attached to a spring-loaded valve. A tug on it not only cleaned the window with a stream of water, but made me feel as though I were somehow helping the fellow who was running the machine. With half a dozen levers, he was turning, shoving, rolling, and otherwise manipulating ten-ton logs as easily as if he were eating dim sum with chopsticks.

This mill doesn't fool with small trees as do those in much of the nation. Redwood logs can be the diameter of a Cadillac limousine and several times as long. The band-saw blade for the "headrig" was thirty feet around and must have weighed one thousand pounds. I watched as the sawyer sliced the log into "cants" a foot thick. Rattling conveyers hauled them off to the edgerman, who used a laser scanner to select the optimum-size boards. Prime lumber went one way, scrap mysteriously disappeared into a hole in the floor. At the far end of the huge building, I gazed in wonder as the trimmerman, operating a gang of cross-cut saws, sliced defects out of a forty-foot board. It took only a couple of seconds for him to decide which saws to drop. A conveyor sent the boards to the sinister "green chain," where twenty-odd brawny mill workers sorted the sawed lumber by hand in what traditionally has been considered the roughest job in a sawmill. A fellow driving a careening overhead monorail car came by to pick up the sorted green lumber and transfer it either to a drying kiln or to the air-dry stacks in the fifty-acre yard.

The Pacific Lumber Company's mill in Scotia, I learned, is a bit unique in that it also includes a factory where cured lumber is planed, edged, and sometimes textured. Most of these operations were performed by teams, or gangs, several of which, I was interested to see, were gangs of women. Redwood is so expensive these days that it is profitable to slice out individual knots and then glue the ends together to make a clear, hardwood board of any desired length.

Will we ever run out of trees, I wondered, and see this mill close like all the others? Fortunately, I learned, redwood literally grows like a weed from the stump of a downed giant, and given modest care, these forests will provide lumber for generations.

Nearby **Rio Dell** is a bigger town than Scotia and a graphic example of the difference between the neatness yet sameness of a centrally planned company town and one that just sort of grew. This town is a hodgepodge of nice houses and some that need paint, neat gardens and others crowded with parked house trailers, all intermixed in a way that is more typical of the Northwest. But it is hardly a pretty town.

Rio Dell marks the spot where the Eel emerges from its steep-sided canyon and begins to meander out on the vast floodplain surrounding Humboldt Bay and thus is the logical ending for this segment of our journey. To continue on to Ferndale, the town we'll visit in Chapter 7, turn left on Blue Slide Road and drive out along the southwest bank of the Eel. We won't take this route, though, because there is a special reason to backtrack a bit to explore an area few tourists know anything about.

FOOD AND LODGING

✔✔ **Scotia Inn** Restaurant, bar, and 10 rooms in restored company hotel. Scotia 95565. (707) 764-5683.

✔ **Humboldt Gables Motel** 20 units. 40 West Davis Street, Rio Dell 95562. (707) 764-5609.

✔ **Humboldt Redwoods State Park** Burlington Campground—250 sites; Albee Creek Campground—34 sites; Hidden Springs Campground—150 sites; Marin Garden Club Grove—walk-/bike-in camping.

CALIFORNIA'S LOST COAST • (Three-hour side trip)

The road we followed to Rockefeller Grove continues on through the park, climbs a ridge, crosses some grassy prairies, and drops into the valley of the Mattole (the "e" is silent) River. "Before CAMP, I wouldn't send anyone out there," said Linda Hilburn, who works at the park headquarters. "Guys with Uzis [an Israeli submachine gun] would stand in the road and demand to know what your business was. But it's okay now. The marijuana growers have gone somewhere else, I guess."

The road is narrow and twisty but paved throughout. You should check locally, though, for Linda told me that storm damage is frequent, and since the road has so little traffic, it is practically the last in the county to be repaired. And it rains a lot. **Honeydew,** a little hamlet fifteen miles from Highway 101, is the wettest spot in California. Storms come off the coast, get pushed up by the four-thousand-foot King Range, become colder, and drop most of their load in one place. Fifteen *feet* of rain fell in the winter of 1957–58.

The Mattoles were a tribe of Athabaskans who, with their neighbors the Sinkyones, tried to resist the white man's invasion and suffered dearly for their intransigence. In 1864 the *Humboldt Times,* according to author Mike Hayden, reported:

> Lt. Frazier, Co. E, C.M., with a detachment of twelve men stationed at Upper Mattole, started on a scout about the 1st . . . and [on] the night of the second succeeded in finding some Indians at Whitehorn Valley on the Mattole River about 25 miles south of Upper Mattole. At this place, he captured thirteen squaws and killed four bucks—none escaping. The Indians offered no resistance, being completely surprised.

Both tribes were nearly exterminated.

It seems quite inappropriate to be in a hurry along the country lane between Honeydew and Petrolia, another tiny village. The pretty little **A. W. Way County Park** is a nice place to have a picnic. When a fellow standing by his mailbox gave me a friendly wave, I stopped to chat. It didn't seem necessary to pull off the road; I hadn't seen another car in nearly an hour. A. R. Miner, it seems, had been blind for forty years, and I guess he thought I was the friend he was expecting along to take him to the Baptist church in Honeydew. But he liked to talk, especially about the old days before the valley had been logged over. "I can't see it now," he said, "but people tell me it's not too pretty anymore." I disagreed. Though the redwoods were gone, the hills were green with a spring growth of rye grass, and I knew he must have sensed how lovely the day was by the warmth of the sun on his face.

Petrolia marks the halfway point in our backcountry drive. Ferndale is thirty miles farther north. From here our road leaves the river, goes over a hill, and then drops down to the Lost Coast. For six miles you drive along an absolutely spectacular grassy, sheep-dotted marine terrace only a few feet above the ocean. On blustery days, spindrift pelts your windshield, and in places waves batter offshore rocks so hard that ocean spray covers the road. My guess is that during the winter it's helpful to have a tide table in your glove compartment. During a storm you may have to wait for an ebb before attempting the drive.

A mile before returning inland, you get a nice view of **Cape Mendocino,** named by João Rodríguez Cabrillo a full forty years before Sir Francis Drake sailed along this coast. It is the most westerly point in California. I have a copy of Dutchman Joan Bleau's map of the world, printed in 1645, which clearly shows the cape with its correct spelling. My modern map of the area indicates that there is a village called Capetown located along the road. The fog hadn't burned off when I drove by, a possible explanation for why I couldn't find the place.

The geology changes abruptly at Cape Mendocino. The country we been exploring all the way from San Francisco has been uplifted. Up ahead the land was pushed down, creating numerous estuaries and lagoons that we'll explore next.

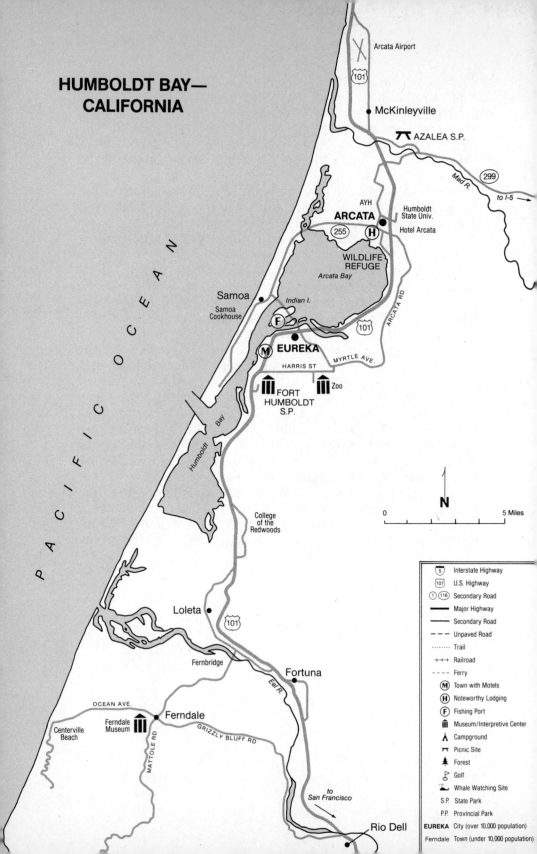

HUMBOLDT BAY—
CALIFORNIA

P A C I F I C   O C E A N

Arcata Airport

McKinleyville

AZALEA S.P.

Mad R.

299

to I-5

AYH

ARCATA

Humboldt
State Univ.

255

H

Hotel Arcata

WILDLIFE
REFUGE

Arcata Bay

ARCATA RD

Samoa

Indian I.

Samoa
Cookhouse

101

F

M

EUREKA

MYRTLE AVE.

HARRIS ST

FORT
HUMBOLDT
S.P.

Zoo

Humboldt Bay

College
of the
Redwoods

0   N   5 Miles

Loleta

101

Fernbridge

Eel R.

Fortuna

OCEAN AVE.

Centerville
Beach

Ferndale
Museum

Ferndale

MATTOLE RD

GRIZZLY BLUFF RD

to
San Francisco

Rio Dell

5	Interstate Highway
101	U.S. Highway
1 116	Secondary Road
▬	Major Highway
—	Secondary Road
- - -	Unpaved Road
·······	Trail
+++	Railroad
- - -	Ferry
M	Town with Motels
H	Noteworthy Lodging
F	Fishing Port
▥	Museum/Interpretive Center
⋏	Campground
⊤⊤	Picnic Site
♠	Forest
⚲	Golf
⌣	Whale Watching Site
S.P.	State Park
P.P.	Provincial Park
EUREKA	City (over 10,000 population)
Ferndale	Town (under 10,000 population)

• 7 •

HUMBOLDT BAY

A Metropolitan Enclave on a Lonely Coast

As the little county road from Petrolia struggles down off Wildcat Ridge, it leaves the so-called Lost Coast behind and emerges onto a large area almost as flat as Kansas. This is the floodplain of the Eel River. Suddenly, as if squashed by some unseen fist, the coastal mountains cease to plunge steeply into the sea. Instead, for the next forty miles the shoreline becomes a series of sand dunes protecting a few lagoons, a huge bay, and great treeless grasslands, some of which stretch inland for more than ten miles. It is a drowned coast, much like the entire eastern seaboard. Geologists speculate that the Pacific and North American plates have been at war here for 150 million years with the North American plate seemingly the winner, forcing the Pacific plate to dive deep into the ocean, literally drowning the mountains that once graced this part of California. For years the dunes kept their secret well, for it was a long time before American explorers discovered a suitable harbor along this lonely coast (see Eureka! I Have Found It!, page 96). But the secret was revealed; the cities and towns that have grown up around Humboldt Bay now have a population of over eighty thousand, forming California's largest coastal metropolitan center north of San Francisco Bay.

Shortcut Access to Humboldt Bay

Several major airlines serve the Humboldt Bay region from an airport located near the bedroom community of McKinleyville, eighteen miles north of Eureka. Car rentals are available at the terminal.

EUREKA! I HAVE FOUND IT!

During the Gold Rush it was the land up ahead, not that behind us, that was really the Lost Coast. Cape Mendocino was, after all, first spotted in 1642. Nothing lost about that country. But up ahead lay a giant problem. Nobody could find what they needed most, a harbor to serve the burgeoning gold fields of the Trinity Mountains. Poring over old charts, mariners found a cove called Trinidad. Half a dozen ships sailed north from San Francisco in 1850, seeking the harbor, but the ubiquitous sand dunes kept their secret well. In his book *Redwood Country*, Alfred Powers cites a contemporary verse:

> Ere long the country was o'errun,
> And gold could not be had,
> And many people then began
> To talk of "Trinidad."
>
> And some affirmed that they had seen
> A man, who heard one say
> He knew a person who had been
> In sight of that same bay.
>
> The story spread like any lie,
> A party sailed in haste,
> But soon returned—the reason why,
> They could not find the place.

Over the centuries, mariners learned that rivers usually scooped out some sort of harbor, so they looked for fresh (or at least less salty) water, which usually meant a river was disgorging into the sea. Argonauts, poking around in their quest for the yellow metal, had discovered a number of rivers, including the Eel, the Van Duzen, the Mad, and the Trinity. All were heading toward the Pacific at the latitude of these cursed sand dunes. Navigators managed to find the Eel, which by the time it reached the sea had absorbed the Van Duzen. They found the Mad, too, but neither provided a suitable harbor. The Trinity swung too far north and joined the Klamath, so they were stumped. There was a great harbor, of course, the one that graces our modern maps. It had actually been discovered in 1806 by one Jonathan Winship, a poacher in the employ of the Russian American Fur Company. But the Russians weren't talking.

So the search went on as well it might. Lot sales alone could make a fellow rich. Credit for the rediscovery is usually given to Captain Ottinger of the *Laura Virginia,* but Captain James T. Ryan is the one most closely associated with the find. Putting his boat up on a mud flat, he stepped ashore and, displaying a fit of exuberance, is supposed to have done exactly what Archimedes did when he made his great discovery—he lapsed into Greek, shouting out the word "Eureka." His exhilaration must have waned a bit when he later came upon a redwood tree, for carved thereon was the latitude and longitude of the place and the words "Dec. 7, 1849 J. Gregg." So it turned out that the first American to find the bay was not a sailor, but an adventurer who came overland—Dr. Josiah Gregg, author of the western classic *Commerce of the Prairies,* published in 1844. Gregg was astonished to learn that no river of any consequence flowed into northern California's finest harbor. No wonder the sailors couldn't find it.

Captain Ottinger's mate, one Hans Buhne, named the bay after the noted explorer and cartographer of the day, Baron Alexander von Humboldt, who earlier had gotten his name attached to another famous western landmark, the forty-niners' lifeline to the gold fields, Nevada's Humboldt River. Meanwhile, the politicians in Sacramento must have gotten caught up in Ryan's enthusiasm; during the Constitutional Convention that year, they chose "I have found it" for the state motto, and the word "Eureka" now graces the Great Seal of California.

Ferndale • Population: 1,400

The first town you come to is arguably the nicest. Snuggled against the steeply canted abutment of Cape Mendocino is a Victorian village much like the town of Mendocino, which we visited earlier. Over the years Ferndale has managed to keep its 1870s charm, but it is too far from any large city to have evolved into a "quaint tourist spot." It has a nice lived-in, rather than a museum, feel—fixed up but not gussied up. There aren't any boutiques or stores with cute names, unless you count the Yancy Feed Company, whose sign boasts: "Our Animals Pig out in Style." Shops, not shoppes, line Main Street.

Ferndale was first settled in 1852 but faded once the easy-to-reach timber was gone. The countryside lay dormant for a while, but then emigrant Danes, Portuguese, and Swiss began establishing farms on the rich, cutover floodplain. The loamy soil was well suited to dairying, and those who worked their land became as rich as the milk their herds produced. During the 1870s the early settlers began turning their farms over to their children. They moved into town, and Ferndale became known as Cream City.

Envious outsiders called the mansions that sprang up along Brown and Berding streets "butterfat palaces." If these events had occurred thirty years later, the town would probably not have been of particular interest to us today, but they happened at the height of California's love affair with the so-called Victorian style of architecture, so Queen Vickie got her name appended to this little town in faraway Humboldt County.

At first sight, Ferndale seems to be a nice place to spend an afternoon, no longer, but soon you sense the urge to linger. "Just across the Fern Bridge you feel a tug on your back bumper," said Jane Hughes, who recently moved here from Los Angeles and was helping out with the cooking at one of the B&Bs. "It isn't that there is a lot to *do* here. You just seem to want to spend more *time* doing it." At seven in the morning, the ladies were having a coffee klatch at the bakery while the men were a block up the street playing pinochle at Becker's Pool Hall. "It's called the Greek Investment Club," Jane told me, "but of course most of them are Portuguese."

While gulping down a cup of watery coffee, I overheard a middle-aged fellow complaining to a seatmate: "I don't know why he doesn't put his yearlings on the southwest pasture. One of these days he'll learn, I guess."

No one seemed in a hurry to do anything, least of all the stocky woman who ran the place. Twice I heard a fellow ask her when she was going to fire up the cooking range. Twice I saw her ignore the request. Instead, I listened to a fifteen-minute discourse on why the local team lost to Loleta in last night's slow-pitch softball game.

A midday stroll up Main Street is revealing. George's Glass and Body Shop is across the street from a Depression-style building housing the unpretentious Fern Cafe. Peers Motor Sales looks like a car dealership you would find in any small town, but here it is next door to a false-fronted post office (combination locks on the brass-doored boxes), which in turn is across the street from a Roman-Renaissance-style bank that you're tempted to patronize, even if you don't need the money, because standing in line in front of a hundred-year-old frosted-glass teller's window seems like it would be fun. The old movie house is now the **Ferndale Repertory Theatre,** and there are a couple of art galleries. But mixed in together with a few gift stores you find ordinary places like a TV repair shop, a beauty salon, and the Texaco station. The Palace, with its ancient back bar, perhaps could have been the set for a Hollywood movie, but according to the barkeep, "The owner was too cheap to replace the beveled-glass mirror after a fellow threw a chair through it during a brawl a couple of years ago."

The people who live here seem to have a passion for the past and are determined to keep their town looking nice. It got its "Victorian village" appendage some years ago after everyone stopped what they were doing and collectively repainted the whole business district. The cemetery, circa 1878, is as well tended as Forest Lawn and prettier, especially when the azaleas are in bloom. You could spend a day in the **Ferndale Museum,** poring over old photographs and examining bits of nostalgia, including relics from Panama Mail Line's *Northerner*, which went aground five miles east of here in 1860. One hundred and eight passengers were saved, thirty-eight were lost. There is a monument to the tragedy at the lovely yet lonely **Centerville Beach,** located at the end of Ocean Avenue.

Not all the interesting history is old. Donna Huckaby, a graphic artist and part-time curator, told me how people feel about their lovely old concrete-arch structure that spans the meandering Eel River. "CalTrans [the State Division of Highways] decided to replace it, and we got up in arms," she said. " 'What's wrong with our bridge?' we wanted to know. 'It's long enough to reach from one bank to the other, and that's more than you guys can say about the one you built on 101.' " (Of a pair the state built fifteen miles upstream, one now goes only halfway across, a casualty of the flood of 1964.) "Well, CalTrans bemoaned the fact that Fern Bridge was just too narrow. So a fellow I know went down to San Francisco and measured the width of the lanes on the Golden Gate Bridge. Can you believe it, they were six inches narrower! 'Widen the Golden Gate if you want a bridge to play around with,' we gleefully told them. When you're done with that, come back and talk to us.' "

There used to be a couple of hotels on Main Street, but they burned down years ago. Now there is talk that the lovely old building on the corner of Ocean Street will be redone. If so, it has the potential to be as nice as anything on this trip. There are three thriving B&Bs, however, the largest of which is the gaudily painted Queen Anne–style Gingerbread Mansion, built in 1898.

FOOD AND LODGING   Ferndale, California 95536

✔✔✔ **The Gingerbread Mansion**   8-room B&B. 400 Berding Street. (707) 786-4000.

✔✔ **Ferndale Inn**   4-room B&B. P.O. Box 887. (707) 786-4307.

✔✔ **Shaw House B&B**   703 Main Street. (707) 786-9958.

● **Roman's**   Restaurant. (707) 725-6358.

Fernbridge's Main Street becomes County Road 211 as it heads north toward Humboldt Bay. You cross a number of dry creek beds, former distributaries of the Eel that had at one time provided havens for the tiny coastal packets that took the cheese made hereabouts to San Francisco. You can still watch a couple of burly men making cheese the old-fashioned way at the Loleta Cheese Factory. Turophiles will be pleased to learn that cheddar was first made in California by one Clarissa Steel, who brought the recipe across the plains in 1857. She cajoled a lo-cal Indian boy into roping a few wild cows that were said—incorrectly, it turned out—to be unmilkable. Tasty food was hard to find in California in those days; Clarissa enjoyed what one contemporary described as "a leap into immortality." Mon-terey Jack, also made here, was invented at that California town in 1882 by a bearded fellow named David Jacks. They spice up the somewhat bland product here by adding your choice of caraway seeds, garlic, green chiles, jalapeño chiles, or smoked salmon.

Eureka • Population: 24,200

Those used to sweltering summer heat will be pleased to learn that Eureka is the coolest city in the nation, averaging 60 degrees in July and August. The ocean and the fogs have a stabilizing effect on the weather no matter what the season, so January is only seven degrees cooler.

Though Eureka is primarily a mill town, it is best known for a single building, the **Carson House Mansion,** said to be the most photographed residence in America. This quintessential Victorian, owned by timber baron William Carson (he and his partner, John Dolbeer, owned half of Humboldt County), was built in the carpenter-gothic style. It is now a private club, and you can't go inside to see the exquisite interior detailing, which includes mahogany trim from South America, teak from the Orient, and hardwoods from New England. Ignoring the hand that fed him, Carson relegated redwood, milled on the flats di-rectly below, to the foundation joists, studs, and rafters. Some say the turreted building is gorgeous; others think it is hideous. I side with an uncredited author of the 1939 Federal Writer's Project book *California,* who wrote:

> It stands, carefully preserved, amid sprucely tended grounds. Its jagged roof line, visible from almost any quarter of the city, the tortured ornamentation, and the trim paint give it the air of a prop for a Silly Symphony.

Hollywood's *The Valley of the Giants*, based on Peter B. Kyne's novel of greed in the lumber country, was filmed here. The handsome house across the street was a wedding gift to Carson's eldest son.

The city used the mansion as the cornerstone for the revitalization of its dockside warehouse district. At one time logs were slid down to waiting ships on what was called a "skid road." Eurekans maintain this was the origin of the term (often improperly called "skid row") used to describe seedy places like this used to be. Taking a hint from other waterfront cities, Boston, Omaha, Port Townsend, Portland, and San Francisco, the town fathers established a historic district and made money available for the restoration of the old brick buildings. The lovely promenade, which stretches ten blocks west of the Carson House, is graced with a gazebo, fountains, and numerous benches and is lined with interesting stores and restaurants. The project, dubbed Old Town, spurred the upgrading of the nearby retail district, though unfortunately that may have gone for naught. A slick new shopping center is opening south of town.

An old terra-cotta-walled bank building has been converted into the **Clarke Memorial Museum,** which has a wonderful collection of old-time odds and ends and boasts the finest collection of Indian baskets found along this coast. The **Humboldt Bay Maritime Museum** is housed in a white-clapboard saltbox building that overlooks the bay. The highlight of their collection is a set of photographs of Eureka's most ignominious disaster. In 1917, the submarine *H-3* had gone on the beach. The navy, believing that the salvage bids they had received were too high, dispatched the flagship of the Pacific Fleet, the USS *Milwaukee,* to Humboldt Bay to pull her off. The cruiser promptly went aground, a total loss. The War Department, exercising great wisdom, subsequently judged the bids right and proper. The museum owns a restored 1910 ferry boat that sailed across the bay to Samoa before the bridge was built. *Madaket* now makes 1¼-hour harbor cruises during the summer, sailing from the foot of C Street. While on the cruise I learned that 90 percent of California's oysters come from Humboldt Bay.

Fort Humboldt State Historic Park, located on a bluff south of town, is a nice place for a picnic. Little is left of the post that army men of the day considered the end of the world (see A Place Like This Could Drive a Man to Drink, page 102), but the state has assembled a collection of steam locomotives and logging machinery and built a small interpretive center where logging practices are explained. Eureka also boasts a nice zoo, unusual for

A PLACE LIKE THIS COULD
DRIVE A MAN TO DRINK

The federal government established Fort Humboldt in 1853, a time when the people who had lived here for a thousand years began to get uneasy about all the white men scurrying around looking for a shiny yellow metal that had absolutely no use whatsoever. The troops were supposedly garrisoned here to protect the Indians from the whites, but mostly it worked the other way around. For months on end there was nothing to do in this dank outpost where the seemingly unceasing rains of winter finally gave way to the continual fog of summer. The dreariness of it all would have stifled the enthusiasm of the most self-confident soldier.

Into this dismal place came a young captain, Ulysses S. Grant, fresh from an assignment at an equally out-of-the way post, the Columbia Barracks at Vancouver, Washington. It was not a good time in Grant's life. He had wedded a couple of years earlier and had sired two children, one of whom he had never seen. His pay was insufficient to allow him to bring his family to the far West; he was homesick. Two business ventures had failed; one when he loaned $1,500 to a scoundrel in San Francisco, the other when he started a potato farm at Vancouver, only to watch as a Columbia flood wiped out his crop. Furthermore, he despised his superior officer, Lieutenant Colonel Robert Buchanan, who despised him in kind. It was not surprising, therefore, that the young officer established a longtime friendship with a Mr. John Barleycorn. As his biographer, William S. McFeely, put it:

> What surely is more important than estimating the quantity of whiskey consumed or speculating on Grant's favorite brand (we do not know what it was) is understanding the extent of the depression that occasioned the drinking.

The bottle became his companion. On April 11, 1854, while listed on the company roll as sick, U. S. Grant wrote a letter resigning from the army.

---

a city this size, located in Sequoia Park near the southeastern edge of town.

All told, Eureka has one thousand rooms for tourists, most of which are in motels along Highway 101. In keeping with the town's Victorian heritage, however, you'll find a number of B&Bs, the most interesting of which is the ornate Carter House. It's almost as gingerbready as nearby Carson House but in fact is brand new. Queen of the city's hostelries is the sixty-year-old Eureka Inn, northern California's most famous hotel. The old half-timbered Elizabethan dowager has recently been refurbished with several conference and banquet rooms. Cozy chairs surround a large fireplace in the two-storied, redwood-paneled lobby dominated by an English candle-fixtured chandelier. French doors look out on a well-tended garden and a heated swimming pool. The hotel has a popular bar with nightly entertainment, a cafe, a large dining room, and a publike ale house in the basement.

Somebody (I can't find out who) thought the sand spit across the bay looked like the harbor at Pago Pago, so he (or she) named the place **Samoa.** Ugly sawmills and paper mills line the peninsula, but there is a special reason to visit the place. The Samoa Cookhouse is exactly that—a cookhouse, the last survivor of an institution along the redwood coast. The men who worked in the camps ate at a cookhouse (sometimes called a smokehouse); they had no other choice. The timber companies, knowing the foibles of their woodsmen, wisely served no booze. Waitresses, who had to be single, lived upstairs in dormitories that, no doubt, were off limits to those with amorous intentions. The ladies tended oilcloth-covered tables set with dime-store flatware, white crockery plates, and coffee mugs that weighed half a pound. Water was poured from crocks, food was passed around family style, and you ate as much as your belly could hold and a little bit more. That's exactly how it is at Samoa Cookhouse today, except that the waitresses don't have to be single anymore, and they probably live in town. The place, which seats several hundred at twenty-odd tables, opens at six A.M. and continues serving through supper. You eat whatever the cook decides to make that day, which is invariably too much.

FOOD AND LODGING   Eureka, California 95510

✔✔✔ **Carter House Inn**   7-room B&B. 1033 3rd Street. (707) 445-1390.

✔✔✔ **Eureka Inn**   109-room hotel. Rib Room Restaurant, bar, entertainment, pool. 7th and F streets. (707) 442-6441.

✔✔ **Carson House Inn**   60-room motel. 1209 4th Street. (707) 443-1601.

✔✔ **Eagle House Inn**   Restaurant, bar, nightclub, and B&B in an 1888 stick-style hotel. 2nd and C streets. (707) 442-2334.

✔✔ **Hotel Carter**   18-room new hotel. 3-1 L Street. (707) 445-1390.

✔✔ **The Iris Inn** B&B. 12th and H streets. (707) 445-0307.

✔✔ **Old Town B&B Inn** 5-room B&B. 1521 3rd Street. (707) 445-3951.

✔✔ **Red Lion Motor Inn** 180-room motel. 1929 4th Street. (707) 465-0844.

✔✔ **Thunderbird Lodge** 116-room motel. 232 West 5th Street. (707) 443-2234.

●●● **Ramone's Opera Alley Cafe** *Nuevo* California food. Old Town. (707) 444-3339.

●● **Lazio's** Longtime fish restaurant and bar that shares its space with an oyster-processing plant. Foot of C Street. (707) 442-2337.

●● **Marina Cafe** Popular new restaurant on Woodly Island overlooking the yacht harbor.

●● **Panama Jack's** Modest meals served in what they call a "postdeco neon decor."

●● **Waterfront Oyster Bar & Grill** (707) 443-9190.

● **Samoa Cookhouse** (707) 442-1659.

Arcata • Population: 12,400

Even if you're not looking for cookhouse food, the nicest way out of Eureka is to take the two-mile-long Samoa Bridge, which crosses Indian Island, the onetime home of the Wiyots. One night in 1860, some whites, noting that the men of the tribe had gone on a hunting trip, stole ashore and slaughtered the women and children—a hundred in all. Sensing an opportunity to make a statement, a young printer's devil and part-time reporter who worked at Arcata's *The Northern Californian* took advantage of his publisher's absence and wrote an editorial damning the raid. The article aroused such an outcry that the lad was summarily run out of town. His name was Bret Harte.

The road to Arcata follows the sand spit separating Humboldt Bay from the ocean. The swampy northern rim of the bay, once the city dump, has been reclaimed and is now the lovely **Humboldt Bay National Wildlife Refuge,** home to several hundred species of birds. Arcata boasts that it is the only city in California with a municipal forest, a six-hundred-acre second-growth redwood park laced with trails built by students. A self-guiding trail explains how the land was originally logged. A few miles north of town on State Highway 200 is another park built by the Civilian Conservation Corps during the Depression.

Azalea State Reserve is a pleasant picnic spot, especially in the spring.

Arcata, formerly called Union Town, is situated on the old trail to the northern mines and was once bigger than Eureka. While standing in the town's rather pretty central square, I had no difficulty at all imagining the place all abustle with wagons being loaded with merchandise bound for the gold fields. On a single block facing the square I spied The Sidelines, The Alabi, Toby and Jack's, and Everett's, all saloons, and if that wasn't boozy enough, the Arcata Liquour Store, too. It seemed appropriate, therefore, when I came upon a nearby drinking fountain, built in 1912 by the ladies of the Women's Christian Temperance Union. It was out of order. But there is graciousness here, too. The Hotel Arcata, circa 1915, has been redone and furnished with antiques and has an elegantly decorated restaurant. Across the square, the old Jacoby's Storehouse, a three-story brick building, has been converted into shops and eateries.

Though an old city, the atmosphere here is as modern as anywhere in California, due in part to the fact that Arcata is a college town. Humboldt State University, one of the most popular in the state, is famous for its forestry and ecology departments and is also strong in the performing arts. As a result there is lots to do. The university puts on drama, dance, and chamber concerts all year, and when I was there it was doing *Boris Gudonov* (critics said that the performance was Gudonov!). At dinner one night I sat next to a group of ladies celebrating their victory in a soccer match, indicative of the fact that we're still in California. Soccer is not a popular sport at the fishing and lumber towns we'll visit farther north.

FOOD AND LODGING   Arcata, California 95521

✔✔ **Arcata Hotel**   Restored downtown hotel and restaurant. 708 9th Street. (707) 822-6506.

✔✔ **The Lady Anne Victorian Inn**   B&B. 902 14th Street. (707) 822-2797.

✔✔ **The Plough & the Stars Country Inn**   5-room B&B. 1800 12th Street. (707) 822-8236.

✔ **Arcata Crewhouse Hostel**   AYH hostel. Summer only. 1390 I Street. (707) 822-9995.

●● **Pete's Bella Vista Inn**   Victorian restaurant three miles north in McKineyville. (707) 839-3395.

● **Paradise Ridge Cafe**   Natural-foods restaurant. (707) 826-1394.

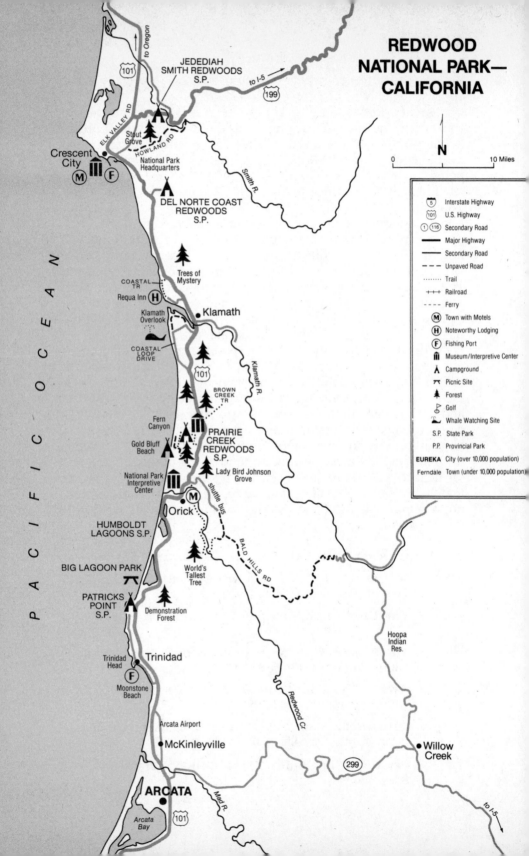

·8·

REDWOOD NATIONAL PARK

The Redwood Coast

We now take our leave of California—not in the literal sense, of course, for you still have 120 miles of country roads to follow before reaching Oregon. But it seemed to me that this was the end of the "California" state of mind (I hesitate even to try to amplify this statement, for to do so is to skirt on the edge of oversimplification). My objective is to alert you to the differences in the way things are up ahead and of the changed attitude of the people who live there. For the most part, meals and lodging are cheaper the farther north you go. This is partly because the market is smaller and partly because Oregonians are simply outraged by San Francisco prices and won't pay them. Whereas Californians are trendy, Oregonians seem to have a rugged independence, an urge for self-determination, and a Jeffersonian sort of democracy. Indeed, in the early 1940s, a movement surfaced (both *Time* and *Life* magazines covered it extensively) to make California's Humboldt and Del Norte counties and Oregon's Curry and Josephine counties into a separate state to be called Jefferson. Pearl Harbor ended that idea, but the attitudes remain. The people here live closer to the land. At least on the back roads, pickups outnumber sedans by a wide margin. I wouldn't call this the Bible belt, but moral values seem more midwestern. People live modestly—mobile homes are a common sight— and houses are heated by wood stoves. You're entering steak-and-potatoes country.

A few miles north of Arcata, you cross the curiously named

Mad River (explorer Josiah Gregg's men were angry when he stopped to take astronomical observations), one of the prettiest along this coast. State Highway 299, which angles southeast from here, follows the Mad for a dozen miles before beginning its tortuous 130-mile roller-coaster run to Interstate 5. Though a scenic drive, it is slow and therefore not really a shortcut to the redwood coast.

If you have traveled all the way from San Francisco on Highway 101, you've now driven three hundred miles without once seeing the pounding Pacific. That bit of misfortune is about to be corrected in a most dramatic way. The freeway traverses the flat countryside of the Mad River delta, makes a bend around a seventy-foot-high bluff, and then turns to face a mile-long, driftwood-studded beach awash with monstrous wind-driven breakers. In the background, a forested cliff drops precipitously into the surf. Offshore sea stacks puncture the horizon. Nearby **Moonstone Beach** is a fine place to stop and capture the magic of this unpacific coast.

Trinidad • Population: 400

Leave the freeway here and head toward Trinidad. A forested island, seemingly floating among the sea stacks, comes into view. A closer examination reveals that it is not an island at all, but **Trinidad Head,** one of the most historic spots on the Northwestern Pacific Coast. A recently constructed trail that circles around the headland leads to a replica of the cross the Spaniards left when they came ashore (see I Claim This Land for Spain, page 109). It's a lovely walk, with numerous benches to tempt you to slow down and sit for a bit while watching the crashing waves. As you round a bend the quietness of a leisurely stroll is suddenly shattered by the din of barking sea lions (seals rarely bark) who make their home on a nearby island. The lighthouse is on the extreme seaward side of the head. Though 190 feet above the ocean, the lamp was doused by a wave during a violent storm in 1914.

Trinidad, a place the Indians called Tsurai, is a lovely little town, situated on an almost level bluff a few hundred feet above the ocean. It marks the southern limit of the Yurok tribe, which populated most of the coast between here and the Oregon border. They were the most advanced of all the California Indians, skillful at building canoes, which they used to fish the tidal waters of the Klamath River. An example of their craft, carved from a thousand-year-old redwood, is resting on a grassy lot at the north end of town. Ruth Kirk, innkeeper at the cozy cliffside Trinidad

I CLAIM THIS LAND FOR SPAIN

On June 11, 1775, Bruno de Heceta in the galleon *Santiago*, and his lieutenant, Juan Francisco de Bodega y Quadra, captain of the thirty-six-foot schooner *Sonora,* dropped anchor here, naming the cove Puerto de la Trinidad because it was Trinity Sunday. As you look at the lovely headland, it is not hard to imagine the little party marching resolutely up the hillside. While the padres chanted "Te Deum Laudamus," they planted a cross inscribed *Carolus III Dei G. Hyspaniarum Rex,* fired some guns, and claimed the land for Spain. The Yuroks, who gazed upon this little ceremony, must have been more than a little puzzled. Could these bearded creatures be people? It didn't seem likely; they showed absolutely no interest in the squaws. But of course the Yuroks couldn't read Latin and therefore had no idea that, at least by some people's laws, the land was no longer theirs. It was not yet time to worry, however; the Spaniards never came back.

Though this was the first landing by Europeans on the northern California coast (after Drake), several navigators had previously sighted the promontory. In 1595 the Portuguese sailor Sebastian Carmeno called it Cape Mendocino, a mistake repeated by Vizcaíno in 1603. Incidentally, the Trinity River, the Trinity Alps, and Trinity County are all named after this headland because an early pioneer, Pierson B. Reading, mistakenly believed that the river he was following emptied into this bay.

B&B, told me that one descendent of the tribe still lives here. Axel Lindgren's grandmother was the last medicine woman of Tsurai.

A replica of the lighthouse sits atop a bluff overlooking the tiny harbor nestled between the town and Trinidad Head. The **Mendocino Marine Laboratory** has a small aquarium displaying the marine life of these waters. Of special interest is a tank where salt water rises and falls, illustrating the fantastic world of the tide pool. The bluffs north of the head are public, and nearby **Trinidad State Beach** has some nice trails and tables for picnicking.

FOOD AND LODGING   Trinidad, California 95570

✔✔✔ **Trinidad B&B**   4 rooms with a spectacular ocean view. P.O. Box 849. (707) 677-0840.

✔✔ **Bishop Pine Lodge**   13 rustic cottages. 1481 Patrick's Point Drive. (707) 667-3314.

✔ **Ocean Grove Lodge**   12 cabins. P.O. Box 873. (707) 677-3543.

✔ **Patrick's Point State Park**   88 campsites.

●● **Merryman's Dinner House**   Restaurant overlooking Moonstone Beach. (707) 677-3001.

● **Seascape Restaurant**   At the pier. (707) 677-3762.

A nice alternative to the freeway is to take the old stagecoach road, which heads north out of town. **Patrick's Point State Park** has campsites scattered about in a bishop pine forest and pleasant trails that lead to scenic bluffs, one of which is called Wedding Rock. Eighty-eight stone steps lead to the summit, where on a good day you can see the entire coast from Cape Mendocino to the mouth of the Klamath River. A small interpretive center has some Yurok artifacts, and exhibits explain a bit about their life-style.

Like most large timber companies, Louisiana-Pacific is sensitive to the public's perception that their cutting ruins the landscape, so they have set aside a logged-over area as a **Demonstration Forest.** Through signs and handouts they try to get out their side of the issue. A brochure explains that lightning-caused fire has always ravaged these forests, and even the Indians cared little about the trees: they wanted fast-growing brush for the deer to feed on, so they often purposely set the place ablaze. The early settlers had little use for the trees, either. They cleared the land to make pastures. But the redwoods pertinaciously came back. A sign shows how a new tree, growing from an old stump, now has four times the lumber its parent did. Clear-cutting is defended as a better way of forest management because natural regeneration, especially in shady areas, takes too long, and trees left standing are vulnerable to being blown down, which destroys their young neighbors. The handout reminds you that this is "taxpaying industrial forest land" and closes with the following statement:

> L-P manages its timberlands to produce a perpetual crop, harvesting, reforesting, protecting the growing crop and finally harvesting again. Many acres of the timberlands are open to the public for swimming, hiking, fishing, hunting, "rockhounding," boating and other recreational activities.

The friends I have who work in the timber industry really do feel they're doing a good job of managing their forests. "We need the jobs, and we need the lumber, and we're taking great pains to hold down soil erosion. So why is everybody on our back?" They feel justified in their bumper sticker: "Sierra Club—Kiss My Axe." But we'll get a different view of things a little later on when we take the shuttle bus to the world's tallest tree.

Highway 101, now mostly two-lane, wanders through **Humboldt Lagoons State Park,** which embraces three lakes formed when sand dunes dammed the mouths of small streams. Included in this area is **Big Lagoon County Park,** which has picnicking facilities and is a favorite place to launch small boats. Stone Lagoon is said to have the best fishing, but the most popular is Freshwater Lagoon, where the highway traverses a spit separating it from the sea. RVs by the hundreds line up nose to tail along a two-mile stretch of road shoulder. Their owners comb the beach, gossip with their neighbors, or just spend a few days taking in the salt air.

REDWOOD NATIONAL PARK

For the next thirty-five miles, we will be driving through some of the most magnificent forests in the world. The Save the Redwoods League led the way in keeping much of this land in its virginal state. Through their efforts, three state parks were established: Prairie Creek Redwoods, Del Norte Coast Redwoods, and Jedediah Smith Redwoods. Then, in the 1960s, faced with the potential loss of fifty thousand acres of prime lands to the logger's axe, the federal government stepped in and created the national park. Attending the dedication ceremonies were President and Lady Bird Johnson (she worked hard to get the legislation passed); officers of the *National Geographic,* which did much to focus public awareness on the potential loss of the trees; and Richard Nixon, who ironically many years before had defeated the original sponsor of the park legislation, Helen Gahagan Douglas. It turned out to be the most expensive park ever purchased. Brent Twoomey, who leads tours to the tall trees area, gets mad every time he thinks about the process. "The government practically gave this land to the timber companies under the Homestead Act," he said. "When it came time to buy it back, the companies jacked up the price of redwood so they could gouge us. Then they cut so much timber in nearby land that erosion threatened the tall trees themselves. So the government had to step in again, this time purchasing forty thousand additional acres. Not a tree stood on thirty thousand of those acres. They spent thirty-three million more dollars to repair the damage the timber companies had wrecked. Seven hundred and fifty thousand seedlings were planted. A hundred and sixty miles of logging roads and a couple of thousand miles of skid trails were bulldozed out of existence. It's a sad thought, but our government spent more money for this park than they originally did buying the whole damn country." Then, as if to temper his words, he said: "You know, though, even Humboldt County went for the park acquisition bond issue on the last ballot."

Start your tour with a visit to the **National Park Interpretive Center** located a few miles south of the town of Orick or at the **Prairie Creek Ranger Station** ten miles up the road. Both places have bookstores, naturalists on duty, and exhibits displaying the wonders of the area.

Shuttle Bus to World's Tallest Trees. A rather strenuous eight-mile (each way) trail leads to the grove, but the logging roads that go closer to the site are closed to the public. Most people, therefore, take the shuttle bus (modest fee), which during the summer leaves from the National Park Information Center. The adventure takes about six hours, including an hour-long climb back up to where the bus dropped you off.

When I took the trip the driver, Brent Twoomey, talked about how the timber companies are "mining trees as old as the dinosaurs." Only 4 percent of the original forest still stands. He paused at an overlook where we could see the logged-over lands. "You know, in the 1920s *National Geographic* predicted that the tallest tree would be found in this canyon. The place was fog-bound all summer. Look at it now. I'm using the air conditioner, something I never used to have to do (the day was indeed sunny and warm). This bare ground makes the place too hot. Humans have reversed the weather in the last place on earth that the redwoods naturally grow. You'll see that the top of the world's tallest tree is dead. People claim lightning caused it, but they're wrong. Without the fog they're all going to die."

He talked about the impact on the environment. "It takes two thousand acres of old growth for a spotted owl to feel normal. Imagine the howl from the timber companies to setting aside one hundred thousand acres for a bunch of birds. The gravel in Redwood Creek is seven to twelve feet thick, most of which came down after the logging. The water table has been affected. But all the companies want to do is up the cut."

The bus makes four trips a day in the summer. An alternative to the round trip is to ask the driver to pick you up at the **Redwood Creek Trail Head,** which is located near the bus's route about four miles from the interpretive center. Then, after wandering around the grove, you can walk the eight miles back to your car.

Orick • Population: 650

The Oruks, an Indian tribe, lived along Redwood Creek. Whoever named the place didn't get the spelling quite right. Orick is a modest hamlet with a couple of cafes, several inexpensive motels, a gas station, grocery store, and five shops selling redwood burls. One popular purchase is a slab cut four inches thick, polished to a high gloss, and mounted on legs. It makes a fine coffee table.

GOLD BLUFFS BEACH/FERN CANYON •
(Two-hour side trip)

Three miles north of Orick, an unsigned road heads west toward the ocean. It has a name, Davidson Road, and though unpaved it is very popular because it leads to the beautiful Gold Bluffs Beach. The two-hundred-foot-high cliffs reflect a golden hue, but the beach wasn't named for its color. Early prospectors reported the finest placers ever discovered—sands so rich the ocean itself was the sluice. A San Francisco paper reported:

> [The ocean] had been rocking and washing up gold from the bottom of the sea for unknown ages, and had chanced to throw it in tons and shiploads beneath the hitherto undiscovered Gold Bluffs.

The only reason the assay office wasn't overwhelmed, I guess, was that there was no place to land a boat on this wave-smitten beach, and a seventy-five-pound sack of pure gold was about all a man could carry out on his back.

The iron pyrite–strewn (fool's gold) black-sand beach and the dunes behind stretch for six miles up the coast, a three-hundred-yard-wide platform of European dune-grass–rimed swales that snuggle below the bluffs. The state has built a number of campsites here, each with a windbreak-shrouded picnic table that makes outdoor dining a bit more civil when the gusts come out of the north. The fog often drifts in after dark; campers lose contact with everything but their own little band, huddled around the campfire as the gas lantern casts a zinc-coated aura on the swirling mists. I've heard it called California's greatest car-camping site, and I guess it is—if you really want to feel like you're away from civilization, at least. An elk herd lingers in this area, adding to the drama.

The road ends halfway up the beach at the mouth of **Fern Canyon,** a place of exquisite beauty. The two-hundred-foot-deep, square-sided chasm, created when Home Creek forced its way through the bluffs, is covered with the black-stemmed five-fingered fern, the delicate lady fern, and the masculine sward fern, all interspersed with lichen and spongy mosses. When I was there a little stream, maybe the size a garden hose would produce, came tumbling down from the canyon rim. Before it had gone a yard, the moss had massaged it into a sheet of water, then transformed it into individual rivulets, and finally cast it into a thousand droplets, each shining like a fresh-cut diamond lying on a bolt of green felt. An art class that had come up from Humboldt State was trying to capture the magic. "See the colors of the water in the stream?" asked a fellow standing behind his easel. I saw greens and blues, but the paints he was using were from the red and orange end of his palette.

One of the loveliest forests I've ever walked through is the **Lady Bird Johnson Grove,** located a couple of miles east of Highway 101. All the groves we have visited so far have been located in the bottom of canyons. This one is on a ridge a thousand feet above the creek bed and thus has a more open feel. You can actually see the sky, and since the trees are spaced out a bit, you have the unique opportunity to actually photograph an *entire* redwood. Though that sounds a bit bizarre, you have to remember that these trees are monsters. Early explorers were flabbergasted. Though neither ever saw a redwood, Lewis and Clark were suitably impressed with the Douglas fir, which was far larger than anything they had seen in their native Virginia. William Clark's diary reads:

> They rise to a height of two hundred and thirty feet and one hundred and twenty feet of that height [is] without a limb. One of our party measured one and found it forty-two feet in circumference at a point beyond the reach of an ordinary man.

Meriwether Lewis was a bit less precise. "Saw some big sticks today," he wrote.

The Arcata Redwood Company invites you to make a self-guided sawmill tour of their plant near the turnoff to the Lady Bird Johnson Grove. You can't watch the debarking operation as you can in Scotia (Chapter 6), so the tour is not quite as spectacular, but it does provide an insight into how logs become lumber.

PRAIRIE CREEK STATE PARK

The state park operates an interpretive center in an old redwood building built by the Civilian Conservation Corps during the Depression. Nearby is one of the more exciting campgrounds

on the north coast because it sits adjacent to Boyes Prairie, home
of a herd of about forty Roosevelt elk. This animal, also called
wapiti elk or red deer *(Cervus roosevelti)* is second only to the
moose in size among the deer family. Males grow to seven hundred pounds and support massive racks, which one observer
called "animated hat racks." The elk are clearly visible from the
highway most of the time, munching grass in the middle of the
meadow. Most tourists can't resist rubbernecking, much to the ire
of the log truck drivers who barrel down this two-lane highway
at a pretty good clip.

Twenty-odd paths lead out into the state park, one of which,
called Revelation Trail, is designed so that sightless people can
capture the feel, sound, and smell of the forest. Features are
described in braille. Fern Canyon is a bit over four miles from the
state park headquarters by the lovely, moderately graded James
Irvine Trail. Rangers say it's a delightful walk, especially when
you have someone take the car around to Gold Bluffs Beach to
give you a ride back. A nearby fish hatchery is open to visitors.
Park rangers claim five hundred kinds of mushrooms and eight
hundred species of flowers grow in this damp area.

I chose, however, to walk the little-used trail that wends up
Brown Creek because I wanted to get a solitary sense of these
groves. In a nearby forest I found a couple of dozen redwoods
named after men prominent in the forest industry: Gifford Pin-
chot, first director of the National Forest Service; Frederick
Weyerhaeuser, Sr.; Carl Schenck, founder of the Biltmore School
of Forestry, the nation's first; and Frederick Law Olmsted, the
noted landscape architect. A giant had fallen, smashing one of the
markers, and I reflected that perhaps that too was how it should
be. Trees, like people, are part of the transitory shapes of time—
they die.

COASTAL DRIVE LOOP ROAD • (Half-hour side loop)

A scenic eight-mile side loop turns west at the northern end
of Prairie Creek Redwoods Park. A few miles of forest driving
brings you onto a bluff high above the Pacific. Signs at several
turnouts describe what's going on in the natural world before
you. The climate, geology, wildlife, plant habitation, and marine
life are all explained in a way that makes you realize that the
National Park Service is concerned with protecting not only the
trees, but the entire coastal ecosystem, and one of the best ways
to do that is to have an educated, caring public. And the public
does care. Thousands of angry citizens went to Mendocino recently to protest possible offshore oil drilling directly opposite

where you are standing. You can return to 101 via the paved Alder Camp Road or continue along the bluff on the gravel, one-lane road that leads to **Klamath Overlook,** a lovely spot. Below is a private RV park that is crammed to the gills during the salmon season starting in June.

Klamath • Population: 100

There's hardly a town at all at Klamath anymore. Most of the structures that you see are house trailers. Residents have learned the power of this river during flood and have planned for a speedy escape should the need arise. A side road goes a few miles up the north side of the river and then stops abruptly. This is the edge of tribal lands—the Yuroks and Hupas claim a road would destroy their ancient burial grounds. Another road goes downstream along the north bank of the Klamath to the historic Requa Inn, an old roadhouse that still offers quaint rooms, has a cozy living room, and boasts a fine restaurant. Nearby, the spectacularly scenic Coastal Trail wiggles along the flank of a roadless bluff that drops precipitously into the sea.

Klamath River, the second largest in the state, has its headwaters near Oregon's Crater Lake. It is one of the premier salmon streams in the country, but it's not without problems. At times, fishermen stand shoulder to shoulder along the bank and boat bow to boat bow out in the lagoon. The Klamaths, who live on the Hupa Reservation twenty miles upstream, claim they have special tribal rights that allow them to use gill nets. Not surprisingly, they would quite prefer the whites to simply go away. A lady who sold me some smoked salmon at a nearby shop said this year was going to be really bad. "They are opening the commercial season the same day the sport season starts, and what with the Indians making their claims, it's going to be a mess. I hope we don't get some bloodshed."

Half a dozen miles north of the river is a private operation called Trees of Mystery. Thirty-foot concrete statues of Paul Bunyan and Babe, his blue ox, loom over the immense parking lot. When I toured the place, a sign at the entrance read "Please pay when leaving." It didn't say how much. After walking the three-quarter-mile trail, I learned that the real mystery is why anyone would pay five bucks to visit a place where the main event is listening to a love song called "Trees" blaring out from a couple of speakers hidden behind a ring of second-growth redwoods.

A bit farther on you pass a quiet lagoon filled with water lilies, a scene just as common in New Jersey or Minnesota but here only a dozen yards from the Pacific. The first whites to traverse this countryside (see Jedediah Smith: Mountain Man, page 153) had a terrible time of it.

> All hands working to get our horses on as they are so worn out, that it is almost impossible to drive them through the Bush. We have two men everyday that go ahead with axes, to cut a road, and then with difficulty—we can get ahead.

The drive north turns inland as it meanders through **Del Norte State Park,** the last stand of redwoods located directly on Highway 101. The highway then drops down onto the fifteen-mile-long coastal plain abutting the harbor at Crescent City.

FOOD AND LODGING   Klamath, California 95548

✔✔ **Requa Inn**   Historic riverside tavern and restaurant. 16 rooms. 451 Requa Road. (707) 482-8205.

✔ **Motel Trees**   23-room motel and coffee shop opposite Trees of Mystery. (707) 482-3152.

✔ **Del Norte Coast Redwoods State Park**   145 campsites.

✔ **Prairie Creek State Park**   Elk Prairie—25 campsites; Gold Bluffs Beach—25 campsites.

Crescent City • Population: 3,100

Crescent City is the seat of Del Norte County, one of California's smallest, with a population of eighteen thousand. "We're a bit countryish up here," the lady at the motel told me. "We pronounce it Del Nort, but of course the Spanish would say 'nort-ay'." The town has a sizable harbor jammed with commercial fishing boats. Between the boat basin and the business district is a lovely park—an area that was considered the downtown prior to Good Friday, 1964 (see Tsunami, page 118). I learned a bit about the history of the area by visiting the fine **Crescent City Museum,** located in the old jailhouse. A first-order Fresnel lens, removed from an offshore lighthouse, dominates one wing. Photos show the wreckage of *Emidio,* a tanker sunk by a Japanese submarine in 1941, which drifted ashore here, and of the tragic end of *Brother Jonathan,* which sank in 1865 with a loss of nearly two hundred lives. Additional marine history is displayed in the privately owned **Battery Point Lighthouse,** built in 1856. Provided the tide is not too high, you walk to the lovely old building that sits on an isolated headland. Information on the forest lands is available at the **Redwood**

National Park Headquarters, located a couple of blocks off of Highway 101. A private aquarium called Undersea World is nearby.

Crescent City is the principal stopover point for people traveling along the coast. The highway is lined with motels. Most tourists head for Citizen's Dock, where you dine overlooking the fishing fleet.

~~~~~~~~~~~~~~~~~~~~~~~~~~~~~~~~~~~~~~~

TSUNAMI

When Anchorage got its awful jolt at seven-thirty in the evening on March 27, 1964, it is unlikely that anyone in Crescent City knew what the word "tsunami" meant, and if they did, they probably couldn't have pronounced it (the "t" is silent). No one here felt the quake; its epicenter was three thousand miles away. By 10:30 P.M., though, when television announcers began talking about what they incorrectly called a tidal wave (tides are not involved), people's interest began to perk up. Tsunamis, it seems, have been known to travel five hundred miles an hour. But this one didn't look bad. Midnight reports from both Honolulu and Washington's Neah Bay noted only moderate swells. The news media hadn't yet learned that three unfortunates had been swept out to sea at Depoe Bay, Oregon. Mariners reported nothing at all, but that was not surprising. Deep water can hide a dreadful force. A long, sloping, funnel-shaped continental shelf is required to turn a tsunami into a lethal force, exactly like the shoal called the Mendocino escarpment, which lies off Crescent City's shore.

The first bore hit at 1:00 A.M. The *San Francisco Examiner's* William Boquist described the scene:

> It does not resemble a wave. It's a terrifying mass of water that raises up and comes in like the churning waters from a broken dam.

The bore was three feet high, an enormous amount of water when you consider it was half a mile wide. Forty minutes later another hit, then, eerily, the harbor emptied itself. Boat owners, who had headed out to the presumed safety of the sea, suddenly found themselves hard upon an unfamiliar bottom. The third bore wasn't as bad, but by now debris from buildings and piers wrecked by the first waves had become quite effective truncheons. Then, at roughly 2:20 A.M., the giant hit, a twelve-foot monster that surged a third of a mile into Crescent City's downtown. Resident Bob Ames recalled:

The water was four feet up above the sidewalk. We decided we couldn't get out, so we went upstairs. . . . My mom and dad, Bert, Brad, and I all converged on the stairs at once. Then the fuses blew, and we had just gotten up there, when the windows started breaking. There was a car with two people inside floating up L Street. A house came floating by between our building and G&G Liquors. We could hear a lady inside yelling for help.

In two and a half hours it was all over. The fourth wave was the last, but Bob Ames and the others who huddled there in terror didn't know that. Nine city blocks, $20 million worth of property, were destroyed while they watched. Citizens Dock was in shambles. Eleven people had lost their lives.

By eleven that morning the tsunami was pounding the shores of La Punta, Peru.

FOOD AND LODGING   Crescent City, California 95531

✔✔ **Curly Redwood Lodge**   36-unit motel built from a single redwood tree. 701 Redwood Highway South. (707) 464-2137.

✔✔ **Northwoods Best Western Inn**   52-unit motel. 655 Highway 101 South. (707) 464-9971.

✔✔ **Pacific Motor Hotel**   62-unit motel, pool. P.O. Box 595. (707) 464-4141.

✔✔ **Thunderbird Lodge**   48-unit motel. 119 L Street. (707) 464-2181.

✔ **Jedediah Smith State Park**   108 campsites.

● **Harbor View Grotto**   Restaurant and bar. (707) 464-3815.

JEDEDIAH SMITH REDWOODS STATE PARK •
(Two-hour side loop)

"When I want to get my head back in order, I drive out along Howland Hill Road," a waitress told me at dinner. "The beauty of the place helps you get things sorted out."

I discovered what she meant. Drive east on Elk Valley Road for 1½ miles and turn right. Howland Hill Road soon turns to gravel, climbs steeply to a low summit, and then drops into the Mill Creek watershed following the route of the old Crescent City & Yreka Plank Turnpike Road built in 1858. No one has seen fit to widen it, so you may have to back up to pass an occasional oncoming car. That's just as it should be because even when driving you feel an intimacy with these woods. The day I went there, I had to stop to remove a pile of charred cordwood that was blocking my way. Someone had—unsuccessfully, it turned out—tried to build a campfire, and the center of the road seemed as good a place as any to do it. The road hugs a moss-covered stream bank spotted with redwood sorrel, a ubiquitous little plant that looks like a heart-shaped three-leaf clover. Sunlight, by contrast, is a rare commodity on the forest floor. A scenic two-mile trail leads to Fern Falls and the Boy Scout Tree. Park rangers laud the virtues of **Stout Memorial Grove,** one of the most stately stands around. The Stout Tree, said to be the largest of all the still-existing coast redwoods, is 340 feet high and measures 20 feet in diameter at shoulder level. To put that in perspective, 20 feet is the width of a modest house. The dirt road continues for a few miles, becomes paved, crosses a couple of bridges, and joins U.S. Highway 199.

Shortcut Return to Interstate 5

The Redwood Highway officially ends at the junction of Highways 101 and 199, though the Redwood Empire Association, a trade group promoting tourism, includes members from Josephine County, Oregon, because many people leave the coast here to take the faster inland highways. It's a 1½-hour drive to Grants Pass, but there is a reason not to hurry. **Oregon Caves National Monument** is located at the end of a twenty-mile steep but paved road that branches off from Highway 199. The National Park Service conducts hour-long tours of the cavern that feature many unusual limestone formations and a phalanx of stalactites and stalagmites. A grand old lodge near the cave entrance is open during the summer.

We'll return west on Highway 199, though, and continue our northward trek on Highway 101. Though this may be the end of the Redwood Empire, it is not the end of the redwoods. We'll visit an Oregon grove in the next chapter.

PART THREE

The Oregon Coast

OREGON'S ISOLATED
SOUTH COAST

Forests Marching down to the Sea

A look at a large relief map of the Northwestern Pacific Coast reveals an almost continuous string of mountains, the Coast Range, rising within a few miles of the ocean and extending inland until they dissolve into several large north-south-running valleys. California's Central Valley stretches out for four hundred miles, and to the north Oregon's Willamette adds another 110 miles to this inland trough. But in between these two rifts lies the chaotic jumble of the Klamath Range, which, with its subgroups, the Siskiyou and the Trinity mountains, march inland one hundred miles, colliding directly with the volcano-studded Cascades. Geologists think the Klamaths were once part of the Cascades, but 150 million years ago, for reasons no one seems to understand, they moved west, forming an island. Since that time, the Pacific and Juan de Fuca plates have been sliding under the North American plate, forcing it higher and draining the two valleys and, at the same time, building a mountainous link between the onetime island and the mainland. During this process, very hard rocks were scraped off the descending plates and deposited along the southern Oregon coast, rocks that have defiantly stood up to the crashing sea. Fortunately these events combined to make the country up ahead one of great scenic beauty. Robert Haswell, an officer aboard Captain Gray's *Washington*, was one of the first to describe this coast. Two hundred years ago he wrote:

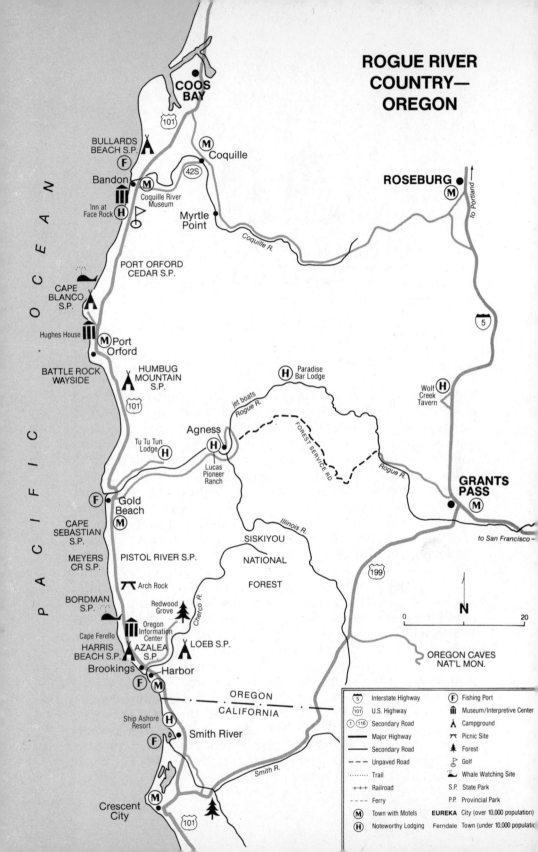

ROGUE RIVER COUNTRY— OREGON

COOS BAY

(101)

BULLARDS BEACH S.P.
(F)

(M) Coquille

Bandon
(M)
42S
Coquille River Museum

Inn at Face Rock
(H)

Myrtle Point

Coquille R.

ROSEBURG ●
(M)

to Portland →

PORT ORFORD CEDAR S.P.

CAPE BLANCO S.P.

Hughes House
(M) Port Orford

BATTLE ROCK WAYSIDE

HUMBUG MOUNTAIN S.P.

(101)

Paradise Bar Lodge
(H)

jet boats
Rogue R.

Wolf Creek Tavern (H)

5

Agness

Tu Tu Tun Lodge
(H)

(H)
Lucas Pioneer Ranch

FOREST SERVICE RD

Rogue R.

GRANTS PASS
(M)

(F) Gold Beach
(M)

to San Francisco →

CAPE SEBASTIAN S.P.

MEYERS CR S.P.

PISTOL RIVER S.P.

Illinois R.

SISKIYOU

NATIONAL

FOREST

199

Arch Rock

BORDMAN S.P.

Redwood Grove

Chetco R.

Cape Ferello

Oregon Information Center

HARRIS BEACH S.P.

AZALEA S.P.

LOEB S.P.

N

0   20

OREGON CAVES NAT'L MON.

Brookings
(F) (M) Harbor

OREGON
CALIFORNIA

Ship Ashore Resort
(H)

(F) ● Smith River

Smith R.

(5)	Interstate Highway	(F)	Fishing Port
(101)	U.S. Highway	🏛	Museum/Interpretive Center
(1) (116)	Secondary Road	🏕	Campground
	Major Highway	🔭	Picnic Site
	Secondary Road	🌲	Forest
- - -	Unpaved Road	⛳	Golf
····	Trail	🐋	Whale Watching Site
+++	Railroad	S.P.	State Park
- · -	Ferry	P.P.	Provincial Park
(M)	Town with Motels	**EUREKA**	City (over 10,000 population)
(H)	Noteworthy Lodging	Ferndale	Town (under 10,000 population)

Crescent City
(M)

(101)

PACIFIC OCEAN

. . . a delightful Country, thickly inhabited and Cloathed with woods and verdure with maney Charming streems of water gushing from the vallies.

Smith River • Population: 250

We will explore the one-hundred-mile stretch of highway between the mouths of Oregon's Chetco and Coquille rivers, arguably the prettiest section of U.S. 101 between Canada and the Mexican border. But first you have the pleasure of traversing the lowlands surrounding the mouth of California's Smith River. This is dairying country, interspersed, surprisingly, with lily fields. Ninety percent of the production of America's lily bulbs comes from the farms between here and Brookings, Oregon, and judging from some of the mansionlike farmhouses that stand just below the hills to the east, it must be a profitable crop indeed.

The Smith, like the Klamath and a whole bunch of other rivers we'll cross farther north, is a world-class angling stream, productive almost all year long. In July and August fishermen troll for salmon just outside the bar. Rules specify a barbless hook and a twenty-inch minimum size. Then, starting in September, the kings (chinook) enter the lagoon, followed a month later by the silver (or coho) salmon. Steelhead return to their native streams starting in December. "Steelies" are the premier sport fish on the Pacific Coast, rivaling Florida's bonefish in fighting spirit. A record-setting 27.5-pounder was caught in this river. Cutthroat trout return for a March–May migration, and just to round things out, some rivers have a summer steelhead run of what the locals call half-pounders. Most are quite a bit larger than that.

Thousands of people come to fish these waters, most of whom bring along their house trailers or drive motor homes. As a result, RV parks proliferate, and the vehicles here are parked together cheek by jowl. An example is the Ship Ashore Resort on the north bank of the Smith overlooking the lagoon. There must be room for three hundred rigs on the grassy field at the center of the complex. Nearby, a temporary ditch was built to float an old yacht to a site next to the highway. It's now a gift shop with a rather interesting museum of nautical paraphernalia belowdeck.

FOOD AND LODGING

✔✔ **Ship Ashore Resort**   32-unit motel, restaurant and bar. Smith River, California 95567. (707) 487-3141.

Brookings/Harbor • Population: 3,900

In crossing the state line, you immediately go from the north coast, with its inference of cold and dampness, to the south coast, a term the locals use to imply that their pleasant little enclave in southwestern Oregon is a nice place to live. "We have the warmest winter weather in the state," Art Collins, manager of the Chamber of Commerce, told me. "We're in the banana belt; flowers bloom year round." Art didn't mention that they also get over eighty inches of rain in a typical year. Brookings and the separate town of Harbor on the south side of the Chetco River are having a boom, Art told me; lots of retired people are moving here. Considering some earlier reports about the value of this countryside, and a plea from a former governor (see Oregon: "A Vast, Worthless Area," below), that may be a bit of hyperbole. Oregon, incidentally, is pronounced "or-re-gun," with the accent equally on all syllables.

OREGON: "A VAST, WORTHLESS AREA"

There is some dispute among historians as to whether he actually said it, but everyone wants to believe he did, simply because it makes such a good story. Daniel Webster, thundering before Congress, let his fellow legislators know just what he thought about Oregon.

What do we want of this vast, worthless area, this region of savages and wild beasts, of shifting sands and whirlpools of dust, of cactus and prairie dogs? To what use could we ever hope to put these great deserts or these great mountain ranges, impenetrable and covered to their base with eternal snow? Mr. President, I will never vote one cent from the public treasury to place the Pacific Coast one inch nearer Boston than it is now.

It was an outrageous statement, as millions of native-born Oregonians will attest to and as thousands of modern-day emigrants to the Beaver State have proved. "Don't Californicate Oregon" was a slogan that began to appear on bumper stickers when it seemed like every retiree from Los Angeles had decided to move north. Even the governor got into the fray. In the mid-1970s, Tom McCall told a group of conventioneers:

Welcome to Oregon. While you're here, I want you to enjoy yourselves. Travel, visit, drink in the great beauty of our state. But for God's sake, don't move here.

That bit of nonwelcome made headlines throughout the country. Happily, the current administration is delighted to see newcomers settle in this lovely state.

Many old-timers would argue that Brookings gets its charm from the fact that in 1913, the Brookings Timber and Lumber Company decided to do things right. They hired the renowned Berkeley architect Bernard Maybeck, who chose to lay out the streets following the landform rather than in the classic north-south grid. The Chetco Inn illustrates Maybeck's style. Owner Victoria Roberts told me that the restoration has been an arduous, ongoing process with the end not yet in sight. The handsome old company headquarters building across the street has been con-verted into a shopping mall. As tiny as Brookings is, it has one of the nicest city parks I have ever seen, built by the Civilian Con-servation Corps during the Great Depression. The town celebrates spring with an azalea festival.

The little harbor at the mouth of the Chetco has enjoyed quite an expansion in recent years because it faces south, away from the prevailing winds. The bar is said to be the safest in Oregon—even car-top aluminum boats can be taken out to sea on most days. In 1985 eleven thousand salmon were caught in one single July week. Party boats furnish everything you need, including license, tackle, and know-how. Farther north, on Van-couver Island, the sport catch will be even higher. South of town is the delightful **Chetco Valley Museum,** housed in the 1855 home of an early settler. The world's largest Monterey cypress—twenty-seven feet nine inches in circumference, is on the grounds. During the summer, Strahm's Lilies Inc. invites you on a self-guided tour to learn a bit about the hybrid process of creat-ing new and ever more beautiful varieties of this perennial fa-vorite.

Brookings had its "day of infamy" in 1942 when a Japanese submarine surfaced offshore. The crew assembled a small sea-plane, which the pilot took on the only bombing run of the United States mainland. He scored a direct hit on a myrtle tree up near Mount Emily.

Loeb State Park, located eight miles up the Chetco River, is the site of the state's largest stand of old-growth myrtlewood. Oregonians are very proud of this tree; numerous businesses carve the wood into bowls and artifacts. When park hostess Alice Carlton pointed one out, I remarked that it looked the same as our California laurel, which we also call a bay tree. "You're right," she said, "but we think a special kind of laurel. It grows only here and in the Holy Land, you know." Sir David Douglas, the British botanist for whom the Douglas fir is named, seemed to be damning this country with faint praise when he wrote:

This elegant evergreen tree forms the connecting link between the gloomy pine forests of northwest America and the tropical-like verdure of California.

A bit farther up the road is one of Oregon's two redwood groves, the last we'll see on this sojourn. A mile-long trail, steep in spots, wends through the stately forest.

Lovely **Harris Beach State Park,** located several miles north of town, has several pathways leading down to the strand. The beach is partially protected from the wind by Goat Island, at twenty-one acres the Oregon coast's largest. The island's population, I read, "includes pelicans, murres, puffins, cormorants, auklets, loons, shearwaters, petrels, terns, and many kinds of gulls." Across the highway is the **Oregon State Information Center,** where a staff has answers to the questions most tourists ask.

FOOD AND LODGING   Brookings/Harbor, Oregon 97415

- ✔✔ **Best Western Brookings Inn**   41-unit motel. P.O. Box 1139. (503) 469-2173.

- ✔✔ **Chetco Inn**   30-room hotel built in 1915. 417 Fern Street. (503) 469-9984.

- ✔✔ **Pacific Sunset Inn**   41-unit motel. P.O. Box AL. (503) 469-2141.

- ✔✔ **Spindrift Motor Inn**   35-unit motel. P.O. Box 6023. (503) 469-5345.

- ✔✔ **Sea Dreamer Inn**   B&B. 15167 McVay Lane. (503) 469-6629.

- ✔ **Loeb State Park**   53 campsites.

- ✔ **Harris Beach State Park**   151 campsites.

BOARDMAN STATE PARK

We now head north on a new and very scenic part of Highway 101. The old road went up the mountainside to avoid this treacherous stretch of coast. Unfortunately it wandered through the trees; you couldn't see very much. The new highway struggles through a ten-mile-long state park, named after the well-loved Samuel Boardman, chief of Oregon's state park system, who retired in 1950 at the age of seventy-five. Beach trails traverse much of this linear park, but most people pause at one or more of the vista points that line the road or picnic at several day-use spots along the way. I'll mention all the best shopping points in the hope that you won't hurry too quickly through this wonderland.

Lone Ranch Beach has excellent tide pooling. One of the prettiest vista points is at Cape Ferrelo, named for the Portuguese navigator Bartholome Ferrelo. No one knows whether Ferrelo ever sighted this cape during his voyage in 1542. Whaleshead View Point overlooks an offshore rock that resembles a whale's head, complete with a blowhole that—at certain tides, at least—spouts right on cue. The little cove on the north, a favorite landing spot for rumrunners during Prohibition, is now a nice place for a picnic. A half-mile trail leads through the woods to some shoreline dunes. Nearby, a short trail leads to Natural Bridge Viewpoint, where you look out over the remains of an ancient sea cave that collapsed, leaving several natural bridges. Arch Rock Viewpoint has picnic tables in a parklike setting, and Mack Arch Viewpoint looks out over an interesting, two-hundred-foot-high offshore rock formation.

The highway drops down to the sand dunes of **Pistol River State Park.** One James Mace is said to have lost his pistol in this river in 1853. Nearby is the site of one of the many battles of the Rogue Indian wars (see They Certainly Weren't Rogues, below). Meyers Creek beach is an excellent place for clamming. Towering Cape Sebastian soars seven hundred feet above the surf. A narrow but paved road leads partway out onto the headland. A more interesting experience, however, is to take the two-mile trail that leads down to the surf. Several belvederes make fine places to look for whales. Sebastián Vizcaíno named the promontory after the patron of the day he sailed by, Saint Sebastian.

THEY CERTAINLY WEREN'T ROGUES

Blood enough to be remembered, one would think. Yet the Indian wars of southern Oregon, though among the most ferocious of our pioneer annals, have been largely forgotten. Part of the obscurity arises from the geography. In southern Oregon the coastal and Cascade mountain ranges merge in a convulsed jumble of forested peaks, deep canyons, and isolated grassy valleys. As a result the skirmishes that raged through them were as detached as they were brutal, a complexity of little wars rather than a clearly patterned, unified campaign.

So wrote David Lavender in his book *Land of Giants.* The war began almost the instant white men stepped ashore at Port Orford in 1851 when a tribe of warriors brandishing knives and launching arrows bravely charged into the mouth of a cannon and were summarily dispatched to the happy hunting ground. More whites arrived, more Indians were either murdered or succumbed to the white man's diseases. Between 1852 and 1854 the white population on the Rogue went up as the Indian population declined—from 1,100 to 500 in a two-year span. Joel Palmer, the superintendent of Indian affairs, wrote:

> I found the Indians of the Rogue River Valley excited and unsettled. The hostilities of last summer had prevented the storing of the usual quantities of food; the occupation of their best root-grounds by the whites greatly abridged that resource; their scanty supplies and the unusual severity of the winter had induced disease, and death had swept away nearly one-fifth of those residing on the reserve.

Yet more Indians came down out of the mountains, determined to drive the white men out.

The skirmishes got bloody. Indians on the Klamath massacred ten miners. In revenge the whites shot or hanged the first twenty-five Indians they came upon, even though they were nowhere around when the killings were done. On the Coquille, miners slaughtered sixteen Indians; on the Chetco, twelve. Near the Pistol River, thirty-four "minutemen" withstood the repeated charge of warriors displaying a desperate courage. Settlers at Gold Beach took refuge in the hastily built Fort Miner, where they were under seige for two months (during which time, strangely, two white-Indian weddings were performed). John Geisel and his three sons were killed; his wife, Christina, and two daughters were taken captive and later returned for ransom. Christina, who became a symbol of the insurrection, lived until 1899, when she was murdered for her pension check.

The last battle was at Big Bend, near Illahe on the Rogue. It lasted thirty-four hours, during which time eleven soldiers were killed and sixteen wounded. The Indians lost more than one hundred. Captain Edward Ord's journal of June 8, 1856, described the surrender:

> At 2 P.M. lot of Indians 4 men 9 squaws & some children came limping and crying [the squaws] into camp—a girl 12 years was drowned coming down the river—poor devils—the decrepid and half blind old woman are a melancholy sight—to think of collecting such people for a long journey through an unknown land—no wonder the men fight so desperately to remain.

French fur traders called this La Rivière aux Coquins, or "River of the Rogues," because of their contempt for the local tribes. Judging from the valor these Indians displayed, I think most people today would agree that the French were wrong.

Twelve hundred survivors were marched to Port Orford and

taken to reservations on the Yamhill and Siletz rivers. After the Geisel massacre, bounty hunters rounded up some stragglers and marched them to the site of the foray. F. A. Stewart, a witness, wrote:

> A number of citizens rose up from the low brush, and poured a preconcerted and well directed volley upon the doomed Indians, all of whom, nineteen in number were slain, and thus was the Geisel massacre avenged, as far as was in the power of man to do.

A few miles north of Gold Beach there is a monument to the Geisel family. No monument to the Indians exists.

Gold Beach • Population: 1,500

The hills around the mouth of the Rogue River began to swarm with miners after gold was discovered farther upstream in February 1852. By June the beaches here were turned into placer mines; huge pipes were built to transport water to wash the sands. The most successful sluicing occurred where ocean waves had concentrated deposits of black sand containing gold, platinum, and chromite. But nobody, it seems, did very well. Even the optimists admitted that you had to wash thirty thousand *tons* of sand to get an ounce of gold, even in the richest places. That's a lot of sand. Then in 1861 a flood swept the black sand out to sea, taking the gold with it—if indeed there ever really was any.

Though Gold Beach is a quarter the size of Brookings, it seems larger, mainly because it is a resort town, thanks to its location at the mouth of the Rogue River. It is also the Curry County seat and home to the county fair and the **Curry County Historical Museum,** which has displays of Indian artifacts, mining equipment, and farming and logging machinery.

An old relic from the town's maritime days rots away near the boat basin. The *Mary D. Hume* was built in 1880 by lumber and fishing baron R. D. Hume, the largest landowner in Curry County. In 1978 she had the distinction of being the oldest ship still in operation on the Pacific Coast. It is obvious that Gold Beach's harbor is not as well protected as the one in Brookings. Massive stone jetties poke out into the ocean in an attempt to keep the bar open without constant dredging. The use of jetties for this purpose was perfected by James Eads, the fellow who invented the diving bell and builder of the first bridge across the Mississippi at St. Louis in 1874. His theory, which he demonstrated on the lower Mississippi, was to confine the river so that the current would accelerate, thereby scouring out its own channel and depositing its load of silt far out at sea. The system worked on the Mississippi. It failed here. I watched the harbor entrance on a day with a two-foot-minus tide and a moderate to strong breeze coming out of the west. Surfers would have enjoyed the three-foot waves that were pouring in between the jetties.

FOOD AND LODGING   Gold Beach, Oregon 97444

✔✔ **Best Western Inn of the Beachcomber**   50-unit motel, pool. 1250 South Highway 101. (503) 247-6691.

✔✔ **The Inn at Gold Beach**   41-unit motel. 1435 South Ellingsburg. (503) 247-6606.

✔✔ **Ireland's Rustic Lodges**   29 cottages and motel units. P.O. Box 774. (503) 247-7718.

✔✔ **Jot's Resort**   Huge 140-room motel (many with kitchens) overlooking the mouth of the Rogue. Restaurant and bar. P.O. Box J. (503) 247-6676.

✔✔ **Western Village Motel**   27-unit motel. P.O. Box 793. (503) 247-6611.

●● **Nor Wester Seafood Restaurant**   Restaurant and bar overlooking harbor. (503) 247-2333.

●● **Rod 'n' Reel**   Restaurant and bar. (503) 247-6823.

ROGUE RIVER EXCURSIONS

Though the Rogue is by no means the best fishing river in the West, it certainly is the best known, thanks mainly to a former dentist from Zanesville, Ohio. In 1916 Zane Grey went on a fishing expedition to the Rogue and promptly fell in love with the place. For more than twenty years, the writer kept coming back, even though he apparently didn't have a whole lot of luck. In his book *A Guide to Oregon South Coast History*, Nathan Douthit has a marvelous quote by longtime river guide Glen Wooldridge:

> He always traveled with a full crew, his secretaries, a cook, a cameraman, and there would be tents and lots of equipment to haul in. But I never did think much of him as a fisherman. He just couldn't seem to get the hang of catching a steelhead.

Grey's novel about the conflicts between the commerical fisherman of the lower river was serialized in the magazine *Country Gentleman* under the title "Rustlers of Silver River" and republished after his death as *Rogue River Feud*. Grey's writing attracted a host of celebrities to these waters, including Herbert Hoover and Hollywood stars George Murphy and Ginger Rogers. Famous people still come here, to fish, to run the white-water rapids, or just to escape into its roadless interior.

Glen Wooldridge's trips became so popular that he made quite an effort to tame the river—presumably so that what he called "the dudes" wouldn't get too wet. Many of the rocks at the river's most fearsome rapid, Blossom Bar, were blasted out of existence. Glen recalled that most of his customers fished with lures or bait, but fly fishermen, he maintained, "just couldn't stand to see a fish caught on anything but a fly." He could never understand why, but we fly-casters know. My father, a contemporary of Wooldridge, had nothing but scorn for the nonpurists; he wouldn't even call them fishermen. "Bait operators" was his term.

Float Trips

White-water rafters now swarm over the river from spring to fall. They come because the river is reasonably challenging, both water and the days are warm, and it's a chance to get out into a wilderness area without having to walk or ride a horse. Modern, inflatable equipment has made the sport safer and easier to learn. Most people book three- to five-day trips offered by numerous white-water outfitters based in Grants Pass, Oregon. Many offer three types of transport. Single-person inflatable kayaks are said to be easy to master. Your guide/teacher follows in a larger craft with the dunnage. I enjoy paddle rafting, where four boatmates work as a team under the direction of the boatman, who steers you through the rapids energetically shouting out orders—"all ahead," "left ahead," "all back"—as you furiously paddle away, trying to avoid the rocks. Excursion rafts are slightly larger. The boatman sits in the middle, working two long oars, while two or three passengers sit on the dunnage, holding on tight as they careen over the falls. Nights are spent either camping out or sleeping in the luxury of a number of resorts that line the river. You are then bused back to Grants Pass over a dirt forest service road. For a packet of information, write to the Grants Pass Visitor and Convention Bureau: P.O. Box 970, Grants Pass, Oregon 97526.

Jet Boats

In 1895 an adventuresome boatman contracted to take the mail to Agness, thirty-two miles upstream from Gold Beach. Back then the round trip took four days. Now you can do it in six hours, including a two-hour lunch stop at the famous old Lucas Pioneer Ranch. One outfitter boasts that they still deliver the mail, but this is largely a fiction. A paved road now leads all the way to Agness, but taking the boat is more fun; the river is calm, and the weather warms up considerably once you get a few miles upstream from Gold Beach. Yet Agness is out in the woods. I was amused by a sign reading

Agness

Elevation • 185 feet

Population • Small

With the invention of hydrojet propulsion (water is pumped through a nozzle), boats can now go into the wilder parts of the river where the water is more challenging. With three V-8 engines producing a total of one thousand horsepower, the boatman can power a forty-person craft up and over all but the most ferocious rapids. The twenty-mile section upriver from Agness is the most exciting part; there are no roads, the water is much faster, and the canyon narrower. Passengers are required to wear life jackets. The boatman makes the most out of each cascade, angling in to a fall, whirling about, and creating as much spray as it is safe to do. He can reverse the thrust of the jets, bringing the craft to an abrupt stop in an avalanche of water that drenches almost everyone. "Just checking my breaks before heading downhill," my driver said with a grin.

Antics like this provide the excitement, but there are other reasons for going farther upstream. I spotted an osprey's nest as we rounded a bend. A bald eagle perched on the limb of an oak tree. It seemed almost staged, and maybe it was, but there was wildlife everywhere. A brown bear watched us pass with idle interest, yawning and scratching in seeming unconcern. A curious fawn looked up and then, at her mother's beckoning, scudded off into the woods. A great blue heron soared above along with another, less handsome fellow, a turkey vulture.

The boats are turned back at Blossom Bar, where even Glen Wooldridge's blasting wasn't enough to allow them to pass. Lunch is offered at the lovely Paradise Bar Lodge, where a staff prepares country cooking for the hundred or more people who make this day-long trip on a typical summer day.

JET BOAT OUTFITTERS   Gold Beach, Oregon 97444

✔ **Court's**   P.O. Box 456. (503) 247-6022.

✔ **Jerry's**   P.O. Box 1011. (503) 247-4571.

✔ **Mail Boat**   P.O. Box 1165. (503) 247-7033.

A delightful way to see this country is to take one of the boats upstream and spend the night in the middle of a wilderness. No roads lead to Paradise Bar Lodge, which has motellike rooms, a large living room stocked with books, a full bar, and a fine kitchen. The resort sits on a white-oak-studded ledge several hundred feet above the water (all the resorts are this high because the river floods a lot). Out back is a grassy pasture that serves as an airport when cattle aren't grazing or guests aren't pitching golf balls (a sign reads "Cow Chip Country Club"). For exercise you can walk a portion of the forty-mile trail, which follows the north bank of the river.

A less adventuresome, but more elegant way to enjoy the backcountry is to drive seven miles up North Bank Road to Tu Tu' Tun Lodge. This first-class resort takes its name from a subtribe of Rogues, who, incidentally, called this river "Trashit," not a good name for such a fine place to stay. Guests have dinner together, which encourages a sense of community—and the living room is also stocked with books. There is no TV. The grounds include a pool, a pitch-and-putt golf course, and a pier where a jet boat will pick you up if you call beforehand. River guides are available for fishermen.

FOOD AND LODGING   Gold Beach, Oregon 97444

✔✔✔ **Tu Tu' Tun Lodge**   16 river-view rooms. 96555 North Bank Road. (503) 247-6664.

✔✔ **Paradise Bar Lodge**   Wilderness resort. P.O. Box 456. (503) 247-6504.

✔ **Lucas Pioneer Ranch**   Restaurant and cabins. Agness, California 97406. (503) 247-7443.

The highway north of Gold Beach follows a marine terrace similar to the one we crossed in southern Mendocino County. A giant monolith looms up, shaped like a cone. **Humbug Mountain** is said to be the highest shoreline peak along the entire Pacific Coast, and it drops directly into the sea. There is not even a resemblance of a beach. Crested waves don't form here, the water is too deep, so there is just a sloshing against the side of the cliff, much like ocean swells lapping at the side of a ship at sea. Even the most ferocious storms do little damage to this precipice. Highway 101 simply avoids the hazard by going around the backside. A steep, three-mile trail leads to the 1,700-foot summit. The view to the south from top is terrific.

Port Orford • Population: 1,035

The Oregon coast is 362 miles long. Of the eleven harbors gracing this shoreline, only one is natural, meaning that boats don't have to cross a bar to get out to sea. Cape Blanco, jutting westward, shields Port Orford from all but the southwesterlies. But just because it is natural doesn't mean it is safe. Commercial fishermen take no chances. When in port they hoist their craft out of the water and store them on dollies that they can roll around on the quay. Port Orford is a pretty little village, perched on a gentle bluff one hundred feet above the sea. It claims to be the westernmost incorporated city in the United States, outside of Alaska. It isn't really a tourist town, but it does have a nice beach, and innkeeper Jack Lawson told me that they, not Brookings, have the best weather on the coast.

A controversy is brewing here over a most unlikely subject, the ugly sea urchin. According to a UPI story, California fish and wildlife officials wanted to get rid of urchins because they were eating the kelp. Sea otters eat kelp, too, and they are prettier. "So these guys were just going out with hammers or something and smashing urchins," said Port Orford diver Rob Young. "The Japanese caught wind of this and said, 'Hey, don't do that.' " It seems that they use the gonads of this hapless creature in uni rice, a dish that is supposed to impart aphrodisiac properties. "Divers in California were making $1,000 a day," said Young. "The traditional beds are becoming depleted, however, so divers are starting to look northward to Oregon." Officials here don't want to see their urchin population destroyed, so the legislature is studying a bill to control the harvest. The divers, not surprisingly, are madder than a wet—well, a wet urchin.

One of the more intriguing stories hereabouts is the mystery of the Port Orford meteorite. Where did it land, and why hasn't anybody been able to find it again? While exploring this coast in 1856, Dr. John Evans of the U.S. Geological Survey took a specimen back to Washington that proved indeed to be a celestial stone. He died unexpectedly, however, before telling his colleagues where he found it. The only clues were his log describing his approximate route and a letter in which he said: "It is located on a bare bald mountain, on the western face, which can be seen from long distances from the sea." Since then thousands of geologists and rock hounds have searched in vain. One theory places it at Sugarloaf Mountain, fifteen miles east of here. Another pinpoints it at tiny Mud Lake. Searchers are intrigued by University of Oregon Professor E. M. Baldwin's comment: "Mud Lake is not caused by an earth slide, there is just no reason for it to be where it is." But apparently there is no meteorite at Mud Lake's bottom.

FOOD AND LODGING   Port Orford, Oregon 97465

✔✔ **Neptune Motel** Apartments overlooking the harbor. P.O. Box 855. (503) 332-4502.

✔✔ **Sea Crest Motel** 18 units on a bluff overlooking the ocean. P.O. Box C. (503) 332-3040.

✔ **Cape Blanco State Park** 58 campsites.

✔ **Humbug Mountain State Park** 105 campsites.

•• **Truculent Oyster/Peg Leg Saloon** Restaurant and bar.

CAPE BLANCO STATE PARK

Five miles north of town, turn west on the paved road that leads to what the locals claim (incorrectly, as we will see in Chapter 14) is the westernmost point you can drive to in the "lower forty-eight." Named by the Spanish sea captain Martin de Aguilar, Cape Blanco is a grassy, undulating bluff that juts a couple of miles out into the Pacific. George Vancouver saw the point too and named it after his friend the earl of Orford, but the Spanish name stuck. A lovely lighthouse, looking like a New England church with a round rather than pyramidal steeple, lies at the tip of the point behind a chain-link fence. The Coast Guard still operates the light.

The place is reminiscent of western Ireland. Mists swirl about, sometimes hiding the sheep that graze on the lush grass. I was not surprised to see that the six graves in an iron-fenced cemetery were settlers who indeed had come from Ireland. In 1860 two of them, Patrick and Jane Hughes, built a lovely Victorian home on a bench along the Sixes River. The brown and yellow **Hughes House** is now operated by the state and open to the public. Though sparsely furnished (including some awful nylon carpet), the tile-covered masonry cook stove in the kitchen is quite impressive. The setting is as tranquil as any place we will visit on this sojourn—a lovely spot for a picnic.

This area is famous for the tree that grows only along this stretch of coast. Sir Thomas Lipton, the tea magnate, demanded that all five of his America's Cup challenge boats (all named *Shamrock*) be made from Port Orford cedar. Florists like the needles for their lovely green delicacy. A blight has hit, however. The nematode, a kind of worm, is attacking the roots, and many of the trees you see along the highway have turned brown. **Port Orford Cedar State Park** is a few miles north of Cape Blanco.

Bandon • Population: 2,300

Lord George Bennett, who founded the village in 1873, named it after his hometown in Ireland. Dorothy Mills, a docent at the historical museum, told me, however, that old-timers insist the place should be renamed Elizabethtown to honor the faithful service of the steam schooner SS *Elizabeth*, which, during the first quarter of this century, made an incredible six hundred round trips to San Francisco. *Lizzie*, "the old milk-maid of the Pacific," as she was affectionately called, never did meet her fuel and labor costs, but the owners of this diminutive vessel continued to keep her in service anyway. The December 15, 1915, edition of the local paper, the *Western World*, said rather matter-of-factly:

> There are three ways of getting to Bandon:
> 1) Take steamer *Elizabeth* from San Francisco for $10;
> 2) take either the *Alliance* or the *Breakwater* from Portland to Marshfield [Coos Bay], then take a train to Coquille at 9 o'clock, connecting with the Coquille River boat, landing you at noon the same day in Bandon, combined fare not counting lodging $12; or
> 3) over stage from Roseburg to Myrtle Point from which you take the river boat to Bandon as before, fare, being $5 for stage and $1 for boat. We recommend the boat clear through in the wintertime at least. It is quicker and pleasanter for those not afflicted with seasickness.

Dorothy Mills didn't quite agree with the last statement. "Whichever route you took, you probably wished you had taken another," she said with a grin. If the winds weren't against you, the trip from the Golden Gate took forty hours.

Today, Bandon is a pleasant town at the mouth of the Coquille River. Old Town, as the shopping district is called even though it is not very old (see Bandon's Curse, page 139), has been recently spruced up with an eye to the tourist trade. One clapboard building has been remodeled and given the name Continuum Center. Another, with a balcony over the sidewalk, is called Bandon Mercantile, and the old, Ionic-columned Masonic Temple, which survived the fire, has shops on the ground floor. These and other buildings house myrtlewood gift shops, jewelry stores, antique shops, art galleries, and half a dozen boutiques.

The almost handsome (white with green shutters) Coast Guard Building, built in 1939, has been converted into the **Coquille River Museum,** one of the best historical exhibits on this coast. Photographs depict Bandon's maritime past, show the destruction the fire wrought (even to the point of displaying a clump of gorse), and describe the logging that went on here-

BANDON'S CURSE

Though Lord George Bennett is credited with the town's founding, he also, quite literally, planted the seeds of its ruin. In an attempt to harness the wayward dunes of this area, he planted Irish gorse, a spiny, ugly bush that thrives in salty, sandy soil. One hot September day in 1936, some loggers were burning slash in a nearby forest. Flames reached the resinous bush, and within hours fireballs of gorse were shooting high into the sky. By evening the fires were beginning to threaten Bandon itself, many of whose citizens were ironically watching a movie titled *Twenty-Six Hours to Live*. The title, sadly, proved prophetic for some. The holocaust couldn't be stopped—flames came roaring down upon the business district, gutting building after building. Cars jammed First Street, their tires melting on the hot pavement. Ammunition exploded in a hardware store. Even the grass on offshore Table Rock caught fire. People ran for their lives, many seeking refuge in the bay itself. Heroic Coast Guardsmen launched boats and took most across the harbor to safety. Later, survivors said it seemed as though the ocean itself were burning.

By the time it was over, sixteen buildings still stood, five hundred had burned. Sixteen people died outright and many more later, victims of what was then called smoke pneumonia. The town was rebuilt, of course, but the ultimate survivor was the gorse. Landowners today hire D-6 bulldozers to try to get rid of this curse, unfortunately with little success.

---

abouts. One picture that caught my eye was of a magnificent, just completed trestle built by the Selly & Anderson Railroad. The structure was elegantly made with ample bracing up and down and from side to side, but unfortunately not along the direction a train would be traveling. In a moment of hesitation, the engineer of the very first locomotive across put on his brakes. The train, the tracks, and the trestle kept going. It would have been funny except that six out of seven of those aboard died, three immediately and three later, due to scalds from the exploding engine.

During the summer, a public boat sails up the Coquille River and over to **Bullards Beach State Park,** which is located directly across the harbor. Many take bicycles, which can be rented near the dock. Though the town is becoming touristy, it is still a working commercial fishing center, as I learned when an odoriferous eighteen-wheeler rumbled past as I was strolling down Riverside Road.

FOOD AND LODGING   Bandon, Oregon 97411

✔✔✔ **Inn at Face Rock**   44-room resort on a bluff overlooking the ocean. Restaurant and bar. Golf. 3225 Beach Loop Road. (503) 347-9441.

✔✔ **Harbor View Inn**   25-unit motel. P.O. Box 1409. (503) 347-4417.

✔ **Caprice Motel**   15 units. P.O. Box 530. (503) 347-4494.

✔ **Sea Star Hostel**   AYH hostel. 375 2nd Street. (503) 347-9533.

✔ **Bullards Beach State Park**   192 campsites.

●● **Andrea's Old Town Cafe**   Home cooking. (503) 347-3022.

●● **Wheelhouse**   Harbor view restaurant and bar. (503) 347-9331.

We have now reached the northern end of the Klamath Mountains. Geologically, the land farther north is much different. The rivers are less wild, and tidewater often extends inland twenty or more miles. Since a good road comes in from Interstate 5, we've also come to the end of Oregon's isolated coast.

· 10 ·

OREGON DUNES NATIONAL RECREATION AREA

A Seashore Piled High with Sand

In many ways, the next eighty miles of Oregon coast resembles more what you would expect to find along the middle Atlantic seaboard than the Pacific Northwest Coast. Sand spits and dunes line the shoreline. Bays, sloughs, and tidewater lakes give an otherwise straight shore an indented profile, almost as notched out as along the coast of Virginia. The comparison is not too farfetched—both seaboards are what geologists call "drowned" coasts. Here, when the glaciers of the last ice age melted, the sea rose three hundred feet and flooded much of the land. So to avoid these bays and sloughs, Highway 101 moves inland, just as Highway 1 does in the East. Even where you are not far from the ocean, you can't see the waves; they're hidden by hummocks and bluffs and dunes and stands of spruce. The result is that you're now presented with yet another dimension to this fascinating, ever-changing Pacific shoreline.

Shortcut Access to the Oregon Dunes

The south-central Oregon coast is much less isolated than that bordering northern California. State Highway 42 wiggles over the mountains from Roseburg, an old lumber town on Interstate 5. When the one hundred thousand or so people who live in Oregon's third-largest metropolitan area (Ashland, Medford, and Grants Pass) want to go to the beach, this is where they come. As a result we will see more tourist facilities as we proceed

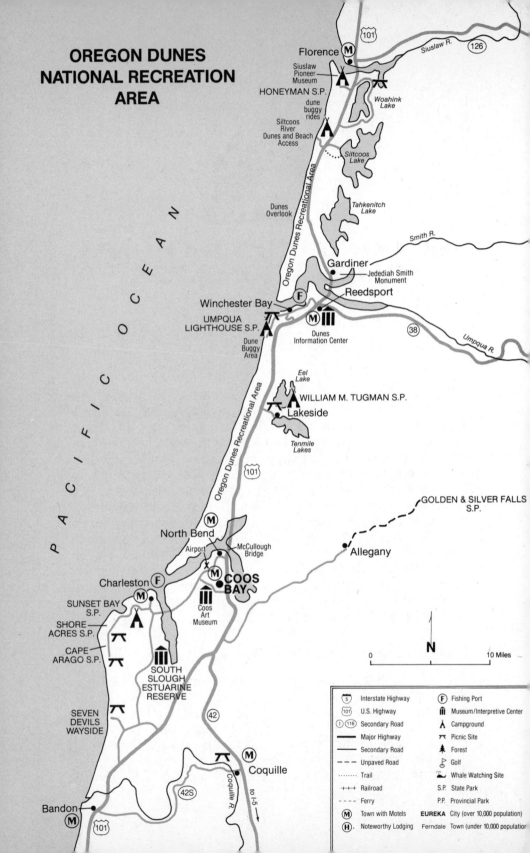

OREGON DUNES
NATIONAL RECREATION
AREA

Florence

Siuslaw
Pioneer
Museum

HONEYMAN S.P.

dune
buggy
rides

Woahink
Lake

Siltcoos
River
Dunes and Beach
Access

Siltcoos
Lake

Dunes
Overlook

Tahkenitch
Lake

Smith R.

Gardiner

Jedediah Smith
Monument

Winchester Bay

Reedsport

UMPQUA
LIGHTHOUSE S.P.

Dunes
Information Center

Umpqua R.

Dune
Buggy
Area

Eel
Lake

WILLIAM M. TUGMAN S.P.

Lakeside

Tenmile
Lakes

GOLDEN & SILVER FALLS
S.P.

North Bend

Airport

McCullough
Bridge

Allegany

Charleston

COOS
BAY

SUNSET BAY
S.P.

Coos Art
Museum

SHORE
ACRES S.P.

CAPE
ARAGO S.P.

SOUTH
SLOUGH
ESTUARINE
RESERVE

SEVEN
DEVILS
WAYSIDE

Coquille

Bandon

to I-5

N

0   10 Miles

P A C I F I C   O C E A N

Oregon Dunes Recreational Area

Oregon Dunes Recreational Area

Siuslaw R.

	Interstate Highway		Fishing Port
	U.S. Highway		Museum/Interpretive Center
	Secondary Road		Campground
	Major Highway		Picnic Site
	Secondary Road		Forest
	Unpaved Road		Golf
	Trail		Whale Watching Site
	Railroad	S.P.	State Park
	Ferry	P.P.	Provincial Park
	Town with Motels	**EUREKA**	City (over 10,000 population)
	Noteworthy Lodging	Ferndale	Town (under 10,000 population)

north, and plenty of T-shirt shops and saltwater taffy emporiums, but we will also explore some serene bayous and visit the longest and highest series of sand dunes in the United States.

There is one noteworthy place to stay along I5 between Grants Pass and Roseburg. **Wolf Creek Tavern,** now owned by the Oregon State Parks Department, provides food, beverages, meeting rooms, and overnight accommodations just as it has for more than a hundred years. The ladies' parlor, the men's sitting room, and the dining room have been restored with hand-rubbed wainscoting, period wallpaper, and lace-draped windows. Public rooms in the front are furnished in turn-of-the-century style, while the guest rooms in the rear, which were added in the 1930s, reflect the *moderne* tastes of that era.

COQUILLE RIVER VALLEY • (Two-hour side loop)

For all its charms, it is sometimes best to leave the shoreline for a bit to get a more complete sense of what western Oregon is all about. The rivers that discharge into the Pacific along this stretch of coast are placid and bucolic, with tidewater often stretching inland for many miles. One of the most beautiful is the Coquille, which meanders through a wide, pasture-covered valley. State highway 42S skirts along the south side of the river, passing through the tiny hamlet of Riverton. A few miles from the coast, the weather changes abruptly; marine fogs simply don't penetrate very far inland. Early mornings find the quiet river broken with the wakes of a dozen skiffs; fishermen are out trolling for salmon. This is dairy country; the milk, I learned, is condensed and then shipped to Oakland, where Safeway turns it into ice cream.

Coquille • Population: 4,045

Coquille, the seat of Coos County, is as pretty a village as you are likely to find. The **Coquille Valley Art Center** and a new golf course suggest that perhaps this valley is becoming a retirement center, but there is a plywood mill here, too, and the fellows you see on the street or downing a beer in a bar are likely to be wearing the traditional dress of the logger or forester—blue jeans, a vertical-striped cotton shirt, and wide red suspenders. The little park along the river is a super place for a picnic.

Twenty-two years ago, I learned from a fellow playgoer, the movie theater closed and people were wondering what to do with their evenings. So the wife of a local physician, a lady still quick on her feet, set about creating a song-and-dance company that has amused summer audiences ever since. Every Saturday night, from Memorial Day to Labor Day, the Sawdust Theatre puts on a "melodrama with olio"; patrons hiss the villain and cheer on the hero, all the while enjoying a beer and clapping to the beat of the cancan dancers. The show is often sold out months in advance, but drop in anyway. There are always cancellations.

FOOD AND LODGING   Coquille, Oregon 97423

✔ **Myrtle Lane Motel**   20 units. 787 North Central. (503) 396-2102.

SOUTH SLOUGH NATIONAL ESTUARINE RESERVE

Highway 42, which bisects Coquille, heads north to the city of Coos Bay. Whether you are coming in from the east or are continuing north from Bandon on 101, it is best to detour out toward the ocean to visit a special attraction. So far on this trip, we have visited a national recreation area, a national seashore, a national historic site, a national bird sanctuary, a number of national forests, and a national park. The fact that we are now going to visit a national estuarine reserve illustrates, I think, the emphasis many government policymakers now place on how to treat our national resources. Scientists are just beginning to understand the role wetlands play in our ecology, and this is an excellent place to get an idea of what's on their minds. The four-thousand-acre reserve is a joint project of the National Oceanic and Atmospheric Administration (Department of Commerce) and the state of Oregon. A few miles north of Bandon, turn left on Seven Devils Road and follow the signs to the **South Slough Interpretive Center.** "An estuary," Ron McDuffy, the host at the center, told me, "is where a river meets tidewater. The boundary between fresh and salt water is constantly sloshing back and forth with the changes in the seasons, the amount of rainfall, and the stage of the tides, all of which makes for a unique plant and animal habitat.

"Wetlands," he continued, "include swamps, bogs, mud flats, and fresh- and salt-water marshes. They were once considered useless—suitable only for reclamation projects—but now we know differently. Unfortunately, we didn't learn that until 90 percent of the Coos Bay estuary had already been diked off." The interpretive center overlooks a lovely stretch of water, calm save for the ripples of a couple of slowly moving canoes.

By following several short trails, you can discover some of the secrets of this strange world. Literature and exhibits explain how the marshes act as purifiers, cleansing the estuary's waters. You learn how, starting with phytoplankton, the food chain works up through the countless small animals that serve as food for the clams and shrimp, which in their turn provide the next hungry critter's meal. The estuary is home to twenty-two species of commercially important fish and shellfish and is a major resting area for migratory birds along the Pacific Flyway. Bird sightings include brown pelicans, horned grebes, the common loon, ducks and geese of all kinds, gulls, scooters, cormorants, oyster catchers, black terns, surf birds, wandering tattlers, and Clark's (of Lewis and Clark) nutcrackers.

One result of all this wetlands study is that Oregon now requires a permit of anyone planning on removing, filling, or altering more than fifty cubic yards of material from any waterway. The days of uncontrolled diking, draining, and landfilling are over.

Charleston • Population: 700

South Slough extends northward to Charleston, one of three cities that make up what locals call the "Bay Area." Its location at the mouth of Coos Bay makes it the obvious anchorage for the area's large fishing fleet. Party boats abound, and there is room for five hundred RVs, but there is also a sizable commercial fleet and a couple of fish canneries. Oysters are farmed inside the bay.

SUNSET BAY, SHORE ACRES, AND CAPE ARAGO STATE PARKS

Charleston is the access point for one of the prettiest sections of the entire Oregon coast. Sandstone deposits were lifted fifty above the waves and tilted downward, back toward the land, exposing a ragged face that has been eroded by the waves into a series of highly sculptured, salmon-colored ramparts jutting up from the sea. The rocks seem to glow in the afternoon sun. Coves, the prettiest of which is Sunset Bay, snuggle in the bosom of mesa-topped headlands that shield the beaches from the westerlies. Sunset Bay, therefore, has the best swimming on this part of the coast. A very popular campground is nearby. Cape Arago is a lovely spot, too; a trail here leads to a bluff where you can look out on a shoreline stretching clear back to Bandon. Historians aren't sure, but perhaps it was here that Sir Francis Drake took refuge from a storm. A plaque reads:

> . . . wee were forced by contrary windes, to run in with the shoare, which we then first descried; and to cast anchor in a bad bay, the best roade we could for the present meete with . . .

Maybe, but the pièce de résistance for this area is Shore Acres, a place of uncommon beauty. Louis Simpson, son of Coos

Bay timber baron Asa Simpson, chose this spot for his summer home. The mansion he built in the early 1900s was destroyed by fire and its partially completed replacement torn down, but the gardens he created are here for all to enjoy. The state owns the property now, and they have done a splendid job of preserving Simpson's dream. Where the mansions once stood, a glass-enclosed gazebo now provides shelter for people watching the crashing of the sea. Waves come pounding out of the west, find cracks in the cliff, and rush headlong toward their narrowing ends, terminating in foamy geysers that, at high tide, shoot ten or fifteen feet into the air.

Simpson used Versailles as his model, planting formal, box-hedged gardens filled with hydrangeas, roses, azaleas, rhododendrons, and exotic plants brought from around the world by the captains of his extensive fleet of lumber schooners. There are thirty kinds of rhododendrons, six varieties of azaleas, and fifty other species of shrubs and trees. Perennials are selected so that there is almost always something in bloom. Oregon State Park planners designed the entrance in such a way that you first leave the parking lot, make a jog between some weathered fences (which by their neutrality of shape and color serve to erase from your mind images of an ordinary world), and then abruptly force you to turn and face the magnificent garden, here framed by an overhang of carefully pruned conifers. The gateway itself, I felt, is a tribute to someone's skills: the designer has created a transition zone that makes you feel good about where you are going. *New Yorker* writer Tony Hiss would be impressed. A lily pond, landscaped to suggest a Japanese tea garden, sits at the far end of the formal area. The trails Simpson built so that guests could walk down to secluded coves still exist and add to the naturalness of the area. To put it simply, Shore Acres is an enchanting place.

FOOD AND LODGING   Charleston, Oregon 97420

- ✔ **Captain John's Motel**   Modest motel frequented by sport-fishermen. 8061 Kingfisher Drive. (503) 888-4041.

- ✔ **Sunset Bay State Park**   137 campsites.

- •• **Portside Restaurant**   Seafood restaurant and bar overlooking the harbor. (503) 888-5544.

GOLDEN AND SILVER FALLS STATE PARK •
(Two-hour side trip)

Coos Bay and California's Humboldt Bay are similar—although both are major ports for oceangoing freighters, neither has much of a river emptying into its confines. The Coos River doesn't begin to match the charm of the Coquille, but there is a reason to detour inland for a look at what Mother Nature has to offer. A county road turns off 101 at the south end of town and heads northwest to the hamlet of Allegany, where it turns to gravel as it struggles up a steep-sided canyon toward a couple of small but very pretty waterfalls. Golden Falls is a ribbon of water that twists down from a one-hundred-foot-high limestone cliff, splashing into a pool nestled in the midst of a rain forest. The combination of crystal water and mossy tree trunks provides a beguiling sight. By contrast, the cliff that defines Silver Falls looks more like a sixty-foot-high overflowing champagne glass. The water wells up over the lip in sheets that cling tenaciously to the inward-sloping form; finally the overhang becomes so great, the water is forced to coalesce into half a dozen runnels that tumble rather awkwardly toward the scree-covered slope below. Quarter-mile trails lead to each cataract.

Coos Bay-North Bend • Population: 25,000

Until the mid-1940s, Marshfield was the official name of the Oregon coast's largest city. The citizens voted to change the name to Coos Bay because that was simply what everyone called it anyway. The contiguous city of North Bend—for quite provincial reasons, I suppose—refused to go along, so now you either have to hyphenate the two names or use the unexciting name "Bay Area" (San Franciscans certainly aren't enamored with that term, either). The twin cities hide their charms from the casual traveler. A drive up 101 leads past run-down businesses, stinking paper mills, and ugly railroad marshaling yards. Your instinct is to keep moving, but there are reasons to pause.

Coos Bay's Central Avenue has been converted into a pleasant mall, though many shops have fled to a huge, rather ugly shopping center in North Bend. The art deco former post office now houses the **Coos Art Museum,** the largest fine-arts gallery we'll see on this coast. I'm hardly an expert on such matters, but it seemed to me that the acquisitions curator had done a splendid job on a less-than-unlimited budget, spending the money that was available on first-class etchings, serigraphs, and other forms of multicopy original art.

The **Coos County Historical Society Museum** is located along Highway 101 in North Bend. One interesting exhibit explains how, through the Oregon and California Railroad Act of 1866, much of the land in the West got to be in private hands and also how, because of abuses in that act, the General Land Office was created to protect what was left. Two and a half million acres of former Oregon and California lands are now administered by the Bureau of Land Management or the U.S. Grazing Service. Another interesting exhibit not only displays the baskets woven by the Coos Indians, but also has a photo of "Old Blind Kate," the woman who wove some of them. She was one of the last of a family that had lived here for eight thousand years. Photographs and artifacts illustrate the extensive coal mining that used to go on hereabouts.

Coos Bay is said to be the largest lumber port in the world, thanks to its deep-water facilities. The Weyerhaeuser Company invites visitors to tour the sawmill during the summer. The House of Myrtlewood shows off its factory, which is housed in the same building as one of the largest gift shops around. The Marshfield Sun Printing Museum displays turn-of-the-century machinery used to publish the local newspaper. Coos Bay is the home of Southern Oregon Community College, hosts the Oregon Coast Music Festival in July, and has scheduled air service.

FOOD AND LODGING   Coos Bay, Oregon 97420

✔✔ **Best Western Holiday Motel**   76 units. 411 North Bayshore Drive. (503) 269-5111.

✔✔ **Thunderbird Inn**   168-room motel, dining room and bar, pool. 1313 North Bayshore Drive. (503) 267-4141.

✔✔ **Pony Village Motor Lodge**   110-unit motel next to a large shopping mall. Restaurant, bar, pool. Virginia Avenue, North Bend, Oregon 97459. (503) 756-3151.

●●● **Hilltop House Restaurant**   North end of McCullough Memorial Bridge overlooking a bayou. (503) 756-6615.

OREGON DUNES NATIONAL RECREATION AREA

Highway 101 now crosses the longest of the five major bridges built in the 1930s to replace the ferry system that used to slow things down so much. The mile-long Conte McCullough Memorial Bridge, named for the well-respected engineer who designed these structures, is a handsome series of concrete arches, connected in the middle by a graceful steel truss, painted green. For the next fifty miles, the highway keeps out of sight and sound of the ocean, plodding through stunted forests and alongside swampy lands dotted with grassy, freshwater lakes. A smelly paper mill suggests that the road up ahead is going to be the dullest section of 101 we've seen so far. But the countryside itself is anything but uninteresting. You only have to go off the high-way a short distance to discover a unique world of water and sand.

Coos Bay marks the southern boundary of the Oregon Dunes National Recreation Area, a unit of the Department of Agriculture's National Forest Service. My guess is that the word "recreation" was chosen rather than "park" because the land here is put to two uses, one conservative, one exploitive. Since early days, Oregonians have used their beaches for roadways, first out of necessity and later because those with four-wheel-drive vehicles found that beach driving was just plain fun. The invention of dune buggies created a whole new off-road sport that has become very popular indeed. No one claimed that bouncing over sandy plains, dunes, and hummocks was actually good for an environment, but neither did anyone prove the opposite, so the National Forest Service has essentially said, "Come on out with whatever vehicle you want and have a good time." Though half the area is off limits to the dune buggies, many miles of sand are open, making this one of the most popular off-road sites in the country.

I had several chances to observe the sport. There seemed to be three types of vehicles: modified Volkswagens fitted with roll bars, standard Jeeps, and balloon-tired three- and four-wheel minicars, steered by handlebars. National Forest Service regulations require that each carry a flag and have a muffler to dampen the noise. The reason for the flag became clear when I asked a fellow, dressed in knee-high, Velcro-strapped leather boots, what the most fun was.

"See how the grass has made a string of little hills, all sort of tied together? You weave in and out of the troughs like you're running a slalom course," he said. (The troughs are about six feet deep.) "It's great fun careening off the side of first one hummock and then another. Problem is, maybe somebody is taking the same track, only coming the other way. There's a gal in one of the vans right now. Don't know what's wrong with her, but it looks kind of bad."

"Do you need a license?" I asked.

"Naw, any bozo can do it," he replied.

At that moment, perhaps to strengthen his point, a fellow on a three-wheeler with his ten-year-old daughter riding behind came roaring across the paved road, hit a drainage ditch, and catapulted into the brush, landing upside down. While he was still trying to right the vehicle and get the engine turned off, I inquired if they were all right.

"Yah, she's okay," he hollered, but I noticed that he hadn't yet looked to see that she was clutching her elbow and crying buckets. At least she was wearing a helmet. Another person told me that parents sometimes don't watch where their toddlers are walking, and several have been killed when they found themselves on the blind side of a sand cornice when it was being used as a launching platform.

An outfitter near Florence runs giant dune buggies, holding twenty or more people, out onto the sand. It is more a sightseeing event than a joy ride, although you do go down the backside of some steep dunes. The driver I rode with said that the day before, he watched as two people crashed into each other. "She broke her back, he broke his neck. Took two hours to get an ambulance here." He later said rather apologetically that 100 percent of the fatalities are from three-wheelers. I watched young and old alike careening off cornices, doing wheelies in the sand, and obviously having a good time. But it seemed as though I were watching bumper cars being played at forty miles an hour—only with no bumpers. And several of the campgrounds I saw were so dirty (oil cans strewn about) and so crowded (it was the Labor Day weekend) that they looked like Depression-style hobo jungles.

The National Forest Service does a good job explaining how the natural forces create the dunes and what you should look for when wandering about. Jeannie Bibbey at the **National Recreation Area Interpretive Center** in Reedsport explained that some dunes are over five hundred feet high. Heavy winter winds give shape to the major outlines, then the gentler winds of summer form the lovely cross-ridges. Every little shift erases yesterday's tire tracks and footprints. Blowing sand rarely rises more than a few inches off the ground. Grains get swept off hard surfaces and collect on soft ones. The valleys collect water and are hard, while the mounds are soft, so that's what builds the dunes. Grasses build dunes, too, not only because of the stabilizing effect of their roots, but because the blades trap the blowing sand.

"The dunes used to move inland at a rate of three to five feet a year," the dune buggy driver told us. "For some reason, that seemed to offend people, so back in the twenties the place was planted with European beach grass. Now they move a couple of inches."

It seemed to me that that was quite an assault on nature, so when I visited the National Forest Service's Dunes Overlook, I asked docent Jeannie Monahan why people wanted to stabilize the dunes. "So they can build more motels," was her testy reply. "We've also got too many cats," she said. "They're eating the birds, which used to feed on the caterpillars. Now we're up to our ears in caterpillars." Just then a chipmunk darted out of the grass, snatched a proffered bread crumb, and scurried back. Is that going to alter his natural food-gathering skills? I wondered. Man and nature, I guess, are just going to have to learn to live together—somehow.

The most convenient place to get a sense of the sand is here at the **Dunes Overlook,** about thirty miles north of the Coos Bay Bridge. Scientists have given names to the various landforms. Stretching inland from the ocean are, first, the grassy foredunes; then come a series of hummocks, followed by the deflation plain, a dampish area where the sand has been scoured out by the wind. Transverse dunes form sinuous, wavelike mounds parallel to the coastline, a prelude to the monarchs, the so-called oblique dunes that attain such remarkable heights. Interspersed among this labyrinth are numerous rainwater ponds and a series of tree islands, which at one time were in a state of equilibrium but are presently being attacked by a naturally occurring wind erosion process. The overlook itself is in a transition forest of shore pine, Sitka spruce, western hemlock, red cedar, and Douglas fir. Access trails lead from the overlook onto the sand and also (going from south to north) from the Bluebill, Eel Creek, Tahkenitch, and Siltcoos campgrounds. The best time to walk out on the sand is early morning or late afternoon when the shadows are the longest.

The entire forty-five miles between Coos Bay and Florence is, by Oregon standards, a giant vacationland. A series of inland freshwater lakes, created when the dunes dammed up small streams, provide excellent places to fish, sail, or swim in the warmish water. The greenness and grassiness of the shorelines is quite a contrast to the lakes farther south. The vegetation along these shores resembles that in Minnesota or Wisconsin. The National Forest Service operates fourteen developed campgrounds with space for over four hundred tents or RVs. State and county parks have spaces for seven hundred, and a host of private RV parks brings the total to over two thousand campsites. **William Tugman State Park** on Eel Lake has a lovely picnic area. Perhaps the most popular dune buggy area is just south of the resort community of Lakeside. Several firms provide buggy rentals. The town overlooks **Ten Mile Lake,** a fishery noted for its catch of largemouth bass. The highest dune in the area (said to be higher than any in the Sahara) is just west of Clear Lake.

Now, instead of proceeding directly up Highway 101, turn west at the signs directing you to **Umpqua Lighthouse State Park.** The lighthouse, built in 1857, overlooks the mouth of the Umpqua. Nearby, an attractive Colonial-revival, lap-jointed wooden Coast Guard station house is now the **Coastal Visitor Center.** The museum houses artifacts and photographs of early-day marine and logging activity. Fort Umpqua was established across the river on the North Spit in 1856. When an unannounced inspection team paid a visit in 1862, they found nobody home. Both the soldiers and the Indians they were supposed to be guarding had gone fishing. That seemed reason enough to close the place down. Another popular dune buggy area is along the shore just south of the lighthouse.

Winchester Bay • Population: 500

Next to the Columbia, the Umpqua is Oregon's largest river discharging directly into the ocean. Like the Klamath and the Rogue, it has its headwaters near Crater Lake in the Cascade Range and is another world-class salmon stream. Near its mouth, the once sleepy village of Winchester Bay has blossomed into the largest sportfishing port on the Oregon coast. The town has a nice, unassuming feel with four or five mom-and-pop cafes and a couple of inexpensive motels. A new marina called Salmon Harbor has slips for nearly one hundred boats and storage for two or three times that many trailers. A half-dozen outfitters run party boats (some have three sailings a day), and the dock area is laced with tackle shops, canneries, and places to have your catch vacuum-packed and frozen. "I cooked up both a fresh and a frozen halibut for a friend," the fellow in the packing shed told me. "He absolutely couldn't tell the difference." Out front was a large sign labeled "Fishing Barometer." The scale was calibrated: Slow, Spotty, So-So (where the arrow was pointing), Good, Very Good, and Red Hot.

Reedsport • Population: 4,915

Author Ken Kesey probably had either Reedsport or Florence in mind when he created the fictional town of Wakonda in his classic book *Sometimes a Great Notion*. Kesey's description of paint peeling off cannery walls, mills with corroding machinery, and a main street of wet asphalt smeared with barroom neon is hardly flattering. Yet to my way of thinking, Reedsport provides a welcome respite from the tourist world all around. The main drag is Broadway Avenue—a redundancy that suggests there might also be a Boulevard Street. It's lined with firms like William's Walgreen Drug, Alexander's Clothing, Macy's Home Furnishings, Don's Downtowner Restaurant, Silver Moon Tavern, Rainbow Inn (cocktails, dancing, Mexican dinners), and Sugar Shack Bakery. The movie theater, long closed, has been replaced by the video rental store. Two rivers converge just upstream, the Umpqua and the Smith, and people who live in their watersheds come here to shop and perhaps to whoop it up on Saturday night. The menu in one cafe says, tongue-in-cheek: "No doggie bags— the SPCA won't allow it." Reedsport is a nothing-special place, certainly, but perhaps the most typical western country town we'll see along this coast. Just across the river is the site of the first battle between American fur trappers and the Indians of the Pacific Northwest (see Jedediah Smith: Mountain Man, below).

FOOD AND LODGING   Reedsport, Oregon 97467

✔✔ **Tropicana Motel**   41 units. 1593 Highway Avenue. (503) 271-3671.

✔ **Western Hills Motel**   21 units. 1821 Winchester Avenue. (503) 271-2149.

✔ **Umpqua Lighthouse State Park**   63 campsites.

✔ **William M. Tugman State Park**   115 campsites.

JEDEDIAH SMITH: MOUNTAIN MAN

In 1822 General William H. Ashley placed a famous ad in the St. Louis *Gazette and Public Advertiser* calling for "Enterprising Young Men . . . to ascend the Missouri to its source, there to be employed for one, two, or three years." The Americans had, at last, decided to mount a direct assault on the Hudson's Bay Company's monopoly on the northwest fur trade. One of those to answer the call was twenty-four-year-old Jed Smith, an explorer who deserves to rank with Lewis and Clark. It didn't take long for the young lad to receive his baptism into the ways of the West. In South Dakota Ashley's men found themselves under attack by the Arikaras, the Missouri River pirates of the time. Twelve *voyageurs* and trappers were killed; Smith survived only by swimming for his life. The following year he led a party into Wyoming's Wind River Range and in the process discovered South Pass, the gentle gap in the Rockies that became the emigrants' "Gateway to the West" (South Pass had probably been crossed eleven years earlier by a party of Astorians on their way home from the Pacific, but since they were lost, they could hardly lay claim to its discovery).

Our hero's wilderness smarts grew, and a couple of years later he joined two other trappers to form Smith, Jackson and Sublette, destined to become one of the most profitable firms in the fur trade. William Sublette was no slouch, either. He ranks with

George Drouillard, John Colter, Caleb Greenwood, and Jim Bridger as a giant among mountain men.

Jed Smith, though, had an insatiable wanderlust. In 1826 he became the first American to cross the deserts between the Great Salt Lake and southern California and the following spring was the first to cross the mighty Sierra Nevada mountains—in this case from west to east. After replenishing his supplies and recruiting more men at the annual rendezvous in Utah, he again headed west. While crossing the Colorado River, his party was attacked by a band of Mojaves. Ten trappers and two Indian women were slain—Jed and nine men survived.

After being expelled by the Mexican governor at Los Angeles, he and his party headed north toward Oregon, driving a herd of three hundred horses. On July 13, 1828, Smith's associate, Harrison Rogers, penned his last diary entry:

> 50 or 60 Ind. in camp again to-day (we traded 15 or 20 beaver skins from them, some elk meat and tallow, also some lamprey eels). The traveling quite miery in places; we got a number of our pack horses mired, and had to bridge several places. . . . Those Inds. tell us after we get to the river 15 or 20 miles we will have good traveling to the Wel Hammett or Multinomah, where the Callipoo Inds. live.

Historians speculate that it was at the point where the Smith River joins the Umpqua that their party of nineteen was attacked by a tribe of Kelawatsets bent on stealing their furs. Jed and two others were upriver at the time, scouting out a route to the Willamette. Only one of Rodgers's group lived to tell the tale. The four survivors continued inland, eventually making it to Fort Vancouver (Washington). The factor, John McLaughlin, sent out a party that recovered most of the furs (they were worth $20,000) and returned them to Smith, but only after extracting a promise that the Americans would forever quit trapping in Hudson's Bay Company territory. Smith kept his promise, but others who followed felt no such compunction, as we shall see.

Three years later Smith's luck ran out. Rivers, it seems, were never kind to our hero. In 1831, while hauling trade goods to Santa Fe, he was ambushed by a band of Comanches near a ford on the Cimarron. His death at the age of 31 delayed publication of his maps and journals, and it wasn't until the the 1930s that he finally gained his rightful place in the history books.

North of town, the highway skirts a few more freshwater lakes, the largest of which is the Siltcoos. The **Siltcoos River Beach Access** area has a number of campgrounds frequented by RVers. Across the highway, a lovely two-mile-long trail goes through a spruce forest, climbs over a low hill, and drops down the remote shore of **Lake Siltcoos,** where there are a couple of walk-in campsites. Lawrence of Florence is a fellow who offers rides on his camel. You climb up a ladder to mount the animal, which poses in front of a snowy-white dune. It makes for a nice photo backdrop, but I learned that the beast hates to walk on sand, so you're led on a short trip through a clump of trees. One firm advertises rides in a seaplane, another dune buggy excursions.

Honeyman State Park, which in the 1960s the *Saturday Evening Post* called one of the ten best public-owned campgrounds in the nation, has a lovely swimming lake, bounded on the seaward side by a stark-white mound of sand. A fine stone building houses a store and deli, making this another excellent place for a picnic. The park extends eastward from 101 to **Woahinik Lake,** where another fabulous picnic area abuts a garden of azaleas. All in all, it would be easy to argue that these inland lakes are prettier than the dunes and certainly more serene.

The northern section of the recreation area is best seen by taking South Jetty Road, which leads to the mouth of the Siuslaw (pronounced "SIGH-oos-law") River.

Florence • Population: 4,950

In my judgment, the bridge spanning the Siuslaw, although the smallest and least expensive of the five structures designed by the noted engineer Conde McCullough, is the prettiest of the lot. Slender art deco–style pylons guard the entry to bowstring concrete arches on either side of a center span, which itself is framed by massive Egyptian obelisks hiding the machinery used to lift the bascule draw structures. The bridge, sitting low on the water, doesn't overpower the snugness of Florence's lovely harbor.

Legend has it that the escutcheon of a wrecked ship, engraved with the name Florence, washed up on the shore hereabouts. The proprietor of a local tavern nailed it up over his doorway, and that is how the town got its name. The building of the bridge and the resulting loss of ferry traffic induced most of the merchants to move up onto the bluff, where they created a rather ugly strip development along Highway 101. The lower town along the river fell into disrepair. That's now been rectified. Florence, like Bandon and Newport, another town we'll visit shortly, has its Old Town at the harbor. The 1901 Wm. Kyle & Sons Building is now the home of the Bridgewater Restaurant, a tin-ceilinged, press-back-chaired establishment that boasts an oyster bar and an overstuffed-sofa-furnished lounge. Old Town isn't large, but it is pretty, with a number of stores, gift shops, and boutiques occupying rehabilitated warehouses.

The city built a gazebo on a pier jutting out into the river. The **Siuslaw Pioneer Museum** is housed in an old church on the south side of the river. Pioneer artifacts are displayed, but the best exhibits focus on the Siuslaw Indians. Manager Eileen Huntington has a wealth of information on how this hapless tribe's life-style changed for the worse after A. M. McCleod of the Hudson's Bay Company came through looking for sea otter pelts. Other attractions include the Dolly Wares Doll Museum and Indian Forest, a family amusement park where various North American Indian dwellings have been re-created.

FOOD AND LODGING   Florence, Oregon 97439

✔✔ **Best Western Pier Point Inn**   50-unit motel on bluff overlooking the river. Restaurant and bar. P.O. Box 2235. (503) 997-7191.

✔✔ **Driftwood Shores Surfside Resort**   Large motel on the beach. Restaurant, bar, pool. 88416 1st Avenue. (503) 997-8263.

✔✔ **Johnson House**   Old Town B&B. P.O. Box 1892. (503) 997-8000.

✔✔ **The Windward Inn**   Fifty-year-old restaurant and bar. (503) 997-8243.

✔ **Honeyman State Park**   380 campsites.

✔ **Park Motel**   15-unit old-style motel. 85030 Highway 101. (503) 997-2634.

Florence marks the northern limit of the drowned coast. The countryside up ahead, which we'll visit next, has a more dramatic seascape.

11

CENTRAL OREGON

Ocean-Bitten Cliffs Along the Devil's Coast

We now leave Oregon's aberration, the drowned coast, and return to a landscape we've become more accustomed to. The next seventy-five miles of coastline is a marine terrace, spiked with numerous lava flows that have created a lovely string of ocean-bitten cliffs interspersed with cozy coves. To early explorers it must have seemed a tortured land, for they named a number of places after that fellow down below. Along this shore you will wander about at Devil's Elbow, watch the frothing sea at Devil's Churn, gaze into the bubbling Devil's Punch Bowl, and, just to show you're not too frightened by such things, swim in Devil's Lake without showing the least bit of concern. But you will also visit a place where plants enjoy an unnatural diet and probe the dark corners of a lighthouse where unexplainable things have occurred. So maybe it's best to be a little cautious about the coast up ahead.

Shortcut Access to the Central Oregon Coast

In 1915, the Southern Pacific Railroad finished a line over the mountains from Eugene to Florence that continued south to Coos Bay, thus ending the central coast's long isolation from the rest of the world. State Highway 126 more or less parallels this route, making Florence just a little over an hour's drive from Interstate 5. Eugene, home of the University of Oregon, has seen a new influx of settlers in recent years and now has a metropoli-

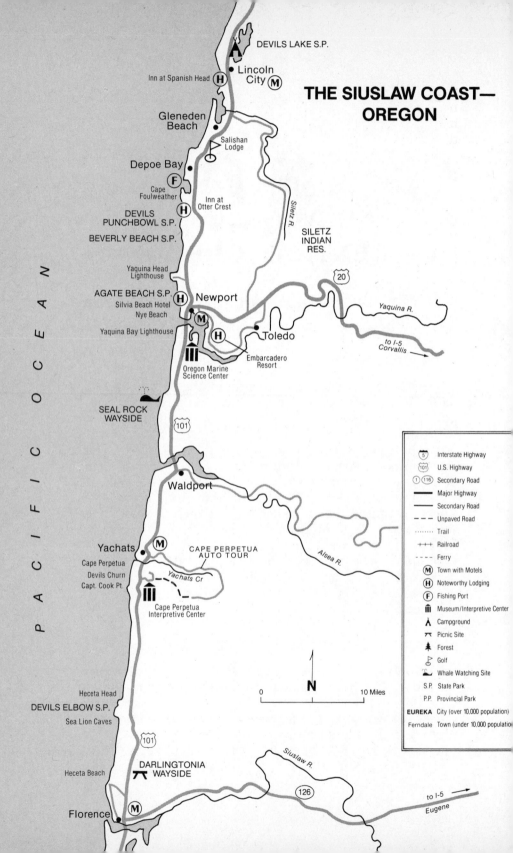

THE SIUSLAW COAST—
OREGON

DEVILS LAKE S.P.

Inn at Spanish Head (H) ● Lincoln
City (M)

Gleneden
Beach

Salishan
Lodge

Depoe Bay
(F)
Cape
Foulweather
(H)   Inn at
Otter Crest

DEVILS
PUNCHBOWL S.P.

BEVERLY BEACH S.P.

SILETZ
INDIAN
RES.

Yaquina Head
Lighthouse

AGATE BEACH S.P. (H) Newport
Silvia Beach Hotel
Nye Beach
Yaquina Bay Lighthouse (M)
(H) ● Toledo

Oregon Marine
Science Center

Embarcadero
Resort

Siletz R.

Yaquina R.

20

to I-5
Corvallis

SEAL ROCK
WAYSIDE

101

Waldport

Alsea R.

Yachats (M)
Cape Perpetua
Devils Churn
Capt. Cook Pt.

CAPE PERPETUA
AUTO TOUR

Yachats Cr.

Cape Perpetua
Interpretive Center

P A C I F I C   O C E A N

Heceta Head
DEVILS ELBOW S.P.
Sea Lion Caves

101

Heceta Beach

DARLINGTONIA
WAYSIDE

Siuslaw R.

126

to I-5
Eugene

Florence (M)

N

0   10 Miles

5	Interstate Highway
101	U.S. Highway
1 116	Secondary Road
▬	Major Highway
—	Secondary Road
- - -	Unpaved Road
....	Trail
+++	Railroad
- - -	Ferry
(M)	Town with Motels
(H)	Noteworthy Lodging
(F)	Fishing Port
血	Museum/Interpretive Center
Å	Campground
⋈	Picnic Site
♠	Forest
⚲	Golf
☲	Whale Watching Site
S.P.	State Park
P.P.	Provincial Park
EUREKA	City (over 10,000 population)
Ferndale	Town (under 10,000 population)

tan population of several hundred thousand. The city dominates the southern reaches of the famous Willamette Valley (pronounced will-AM-it), the incredibly fertile tract that was the raison d'être for the Oregon Trail during the great migrations of the 1840s.

DARLINGTONIA BOTANICAL WAYSIDE

A little state park, located about five miles north of Florence, is an interesting place to pause because a short trail, built on a wooden platform, heads out over a small sphagnum bog, home to the carnivorous cobra lily *(Darlingtoniona californica)*. Several hundred hooded stalks rear up from the swamp like a den of snakes, mouths open in search of prey. The flower produces a scent that inveigles insects into its fuzzy trap. The lilies didn't look hungry the day I stopped by, probably a good thing since there didn't seem to be any mosquitoes around willing to sacrifice themselves to the weird appetite of this botanical oddity.

The countryside now takes on the same rugged look as the southern Oregon coast; up ahead, a thousand-foot mountain seems to plunge directly into the ocean. Thanks to the efforts of the company that owns the land, Sea Lion Head and the caves beneath is one of the best-known spots on Highway 101. While you're inside, buying gifts or looking at the animals, a fellow roams the parking lot attaching stickers to bumpers reading "Sea Lion Caves." The place was discovered in the 1880s by an old seadog out for a row. Poking into what seemed like just another of the many wave-scoured caves along the coast, he was astonished to find himself surrounded by hundreds of barking, wheezing, bawling animals. Lights were installed and a stairway constructed on the cliff so the curious could get a better view. Although the cave itself is interesting, the animals rarely go inside during the summer, preferring a rocky ledge nearby. An elevator replaced the stair some years ago.

Sea lions, of course, are common all along this coast, but they usually prefer basking on the offshore rocks. Here they are in better view, making the entry fee worthwhile. The dominant species is the spotted, tawny-colored Stellar's sea lion, named after George Wilhelm Stellar, naturalist who sailed with Vitus Bering in 1741. They are a gregarious lot, especially during the breeding season when master bulls, some weighing up to six hundred pounds, fiercely defend their harem from encroachment by younger bachelor bulls. A few of the gray-black, much smaller California sea lions also frequent this spot, and there is a large Brandt's cormorant rookery nearby.

DEVIL'S ELBOW STATE PARK

People wax lyrical about Switzerland's Axenstrasse, a spectacular, rock-encrusted highway along the southeastern shore of Lake Lucerne. Though this stretch of Highway 101 is much shorter, it is no less impressive. You climb to seemingly dizzying heights, wiggle around a cliff, and there, half a mile beyond, is another promontory, this one supporting Oregon's most photographed lighthouse at **Heceta Head.** On a clear day, especially early in the morning, you'll capture the quintessential picture of the beauty of this coast. The stark-white tower, with its red-tile roof, perches on a ledge a couple of hundred feet above the pounding surf. The Victorian light-keeper's house stands serenely nearby. The cape was named after Bruno Heceta (pronounced ha-SEA-ta), captain in the Spanish navy who sailed up this coast in 1775. The lighthouse, built in 1893, was automated in the 1960s. Both the keeper's house and the light itself are listed in the National Register of Historic Places.

A hundred yards past the lighthouse viewpoint, the highway plunges into a rocky tunnel, only to suddenly emerge directly atop another of McCullough's famous bridges, this one spanning a tiny stream. What at first seems like another tunnel at the far end of the bridge turns out to be the forest hovering over the road. A short side road leads down to the Devil's Elbow, a cozy cove where you get a splendid view of the handsome bridge. The concrete, open-spandrel center arch is flanked by a double-tiered series of small arches resembling a Roman aqueduct. There are picnic tables here, and you can walk up to the lighthouse to get a nice view back toward Sea Lion Caves. It's a great whale-watching spot.

CAPE PERPETUA

For fifteen miles, Highway 101 slithers along the edge of the continent, clinging to the mountainside like a well-anchored rock climber's rope. You round Captain Cook Point, and up ahead looms Cape Perpetua, one of the highest and largest of Oregon's headlands. James Cook named it after the saint who was martyred in Carthage in 203. For a mile or so you're way up in the air, but then the highway swoops down around a tiny cove and the sea is almost at eye level. A little creek separates Point Cook from Cape Perpetua, its ocean outfall punctuated with sinister-sounding places: **Cook's Chasm** and **Devil's Churn.** The latter is a tapering slot in the lava called a surge channel. Perhaps to counteract the ill-boding sound of these places, the Forest Service has given pleasant names to the paths they built. You can walk along the Restless Waters Trail or climb the Trail of the Whispering Spruce. A paved road leads to the top of the headland, where, on a clear day, you can see 150 miles of coastline. Is there any other spot in the United States where that is possible?

The large **Cape Perpetua Visitors Center** is run by the Siuslaw National Forest, which puts on slide shows and has exhibits and dioramas explaining a bit about the life and times of the modern forest. Perhaps taking a clue from the Army Corps of Engineers (which spent a lot of money on visitors centers in an effort to counteract the public's perception of their having destroyed the salmon run), the Forest Service hopes to dispel the image that they are dupes of the timber industry. "Land of Many Uses" is their longtime motto, and the attempt here is to explain what other uses (some say abuses) besides timber harvesting they have in mind. "Wood, water, wildlife, forage, and recreation" is the new catch phrase, and you learn a bit about how this translates into policies regarding grazing, hunting, fishing, beachcombing, and nature watching and also about some of the steps they are now taking to minimize the damage logging does to these lovely mountains.

CAPE PERPETUA AUTO TOUR • (One-hour side loop)

To get a better understanding of these issues, take the auto tour that leads you on a twenty-two-mile loop out into the woods. The road, paved after the first five miles, climbs up a ridge, passing first through a coastal forest of Sitka spruce and red alder and then into the more widespread inland type of timberland dominated by Douglas fir with a sprinkling of western hemlock (the evergreen with the drooping top) and giant red cedar. Signs along the way explain what you are seeing. After traversing a clear-cut area where slash burning, tree planting, and brush control techniques (they use herbicides) are explained, you are led through what is called a youthful, or pioneer, forest; a middle-aged forest; and finally a mature, or climax, forest. The road loops down into the grazing lands along Yachats Creek, where you see some fish ladders and note how the stream water is used for domestic purposes. A nice picnic area illustrates the recreational aspects of the National Forest Service's policies. Deer abound, especially in the cutover areas where they feed on young brush.

The tour brochure states: "The amount of timber harvested does not exceed the annual growth. This insures a continuous supply and is known as sustained yield." When I asked Bruce Buckley at the Waldport Ranger Station if they really were on a sustained-yield basis, he replied: "Well, that's the objective. But we won't get there for a few more years."

"What about on private land?" I asked.

"A new state law says they have to do that, too, but it doesn't take effect for a couple of years, so right now they're cutting like mad."

It would seem so, considering the multitude of log trucks you have to keep a wary eye out for on these backwoods roads. Bruce told me that they allow clear-cutting but, in an effort to control erosion, restrict the felling to sixty-acre parcels.

Yachats • Population: 450

> *If ya hots, Yachats!*
> *If ya not, ya not!*

Thus have locals resorted to a T-shirt slogan to let people know how to pronounce the name of their lovely little village. Yachats sits on the north bluff of a splendid little cove, a favorite clamming site at low tide. But it is the bluff itself or, more precisely, the material it's made of (called a volcanic spill), that gives the place its specialness. Judy Taylor put it well when she wrote in a guide she provides to her motel guests:

> Basaltic headlands push out against the tide, sheltering coves and beaches between them, yielding only to the power of the waves where fissures have been ground out by the sea.

The cracks in the lava, like the one at Devil's Churn, catch the waves and funnel them down, increasing their speed and power until they crash against the far end, metamorphosing into a towering geyser of salty spray. The scene rivals that at the island of Kauai's Spouting Horn. At a tiny cove, I watched successive waves play catch with a six-foot-long piece of driftwood, first tossing it up on the sand and then fetching it back. An extremely high tide about midnight finally left it stranded.

An entire microhabitat lives atop the lava. Sea gulls shrug off the spray with total indifference, but crows have found their kitchen. The spray collects in little pools (called spray pools, not tide pools, though the tide determines when the water will be replenished) that nurture mosses, which in turn provide a home for little bugs. The crows love those bugs. Geysers and the animated world they nourish are best viewed half an hour before a high spring tide. **Seal Rock,** located half a dozen miles farther north, is another fine place to watch the waves (and the whales).

Judy told me that the favorite sport around town is smelt

fishing. "At high tide, you wade out and scoop the little critters up in a triangular-shaped dip net, just the way the Indians have done for centuries. Everybody freezes them for our big smelt fry in September. We're not much of a family vacation place," she said, "because we don't have a lot of beaches, but we think our town is more interesting. You ought to be here when the purple sailor or vella-vella gets blown on shore. What a stink. 'Vella-vella-smella,' that's what I call it."

A sign along the shore in front of a private home reads:

> Memorial to the Lincoln County Ghost Road.
> County Road 804 still lost to this day,
> unlocated, unclaimed and unneeded.
> Private property.

Sensing a controversy, I made some inquiries and learned that there indeed had been a stage road along the bluff. Before the highway was built, the road coming down from Waldport went along the beach and then, when the sand ran out, had to come up onto this bluff. The property owners filed a quit-claim suit and lost. Because of the publicity the case generated, what was a simple unmarked trail is now apparently going to be developed by the county into a paved path suitable for bicyclists. The property owners should have kept quiet, I guess.

Though Yachats is small, there are some very nice places to stay, and the town has one of the best restaurants on the Oregon coast. I asked Joanne Lambert, owner of La Serre, for the secret of her success. "We started right out with the idea of no hamburgers and absolutely fresh vegetables, and that, I guess, led to everything else." Her policies are working; one of the nights I ate there she was hosting a party for Mo, owner of Mo's, Oregon's most popular string of seafood restaurants.

FOOD AND LODGING   Yachats, Oregon 97498

✔✔ **Adobe Resort Hotel**   56-unit full-service resort along the shore. Restaurant, lounge. P.O. Box 219. (503) 547-3141.

✔✔ **Fireside Motel**   38-unit motel overlooking the "geysers." P.O. Box 313. (503) 547-3636.

✔✔ **Oregon House**   10-unit B&B with gazebo overlooking the ocean. 94288 Highway 101. (503) 547-3329.

✔✔ **Shamrock Lodgettes**   19 units, fireplaces. P.O. Box 346. (503) 547-3312.

•• **La Serre**   Restaurant and lounge. (503) 547-3420.

Newport • Population: 8,305

The bridge across Yaquina (pronounced YAH-quinna) Bay is the most grandiose of McCullough's creations, dominated by a six-hundred-foot steel arch guarded by his trademark, the Egyptian-style obelisk. The northern abutment is flanked by the original **Yaquina Bay Lighthouse** on one side and a more modern Coast Guard station on the other. The lighthouse, which is open to the public, is set in a lovely park that overlooks the bar. It is unique in that the light and the living quarters are in the same structure. The keeper of the light had hardly trimmed the first wick, though, when everybody realized it was in the wrong place. Mariners coming from the north couldn't see the beam; it was hidden by Yaquina Head a couple of miles up the coast. So it was abandoned, and strange things have been happening there ever since (see The Riddle of Muriel Trevenard, below).

THE RIDDLE OF MURIEL TREVENARD

Lischen Miller, poet Joaquin Miller's sister, knew what happened. She described the events in an 1899 issue of *Pacific Monthly*. Herewith is a summary of what she learned.

Situated at Yaquina is an old, deserted lighthouse. Its weather-beaten walls are wrapped in mystery. Of an afternoon when the fog comes drifting in, it is the loneliest place in the world. At such times those who chance to be in the vicinity hear a moaning sound like the cry of one in pain, and sometimes a frenzied call for help pierces the deathlike stillness of the waning day. A light gleams from the lantern tower where no lamp is ever trimmed.

In the days when Newport was but a handful of cabins, across the bar there sailed a sloop, grotesquely rigged and without a name. Her skipper was a beetle-browed ruffian with a scar across his cheek from mouth to ear. A boat was lowered, and in it a man about forty years of age, accompanied by a young girl, were rowed ashore. He explained that he had encountered rough weather, and to his daughter the voyage proved most trying. If, therefore, accommodations could be secured, he wished to leave her until he returned in a fortnight.

Muriel was a delicate-looking, fair-haired girl still in her teens. She spent many hours each day idling with a sketch block and pencil in that grassy hollow in the hill. The fortnight lengthened to a month, yet no sign of a sail rose above the horizon. It was in August that a party of pleasure seekers came over the Coast Range, and they were not long in discovering Muriel. She joined them in their ceaseless excursions and was made one of the group that gathered nightly around the campfire.

The Cape Foulweather light had just been completed, and the house upon the bluff above Newport was deserted. Some member of the camping party proposed that they pay it a visit. With much merry talk and laughter, they climbed the hill. Harold Welch unlocked the door, and they went into the empty hall that echoed dismally to the sound of human voices. Stairs led up to a small landing from which a little room, evidently a linen closet, opened. It was well furnished, and its only unoccupied wall was finished with a simple wainscoting. "Why," cried one, "this house seems to be falling to pieces."

He pulled at a section, and it came away, and behind was a heavy piece of sheet iron. He moved it to one side and peered into the aperture. It went straight back and then dropped abruptly into a soundless well. "Who knows what it is?"

"Smugglers," suggested somebody, and they all laughed, but they were strangely nervous and excited. There was something uncanny in the atmosphere that oppressed them with an unaccountable sense of dread, so they hurried out, leaving the dark closet open, and they passed out through the lower hall into the gray fog.

Harold Welch stopped to lock the door, but Muriel laid her hand upon his arm. "I must go back," she said. "I—I—dropped my handkerchief in the hall upstairs. I am going alone," she said.

Perhaps because her lightest wish was beginning to be his law of life, he reluctantly obeyed her. He had just caught up with the stragglers of the party when the somber stillness of the darkening day was rent by a shriek so wild and weird that they who heard it felt the blood freeze suddenly in their veins.

"Muriel, we are coming! Don't be afraid." But they got no reply. In a few minutes they were pouring into the house, then up the stairs, and there, upon the floor, they found a pool of warm, red blood. There were blood drips in the hall and on the landing, and in the linen closet they picked up a bloodstained handkerchief. But there was nothing else. The iron door had been replaced, and the panel in the wainscot closed, and try as they might, they could not open it.

"It will be a dreadful blow to her father," remarked the landlady where Muriel stayed. "I don't want to be the one to break it to him."

And she had her wish, for neither the sloop nor any of its crew ever again sailed into Yaquina Bay.

Newport was founded by a fellow from Rhode Island in 1864; thus the name. The first July Fourth celebration was, according to a plaque along the bluff: "Attended by 400 patriots and 300 Indians." I couldn't help comparing the town with Monterey, California. It too has a Cannery Row—only here the canneries are still operating, so although Newport is definitely a tourist town, you also sense a realness that is refreshing. The smell of fish permeates the western end of Old Town. Restaurants, gift shops, bookstores, and boutiques abound, along with the seemingly obligatory kite shop and, as if to mimic San Francisco's Fisherman's Wharf, a wax museum and Ripley's Believe It or Not! Across the street is a floating gift shop atop an attraction called Undersea Gardens. Certain forms of gambling are legal in some Oregon resort towns, so you can play blackjack at several night spots. Not being a gambler, I couldn't tell whether the rules are the same as those in Las Vegas; but I suspect here they favor the house a bit more because even on a busy summer weekend there was little action and absolutely no glamour.

The Undersea Gardens boasts that you can watch a scuba diver wrestle with an octopus. Across the bay at the **Oregon Marine Science Center** you can shake hands with one. This museum and aquarium, named for longtime Oregon governor and senator Mark Hatfield, is an adjunct of Oregon State University. The public area, which is free, includes numerous tanks housing local marine life, exhibits explaining the geology of the coast, displays of marine birds, whale skeletons, and ship models, and examples of the ancient art of scrimshaw. A map shows the incredible seven-thousand-mile trek of the gray whale (the word "California" has been dropped from the name), the longest migration of any animal in the world. No wonder botanists call the beast *Eschrichtius robustus*. Tide pools are set up so children can feel the anemones and starfish, and another tank, the favorite for young and old alike, houses a youthful octopus, whose hands you can shake or soft brow you can pet. Newport also boasts the **Lincoln County Historical Museum,** a treasure of Indian artifacts and old logging equipment that is housed in a log cabin. **Burrows House Museum** is in a nearby mansion.

Newport is a resort for both boaters and seashore lovers. Party boats make four- to six-hour trips during the salmon season (June to September) and sixty-mile voyages to Heceta Banks during the tuna run in the fall. Bottom fishing occurs year round, although at times the sea is too rough to go out. Crabbers rent nets and work from the town's pier during a flooding tide. Though only red crab were being taken when I watched, a fellow told me that they do get the much more tasty Dungeness variety from time to time.

Newport has always been a resort town. The better motels are strung out along Elizabeth Street facing long, sandy Nye Beach. Most not only cater to such activities as Lions Club conventions and gatherings of Job's Daughters, but are family places, too. My favorite is the old-time Sylvia Beach Hotel, a three-story, shingle-sided charmer with a library nestled in a third-story gallery overlooking the ocean. Each room is named after a famous author.

FOOD AND LODGING   Newport, Oregon 97365

✔✔✔ **Embarcadero** 110-unit condo resort and marina. Rooms and apartments, restaurant and bar, pool. 1,000 Southeast Bay Boulevard. (503) 265-8521.

✔✔✔ **Schooner Landing** 21-unit condo resort. P.O. Box 703. (503) 265-4293.

✔✔ **Aladin Motor Inn** 117-unit motel. 536 Southwest Elizabeth. (503) 265-7701.

✔✔ **Hotel Newport** 150-room hotel overlooking Agate Beach. 3019 North Coast Highway. (530) 265-9411.

✔✔ **Little Creek Cove** 29-unit condo resort. 3641 Northwest Ocean View. (503) 265-8587.

✔✔ **Moolack Shores Motel** 15-unit motel. P.O. Box 420. (503) 265-2326.

✔✔ **Ocean House** B&B. 4920 Woody Way. (503) 265-6158.

✔✔ **Sylvia Beach Hotel** 267 Northwest Cliff. (503) 265-5428. Restaurant, bar, pool. 3019 North Coast Highway. (503) 265-9411.

✔✔ **Whaler Motel** 61-unit motel. 155 Southwest Elizabeth Street. (503) 265-9261.

✔✔ **Windjammer** 72-unit Best Western motel. 744 Southwest Elizabeth Street. (503) 265-8853.

✔ **Newport Hostel** AYH facility. 212 Northwest Brook. (503) 265-9816.

✔ **South Beach State Park** 250 campsites. P.O. Box 1350.

✔ **Beverley Beach State Park** 280 campsites. Star Route North, P.O. Box k684.

•• **Canyon Way**   Innovative restaurant and bookstore. 1216 Southwest Canyon Way. (503) 265-8319.

•• **Smuggler's Cove**   Upstairs restaurant, bar, blackjack. 333 Southeast Bay. (503) 265-4614.

•• **Welton's Towne House**   Bluff-top restaurant and bar overlooking the ocean. 5251 North Coast Highway. (503) 265-7263.

• **Pip Tide**   Restaurant, lounge (music), blackjack. 836 Southwest Bay. (503) 265-7797.

• **Mo's**   Famous chowder house, now a string of inexpensive eateries along the Oregon coast. 622 Southwest Bay. (503) 265-2979.

YAQUINA BAY/SILETZ RIVER • (Two-hour side loop)

Yaquina Bay offers another fine opportunity to duck off Highway 101 and get a glimpse of the backcountry. County Road 515 snakes around behind the Embarcadero Resort and follows the steepening shoreline as the bay necks down to a fjordlike inlet. Oceangoing freighters use this passage to get to the great mills at Toledo. While driving this road, I suddenly spotted an oyster farm, slammed on the brakes, and backed up to where I could park. Eight of the sweetest bivalves I have ever tasted, served in a red sauce, cost $1.75. The lady doing the shucking apologized for the size: "Sorry these are so big. They're what we call the petite. The smaller ones are better in a cocktail." Later I learned that they have been harvesting oysters for 125 years and that most of the crop goes to Portland's most famous eatery, the Dan and Louis Oyster Bar.

Newport's rise has signaled Toledo's decline as a commercial center for central coast workers. It wasn't always so. The town is the home of one of the largest sawmills in Oregon. The facility was built to process the tremendous stand of Sitka spruce found at the Blodgett Tract near Yachats. During World War I the facility was taken over by the federal government to supply material to build the airplanes of the day. It later became the Pacific Spruce Corporation and is now owned by Georgia-Pacific. Mill tours are offered from time to time.

State Highway 229 heads due north, crosses a low divide, and drops into the Siletz (pronounced sah-LETS) River drainage. The town of Siletz was the principal agency for the reservation and once boasted a number of fine buildings built by the government (see A Meeting of the Waters: The Siletz Reservation, page 169). As late as the 1910s, the tribal people would dress up in full regalia and parade into Newport during summer festivals. Now there is little to attract the tourist save for the lovely countryside. Highway 229 continues north, where you rejoin 101 near Lincoln City.

~~~~~~~~~~~~~~~~~~~~~~~~~~~~~~~~~~~

A MEETING OF THE WATERS: THE SILETZ RESERVATION

If, by some cataclysmic act, all the rivers of western Oregon were to converge upon one spot, fairness would have it be here, for during the last half of the nineteenth century this was the enforced homeland of the peoples who gave their tribal names to most of the rivers we have been exploring, the Chetco, Rogue, Sixes, Coquille, Coos, Umpqua, Siuslaw, Alsea, and Yaquina, and to two more streams we will visit shortly, the Tillamook and Nehalem. These peoples, several thousand of them, had been moved here starting in 1855 after the government had "purchased" six million acres of the land they and their forebears had lived on for ten thousand years. Three cents an acre seemed like a fair price to those making the offer.

Even then, there was still room to spread out, 1.25 million acres. The government could afford to be generous because, according to a 1864 report to the superintendent of Indian affairs:

> The Coast Reservation was selected . . . at a time when the Western slope of the Coast Mountains had been but partially explored, and was supposed to be nearly or quite worthless. . . . Consequently the Coast Reservation was made very large, extending north and south about 100 miles, and averaging in breadth about twenty.

The land included nearly a third of the Oregon coast, stretching from present-day Reedsport to Lincoln City. Yet in spite of the space, things were not tranquil. The tribes spoke seven different languages, including Athapascan, Salishan, and Chinookan, so to communicate they had to resort to "Chinook jargon," the crude language that had evolved among the traders of the Pacific Northwest (Lewis and Clark learned some Chinook jargon). Most tribes were pacific in nature—all but the intransigent Rogues, who had been sent here simply because this was the most isolated spot the whites could find. The fact that they were forced into an unfamiliar, cold, damp climate and constrained to eat what they considered abominable food—oysters, clams, crab, and fish— only exacerbated their restlessness. They constantly quarreled with their neighbors.

Indian agent Joel Palmer and his subordinate, Captain (later

Civil War general) Philip Sheridan, tried to do a good job. Always short of money and often forced to deal with scoundrels (one sold barrels of "mill sweeps" as prime flour), they did manage to get farms started so that the tribes could be more self-sufficient, despite the fact that these coastal people, used to a diet of roots, at first ate the crops before they had a chance to develop and mature. Nevertheless, by 1861 over one thousand acres were under cultivation, and a few years later 1,500 apple trees were in the ground.

The first hint of change occurred in 1864 when a San Francisco trader, Captain Hillyer, discovered the tasty quality of Yaquina Bay's oysters. So the government purchased the bay for $16,500, thus setting in motion the founding of Newport. Not all the settlers were pleased with the situation; many harbored a genuine fear of the natives. Author/teacher William Kent quotes one Irishman as having said, "We went to bed every night expecting to wake up the next morning and find ourselves dead." Nevertheless land sales continued, and by 1875 the southern, or Alsea, portion of the reservation and a northern tract called Grand Ronde had both been sold off. Operations were consolidated at the Siletz Agency. Room to move about in was now reduced by a factor of five.

Intermarriage among the tribes and between white and Indian gradually homogenized the population, and tuberculosis, measles, and smallpox of course took their toll. By 1889 less than forty Tillamooks remained out of an original population of several thousand. By 1892 the total number of Indians living here fell below six hundred.

In the 1870s an attempt was made to close the entire reservation and give the survivors an "allotment" of land. Not surprisingly, the Indians were skeptical—they had been cheated before. Nevertheless, by 1892 fifty thousand acres of allotments had been granted, and other families were encouraged to homestead on quarter-section parcels throughout the state. The rest of the land was sold for $1.25 an acre.

It is unlikely that anyone knows how much property the tribespeople still own, but the Siusula National Forest's map shows Indian land in pink. Three dozen separate parcels are shown, totaling about four thousand acres. By my estimate, three-quarters of that land is not served by a road of any kind.

YAQUINA HEAD

The Oregon State Parks system maintains an incredible twenty-five separate wayside parks between Florence and Newport (one every three miles on average), and they have literally hundreds along the rest of the 350-mile shoreline. It is a tribute to the farsightedness of the state legislators that less than ten miles of this coast is closed to public use, a record that Atlantic seaboard states would be hard put to match. One of the nicest places in which to linger, especially in winter, is **Algate Beach Wayside,** near where composer Ernest Bloch once had a studio.

The whole coast is a rock hound's playground, for each winter nature thoughtfully gives up a fresh supply of colorful agates. Great storm-driven waves sort through the gravels, pushing the lighter-weight stones characteristic of gem material to the top. The best time to hunt is during a receding tide, preferably near sunset. High tides mix things up a bit, and because the stones are very hard, they stay wet longer. By facing the setting sun you can see them sparkle, so they are easier to find. Opaque jaspers are the most common, but you'll also come upon agatized wood, coral, sea fossils, regular and clear agate, ribbon agate, and bloodstones. The moonstone agate is a brilliant, clear stone; the carnelian, a bright transparent red. Ribbon agates, I learned, have colors formed in layers, whereas cloud agates are transparent but with a dark central formation. All require polishing to bring out their beauty. Agate, classified as a gemstone, is the birthstone for June.

At the north end of Newport you pass a curiously named point called Jumpoff-Joe. A few years ago the land obliged and, lemminglike, did just that. Four hundred feet of cliff slid into the ocean, taking some houses with it. Farther north, a road leads out to the pretty **Yaquina Head Lighthouse,** built in 1871. The view here is lovely. Another side road leads out to the **Devil's Punch Bowl,** a collapsed sea cave where the ocean, at high tide, swirls about like a boiling pot.

Otter Crest/Depoe Bay/Gleneden Beach • Population: 1310

A section of old Highway 101 ducks off to the west and hugs a very pretty coast, punctuated first by a tiny spit called Otter Crest and then by the huge **Cape Foulweather.** When developers chose this site for a first-class condo-resort, I guess they decided that the name "Inn at Otter Crest" might attract more guests and investors than a more appropriate one, Inn at Cape Foulweather. The resort is spectacular, with a dozen two-story buildings framed by a rhododendron garden. Each unit looks out over the rugged surf. Most guests park away from their rooms and either use a golf cart to get their luggage around or take an outdoor inclined elevator that resembles a European-style funicular. Rooms are rented by the night, and the restaurant, which occupies a dramatic site on a bluff, is open to the public.

Captain Cook's first landfall after discovering the Sandwich Islands (Hawaii) was here on March 7, 1778. He never found a suitable harbor along the Oregon coast to put in and restock *Resolution* and *Discovery*, but his aide, John Laynard, an expatriate from Connecticut, kept a log that inspired Thomas Jefferson to send Lewis and Clark out to have a look around (see Chapter 20). Hundred-mile-an-hour winds are not unusual, it is said, but the June day I happened by was beautiful.

Tiny **Depoe Bay** looks like a keyhole slot in the devil's coast. It's been described as the world's smallest harbor or just "the Hole." Whatever, it bears a striking resemblance to another lovely place we visited earlier, Noyo Harbor in Mendocino County. There is no bar here; the streams that feed the six-acre harbor are simply too small to carry enough sand to create one. Mariners, though, have a tough time navigating the tricky, two-hundred-foot-wide, four-hundred-yard-long dog-leg channel that leads out to the crashing waves. The town was named after a local Indian character named Charlie Depoe, who in turn got his name because he lived on the site of a onetime army depot. Old-timers say he got a little uppity in later life and changed his name to DePoe, but the post office wouldn't go along. The town is pronounced like the railroad station, though, not the warehouse. Gift shops and ocean charters (both for fishing and whale watching) provide the main activities here. One restaurant boasts, "Seafood so fresh the ocean hasn't missed it yet," and has evening entertainment. Out front I spotted a news rack displaying that day's *New York Times*. The world is getting smaller, I guess.

The famous Salishan Lodge, built in the 1960s, has become the prototype for modern resort design. The idea was to build motellike rooms in small buildings tucked into a mile-square gardenlike setting, provide decks so guests could savor the country air, and give each room a cozy feel by adding a fireplace. Then design a central building with a couple of well-furnished restaurants (with a first-class chef, of course), and a lounge with live music, a reading room, and plenty of conference rooms. Provide a fitness center, a spa, and an indoor pool and, since it rains a lot, build an indoor tennis court. Add a place to go shopping when you're through working on your fitness program, and surround the complex with condos, reachable by controlled-access roads so that everybody feels safe. Finally, construct a championship golf course and an airport suitable for Lear jets. The scheme worked, as Salishan has proved over the years. In some circles, it is the most well-known resort in the Pacific Northwest and is certainly one of the finest.

The resort straddles both sides of Highway 101 at the southern edge of the sandy, shallow Siletz Bay. The Salishan Market Place has stores selling kitchen wares, exotic coffees, leather handbags, fancy chocolates, silver flatware and jewelry, and men's and ladies' clothing; it's an upscale mall much like you would find in any high-class eastern suburb. A nearby roadhouse, apparently spoofing this opulence, calls itself Salishack.

FOOD AND LODGING

✔✔✔ **Inn at Otter Crest**   144-unit condo-resort. Restaurant and bar, pool. P.O. Box 50, Otter Crest 97369. (503) 765-2111.

✔✔✔ **Salishan Lodge**   First-class resort, four dining rooms, bar, and so on. Highway 101, Gleneden Beach 97388. (503) 547-6500.

✔✔ **Channel House**   6-room B&B overlooking the ocean. P.O. Box 56, Depoe Bay 97341. (503) 765-2140.

✔✔ **Holiday Surf Lodge**   84-unit motel. P.O. Box 9, Depoe Bay 97341. (503) 765-2133.

✔✔ **Inn at Spanish Head**   130-unit resort with elevator to beach. Restaurant and bar. 1009 South Highway 101, Lincoln City 97367. (503) 996-2161.

●●● **Chez Jeannette**   Dressy, dinner-only French restaurant. (503) 764-3434.

●● **Captain Jim's Galley**   Restaurant and bar overlooking Depoe Bay. (503) 765-2836.

Lincoln City • Population: 6,035

Lincoln City, an amalgam of five little beach towns, has become quite a retirement center. The median age of the residents is fifty-one, compared with a statewide average of twenty-nine. The Chamber of Commerce used to call this stretch of Highway 101 "twenty miracle miles," but then-governor Mark Hatfield said it was more like "twenty miserable miles," an utterance that, not surprisingly, got the townsfolk all riled up. But it did spur them into action. In 1966 the town got an award from Lady Bird Johnson for her nationwide "clean-up, paint-up, and fix-up" campaign. Unfortunately, though, they didn't have much to work with because the town had developed along a seven-mile strip of highway with no central core. Vickie Jones, who works up on the north end of town, told me, "It's a small place without very many people, but long enough so that if I do something wrong on the south end of town, by the time I get back up here, everybody knows about it. The traffic on summer weekends is awful," she added. So your impulse is just to get past it and on to the prettier country up north.

But a lot of people must like to vacation here, because there are fifty motels with a whopping 1,800 rooms. Most are located along the beach. **Devil's Lake,** just east of town, is a refreshing place to swim, paddle a canoe, or just loll around at one of the grassy picnic areas.

FOOD AND LODGING   Lincoln City, Oregon 97367

✔✔ **Coho Inn**   69-unit motel. 1635 Northwest Harbor. (503) 994-3684.

✔✔ **Lincoln Sands Resort**   33-unit motel. 535 Northwest Inlet Street. (503) 994-4227.

✔✔ **Sailor Jack Oceanfront Motel**   41 units. 1035 Northwest Harbor. (503) 994-3696.

✔✔ **Shilo Inn**   190-unit motel. 1501 Northwest 40th. (503) 994-3053.

✔ **Devil's Lake State Park**   100 campsites. 1542 Northeast 6th.

Shortcut Escape to Portland

State Highway 18 angles northeast to Portland, passing through part of Oregon's wine country. Yamhill County boasts fifteen wineries, most located in the McMinnville/Amity area. Several have tasting rooms amid the vineyards. The eighty-five-mile drive to Portland takes about two hours.

12

THE TILLAMOOK COAST

"Trees, Cheese, and Ocean Breeze":
An Oregon Caper

The coastline we are about to explore is punctuated with a number of rocky promontories: Cascade Head, Cape Kiwanda, Cape Lookout, Cape Meares, Cape Falcon, and Arch Cape. Each in its own way has alluring qualities, but the seashore in between, with its sandy beaches and bucolic grasslands, has many charms, too. This suggests that you would be well rewarded by spending some time gamboling on, and between, these capes (doing an Oregon caper, if you'll excuse the pun).

NESKOWIN SCENIC DRIVE · (One-hour side loop)

Start the adventure by going the other way. Duck off Highway 101 and head east on the road to Portland. In a bit you come to a place that everyone talks about, the diminutive (six tables and five counter stools) Otis Cafe, noted for its kitchen. Haute cuisine? No way. Breakfast and lunch are the main event here, though dinners are now being served Thursday through Sunday. The down-home cooking features single entrées such as roast pork one night and turkey the next.

To continue, turn left here and cross the Salmon River to the ten-building town of Otis (the cafe is in Otis Junction). Signs direct you to the Neskowin Scenic Drive, a ten-mile side trip that follows old Highway 101 (now Forest Service Road 12). Within a mile you're in a rain forest—tree limbs arch over the road, and you seem to be driving through a tunnel. Signs explain about the Cascade Head Experimental Forest, established in 1934 to study

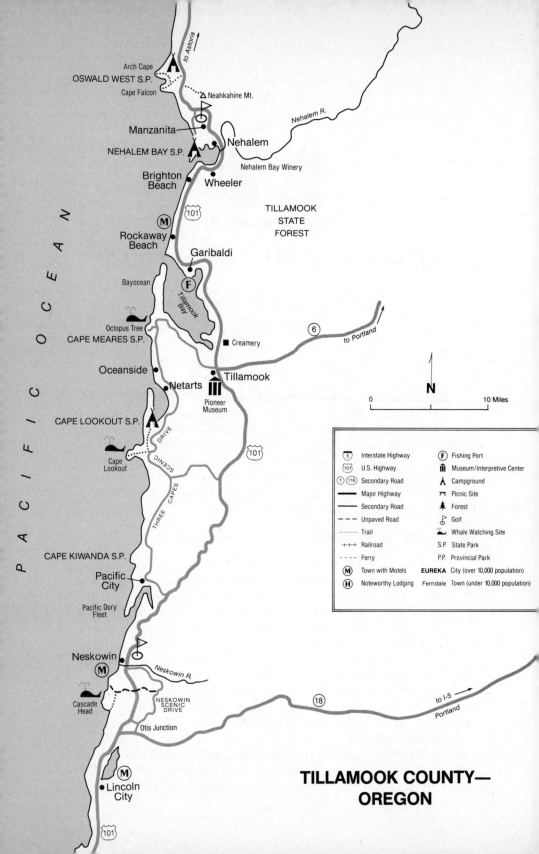

TILLAMOOK COUNTY—OREGON

PACIFIC OCEAN

to Astoria

Arch Cape
OSWALD WEST S.P.
Cape Falcon
△ Neahkahine Mt.
Nehalem R.

Manzanita
Nehalem
NEHALEM BAY S.P.
Nehalem Bay Winery

Brighton
Beach
Wheeler

TILLAMOOK
STATE
FOREST

(M) (101)
Rockaway
Beach

Garibaldi

Bayocean
(F)
Tillamook Bay

Octopus Tree
CAPE MEARES S.P.

(6)
to Portland

■ Creamery

Oceanside

Netarts
Tillamook
(101)

Pioneer
Museum

CAPE LOOKOUT S.P.

SCENIC DRIVE

Cape
Lookout

THREE CAPES

CAPE KIWANDA S.P.

Pacific
City

Pacific Dory
Fleet

Neskowin
(M)
Neskowin R.

Cascade
Head

NESKOWIN
SCENIC
DRIVE

(18)
to I-5
Portland

Otis Junction

Lincoln
City
(M)

(101)

N
0   10 Miles

Legend

(5)	Interstate Highway	(F)	Fishing Port
(101)	U.S. Highway		Museum/Interpretive Center
(1) (116)	Secondary Road	⚑	Campground
	Major Highway		Picnic Site
	Secondary Road	♣	Forest
---	Unpaved Road		Golf
····	Trail		Whale Watching Site
+++	Railroad	S.P.	State Park
- - -	Ferry	P.P.	Provincial Park
(M)	Town with Motels	**EUREKA**	City (over 10,000 population)
(H)	Noteworthy Lodging	Ferndale	Town (under 10,000 population)

the effects of various logging techniques. Foresters have discovered that in this wet climate (annual rainfall exceeds six feet), in a single year trees can gain an inch in diameter and grow more than two feet in height. I was told that six thousand species of mushrooms grow in these backwoods, including golden chanterelle, chicken of the woods, shaggy mane, Japanese pine, king boletus, cauliflower mushrooms, and puff balls. The best mushrooming is in the fall.

Road 12, paved throughout, climbs to the top of a ridge and then drops into the Neskowin River valley. The sense of ruralness here is overpowering. I felt a bit smug at having discovered a portion of the real Oregon, not the touristy one out along the main highway. The Nature Conservancy, incidentally, owns some land out on the tip of **Cascade Head** which can be reached by a short, scenic trail that starts at the end of a gravel road leading west off Highway 101.

Neskowin • Population: 300

Forest Service Road 12 rejoins the highway at the little community of Neskowin. A hundred or so unpretentious yet well-designed houses surround two golf courses.

FOOD AND LODGING   Neskowin, Oregon 97149

✔✔ **Neskowin Resort Condominium**   Large resort overlooking the ocean. Restaurant. P.O. Box 728. (503) 392-3191.

✔✔ **Pacific Sands Inn**   29-unit motel on the beach. 48250 Breaker Boulevard. (503) 392-3101.

● **Otis Cafe**   (503) 994-2813.

You have now crossed into Tillamook County, a name familiar to most because the Tillamook County Creamery Association spends a lot of money on advertising. "Trees, cheese, and ocean breeze" is the Chamber of Commerce's slogan, to which one wag added, "And mud up to your knees." Cows, of course, don't seem to mind mud up to their knees, and as a point of interest, they outnumber people in this county by a slight margin. Tillamook is said to be an Indian word meaning "Land of Many Waters."

THREE CAPES SCENIC DRIVE • (Two-hour side loop)

Highway 101 turns inland north of Neskowin and doesn't return to the Pacific for forty miles, so to continue your coastal exploration, take a series of country lanes that more closely hug the shoreline. Signs direct you along a twenty-mile loop called the Three Capes Scenic Drive, which traverses some spectacular coastal scenery before terminating at the city of Tillamook.

Pacific City is a rather grandiose name for the first little town you come to, but it is a nice place, snuggled amid a string of Scotch broom–covered sand dunes. Though there is no harbor here, it is a major fishing port, an oddity that makes it one of the most interesting spots along the Oregon coast. This is the home of the **Pacific Dory Fleet.** The long, gently sloping beach is hard enough to drive on, so commercial fishermen launch their boats directly into the surf. It is a three-person operation. One fellow boards the craft while it is still on a trailer hooked to a pickup truck, revving up the engine to be sure everything is in order. A second man dons hip boots and wades out into the water, where he waits as the truck and trailer come racing backward toward the surf. When an incoming wave is just right, the driver slams on his brakes, shifts into forward, and goes roaring back toward dry land. The boat scoots off the trailer and into a foot or two of water, where the fellow in the boots gets it turned around and headed out toward the sea before the wave recedes. When the truck driver returns, the engine is restarted, and again, at exactly the right moment, the fellow in the boots shoves the craft into another oncoming wave, the two hop aboard, and they all go roaring out to sea, crashing over the waves like a Grand Canyon rafter negotiating Lava Falls.

Several outfitters provide party boats, sometimes taking sportfishermen many miles out to sea. The dories can go thirty miles an hour. I asked boat owner Jim Nichols if there was a best time for launching. "We like a high tide because there are some sand bars offshore," he replied, "but we go when we gotta go, of course."

Nearby is **Cape Kiwanda,** a fairly low sandstone cliff that juts out into the surf. The shoreline dunes cause the ocean breezes to form updrafts, thereby providing a good place for hang-gliding. Though these sands are not as extensive as those farther south, they make up for it in quality. The absolutely pure white sand, framed by the green of the dune grass and the blue of the ocean, makes for a quite charming scene. At the tiny community of Sand Lake, a side road leads west to a place where dune buggies are allowed.

Cape Lookout State Park surrounds the second headland on this loop drive. It's the longest, and many consider it the most dramatic, of Oregon's many headlands. Less than a quarter of a mile wide but six times that long, and having almost vertical sides, it looks like a tree-topped aircraft carrier heading up into a gale. A two-mile trail meanders through a stately spruce forest before terminating at a belvedere at the tip of the point. Another trail leads down to a large drive-in campground, one of Oregon's most popular because it is nestled in a forest yet is within earshot of the crashing surf.

Another sandy beach separates Cape Lookout from Cape Meares. Two little towns in between, Netarts and Oceanside, serve as low-key resorts. Several taverns, a couple of restaurants, and a few motels compete for trade among the RVers who gather hereabouts. Clamming is popular with razor clams, butter clams, littleneck clams, horse neck clams, empires, and soft-shell clams being taken along with scallops, mussels, and cockles.

FOOD AND LODGING

✔✔ **House on the Hill** 12-unit motel. P.O. Box 187, Oceanside, Oregon 97134. (503) 842-6030.

✔ **Cape Lookout State Park** 250 campsites. 13,000 Whiskey Creek Road West, Tillamook, Oregon 97141.

Cape Meares State Park. The road climbs steeply to the saddle of Cape Meares, where a side road leads to a parking lot overlooking the sea. No one is quite sure whether it was this one or Cape Lookout that Meares meant to give his own name to (see John Meares: Scoundrel?, page 180), and some years later there was also a debate as to which would be the best place to build a lighthouse. A report, written in 1886, settled the matter:

> Cape Meares affords nearly as good a site as far as the view from the sea is concerned, and being lower gives a better situation of light with reference to fog, and besides it would be much easier for construction on account of its accessibility from Tillamook Bay.

A short loop trail, flanked in spots by sweet-smelling wild roses, leads down to the stubby, hundred-year-old light. The lovely offshore rocks are part of the **Three Arches National Wildlife Refuge,** created by Theodore Roosevelt in 1907. Seventy-five thousand common murres nest on every available ledge. Tufted puffins, pigeon guillemots, storm petrels, cormorants, and gulls are also said to frequent the spot. Sea lions are often visible on the lower rocks.

Robert Ripley listed a nearby oddity, **The Octopus Tree,** in his book *Believe It or Not!*. This Sitka spruce has no central trunk but instead six candelabralike limbs that sprout from a ten-foot diameter base. Each limb itself is three to five feet thick and

JOHN MEARES: SCOUNDREL?

Historian Charles Lillard said of him: "Meares and the truth were not boon companions." Author David Lavender was a bit more kind, describing him as "as engaging a scoundrel as ever sailed the Northwest coast." Neither epitaph is particularly derogatory; being a scoundrel and skirting around the truth came with the territory if you wanted to engage in the fur trade in the late eighteenth century. No one ever accused John Jacob Astor of being virtuous. But John Meares, a Britisher, seems to have been one of those adventurers who carried a jinx aboard his ship. In 1786, while wintering in Prince William Sound (in present-day Alaska), he lost twenty-three crewmen of *Nootka* to the sailor's curse, scurvy. Sailing south to present-day Tillamook Bay (which he called Quicksand Bay), he declared the bar uncrossable—yet Gray had crossed earlier in the season. The following year he suffered the ignominious fate of having two of his ships seized by the Spanish, an event that precipitated an international crisis (see The Nootka Convention, Chapter 20). Whether it was bad luck, lack of perseverance, or timidity, no one really knows, but in 1792 he encountered foul weather the day he stood off the mouth of the Northwest's mightiest river and thus lost out to John Gray for the chance to name the Columbia.

Yet John Meares deserves his place in the history books, for on September 20, 1788, while at Nootka Sound, he launched *Northwest America*, the first ship other than a canoe ever to be built on the Pacific Northwest Coast.

extends out horizontally from the base by as much as thirty feet before bending upward into a more or less normal tree. With six rather than eight trunks, I thought it should have been named the Hexopus Tree until I noticed that one limb had broken off. Now it is a Pentopus Tree, I guess.

Three Capes Drive continues along the lovely shore of Tillamook Bay, which John Gray had named Murderer's Harbor because one of his crewmen was killed by Indians while trying to recover a stolen cutlass. The name didn't stick. Piles of oyster shells stand alongside the road. The bay may be shallow and unsuitable for shipping, but it produces mighty fine oysters. Early in this century, the locals like to boast, they were shipped to New York and served at the Waldorf Astoria. This is the onetime site of an erstwhile resort community (see Bye-Bye, Bayocean, page 181).

BYE-BYE, BAYOCEAN

Francis Mitchell was the first to purchase a lot. He figured he could hardly lose. Five hundred dollars bought him a homesite on what everybody said would become the Atlantic City of the West. It was T. B. Potter's idea. A real estate man from Kansas City, he knew a bit about the fortunes to be made in oceanfront sub-divisions. You had to think big, he reasoned—people have to have confidence that they are investing in where the action is. So in 1907 he platted four thousand lots and subsequently built a three-story hotel on the sand spit that separates Cape Meares from the mouth of Tillamook Bay. The hotel wasn't all that pretty, a boxlike flat-topped structure with a covered porch facing the sea. But nearby he built the largest natatorium on the Pacific, a block-long, arched, hangarlike building guarded by six square towers. The saltwater pool was as large as the celebrated Sutro Baths in San Francisco. Boat docks were constructed and a quay built for the weekly steamer from Portland. A 1921 publication stated:

> Bayocean, situated on Tillamook Bay, is destined to become a most popular resort on account of the large amount of money that was expended there for improvements.

All of this may have come to pass, but other poeople had their eye on a different sort of improvement.

The citizens of Tillamook were, like those in many Oregon port cities, concerned about the silting of their harbor bar (see Gold Beach, Chapter 9). So in 1917 they constructed a jetty along the north side of the channel. Lo and behold, that winter a foot or so of Bayocean waterfront washed into the sea. Everybody said it was just because of the bad storms that year, but the erosion continued throughout the summer. The ocean currents had obviously changed. North of the post office, however, the ridge, still visible today, remained fairly high.

However, in 1932 the jetty was built up and extended, and now things simply went to hell in a hand basket. Choice ocean frontage, two hundred feet in width and three miles long, simply disappeared. Deep-rooted trees, brush tangles, roads, homes, and business build-ings were carried away and smashed to bits. The natatorium was gone, along with all but one of the fifty-nine houses that had been built. The sea cut a half-mile swath through the spit, turning Bay-ocean into an island. Francis Mitchell, the first to arrive, was the last to leave—Bayocean became nothing but a memory.

And what of the bar? The jetties never really worked. Today, Tillamook Bay is pretty much useless as a harbor, save for small boats.

Tillamook • Population: 3,920

The city is the county seat and home of the Tillamook County Creamery Association, which operates the largest tourist attraction along the Oregon coast. Three-quarters of a million people a year stop at the factory to see how cheese is made. More than five hundred dairies bring their milk here for processing. Visitors look through windows at what to me is a rather uninteresting operation or watch a videotape explaining how cheddaring turns milk into cheese (rennet is used to hasten the process). The main attraction, frankly, is the immense gift store that doubles as a snack bar, ice-cream shop, and popcorn stand, the latter making the whole place smell like a second-rate shopping mall.

As early as the 1890s, farmers realized that the heavy rainfall pouring down on these rich meadowlands produced luxuriant grass. Cows responded with milk that was more yellow than white (food coloring, however, is added to cheddar). But the prevailing westerlies had endowed their harbor with a bar, and before ships could get to markets in Portland they had to cross it and another at the mouth of the Columbia. Sometimes the sailing ship *Morning Star* (a replica of which is outside the creamery) and later the steamer *Elmore* remained barbound for ten days or more, still in sight of the pastures where their cargo was produced. When the weather relented and allowed a ship to go to sea, it might change its mind again and keep her barbound outside the Columbia, with the cargo in her hold growing older by the day. At times the trip to Portland took three weeks, and when the ship arrived the butter was so rancid it was sold for skid grease. The dairyman got nothing but a freight bill. But by the time the railroad arrived in 1911, the farmers had already decided to turn their milk into longer-lasting cheese, and the rest is history.

The county is justly proud of its **Pioneer Museum,** housed in a 1905 building that until 1932 served as the courthouse. There are the more or less usual exhibits of old furnishings, telephone equipment, cameras, farm tools, and the like, but the special attraction is a collection of stuffed birds and animals. You can study in detail the rare and common raven, trumpeter swan, egret, Canada goose, horned owl, red-tail hawk, magpie, valley quail, mountain crane, grouse, adelle penguin, canvasback duck, merganser, brown pelican, bald eagle, golden eagle, and wood duck and such animals as the western otter, red fox, fur seal, and whistler marmot. The basement houses a collection of old automobiles, wagons, and sleds. Rock hounds will enjoy a fine collection of agates and minerals.

Tillamook is a farm community, not a resort, so there are not a lot of places to stay. An old navy blimp hangar built during World War II dominates the southern horizon.

FOOD AND LODGING   Tillamook, Oregon 97141

✔✔ **Best Western Mar-Clair**   47-unit motel. 11 Main Avenue. (503) 842-7571.

Garibaldi • Population: 999

An old photograph shows the landfill at the upper reaches of Tillamook Bay covered with a dozen buildings, a couple of sawdust incinerators, myriad conveyor belts, and a number of forklift trucks, surrounded by all the other trappings of a giant sawmill. The bay itself is awash with acres and acres of floating logs, ready to be turned into lumber. A smallish steamship lies at the loading dock, awaiting a cargo for San Francisco or Portland. Nothing is left of this image, save for the hundred-foot-tall brick smokestack (demolition costs were too much, I suspect) hovering over a strangely out-of-place collection of small boat trailers, RVs, bait shops, boatyards, a second-class motel, and a modern-day restaurant abutting a shopping-mall-size parking lot. Garibaldi has simply gone through a metamorphosis from a lumber town to a commercial and sportfishing center.

It's a great place to browse around in because so much seems to be going on all the time. When I was there a fellow was filleting sea bass with such skill that it took less than ten seconds to do one fish. The head, tail, and innards were set aside to be used for crab-pot bait. At nearby Smith's Pacific Shrimp Company, half a dozen women were standing alongside a conveyer, sorting through half-inch-long shrimp that had just come from the de-icing and shelling machines. Most of the harvest is canned, but you can buy a shrimp cocktail here for almost nothing. Several nice eateries are nearby. The old mill workers' houses still line the bluffs. They look like bargains for retirees who want to be near the sea but don't want to live in a gussied-up resort.

FOOD AND LODGING   Garibaldi, Oregon 97118

●● **Old Mill Restaurant**   (503) 322-0222.

Rockaway Beach/Brighton • Population: 1,185

An old locomotive, still ready to make steam by the looks of her, stands near the harbor, a relic of the glory days of Garibaldi. If you are a New Yorker and given to nostalgia, you will be delighted to learn that the tracks lead to a couple of familiar-sounding places—only this isn't the A train to Rockaway or the D train to Brighton Beach. It's the occasionally run steam train to what we on this coast might call "far west Rockaway" and "Brighton by the Pacific." Even the right-of-way has a western rather than eastern feel. While browsing through a book I found at the Astoria library, I came upon a picture of the train to Rockaway, stalled in its tracks by an intransigent Stellar's sea lion bull. The engineer and brakeman are standing in front of the locomotive staring at the beast. Both have dumbfounded looks on their faces.

Highway 101 returns to the shore and heads eight miles north in an almost straight line, following along behind a string of sand dunes, alternately punctuated with shore grass and beach-side motels. Rockaway is the larger of the two towns that serve this modest resort area. Mountains loom up to the east, hovering over the coast like the Pali does in Honolulu. Here, however, the slopes are practically devoid of trees, the sad result of a number of forest fires that have plagued the area (see The Big Burn, page 185).

FOOD AND LODGING   Rockaway Beach/Brighton, Oregon 97136

✔✔ **Silver Sands Motel**   64 units on beach, pool. P.O. Box 161. (503) 355-2206.

✔✔ **Tradewinds Motel**   19 units on beach. P.O. Box 269. (503) 355-2212.

Wheeler/Nehalem/Manzanita • Population: 500

Unlike Tillamook Bay, Nehalem Bay is long and slinky, the drowned mouth of the Nehalem River. This is as pretty a dairying country as you'll ever see, with pastures crowding the four-foot-high banks of the bay. Tiny marinas serve as launching sites for boats carried on trailers or the tops of cars. The town of Nehalem inspires the most nostalgia of the three communities that snuggle up to these placid waters. Balustraded balconies shade planked sidewalks in front of recently fixed-up shops. Nehalem Bay Trading Co. occupies an old mercantile store with a twelve-foot-high white-painted fir ceiling. The Peacock Gallery displays works of local artists, and Food for Thought is a bookstore that serves light meals. I paused at the Nehalem Bay Winery to sample several of their recent offerings. Both their Pinot Noir and Chardonnay had an unfamiliar taste, and their white table wine, I learned, was

THE BIG BURN

Foresters knew things were dicey when the humidity dropped to 20 percent at high noon. They sent a runner into the woods with orders to halt logging operations, but he arrived too late. The rasp of steel cable against a dry stump was all it took. On August 14, 1933, a trickle of smoke signaled the start of a conflagration that three thousand fire fighters could not put out.

Men from the mills and logging camps throughout Tillamook County were rushed to the scene. Grimly they fought to trench and hold the fire. Hazel hoe, axe, spade, and dynamite were used to no avail. Flames licked the tops of two-hundred-foot snags; trees were burning like enormous Roman candles. Flaming bark and fiery needles sailed into the air and were carried far into the adjoining timber.

But things were under control after the first ten days. The fire was contained to a thirty-thousand-acre parcel. Or so everyone thought. Then came a moment every forester dreads. Smoldering stumps flared—the forest simply "blew up." Four-hundred-year-old trees were sucked into the roaring caldron created by the inferno. As the flames roared on, fire fighters reported that it sounded like the pounding of a dozen surfs. Near the coast, chickens went to roost because of darkness caused by the smoke. Soot fell on ships five hundred miles out to sea. Beaches were knee deep in ash. In the space of twenty hours 250,000 acres were consumed, five times as much as in the first ten days. Twelve billion feet of prime timber was destroyed, a third of the stand in the entire county. One man had lost his life. The experience prompted the state to adopt its slogan: Keep Oregon Green.

Slogans weren't enough, however. In 1939 the same area burned again, and then in 1945 a third blaze sizzled up. For six weeks an army of four thousand was recruited from the ranks of loggers, soldiers, and sailors (and even a friend of mine who was a high school student in Portland at the time). A hundred thousand more acres of prime timberland was burned. This time three died. The citizens of Oregon felt something had to be done. In 1948 they passed a $12 million bond issue to help in the reforestation. The problems of replanting led to the founding of scientific forest management programs. The Tillamook Burn is now a state forest, and everyone keeps a wary eye out for demon fire.

spiked with sugar. So although it is a friendly place, I came away feeling that they haven't quite gotten the hang of wine making yet. The grapes come from the Willamette Valley.

Manzanita is fast becoming a retirement community, with a nine-hole golf course and a small airport. There are several motels along the beach and a fun place to eat with an unlikely name, The Uptown Supper Club. The spit that separates the bay from the ocean is a series of dunes dominated by newly planted forests of shore pine. **Nehalem Bay State Park,** unfortunately, is not one of the state's prettiest. Park employees call it "Sandblast State Park."

FOOD AND LODGING

✔✔ **Sunset Surf Motel**   27 units. 248 Ocean Road, Manzanita 97131. (503) 368-5224.

✔ **Nehalem Bay State Park**   300 campsites.

✔ **Oswald West State Park**   36 walk-in campsites.

•• **Uptown Supper Club**   Restaurant and bar. (503) 368-6189.

NEAHKAHINE MOUNTAIN

Neahkahine Mountain, Cape Falcon, Arch Cape, and the lovely Short Sand Beach are all part of **Oswald West State Park,** named for the governor who was most responsible for keeping the state's beaches open to the public. Neahkahine, the brooding, often fog-shrouded peak that rises 1,600 feet above the ocean, has its identification in legends as the "home of the gods." One theory suggests its name is derived from an Indian god called "E-Kah-Ni," but another says that the word "kahnie" is a corruption of the Spanish word *carne,* meaning meat. There was plenty of elk for early explorers, so perhaps we should accept that explanation. Today, the largest animals are the protected Roosevelt elk. The best chance to see them is to walk up the trail to the summit that leaves from a graveled turnout on the north side of the mountain. The four-mile up-and-back walk takes about four hours. From the top you can see south to Cape Meares, north to Tillamook Head, and east to the summits of the Coast Range. China lies slightly over the western horizon.

The engineers who built this highway had a time of it getting around this headland. The road was literally blasted out of the cliff, and numerous carefully built rock walls surround lovely turnouts. At one you can see the sand dunes stretching all the way back to Rockaway Beach.

The campground just above Short Sand Beach is unique in that it has always been for walk-in campers only. When the park was built, the high-tech lightweight nylon and down camping

gear we take for granted wasn't available. Sleeping bags were
made of canvas and kapok, air mattresses were of heavy rubber,
and tents were made of ten-ounce duck. So people needed help
getting their gear into the campground. The Park Department
responded by providing wheelbarrows—big, heavy, iron-
wheeled wheelbarrows. After fifty years they are still doing yeoman duty. The campground is nestled in a spruce forest with an
understory of salal. The berry of this bush, incidentally, is sweet
and when mixed with a few apples makes a fine jelly. Picnickers
use the wheelbarrows, too, to haul things down the quarter-mile
paved path that leads to **Short Sand Beach.** Many consider this
Oregon's prettiest cove, for it is well protected from the winds,
the waves aren't too big, and several waterfalls drop right into
the sea. Trails lead out to **Cape Falcon** and **Arch Cape.**
On the latter, park ranger Jim Newell told me, a tiny little cove
provides a special surprise, at least when the tide is right. "Waves
coming in hit a series of dikes in the rocks. The spacing is such
that different sounds are produced by each little ridge, so the
waves are playing a song. When they hit the sandy shore, they
rattle the pebbles around, adding a percussion section to the
symphony."

Highway 101 tunnels under a section of Arch Cape and then
emerges onto a long, more or less flat coastline that is pierced
only by a single headland. You're looking out over Clatsop County, which we will visit next.

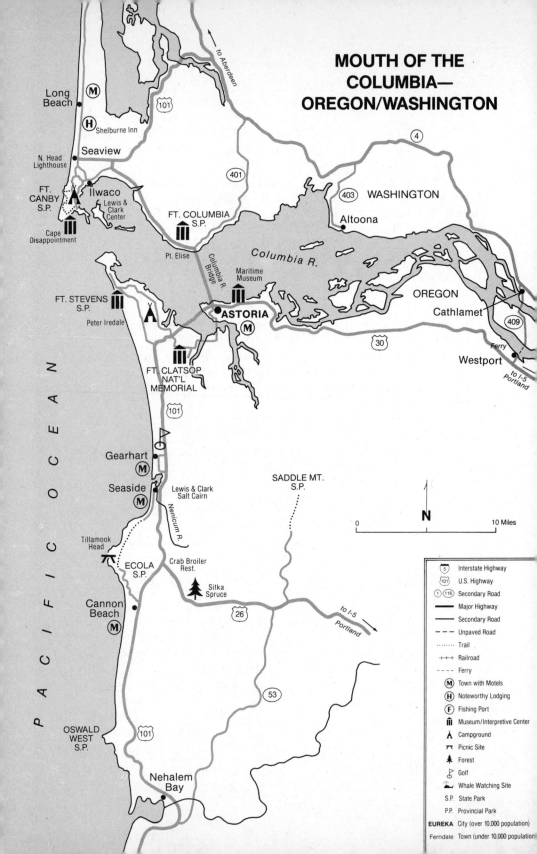

MOUTH OF THE COLUMBIA— OREGON/WASHINGTON

Long Beach

Shelburne Inn

Seaview

N. Head Lighthouse

FT. CANBY S.P.

Ilwaco

Lewis & Clark Center

Cape Disappointment

FT. COLUMBIA S.P.

Pt. Elise

to Aberdeen

WASHINGTON

Altoona

Columbia R.

Columbia R. Bridge

Maritime Museum

ASTORIA

FT. STEVENS S.P.

Peter Iredale

FT. CLATSOP NAT'L MEMORIAL

OREGON

Cathlamet

Westport

Ferry

to I-5 Portland

30

Gearhart

Seaside

Lewis & Clark Salt Cairn

Nenicum R.

SADDLE MT. S.P.

Tillamook Head

ECOLA S.P.

Crab Broiler Rest.

Sitka Spruce

Cannon Beach

N

0   10 Miles

26

to I-5 Portland

53

OSWALD WEST S.P.

Nehalem Bay

PACIFIC OCEAN

Legend

Symbol	Description
5	Interstate Highway
101	U.S. Highway
1 / 116	Secondary Road
—	Major Highway
—	Secondary Road
- - -	Unpaved Road
......	Trail
+++	Railroad
- - - -	Ferry
M	Town with Motels
H	Noteworthy Lodging
F	Fishing Port
🏛	Museum/Interpretive Center
🛆	Campground
⊼	Picnic Site
🌲	Forest
⚑	Golf
🐋	Whale Watching Site
S.P.	State Park
P.P.	Provincial Park
EUREKA	City (over 10,000 population)
Ferndale	Town (under 10,000 population)

13

THE SUNSET EMPIRE

Lewis and Clark Country

The Chambers of Commerce of Clatsop County, Oregon, and Pacific County, Washington, have recently been trying to promote their charms by calling the area the "Sunset Empire." It's a strange boast, since the fog lingers until noon on many days and often returns before sundown. Nevertheless, the miles and miles of beaches stretching north and south from the mouth of the Columbia River have for years been the playground for Portlanders and others living in the hotter climes behind the Coast Range.

A change in the topography appears as you proceed north. Though there are still two more magnificent capes to explore, the beaches are longer and the coastal mountains start rising farther inland. The area between sea and forests is called the Clatsop prairie, a place where Lewis and Clark chose to spend the winter, thereby becoming the first tourists to stay more than a day or two on this northern coast. Their soggy experience (see "Vile, Thicke Mistes and Stynking Fogges," page 190) would hardly suggest that the Sunset Empire had any acquaintance at all with old sol. But beaches attract inlanders, and the place is awash with vacationers during July and August when the weather is said to be the best.

Shortcut Access to the Sunset Empire

U.S. Highway 26 (the Sunset Highway) angles northwestward from Portland, aiming toward the exact place where the sun

"VILE, THICKE MISTES AND STYNKING FOGGES"

Captain Cook named the very first North American landmark he sighted Cape Foulweather for reasons not too hard to understand. Farther north a frustrated mariner called another site Destruction Island, and Cape Disappointment got its moniker because bad weather prevented Captain Meares from crossing the Columbia bar. These explorers were simply echoing the feeling of the first navigator to sail along this coast, Sir Francis Drake, who on June 5, 1579, penned in his log: "Many extreme gusts . . . vile, thicke mistes and stynking fogges."

Early overland explorers expressed similar feelings. Two and a quarter centuries after Drake, while holed up near the mouth of the Columbia, a frustrated Captain William Clark wrote:

> The rainey weather continued without a longer intermition than 2 hours at a time, from the 5th in the morning until the 16th is eleven days rain, and the most disagreeable time I have experenced confined on a tempist coast wet, where I can neither git out to hunt, return to a better situation, or proceed on: in this situation have we been for Six days past.

Lewis and Clark spent 106 days on the Oregon coast; it rained every day save 12. No wonder people say, "Oregonians don't tan, they rust." Modern writers too have shown disdain. Novelist Bernard Malamud called the rain "ubiquitous, continuous, monotonous, formless."

It is the fog, though, that holds more mystery. In *Sometimes a Great Notion,* Ken Kesey wrote:

> Fog is draped over the low branches of vine maple like torn remnants of a gossamer bunting. . . . Above, up through the branches, the sky is blue and still and very clear, but fog is on the land. It creeps down the river and winds around the base of the house, eating at the new yellow-grained planks with a soft white mouth.

Whether the story is true or not you can judge for yourself, but it is said that when some loggers hereabouts were roofing a bunkhouse, the fog was so thick that they shingled forty feet into space before discovering they had long since passed the last rafter.

It does rain a lot—160 days a year, mostly days of drizzle rather than a torrent; but on 200 days it doesn't rain, and many of them are beauties. Of the fifty-odd days I took researching this book, it rained only on two, and then not for more than a couple of hours. The fog hangs around, though, unfortunately right in the middle of the tourist season. "Last August we had twenty-nine straight days of unrelenting fog," groaned a ranger at the Cape Perpetua Visitors Center.

makes its daily exit from the American continent. The seventy-five-mile drive takes about 1½ hours unless you pause at a couple of spots to have a look around. One place of interest is **Camp 18 Logging Museum,** located twenty miles east of Highway 101. Spread out over a couple of acres of cutover land is a fantastic collection of steam donkeys, tractors, high-wheel skidders, various shaped blocks, and sawing machines of all types. Another place to pause is at a little park set aside by the Crown Zellerbach Company to protect the world's largest Sitka spruce. The monster is 216 feet tall and a whopping 56 feet around with enough wood to build 6 two-bedroom houses. The world's largest Douglas fir was nearby, but the nine-hundred-year-old giant blew down a few years ago.

Those lucky enough to be in this area on a clear day and having both time and stamina will do well to climb three-thousand-foot **Saddle Mountain,** the highest peak in the northern Coast Range. A twisty but paved road leads seven miles to the trailhead, 1,900 feet below the summit. There is some dispute about whether the trail to the top is three or four miles long, but in his book *Oregon Coast Hikes*, Paul Williams says: "Whichever, it will seem like five or six." On a perfect day you can see not only the coastal communities we will be visiting in this chapter, but also the great volcanoes, Mounts Rainier, St. Helens, and Hood.

Cannon Beach • Population: 1,215

When I first vacationed at Cannon Beach with my family in the 1960s, it was a sleepy little village with a couple of motels, a fine old grocery store with some school desks out front where you could drink coffee and munch on a ham sandwich, a cafe that opened at 6:00 A.M., and seven miles of sand. Osburn's Grocery Store is still here (and gone upscale), and the motels are, too, but they have been joined by a bevy of resorts and tourist-oriented businesses. Cannon Beach got the reputation of being an artist's community, and since it is not too far from a big city, development followed, right on cue. Out-of-county money looked over the place and thought "whaling village." Their plans were a bit Disneylandish, but fortunately they did a more or less sensitive job, so the town still has a lot of seaside charm, in spite of the fact that old gray shingle-sided bungalows have been replaced by three-story gray shingle-sided motels.

A "downtown" has sprouted up along a couple of blocks on Hemlock Street with board-and-batten-sided buildings housing nearly a dozen galleries, numerous cafes, bistros, chowder houses, and restaurants, a cookie store, candy shop, ice-cream parlor, two bakeries, a wine shop, lots of gift stores, and several seafood markets. People come from miles around to stroll the sidewalks, window-shop, and have a pleasant lunch. The Coaster Theater puts on a Dickens show at Christmastime and three or four plays during the summer, augmented by concerts, dance shows, and variety acts, so there is usually something to do after sunset. Portland State University conducts a program called Haystack Summer Workshop, where professors teach short courses in writing, photography, and the fine arts.

Cannon Beach's trademark is a large offshore volcanic plug called Haystack Rock. The town got its name because Lieutenant Neil H. Hawison, U.S.N., let his three-hundred-ton schooner *Shark* founder on the beach near Seaside in 1846. When she broke up, a small cannon, lashed to her decking, drifted south and washed ashore here. Cannon Beach has fifteen motels with about five hundred rooms.

FOOD AND LODGING   Cannon Beach, Oregon 97101

✔✔✔ **Best Western Surfsand Resort**   52-unit motel, restaurant, bar, pool. P.O. Box 219. (503) 436-2274.

✔✔✔ **Surfview Hallmark Resort**   110-room motel, restaurant, bar, pool. P.O. Box 547. (503) 436-1566.

✔✔✔ **Tolvana Inn**   170-room motel with kitchens, restaurant, bar, pool. P.O. Box 165. (503) 436-2211.

✔✔ **Haystack Resort Motel**   P.O. Box 775. (503) 436-1577.

✔✔ **Sandcastle Inn**   8-room B&B. 1116 South Hemlock. (503) 436-1392.

✔✔ **Tern Inn**   B&B. P.O. Box 952. (503) 436-1528.

●● **The Bistro**   Restaurant. (503) 436-2661.

●● **Cafe La Mer**   Dinner only. (503) 436-1179.

●● **Crab Broiler Restaurant**   Fifty-year-old garden restaurant at the junction of Highways 101 and 26. Bar, gift shop. (503) 738-5313.

●● **Morris' Fireside Restaurant**   Log cabin eatery and bar. (503) 436-2917.

ECOLA STATE PARK

The Clatsop Indians who hung around Lewis and Clark's winter encampment told the explorers about a whale having washed up on the shore just south of the forested spit we now call

Tillamook Head. Several of the party decided to have a look. Sacagawea (contrary to popular belief, this is the correct spelling of her name; there is no "j" in the Shoshone language) made a rare plea, which Meriwether Lewis recorded in his journal:

> The Indian woman was very importunate to be permitted to go, and was therefore indulged; she observed that she had traveled a long way with us to see the great waters, and that now that monstrous fish was also to be seen, she thought it very hard she could not be permitted to see either.

Steep slopes and downed trees made the going difficult, but they were rewarded for their effort. On January 8, 1806, Captain Clark wrote:

> From this point I beheld the grandest and most pleasing prospect which my eyes ever surveyed, in my frount a boundless Ocean; to the N. and N.E. the coast as far as my sight could be extended, the Seas rageing with emence waves and breaking with great force.

You won't have any trouble getting to where they stood. At the north end of Cannon Beach, take the two-mile paved road to Ecola State Park. The scene, looking back toward Haystack Rock, is perhaps the most photographed in Oregon.

Captain Clark liked present-day Cannon Beach, too, but he was a bit disappointed at what he found:

> Arived on a buitful Sand Shore and proceeded to the place the whale had perished, found only the Skelleton of the Monster the Whale was already pillaged of every Valuble part. This Skeleton measured 105 feet. I returned to the Village on the creek which I shall call E co-la or Whale Creek.

There is more than just scenery at Ecola Park. The winding road continues on another couple of miles to a bluff where a short trail leads down to Indian Beach, a popular spot for surfers and sunbathers. A mile offshore is **Tillamook Rock,** spiked with a one-hundred-foot tower. Look carefully at the light. The glass is protected by a steel grating. Incredibly, over the years storms have pelted the lighthouse window with rocks and logs. The light is now automated; no keeper has to brave the awful waves to get to his post. A lovely trail, six miles in length, leads over the roadless Tillamook Head to a trailhead at Sunset Boulevard in the city of Seaside. The walking is easier now than in 1806 when Clark wrote:

See looked wild breaking with great force against the Scattering
rocks and the ruged rockey points under which we wer obleged to
pass and if we had unfortunately made one false Step we Should
eneviateably have fallen into the the Sea and dashed against the
rocks in an instant. . . .

Seaside/Gearhart • Population: 6,193

Most of Seaside is situated on a sand spit separating the
Neanicum River from the ocean. It's the oldest beach resort on
the Pacific Northwest Coast and probably the largest. Cape Cod–
style bungalows, with shingle walls and fieldstone chimneys, line
Columbia and Beach drives. In the 1870s Ben Holladay, the great
stagecoach and railroad mogul, built a sprawling hotel that he
called Seaside House. In his book *Sea Wall*, Ellis Lucia described
the scene:

> In the midst of frontier wilderness, [guests] were treated to every
> comfort in wine, women and song, and the best cuisine prepared
> by French chefs. Trout were brought from the nearby Neanicum
> River still wriggling as they were popped into the pan. Deer, elk
> and birds were shot in the forests. Musicians entertained in the
> salons and gambling rooms, and beautiful women kept the mood
> gay.

In terms of opulence, at least, one could argue that Seaside
has gone downhill ever since. Site of Oregon's Miss America
Pageant, the place has the same sort of family-fun atmosphere as
Atlantic City (before the gambling) or California's Santa Cruz. A
long pier crammed with amusement rides used to jut out into the
ocean. It got so ratty they tore it down. The arcades simply moved
a few blocks east on Broadway, a street the Chamber of Commerce calls the Million Dollar Walk. You can play skee-ball, ride
bumper cars, and play pinball and video games at several amusement centers. Funland and Kiddyland Arcades boasts: "Family
fun since '31." Bingo is played on alternate nights at the American Legion, the I.W.A. Hall, the Elks Lodge, and, during the
summer, at the Catholic church.

Broadway is crammed with half a dozen fast-food outlets,
ten cafes and restaurants, four candy shops, twenty-five gift
stores, a couple of boutiques, several photo stores, and four
T-shirt shops. Vendors rent bicycles, mopeds, and paddle boats
(along the river) and sell fifty-nine flavors of saltwater taffy. An
aquarium has exotic fish and a tank where harbor seals are
trained to clown about while begging for food. The two-mile
concrete walk-way called the Prom separates the sand from the

town. It's a roller-skater's paradise. A small historical museum overlooks the river north of Broadway. Seaside boasts that the "Turnaround" at the foot of Broadway is the end of the Lewis and Clark trail, but as we have seen, some of the explorers went farther south to Cannon Beach.

As far as we know, Lewis and Clark disagreed on only two things. Clark came to enjoy the taste of dog while Lewis did not, but he in turn liked salt with his meals, something Clark couldn't give a whit about. Lewis wrote of his partner: "My friend Capt. Clark declares it to be a mear matter of indifference with him whether he uses it or not." At any rate, a three-man party was dispatched to Seaside to extract salt from the ocean. They spent nearly seven weeks at the task. The salt cairn where they boiled 1,400 gallons of seawater to make twenty gallons of salt has been reconstructed and is now located eight blocks south of Broadway near the beach.

Kite flying is a popular sport, along with the traditional beach activities such as clamming and driftwood hunting. Portions of the beach are open to vehicle use, and a new sport is burgeoning. Surfboards have been outfitted with sails and wheels. Devotees now go racing up and down the sands at what seem like breathtaking speeds.

Gearhart, located along the beach north of the Neanicum River, reflects an older and more stately life-style. The oldest golf course in the Northwest was built here in 1892, and many of the surrounding houses were constructed shortly thereafter. When the tide is right, you can drive all the way from here to Fort Stevens on the same road the old-timers used, the sand. The Indians called this the "Talapus Trail," named after one form of their god Coyote. Talapus kept busy fashioning the headlands and bays and, fortunately for beachgoers, setting a limit to the tide.

FOOD AND LODGING   Seaside, Oregon 97138

✔✔✔ **Gearhart by the Sea Inn** 6-story oceanfront condo-resort. Marion at 10th. Gearhart, Oregon. (503) 738-8331.

✔✔✔ **Shilo Inn** 110-room oceanfront convention center. Restaurant, bar, pool. 30 North Prom. (503) 738-9571.

✔✔ **Best Western Seashore Resort Motel** 51-unit oceanfront motel. 60 North Prom. (503) 738-6368.

✔✔ **Ebb Tide Motel** 83-unit oceanfront motel. 300 North Prom. (503) 738-8371.

✔✔ **Hi-Tide Motel**   64-unit oceanfront motel. 30 Avenue G. (503) 738-8414.

✔✔ **The Boarding House**   7-room B&B overlooking the river. 30 North Holladay. (503) 738-9055.

FORT STEVENS STATE PARK

My reading of the annals of the War Between the States gives no hint that Jefferson Davis or his generals had the slightest interest in capturing Oregon. Nevertheless the Union Army built a huge base here to prevent Confederate ships from entering the Columbia River. It's now one of the largest parks in the state. A small interpretive museum describes some of what went on here over the years. Nearby, old concrete coastal gun emplacements are now beginning to crumble away. This is said to be the only military post in the contiguous forty-eight states to receive hostile alien fire since the War of 1812. A Japanese submarine stood offshore in 1942 and lobbed 17 five-inch shells at the fort, scoring a direct hit on the wire cage behind the batter's box at the baseball diamond. The officer in charge of the base claimed that he didn't return the fire because "I didn't want to reveal my position."

The park has a huge campground, miles of trails, and a freshwater lake to swim in. Visible at low tide is the derelict *Peter Iredale*, an iron-hulled four-masted bark that went on the beach in 1906 while trying to enter the Columbia. It's fun to stand amidships and reflect on her fate. Author Edwin C. Henry wrote a poem about the wreck, which begins:

> *With every rise and ebb of tide,*
> *And every angry storm*
> *A thousand seas have surged inside*
> *Her broken, rusted form.*
> *Defiant to both time and sea*
> *Her sunken stanchions stand;*
> *Her broken ribs and toppled masts*
> *Protruding from the sand.*

Fort Stevens guards the mouth of the mighty Columbia, second only to the Mississippi in the amount of water discharged into the ocean. The river, navigable all the way to Idaho, drains an area almost as large as California, Oregon, and Washington combined. A road leads onto the south jetty, where you can look out on the infamous bar, graveyard to over two hundred ships. It's better, however, to save that experience for the north side of the river, which we will visit shortly.

FORT CLATSOP NATIONAL MEMORIAL

Americans are fascinated by the two-and-a-half-year trek of Lewis and Clark. Their extensive writings paint a picture of men with great scientific curiosity, facing danger and hardship as they struggle across an uncharted land. They were not the first to cross the North American continent. That honor goes to Alexander Mackenzie, a partner in the British-owned Northwest Fur Company, who was scouting for beaver and otter. In 1793, after following the myriad rivers and lakes of the far North, he and his party paddled into tidewater at present-day Bella Coola, British Columbia. The western mountains converge into a single range in the north, and they aren't very high, so the trip wasn't too difficult. His notes were sketchy, however, and for competitive reasons kept secret, so it is to Lewis and Clark that we look to discover the drama of the exploration of the great Pacific Northwest. One only has to recognize the ineptness of those who followed (see The Star-Crossed Astorians, below) to appreciate just how wilderness-wise and prudent these men were. A half day or so spent at their winter quarters is time well spent.

THE STAR-CROSSED ASTORIANS

Washington Irving portrays the Astorians as heroes because they suffered so much. But he was wrong. They were a company of reckless, impulsive, bumbling fortune seekers who should have stayed home. In 1811, barely five years after Lewis and Clark had returned from their epic trek, John Jacob Astor decided to set up operations in the Pacific Northwest. On paper his plan looked good. He would send one party overland, another by sea. But he chose bad leaders.

The *Tonquin,* under the command of Jonathan Thorn, arrived at the Columbia bar during a violent storm. The prudent thing to do was wait it out, but he was in a hurry. In spite of the rampaging seas, he sent four men out in a longboat. When it became apparent they were in real trouble, he dispatched another boat to help. The Astorians' numbers were summarily reduced by eight. Captain Thorn didn't learn much from his mistake. He sailed north to Tofino on Vancouver Island to trade with the Indians (see Chapter 19) and promptly let too many tribesmen aboard. They turned on the crew and massacred the lot, save five who escaped ashore and another who, while hiding in the hold, set fire to the powder magazine, thereby blowing himself, the ship, and the captors to smithereens.

The overland party under the command of Wilson Price Hunt didn't fare much better. When they found themselves on a westward-flowing river, they recklessly built some canoes, abandoned their horses, and started sailing merrily down the Snake. If Hunt had read Lewis and Clark's journals, which had been published that year, he would have known that that wasn't a very smart idea. Western rivers aren't like those back east. His canoes were smashed on rocks, and one man was soon lost in a boiling caldron of turgid, roiling water. Now they were afoot, lost in the clutches of America's deepest canyon. The party split into twos and threes, some on one side of the rampaging river, some on the other, and no place to cross. Snows fell, and they suffered terribly. The survivors eventually made it to Fort Astoria, more or less intact—all but John Day, that is. He was a fine man from Kentucky who had barely kept his sanity during the ordeal in the snows, and on the way home the next year, having contemplated what lay ahead, he went mad as a hatter, turned back, and promptly died. For that bit of self-sacrifice he got a river, a town, and an immense dam named in his honor.

The Canadians, who were trapping north of the Columbia, were amused. Alexander Ross, a partner in the Northwest Fur Company, wrote:

> It made a cynic smile to see this pioneer core, a bunch of traders, shopkeepers, voyagers, and Hawaiians [Owyhees] all floundering in this new walk of life. And the most ignorant of all, the leader.

Astor knew it was time to cut his losses. When war broke out with England in 1812, he sent instructions to sell the place. The man in charge was a former Northwest partner, so he didn't lose any sleep over that decision, especially since the British frigate *Beaver* was lying offshore with its guns trained on the little garrison. Another twenty years would elapse before the Americans regained a toehold in Oregon.

The reconstructed fort and nearby museum are run by the National Park Service, which does a splendid job of introducing you to the drama of the trek. The museum has maps showing their route and artifacts from their journey. Audiovisual programs describe the adventure, and rangers give black-powder demonstrations and show how the explorers' canoes were hollowed out by fire and adze. Lectures are given on such subjects as Sacagawea's role in the adventure (though not the pathfinder she has often been portrayed as, she nevertheless proved her mettle on many occasions), the making of buckskins, the plants, birds, and trees discovered by the explorers, the influence of York, Captain Clark's Negro slave, and the remarkable relationship between the Corps of Discovery and the Indians they encountered along the way.

The National Park Service has declared their route the "Lewis and Clark National Historic Trail" and is coordinating efforts to preserve and maintain the many sites along the way. The enthusiasm of the rangers here at Fort Clatsop is infectious. They might get you excited, too, even to the point of joining the Lewis and Clark Trail Heritage Foundation, a nonprofit organization that publishes a fine journal titled *We Proceeded On* (the name comes from a phrase the captains frequently used) and holds yearly conclaves at various cities throughout the country. We'll get another chance to learn about the Corps of Discovery when we get to the Washington side of the river, so let us proceed on to the mighty Columbia and the oldest city in the Pacific Northwest.

Astoria • Population: 9,950

John Jacob Astor was no shrinking violet; he insisted that the fur trading post he set up to compete with the Canadians be given his name. After all, he put up the money. But when the Northwest Fur Company bought him out a few years later, they had no compunctions about changing it to a more British-sounding Fort George. The site of the post, marked by the headstone of chief factor Donald McTavish, is at the intersection of 15th and Exchange streets. It is the oldest grave in the Pacific Northwest (see The Life and Loves of Jane Barnes, page 200).

The early years weren't too kind to those who came here. Lewis and Clark found that the Indians had been debauched by sea traders and were thievish to an extreme. Astor had his problems, and McTavish's group did, too. When a murderous competition between the "Norwesters" and the Hudson's Bay Company was finally resolved by their merger in 1821 (with the Hudson's Bay Company the survivor), the new factor, John McLaughlin, removed the facility to Fort Vancouver, opposite present-day Portland.

Astoria didn't die, but it lay dormant for twenty years. The British withdrew, and Americans began drifting back. In 1847 one John Shively journeyed to Washington, D.C., to receive from President Polk his appointment as postmaster. His territory—all the lands west of the Rockies. That, incidentally, was the year the government issued its first postage stamps, a five-center with the likeness of Ben Franklin and a ten-center honoring George Washington. Four of the latter were enough to get a letter mailed back east.

Shipping, lumbering, and fishing soon replaced trapping,

and the town began to prosper. Genteel ladies presided over teas and musicales, while along the waterfront, saloons, shanghaiers, and ladies of the night gave Astoria a sordid reputation up and down the coast. Finns, Norwegians, and Swedes began settling in an area called Union Town beneath the present-day Columbia Bridge (where you'll find Suomi Hall). A Scandinavian festival is held every year at the summer solstice. By the time the Spokane, Portland, and Seattle Railroad punched a branch line through in 1898, Astoria was as prosperous as any city in Oregon.

But when the old-growth timber was cut, the lumber industry faltered. Then, with the completion of the Bonneville Dam in 1938, the salmon industry went into a decline. Migrating fish had trouble with the fish ladders and got caught in the turbine blades. Fourteen million salmon a year were caught around the turn of the century. The catch now hovers around the one million mark. The Bumble Bee cannery was the last to close—in 1981, throwing 1,500 people out of work. So the population stabilized at its present level, and the city continues to chug along at a reduced pace. But it is a nice place to visit, and there is lots to see and do.

THE LIFE AND LOVES OF JANE BARNES

In April of 1814, the frigate *Isaac Todd* sailed across the bar, bringing a new factor, a Scotsman named Donald McTavish, to manage Fort George for the Northwest Fur Company. Not wishing to brave the wilds of the Pacific Northwest without some civilization, he brought along his mistress, a voluptuous Portsmouth barmaid named Jane Barnes. Being the first white woman to come to Oregon country, not surprisingly, she aroused the passions of the Clatsop chief. He, it seems, did not understand why Jane refused his offer of what amounted to a king's ransom to induce her to his quarters. After all, he felt no hesitation in proffering any one of his four wives to the white men. Meanwhile, Alexander Henry, one of the more able employees of the firm, offered Jane his "protection," which no doubt made McTavish a bit testy. The two got to drinking and dared each other to row out to the *Isaac Todd*, which at that time was wallowing in waves as bad as any the Columbia could throw at her. The "Norwesters" lost two good men in that bizarre episode.

Jane had seen enough of this wild country—she sailed on the *Isaac Todd* to the Orient, where she reportedly married an official of the British East India Company.

Begin with a drive to the top of Coxcomb Hill to get the lay of the land. The **Astoria Column,** built in 1929, has a spiral staircase leading to the observation deck 125 feet above the ground. Murals, arranged in a spiral, depict scenes from the three major events in the town's history: Captain Gray's discovery of the Columbia, Lewis and Clark's arrival, and the establishment of Fort Astoria. The view from the top is spectacular, especially at sunset. The city streets leading to the hill pass numerous Victorian residences and several churches built in the late 1800s. Notable is the Bethany Lutheran Church, formerly called the Betania Norsk Luthersk by its Scandinavian parishioners; St. Mary's Catholic Church; and the gothic-towered First Presbyterian Church, which features fine stained-glass windows and a large pipe organ.

Pride of the city is the Queen Anne–style **Flaval House** (pronounced fla-VAL), now open to the public. Authentic period furniture graces dining rooms, parlors, and lounges with fourteen-foot-high ceilings. Intricately milled doors and jambs are twelve feet high, and the winding staircase is a tribute to the caring craftsman's art. Flaval House and **The Heritage Center** are both managed by the Clatsop County Historical Society. The latter, which contains photos and artifacts of the early days, is located in the former City Hall, built in 1906. You can also peek into the old jail, which was used until 1976. The largest building on the Oregon coast is the eight-story Astor Hotel, built in the 1920s in a mock Tudor-Gothic style. It has recently been refurbished as a federally subsidized housing project.

The **Columbia River Maritime Museum** is, in my view, as fine a facility as San Francisco's Maritime Museum or the South Street Seaport in New York City. Dedicated in 1982, it traces the rich history of the region with models of famous ships, relics of the longtime fishing industry, and rare exhibits of ocean-related memorabilia. Moored outside is the lightship *Columbia*, which is open to the public.

FOOD AND LODGING   Astoria, Oregon 97103

✔✔ **Crest Motel**   24-unit out-of-town motel on bluff overlooking the river. 5366 Lief Erickson Drive. (503) 325-3141.

✔✔ **Franklin House**   6-room B&B. P.O. Box 804. (503) 325-5044.

✔✔ **Franklin Street Station**   4-room B&B. 1140 Franklin Street. (503) 325-4314.

✔✔ **Red Lion Thunderbird Inn**   124-room riverfront motel, restaurant. 400 Industry Street. (503) 325-7373.

✔✔ **Rosebriar Inn**　9-room B&B in a former convent. 636 14th Street. (503) 325-7427.

✔ **Fort Stevens State Park**　600 campsites.

●● **Pier 11**　Dockside restaurant. (503) 325-0279.

COLUMBIA RIVER FERRY • (Two-hour side loop)

The last gap, 21,697 feet long, in the continuous 1,500-mile strip of asphalt between the Canadian and Mexican borders was bridged in 1966 when the world's longest continuous truss span opened. When the ferry *Chessman* retired from service, an era was closed. Washington and Oregon were now connected at numerous spots throughout the length of the great river (too many, in the view of some). The rivalry between the two states has always been strong, as illustrated by an advertisement placed some years ago in a Seattle newspaper by a hotel in Portland:

> We don't hide a city tax in your hotel bill, and slip it to a bureaucrat. Or even a county tax. Or a state tax. Oh, there are some of you who pay twenty cents to get your car back across the Columbia River when you return to Seattle on your cigarette run, but most of the people we know row.

Fortunately for those who treasure the old ways, it is still possible to cross the Columbia by ferry, but you have to go out of your way to do it. Drive 27 miles east on U.S. Highway 30 to the village of **Westport** and turn left. A little diesel-powered, nine-car ferry makes hourly crossings to the Washington town of **Cathlamet** (pronounced cath-LAM-it). Though the crossing takes only fifteen minutes, you pass by several islands and get a nice sense of the river, which at this spot looks almost exactly the way it did when Lewis and Clark passed by. Both Westport and Cathlamet, incidentally, have saloons with antique backbars, said to have been brought around the horn on sailing ships. Cathlamet has a funky museum, filled with an incredible array of logging equipment, milking machines, and other relics that people didn't want to keep but didn't want to throw away, either. State Highways 4 and 401 lead back to the coast. A little country road heads south to the tiny town of **Altoona,** where on November 7, 1805, Captain Clark penned a memorable phrase:

> Great joy in camp we are in view of the Ocian, this great Pacific Octean which we been so long anxious to See. and the roreing or noise made by the waves breaking on the rockey Shores (as I suppose) may be heard distinctly.

Clark was mistaken. The weather was so bad and the Columbia so wide here that he thought the monstrous breakers had to be Pacific waves. Nine days later the party struggled around Point Elise, the northern anchorage of the Columbia River Bridge and finally did see the "Octean."

At the north end of the Astoria Bridge, Highway 101 turns west and follows the shore of Baker Bay, a sizable body of water separated from the ocean by Cape Disappointment. At the turn of the century the army chose Point Elise as the site of **Fort Columbia,** built to guard the entrance to the river. The fort was closed at the end of World War II, but the buildings have been preserved, and it is now a nice state park with picnicking facilities and a small museum.

Ilwaco, Washington • Population: 600

Ilwaco is a nice little fishing village with a modest museum that has displays of the lumbering, fishing, and cranberry industries of Pacific County. Like its counterpart on the south side of the Columbia—Warenton, Oregon—Ilwaco comes alive at the opening of salmon season. "You can't fall overboard," I heard a fellow say. "You'll just land in the next boat." The fish are now becoming more plentiful, thanks to a massive effort on the part of the federal government to ameliorate the damage done by the upstream dam construction.

CAPE DISAPPOINTMENT

Highlight of a visit to southwestern Washington is a tour of Cape Disappointment, part of **Fort Canby State Park.** One block west of Ilwaco's main intersection, turn south and follow the lee of the last Pacific headland we'll visit for a while. The Coast Guard has a lifeboat training facility here. The narrow road climbs up the deeply forested cape to Washington State's **Lewis and Clark Interpretive Center,** housed in an old gun battery. Here, the curators chose to emphasize the scientific aspects of the great adventure. Large pictures show many of the sites along their route. The museum tour terminates in a spectacular room overlooking the mouth of the river. It's a nice place to pause and contemplate what might have happened if that bar had been a little more forgiving. Captain John Meares called this Cape Disappointment when unfavorable tides and adverse winds prevented him from crossing the bar (spring tides average sixteen feet along this coast). Bostonian John Gray, who had better luck, sailed into the bay on May 11, 1792, and named the great river after his ship, *Columbia*. Mariners have dreaded that bar ever since.

The wreck of the *Peacock* in 1850 convinced the government to build a lighthouse at the tip of the cape, the first on the Pacific Northwest Coast. Had the bar not been so treacherous, Portland, not Seattle, would certainly have become the major shipping port of the Pacific Northwest because railroads heading east could follow the river, thereby avoiding the struggle over the Cascade Range. But if the bar had been safer, it is also quite likely that you would now be standing in Canada, not the state of Washington. The diversion of American shipping to Puget Sound had much to do with the compromise that made the forty-ninth parallel, not the Columbia, the international boundary (see Fifty-four Forty or Fight—Over a Pig! page 254). The Army Corps of Engineers built two long jetties out into the ocean, but even today it's not an easy crossing, as will be quite apparent if you're here on a windy day.

It is perhaps appropriate that the northernmost cape we'll visit for a while is arguably the prettiest. The forest is lush, yet several coastal freshwater ponds and nearby meadows get enough sun to support a brilliant blue display of foxgloves during the spring. Grotesque driftwood shapes cover the sand north of the jetty. A lovely trail leads to North Head Lighthouse, which stands on a promontory above a cove called Dead Man's Hollow, named for the sailors lost in the beaching of the *Vandelia* in 1853.

Long Beach/Seaview • Population: 1,799

On November 15, 1805, Captain Clark stood near this spot and wrote:

> After takeing a Sumptious brackfast of Venison which was roasted on Stiks exposed to the fire, I proceeded on through ruged Country of high hills and Steep hollers 5 miles . . . to the commencement of a Sandy coast. . . . I proceeded on the sandy coast 4 miles, and marked my name on a Small pine, the Day of the month & year, &c.

Unfortunately, the tree he wrote his name on has long since disappeared, and the only surviving graffiti of the many places where he carved his name is on a rock outside of Billings, Montana.

The sand spit separating Willapa Bay from the ocean is said to be the longest stretch of drivable sand in the world—twenty-eight miles. Motels and tourist facilities are stretched out over much of this distance. The bay, home to cranberry bogs and oyster beds, has a moderating influence on the weather, making this country, according to the Chamber of Commerce, warmer than any other Washington coastal community. Half a dozen good-quality motels face the ocean, but by far the most interesting place to stay is The Shelburne Inn. This shingle-sided roadhouse, built in 1896, has recently been renovated and enlarged into a first-class B&B. Seventeen antiques-furnished rooms snuggle above and around one of the best places to eat in the area. The Shoalwater Restaurant, owned separately, first received national attention when the late James Beard (a local boy—his mother was a chef in Gearhart) extolled the innovative regional cuisine he found here. The owners boast that they draw their menus from seasonal local products, including a variety of seafood, wild mushrooms and berries, game, and homemade bread, pastries, pasta, pâtés, and jellies.

FOOD AND LODGING   Long Beach, Washington 98631

✔✔✔ **The Shelburne Inn**   17-room B&B. P.O. Box 250, Seaview, Washington 98644. (206) 642-2442.

✔✔ **Edgewater Inn Motel**   36-unit beachfront motel. 409 10th Street West. (206) 642-2311.

✔✔ **Ocean Lodge**   23-unit beachfront apartment motel. P.O. Box 337. (206) 642-2777.

✔✔ **Our Place at the Beach**   25-unit beachfront motel. P.O. Box 266. (206) 642-3793.

✔ **Fort Canby State Park**   252 campsites. P.O. Box 488, Ilwaco, Washington 98624. (206) 642-3078.

●●● **The Shoalwater Restaurant**   (206) 642-4142.

Surprisingly, Washington's coast is much tamer than Oregon's. Long sand spits, like the one here, guard two large inland bays, forcing Highway 101 to move thirty miles inland. The coastal dunes are overgrown with Scotch broom and European beach grass; no basaltic headlands add character to the shoreline. In addition, thirty miles of shoreline are tribal lands, closed to the public. Though there are several fishing resorts farther north, notably around the mouth of Gray's Harbor Bay, in my opinion they aren't all that interesting and are somewhat out of the way. So I think it's best to leave the Pacific seaboard here and hop on north to the great Olympic Peninsula.

PART FOUR

Northwest Washington

• 14 •

OLYMPIC NATIONAL PARK

"Nature's Safe Retreat, Forever"

President Fillmore signed a bill on March 2, 1853, officially making Washington a territory. Four thousand people lived here at the time. By 1880 the number had swelled to seventy-five thousand, and the coming of the railroad in 1883 brought so many more that by the time statehood was granted in 1889, the population stood at over a third of a million. But there was a land yet to be explored. Territorial Governor Eugene Semple (as reported in Robert L. Wood's informative book *Across the Olympic Mountains: The Press Expedition, 1889–90*) dispatched a report to the secretary of the interior that said in part:

> On the western side of Washington territory, facing the restless ocean and defying its angry waves with a rockbound coast, stands the Olympic range of mountains. . . . The mountains seem to rise from the edge of the water, on both sides, in steep ascent to the line of perpetual snow, as though nature had designed to shut up this spot for her safe retreat forever. . . . It is a land of mystery, awe-inspiring in its mighty constituents and wonder-making in its unknown expanse of canyon and ridge.

In 1778, Captain John Meares, though not the first to spy it, named the highest peak Mount Olympus. He must have thought it was as good a "home of the gods" as any of the six or seven other Mt. Olympuses in the eastern Mediterranean. Yet at the dawn of the Gay Nineties, not one person, white or Indian, had

OLYMPIC NATIONAL PARK— WASHINGTON

Cape Flattery
Neah Bay
She-Bear Beach
Makah Cultural Center
MAKAH INDIAN RESERVATION
Cape Alva
Ozette Lake

STRAIT OF JUAN DE FUCA

Sekiu
Clallam Bay
112

ferry to Victoria

PORT ANGELES
to Seattle
101

Sappho
Soleduck R.
Log Cabin Resort
Mount Storm King
Pioneer Memorial Center
Lake Crescent Lodge
Altaire & Elwha Campgrounds
Olympic Hot Springs
Heart o' the Hills Campground
Hurricane Ridge

COASTAL TR
Mora Campground
Rialto Beach
Forks
La Push
BOGACHIEL S.P.
Sol Duc Hot Springs
Elwha R.

Hoh Rain Forest
Hoh Campground
Hoh R.
Mt. Olympus

Oil City

OLYMPIC NATIONAL PARK

PRESS EXPEDITION ROUTE
Low Divide

Ruby Beach
Destruction Island
Kalaloch Campground
Kalaloch Lodge

Queets R.

N. Fork Trailhead
Graves Cr Trailhead
Enchanted Valley

PACIFIC OCEAN

QUINAULT
INDIAN
RESERVATION

Ranger Station
Lake Quinault Lodge
Quinault Rain Forest
Willaby Campground

Quinault R.

0   10 Miles
N

Moclips
Pacific Beach

Humptulips

101

Ocean City

109

Ocean Shores
Grays Harbor
ABERDEEN
to Portland Seattle
Hoquiam
Chehalis R.
Westport
to Astoria
101

Legend

5	Interstate Highway
101	U.S. Highway
1 116	Secondary Road
——	Major Highway
——	Secondary Road
- - -	Unpaved Road
·····	Trail
+++	Railroad
- - -	Ferry
M	Town with Motels
H	Noteworthy Lodging
F	Fishing Port
🏛	Museum/Interpretive Center
⋏	Campground
⊼	Picnic Site
🌲	Forest
⚲	Golf
	Whale Watching Site
S.P.	State Park
P.P.	Provincial Park
EUREKA	City (over 10,000 population)
Ferndale	Town (under 10,000 population)

ever set foot in those mountains that on clear days were so plainly visible from Seattle itself. The governor used the well-chosen word "mystery" because the land was often obscured by lead-colored rain clouds. He must also have heard stories the Indians told, because he continued:

> Red men and white men have gone all around this section, as bushmen go all around a jungle in which a man-eating tiger is concealed, but the interior is incognito. . . . The Indians have traditions in regard to happenings therein, ages ago, which were so terrible that the memory of them has endured until this day, with a vividness that controls the actions of men.

Even scientists were forced to speculate. The rivers leading out from the mountains didn't seem large enough to disgorge the tremendous amount of rainfall the range seemed to attract. There must, therefore, be a giant inland valley where either the waters perpetually accumulate or somehow find their way to the sea by some unknown underground chasm. It wasn't until 1885 that these mysteries began to unravel, and then only slowly, as we will see. The first penetration into the heart of the range did not occur until 1890.

Seven years later there was talk about establishing a national park because, as people argued, it was absolutely unfit for any other use. President Cleveland created a forest reserve to keep the trees from being cut, and then, in 1909, Teddy Roosevelt proclaimed the area a national monument. Highway 101, which surrounds it, wasn't completed unti the 1930s. The reserve was upgraded to park status in 1938, but even today roads are few and mostly unpaved. Park Ranger Gregg Jackson told me that there are absolutely no plans to build anymore, so in that sense, at least, the Olympic Peninsula is, and perhaps always will be, "nature's safe retreat, forever."

In the last chapter, we left Highway 101 near the Columbia River Bridge. From there it slashes through the woods for a while, skirts around the eastern side of Wallapa Bay, and curves inland past the twin towns of **South Bend** and **Raymond.** South Bend is the center of a large oyster industry and the seat of Pacific County. I poked my head inside the oyster plant and gazed upon forty men and women hard at work at the shucking task. "They get two cents apiece," a fellow said. "A good shucker can make a hundred dollars a day." The Pacific County Court House, a white-domed building, was no doubt inspired by the Pantheon in Rome. It is much too fancy for such a small county; the locals call it "the gilded palace of extravagance," but tourists are among the beneficiaries because it is a delightful place to pause, have a picnic, and look around. The Weyerhaeuser Co. in nearby Raymond conducts sawmill tours on summer weekdays.

Shortcut Access to Olympic National Park

The Coast Range, which is less and less dominant north of Tillamook, more or less peters out at Aberdeen, an industrial city twenty-five miles north of Raymond on Grays Harbor Bay. The westward-flowing Chehalis River, which has its headwaters near the south end of Puget Sound, wanders through a broad valley surrounded by the Wallapa Hills. Serious consideration was once given to building a canal between Grays Harbor and Puget Sound, but the Civil War put an end to that idea. Nevertheless, the sea would not have to rise very much for the Olympic Peninsula to become an island. Aberdeen is only forty-five miles west of the state capital at Olympia, located on Interstate 5. A four-lane highway connects the two cities. Those coming up I5 from the south will save some time by turning left on U.S. Highway 12.

Highway 101, which we have been following since crossing the Golden Gate Bridge, does a curious thing on the Olympic Peninsula. It doesn't just keep going north until it runs out of country, but rather bends around and heads back south almost to Aberdeen, symbolically, at least, making a loop like a shepherd's crook that embraces a mighty group of mountains. We'll follow the loop around in a clockwise direction.

Aberdeen/Hoquiam • Population: 29,000

These two towns form the largest metropolitan area we have visited since Eureka, California. A quick drive-through leaves you disappointed, but there are a couple of interesting things to do. The **Aberdeen Museum of History,** located in a 1930s-style armory, has artifacts from the early days of this lumber town. Hoquiam (pronounced HO-quim) has two old mansions, open to the public. **Hoquiam's Castle** and **Polson Park and Museum** occupy the homes of two lumber barons. The latter has a lovely rose garden surrounded by many exotic trees.

FOOD AND LODGING   Aberdeen/Hoquiam, Washington 98520

✔✔ **Nordic Inn**   66-room motel, restaurant, bar. 1700 South Boone. (206) 533-0100.

✔✔ **Olympic Inn**   55-room motel. 616 West Heron. (206) 533-4200.

✔ **Thunderbird Motel** 36-room motel. 410 West Wish-
kah. (206) 532-3153.

●● **Bridges Restaurant** Old-time downtown eatery. (206)
532-6563.

GRAYS HARBOR RESORTS

Aberdeen and Hoquiam abut Grays Harbor, the most northern of the bays along the American Pacific Coast and one of the
largest. Credit the name to the Bostonian trader Captain John
Gray, who by dint of an insatiable curiosity managed to find not
only this harbor, but Tillamook Bay and the Columbia River as
well, at a time when other explorers were too timid to venture
beyond what they considered safe water. Oceangoing ships now
come twenty-five miles inland to dock at the nearby wharfs. The
dunes and sand spits that guard the mouth of Grays Harbor
support a string of resorts, Seattle's southern window to the
Pacific. **Westport** is on the south spit; **Ocean Shores, Ocean
City, Pacific Beach,** and **Moclips** are on the north. A passenger
ferry makes regular crossings across the mouth of the bay during
the summer, but there is no way to get your car across. However,
as noted in the last chapter, the beaches lack the charm of those
farther north and south. In my view, you will simply find more
interesting places to explore forty miles north of Hoquiam in the
national park. Caution: It is 165 miles from here to Port Angeles
on Highway 101. During the summer, tourist accommodations in
between are hard to come by on the spur of the moment.

OLYMPIC NATIONAL PARK

We ran out of Coast Range back near the Columbia, but as
you drive north along Highway 101, snow-capped peaks up
ahead signal that you're in for something even better. The Olympics are not anything like the coastal mountains, nor like the
Cascades farther east, where a single volcano dominates the
countryside within a radius of fifty or more miles. Here, no one
mountain stands head and shoulders above everything else. Even
Mount Olympus has three tops (the highest is West Peak: 7,965
feet), and nearby, two other peaks are almost as high. Within a
thirty-five-mile circle lie hundreds of scraggy peaks rising over
five thousand feet above tidewater, which in some places is only
twenty miles away. Most of these crags are connected by saw-
toothed ridges covered by eternal snow—ridges whose names
reflect the scabrous nature of the land: Hurricane Ridge, Rugged
Ridge, and The Needles. Fifty or so glaciers are relentlessly grinding away at the shales and sandstones that were thrust up from

the ocean floor thirty million years ago. Dozens of steep-sided canyons pierce this land of splendid confusion, many of which rise hardly more than a few hundred feet above sea level, even as their headwaters are trickling from the tongues of glaciers a few thousand yards away. Place names suggest that this is an intriguing place: Dosewallops, Queets, Lilliwalup, Chetwoot, Ducabush, and Humptulips. Some spots seem inviting: Honeymoon Meadows, Heart o' the Hills, Enchanted Valley, and Lingerlonger Park; yet others suggest asperity: Obstruction Mountain, Giant's Graveyard, Storm King, and Destruction Island. We'll poke into some of the canyons and climb a couple of ridges on the northern and western sides of the park (the most interesting) to discover a few of the secrets that remained hidden here for so many years. Olympic National Park, however, is really three parks in one: the alpine mountains, the rain forest, and the rocky coast. We'll explore the rainy part first.

Almost immediately you find yourself in hilly country with some of the most lush forests imaginable. Conifers hover over the highway, blocking out most of the sky. Much of the western foothills of the Olympics are in private hands, and the land is being logged at a furious pace. While driving less than two miles, I counted ten log trucks coming the other way. The crop is primarily Douglas fir, but you pass several small mills tucked into clearings, where mom-and-pop operations are cutting bolts of red cedar into shingles and shakes.

The western red cedar is a magnificent tree, almost as big as a redwood, with a similar thick, stringy, fibrous bark. It provided both the art and sinew of the coastal Indians' life: the trunk was his house, plank, and oceangoing canoe; the limb, his harpoon; the bark, his dress, fishing line, and bowstring. Totems, the first of which we will see shortly, were mostly carved from red cedar. Where I live, the price of cedar shingles seems to have reached astronomical levels of late, and I wondered if that was because the old-growth trees are all gone.

"Not quite," a park ranger told me, "but they will be by 1990, at least on private land. Scavengers are going out into the woods with bulldozers, digging up old cedar logs that were left over from earlier logging. Back then the common wisdom was that the tree wasn't worth hauling out to a mill. Now we call it 'China wood' because much of it is sold in the Orient."

"What about reforestation?" I inquired.

"Nobody's planting cedar," he said. "You can get a marketable Doug fir in sixty years; it takes two hundred to grow a cedar. Who's going to wait that long?"

"Humptulips" is said to be an Indian word for "hard to

pole." I can only speculate what that might mean. A ghost town now, it was once the logging outlet for the famous "21-9" stand of Douglas fir (township 21, range 9), the greatest forest in the Northwest and perhaps in the world. Timber stood so dense that trees had to be felled in the same direction for lack of space. Locals muse about a garrulous foreman who boasted in a Humptulips saloon:

> Give me enough snoose and Swedes and I'll log 21-9 like it was a hayfield, dump the toothpicks into the south fork and ride 'em to tidewater like they was rocking horses.

QUINAULT LAKE • (Two-hour side loop)

Quinault has a more inland-mountain feel than any lake we have visited so far, with dense forests marching right down to the shore. A thirty-mile road, gravel in spots, goes along the south shore of the five-mile-long lake, ducks into a narrowing canyon, crosses a river, and returns to Highway 101 via the north shore. A stub road ends at the north fork trailhead, where in 1890 the so-called Press Party came stumbling out of the mountains, having completed the first crossing of the central Olympics. (See A Hardly "Pressing" Expedition, below). It's a fifteen-mile hike from the trailhead to **Low Divide,** one of the prettiest backcoun-

---

A HARDLY "PRESSING" EXPEDITION

The trek was called "the Press Exploring Expedition," but the six adventurers who set out on December 8, 1889, to attempt the first crossing of the Olympic Mountains hardly seemed in a hurry. William E. Bailey, proprietor of the Seattle *Press,* had agreed to pay all expenses in exchange for exclusive rights to their story. He thought it would help sell newspapers. James Christe, a thirty-nine-year-old mountain man who headed the group, promised, along with Charles Barnes, to keep extensive diaries, take photographs, make topographical surveys, and bring back samples of the riches that surely were to be found in the unexplored interior. Four other men, ranging in age from twenty-two to thirty-five (the eldest turned back), rounded out the party of adventurers. They boarded a steamer in Seattle taking 1,500 pounds of dunnage, including tents, axes, saws, pots and pans of all kinds, plenty of ammunition, 250 pounds of flour, and 50 pounds of fireworks. The fireworks they planned to ignite from the top of a mountain so that all of Seattle could see where they were.

Wiser people cautioned against a winter departure, but the *Press* was worried that someone else might beat them to the coup, so off they went, changing steamers at Port Townsend and arriving at Port Angeles on December 10. The plan was to build a thirty-foot boat that they would tow, paddle, or pole up the Elwah River. By Christmas construction was begun, and the craft was launched on the thirtieth. It promptly sank. They worked for ten days recaulking *Gertie* and finally got started upriver. Two weeks later found them three miles into the foothills, convinced that the boat wasn't such a good idea. So they spent some more time, building sleds to which they gave fanciful names: Carryall, Go Devil, and Buggy. But sleds didn't work, either; the snow was too soft. The two mules Christe had procured were the most help, but progress is slow when you sink up to your waist in mushy, wet snow. By the middle of February they were still holed up in an abandoned settler's cabin waiting out a storm. The "Press Party" had, to be sure, encountered miserable weather, the worst in many years, but by the third of April, nearly four months into the trek, they were still only twelve airline miles from civilization (that proved fortuitous because it is unlikely they could have survived the fierce winter storms that were then battering the much higher interior).

By mid-April the party had sloshed its way up to a point where the Elwah branched. Two weeks later, as they struggled over a five-thousand-foot pass (the snow was twenty-five feet deep), they realized that they should have gone the other way. By this time the mules had given out, and the fireworks, among other things, no longer seemed like a priority item. Still, they didn't seem to be in too big a hurry. When, during a long clear spell, the trekkers struggled over present-day Low Divide (elevation 3,662 feet), they shot a couple of bear and promptly made camp for four days while they feasted (one member claimed he ate fifteen pounds of bear fat in one day). In fairness, however, it should be pointed out that Christe and Barnes were, during the months of March and April, busily climbing numerous peaks and making their maps.

May 15 found the fivesome in the bottoms of the Quinault River valley, fifty-odd miles from where they had started. Three days later they encountered a white trapper who had engaged a couple of Indians to take him upstream in a canoe. Christe wanted to build a raft. The Indians showed him a trail. Two miles downstream the raft they built hit a pile of drift snags and tossed them all into the water. Only one parcel was recovered, fortunately the one that contained the photographs and the expedition's logs. The men in the canoe returned and ferried the now threadbare and provisionless party down the Quinault River to the ocean, where they hired a stage to take them to Aberdeen.

The adventure ended on May 21, 1890, and the Seattle *Press* had its story. But no fireworks.

try spots in the park. There are a number of camping sites along the way. Another thirteen-mile trail, which leaves from Graves Creek at the end of another stub road, heads up the east fork of the Quinault River to **Enchanted Valley.** Backcountry permits are required for overnight stays in the national park.

But you don't have to bivouac to enjoy the splendors of this parkland. Quite the contrary, you can enjoy the graciousness of a coast-of-Maine–style hotel, complete with a lobby full of wicker chairs, writing desks, and sofas. Today, Lake Quinault Lodge presents the very same charm that induced Franklin D. Roosevelt to stay here in 1937. Although there are a couple of outbuildings with rooms that have fireplaces and balconies, the majority of the guests stay in the main lodge, where many of the rooms are without private bath. There is no TV, no radio, and no phones. Guests mingle in the great lobby, where beams and window trim are stenciled with a bold Indian motif. A fire, built every night, summer and winter, provides a cozy atmosphere. On long summer evenings, those in the dining room watch canoers paddling on a lake owned by a tribe of Indians. Waitresses scurry around bringing food and drink to guests on the porch, which overlooks a huge lawn. The adjacent chimney is graced with a totem, designed like a thermometer but with a gauge that displays the cumulative rainfall since the first of the year. It's calibrated in feet, not inches. The number at the top is seventeen. The saloon has a north woods feel, with glass-eyed elk, moose, mountain lion, and bear staring down at glassy-eyed patrons. Only the indoor pool and sauna add a modern feel to the hotel. Yet all the while, you are surrounded by a forest as magnificent as anyplace in the world.

No motors are allowed on the lake, but you can rent a pedal-powered skiff or a Hobie Cat sailboat. The Quinault tribe controls the rights to the fishing, which is said to be good most of the year. Though no state license is required, you have to purchase a tribal permit, which is available at the Quinault Mercantile Company, a nearby old-time general store, a lovely building with a gas pump by the front porch, oiled-wood floors, and a tin sign on the wall advertising Hires Root Beer. One of the white-painted, wood-mullioned windows has the name "Kodak" painted in gold leaf.

An easy four-mile-loop trail leads from the hotel directly into the **Quinault Rain Forest,** meanders along a ridge, and then returns by way of the lakeshore. A portion of the trail is built over the swampy home of a stand of old-growth red cedar. These are one of the few Pacific trees that seem to prosper in poorly drained soil. Many, however, have died and now stand as stark monuments to a tree that may soon disappear from this earth.

FOOD AND LODGING Quinault Lake, Washington 98575

✔✔✔ **Lake Quinault Lodge**   54-room resort, restaurant, bar, pool. P.O. Box 7. (503) 288-2571.

✔✔ **Rain Forest Resort Village**   38-room motel, cottage complex, restaurant and bar. P.O. Box 40. (503) 288-2535.

✔ **Willaby Campground**   National Forest Service.

OLYMPIC COAST

Highway 101 turns west at Quinault Lake, traversing the northern limits of the reservation. In spots, plantations of western hemlock hug the road, the tops of the drooping trees bowing dutifully to passing motorists. The hemlock never outgrows this absolute refusal to do what all other conifers do, boldly aim for the sky. Soon you are presented with the second of the Olympic Park's charms, the rugged coast.

The seashore along here is very pretty, with sixty-foot forested cliffs guarding the mainland. Rocky coves support lovely tide pools, home to periwinkles, hermit crabs, limpets, starfish, and the curious sea anemone, an animal that sometimes lives a thousand years. The smelt were running the day I walked down to Ruby Beach. "You can always tell," a fisherman told me. "If there are seals and sea gulls, you can bet there are smelt."

Indeed, the beach was crowded with gulls, and half a dozen satiated seals were cavorting offshore. I watched as one fellow with a flat-sided dip net waded out into the surf and scooped up fish so easily that he soon had two buckets full of wriggling, four-inch-long, silvery-sided delicacies. "I come here every year," he said. "The limit is forty pounds a day, so I spend a few days and then take a load back to my freezer in Seattle."

A park ranger told me, "The smelt sometimes get so thick in the rivers you can walk across on their backs, and the cormorants get so stuffed they can't fly."

The highway, however, hides behind a berm, so to capture the magic you have to walk down one of the several short trails that lead to the beach. The large, mesalike offshore island, looking like a battleship with a lighthouse as its conning tower, was a well-known spot in the early days. Sea captains liked to anchor in its lee while they made repairs to their ships or went ashore for game and fresh water. Bodega y Quadra in the schooner *Sonora* landed seven men in 1775. They were promptly massacred by the Hoh. He named the island Ile de Delores (Island of Sorrows).

Twelve years later Captain Barkley in *Imperial Eagle* sent six ashore on a similar mission. They suffered the same fate, prompting Barkley to call it Destruction Island, the name it bears today.

Only one resort graces this remote beach, but it is another grand old beauty. Kalaloch Lodge (pronounced "Claylock") is a bit more modest than Quinault Lodge; it includes a main building with a dozen upstairs rooms and a bar and restaurant that look out onto a tiny, wave-swept cove. Cabins and little log cottages, most of which have fireplaces and kitchens, line a nearby bluff. This is a great spot to watch for whales.

FOOD AND LODGING

✔✔ **Kalaloch Lodge**   42 units, restaurant, coffee shop, and bar. P.O. Box 1100, Forks, Washington 98331. (503) 962-2271.

✔ **Kalaloch Campground**   National Park Service. 179 sites.

HOH RAIN FOREST • (Three-hour side trip)

The weather patterns are responsible for much of the uniqueness of the Olympic Peninsula. The storms, of course, come off the Pacific, and as they move inland the clouds are pushed upward by the steeply rising peaks. As the clouds get higher, they get colder and can no longer hold their moisture. The result is that along the coast the rainfall is similar to what we have seen in Oregon, about sixty inches, but twenty-five miles inland (along a narrow but paved road) the annual rainfall can soar to fifteen feet and more. The Hoh Rain Forest is the wettest spot in North America with a seasonal *average* of 145 inches. One December it rained forty-two inches, and there has never been a month without at least a trace. "Bring scuba gear if you want to see this place in the winter," chortled ranger Ed Whitaker. Yet forty miles farther west, Sequim, lying in the shadow of the Bailey Range and Hurricane Ridge, is one of the driest towns in the Pacific Northwest. They get seventeen inches a year; farmers irrigate their fields.

The Hoh is the premier temperate rain forest in the United States, as inspiring a place as the redwood groves of northern California. The latitude here is north of the state of Maine, yet the growing season is twice as long, thanks to the warming trend of the Japanese current. Sitka spruce dominates the forest, but it is the big leaf maple that is the signature tree of the Hoh: its arching limbs form the prettiest framework to support the mosses, and it is the mosses that give the place such a mellow feel. A sign reads:

There are seventy kinds of epiphytes in the rain forest including Spanish moss, club moss, spike moss, lichen and liverworts. They cling to limbs up to a hundred feet above the ground and grow to a thickness of six inches and more. Epiphytes get their food from the air and therefore have a symbiotic relationship with their host tree.

Ferns and sorrel keep seeds from reaching the ground, so you often see places where young trees have germinated on so-called nurse trees. I saw one spruce whose nine-inch-diameter trunk started four feet above the ground. The spidery roots, which had worked their way down to the ground alongside a rotted-away stump, spread out like the legs on a Chippendale table.

The National Park Service operates an extensive interpretive center here with a naturalist on staff who gives talks and answers questions. The most popular trail leads through the appropriately named "Hall of Mosses." I toured the forest on a bright sunny day that somehow seemed inappropriate, but I came away with some slides I shall treasure.

The Hoh Rain Forest lies alongside the banks of one of the only glacier-fed streams we'll visit on this trip. The snow melt ensures a good summer flow, so the river has year-round fishing, but on hot days the catch is poor because rapid-melting ice loads the river with what those who know about such things call "glacial flour." It turns the water milky white. Roosevelt elk frequent this area, savoring the tiny needles of the hemlock and the grasses in the meadows. Their principal predator is the cougar, though rangers say more elk die from malnutrition than any other cause. Coyotes and bears occasionally attack calves. Two animals are endemic to this area and nowhere else, the Olympic short-tailed weasel and the Olympic marmot. The latter is unique in that the male mates with two females who bear young in alternate years. River otter are common inhabitants of the Hoh. Birds include the ruffed grouse, the pileated wood-pecker, the great blue heron, and the bald eagle.

MOUNT OLYMPUS • (Two- or three-day trek)

This is the principal trailhead for those making an assault on Mount Olympus twenty miles farther up the canyon. Ranger Claire McCabe told me that those skilled in the use of crampons and ice axes can do it without a guide, but she advised having one since climbing on a glacier can be tricky, even in the best weather. "It's one big ice cube up there," commented another ranger. "I'm an old lady when it comes to climbing, and maybe that's why I've lived so long. Even in summer I wear wool pants. If I fall into a cravass, I want something to keep me warm."

And the weather can change in a trice, as I learned one sad spring day on Oregon's Mt. Hood when I watched one hundred mountain rescue guides search for the bodies of a dozen teenagers who had gotten lost in a whiteout.

Forks • Population: 3,060

Forks is the only real town on the western side of the Olympics, serving a huge but sparsely populated trading area. Eleven thousand people live in the area. Most workers are employed in the woods and the mills or cater to tourists and fishermen. Forks has a lumber camp feel with a four-block shopping street. I suspect a couple of saloons do a booming business on Saturday night. **Forks Timber Museum** has exhibits featuring logging equipment and pioneer and Indian artifacts; the National Park Service has an information center a few miles north of town. The steelhead fishing here in November and December is said to be the best in the world.

FOOD AND LODGING   Forks, Washington 98331

✔✔ **Calawah Estates Motel**   32-unit motel overlooking the river.

✔✔ **Forks Motel**   58-unit downtown motel. P.O. Box 510. (503) 374-6243.

✔ **Hoh Campground**   National Park Service. 95 sites.

✔ **Bogachiel State Park Campground**   41 sites.

●● **Smokehouse Restaurant**   Eatery and bar. (503) 374-6258.

WASHINGTON'S WILDERNESS COAST • (Two-hour or six-day side trip)

The state of Washington got cheated out of much of its Pacific shoreline. Vancouver Island pushes south, taking a fifty-mile chunk out of the northern coast, and on the south, the Columbia makes a big jog northward doing the same. Since no roads at all traverse sixty-five miles of the shoreline and an additional ten are reservation lands, closed to the public, less than one hundred highway miles remains, and much of that is through rather uninteresting brush-covered duneland. So, unlike in California and Oregon, a coastal drive is not part of one's itinerary.

To many this is a blessing, because the lack of roads presents an opportunity to see one of the only true wilderness beaches left in the United States outside of Alaska. This and two other spots on our journey, California's "Lost Coast" and Canada's "West Coast Trail," are the only places where the curious traveler can find an extensive shoreline totally devoid of condos, tennis courts, golf courses, and muscle beaches. Virtually all of the continental edge between the mouth of the Hoh River (where Highway 101 turns inland) and the entrance to Juan de Fuca Strait is public land, administered by the National Park Service, and it looks much the same as it did two hundred years ago when the first Europeans set eyes on this rockbound shore. About six days are required to walk this coastline, but you can see a bit of it in a matter of hours by taking the fifteen-mile paved road to the Indian village at La Push.

La Push • Population: 450

The town itself isn't much, a grocery store, tribal hall, Coast Guard station, a small marina, some house trailers, and a few dozen homes. The modest motel is a Quileute tribal enterprise. There is no restaurant or bar. When I asked the lady at the front desk what people do when they come here, she replied: "Just get away from it all."

Park ranger Ed Whitaker was a bit more sarcastic. "In winter they come to see if they can get killed by the beach logs." This coast is literally covered with the bones of the rain forest—great logs, almost as big around as a man is tall and fifty or more feet long, are snatched up by a flood, flung out to sea, and set adrift to find their way onto a leeward shore. Storms toss them about like kitchen matches floating in a rain-swollen gutter.

The National Park Service has constructed short trails leading to a couple of very nice beaches south of La Push, and you can drive to Rialto Beach on the north side of the Quileute River. There's a lovely campground nearby. Rangers give talks on such subjects as Indian lore, intertidal life, botany, geology, and a bit about the birds and mammals who live in these parts.

FOOD AND LODGING   La Push, Washington 98350

✔ **Ocean Park Resort**   39-unit motel-cabin complex. Bring your own food. P.O. Box 67. (503) 347-5267.

✔ **Mora Campground**   National Park Service. 94 sites.

The **Coastal Trail,** much of which runs along the sand, goes from Lake Ozette in the north to a dirt road leading to a place called Oil City (no oil, no city). The La Push–Rialto Beach area marks the halfway point for this forty-mile walk. Numerous headlands that have to be scaled make the walking slow. The trail guide, issued by the National Park Service, is full of cautions:

- Sand Point: Bear problems—hang food high—boil drinking water.
- Yellow Banks: Round at low tide, use rock tunnel at medium tide.
- Cape Johnson: Lots of boulder hopping.
- Goodman Creek: Danger—can't ford at mouth—use overland trail.

MAKAH INDIAN RESERVATION • (All-day side trip)

A few miles north of Forks, Highway 101 begins its bend inland, slicing through dense forestland. So to continue our coastal exploration, you once again make a side trip. Turn left at the hamlet of Sappho and head north on Highway 112. You'll be well rewarded for your time.

Clallam Bay/Sekiu • Population: 475

Voilà! We have finally come about as far north as is possible on the Washington coast, for a little park in the town of Clallam Bay looks out on Juan de Fuca Strait, the legendary Strait of Anian, or Northwest Passage. The mountains on the far shore belong to Canada. Clallam Bay and Sekiu snuggle up to a modest bay about twenty miles inland from the ocean. Once again you are in fisherman's country; RV resorts line the shore, and boat trailers are parked everywhere. Outfitters offer a hundred small boats to rent, and road signs tell whom to call for such necessities as diesel engine and outboard motor repair and hull refiberglassing. This is Seattle's northern window on the sea, the most convenient ocean-fishing port for the bustling cities of Puget Sound. Most people stay in Sekiu, where half a dozen modest motels surround the marina.

FOOD AND LODGING   Sekiu, Washington 98381

✔✔ **The Cove Resort**   12-room motel, restaurant and bar. P.O. Box 189. (503) 963-2321.

✔✔ **Van Riper's Resort**   12-room motel. P.O. Box 246. (503) 963-2334.

Neah Bay • Population: 600

The little country road heading out toward the ocean is slow going but about as pretty as any we have driven on this trip, in places hugging the more or less calm waters of the strait. The pavement ends at Neah Bay, home of the Makah tribe and another sportfishing port. Townsfolk brag that a fellow caught a 241-pound halibut that, according to reports, "looked like a bloated hypopotamus." At the urging of the archbishop of Mexico, Bodega y Quadra sent Lieutenant Fidalgo here in 1792 to establish a colony to be called Bahía Nuñez Gosna. Nothing much came of the venture, and since the place was so isolated, the Makah ("People of the Cape") who lived here were left pretty much alone. That turned out to be a blessing because today Neah Bay is the best place in the United States to get a sense of the life and lore of the north coast tribes. The **Makah Museum and Cultural Center** is, to put it simply, a wonderful place to spend an afternoon.

The Makah have lived here for twenty-five thousand years, we now know, thanks to a Pompei-like disaster that occurred five hundred years ago. In 1970 archaeologists from Washington State University discovered an ancient city (located at an off-limits site fifteen miles south of here near Lake Ozette) that had been entombed by a mud slide. The relics they uncovered in ten years of digging are now sensitively displayed in this new, two-million-dollar museum. Whaling and sealing and plant-gathering exhibits show how they found food. Stone technology, bone working, woodworking, basket making, weaving, and spinning arts are explained, and you get a sense of the spiritual life from displays of toys, miniatures, dolls, and symbolic works of art. Oceangoing canoes are lavishly decorated, totems guard a long house from evil spirits. The Makah culture, I learned, is quite different from that of the tribes we have seen farther south, being similar to the Nootkas on Vancouver Island and in southern Alaska. "It's a pity this lovely place is so far from civilization," I overheard a lady say to a tribal representative. "Well, we would have liked to build it out on Highway 101," he replied, "but they took that land away from us a hundred years ago, and the tribal council felt strongly that our museum should be on our ground." The exhibits here suggest that perhaps it is Seattle that is so far from "civilization."

FOOD AND LODGING   Neah Bay, Washington 98357

✔ **Thunderbird Resort**   29-unit motel. (503) 645-2450.

CAPE FLATTERY

Neah Bay is not quite at the end of the continental United States, but almost. A gravel road continues on to the most northern Pacific strand, a beauty called She-bear Beach, part of the indentation of Makah Bay. Almost no one comes here, so it is easy to reflect on things. It's a sobering thought, but you're looking out at the longest stretch of unbroken water in the world. In 1926 twelve skeletons were found aboard the drifting *Ryo Yei Maru*, a junk whose engines had failed eleven months previously in a gale seven hundred miles off the coast of Japan.

Another gravel road goes out to Cape Flattery, the western-most place you can drive to in this country. Vancouver named the cape when he sailed by on March 7, 1778. A half-mile trail leads out through a damp spruce forest to the cape itself, a vertical-sided promontory one hundred feet above the water. The fog came and went the day I was there; things seemed downright spooky. A nearby island appeared for an instant and then disappeared into the mist. Maybe de Fuca was right, I thought (see Beware of Greeks Telling Stories, page 226), for he described a headland at the mouth of his strait "with an exceeding high Pinacle, or spired Rocke, like a piller." Was this his "spired Rocke"? A lot of people think so.

Curiously, the sea didn't crash against this stony shore; the water was too deep. Instead, waves moved in and out of coves and caves in a heaving manner with a moaning sound, rising and falling like a cold witch's bosom. Indicative, perhaps, of the ruggedness of this coast is the fact that the next place we will visit that actually faces out on the Pacific is only fifty miles farther north, but it takes a minimum of two days to drive there.

CRESCENT LAKE

We return to Highway 101, which is now heading almost due east. The road climbs a little hill, and suddenly you find yourself looking out over a mountain tarn as pretty as Switzerland's Lake of Lucerne or Lake Windermere in northern England. Eight-mile-long Crescent Lake is narrow and deep, with water as clear as Lake Tahoe's. Precipitous, deeply forested mountains soar up from its rocky banks. The shore would be as built up as around Lake George in upstate New York if there weren't so many other beautiful places nearby, so the place has a nice sense of solitude.

Lake Crescent Lodge, located off the highway on a little peninsula, is another relic from a past age. Built in 1916, the two-story, rather modest-looking main building nestles in a lakeside forest with an undercover of bright green lawn. The rustic lobby has a handsome stone fireplace, graced by the immense head and rack of a Roosevelt elk. The old veranda overlooking the lake has been enclosed with wood-mullioned glass windows and now serves as the dining room. A cozy bar is nearby. The upstairs guest rooms are what you would expect for a resort built at this time. Not one room has private facilities. Nearby are the fancier Roosevelt fireplace-cottages, built at the time the president (F.D.R.) made his swing through this part of the world. Modern, motellike units are also available.

A lovely three-quarter-mile path leads to the ninety-foot-high **Marymere Falls,** a filmy ribbon of water that comes tumbling down from a wooded perch. A four-mile, rather strenuous trail leads to the 4,500-foot summit of **Mt. Storm King.** Across the lake, on the north shore, is the more modest Log Cabin Resort.

Several steep-sided canyons poke into the backcountry, some penetrating into the heart of the Olympic Mountains. A famous old spa, Sol Duc Hot Springs, was closed when I made this survey, with reopening plans uncertain, so I opted for a more primitive hot-springs experience. A paved road goes up the steeply sided Elwha River, following the route of Press Expedition for a bit before climbing up a side canyon to a small parking lot. The road used to go two miles farther, but it washed out, so now you have to walk to **Olympic Hot Springs.** There are perhaps a dozen places where mineral-laden water, almost too hot to touch, comes bubbling out of the mountain. Over the years, hikers and campers have dug holes, piled up rocks, and otherwise rerouted the water into steaming bathing pools lying beneath towering firs. Several have enough privacy so that whoever gets there first sets the rules on whether or not bathing attire is required.

BEWARE OF GREEKS TELLING STORIES

Michael Lok, an English merchant, had for almost a score of years suffered from a string of bad luck. Queen Elizabeth I once granted him a charter for a firm called the Company of Cathay, which was to finance explorer Martin Frobisher's search for gold in the New World and, in the process, sail through the sea passage that led around North America to the "Great Spanish Ocean." Frobisher grubbed for riches, found no passage to China, and brought back iron pyrite, no gold. The Cathay Company was no more. Lok had plenty of time while languishing in debtors prison to ponder his misfortune and to dream about the legendary Strait of Anian—the Northwest Passage. Surely it must be there; no less a man than Francis Drake had confirmed its probability. Now, in

1596, he felt his luck was turning. While seated in a cafe in Venice, he chanced upon a Greek navigator by the name of Apostolos Valerianos, who had quite a story to tell.

Valerianos said that four years earlier he had sailed the "Spanish Ocean" and had found, between the latitudes of 47 and 48 degrees, a strait where

> I saw some people on Land, clad in Beasts skins; and that the Land is very fruitful, and rich of gold, Silver, Pearle, and other things, like Nova Spain.

Not wanting to displease his employer, the viceroy of Mexico, this fanciful man had changed his name to Juan de Fuca and had, until then, kept his find secret. Lok, gullible as always, was ecstatic. Hurrying back to England, he begged the queen to finance another expedition, but his plea went for naught, due partly to the advice of a man she trusted, Walter Raleigh. The Greek, it turned out, had quite possibly never sailed west of the Atlantic. But somehow his boast stayed alive, and de Fuca's strait found its way into a book called *Purchas His Pilgrimes, Containing a History of the World in Sea Voyages and Lande Travells by Englishmen and Others.*

Nearly two hundred years later a skeptical Captain James Cook wrote in his journal:

> It is in the very latitude we were now in where geographers have placed the pretended Strait of Juan de Fuca, but we saw nothing like it, nor is there the least probability that iver any such thing exhisted.

In 1778 Cook cast anchor in a bay that he named after an officer on one of his ships, a Mister Bligh (Bligh, and another member of the expedition, George Vancouver, were to make their own marks in the history books some years later). But it was the seventeen-year-old bride of Captain Charles Barclay who in 1787 gave this strait its name because, as she reasoned, it was at the right place and closely matched what de Fuca had to say. So what became the gateway to the Occident, but never the Strait of Anian, got a Spanish name, thanks to a teenager who read books, a Greek with a very large imagination, and an Englishman who couldn't tell fact from fancy.

FOOD AND LODGING

✔✔✔ **Lake Crescent Lodge**   49 rooms, cabins, and motel units. Restaurant, bar, boat rental. P.O. Box 11, Port Angeles, Washington 98362. (503) 928-3211.

✔✔ **Log Cabin Resort** 40 cabins and motel units, restaurant, bar. 6540 East Beach Road, Port Angeles, Washington 98362. (503) 928-3325.

✔ **Park Service Campgrounds** Altaire, 29 sites; Elwha, 41 sites; Fairholm, 87 sites; Heart o' the Hills, 105 sites.

HURRICANE RIDGE PARK ACCESS • (Two-hour side trip)

Remarkably, barely eighteen miles from tidewater at Port Angeles, the countryside has much the same character and feel as at Kline Scheidegg in Switzerland's Bernese Oberland. The stunted evergreens and grassy alps (contrary to popular belief, an alp is a sloping pasture, not a rocky peak), the crisp clear air and a horizon studded with scraggy, glacier-covered peaks, make a sharp contrast to the humid rain forests less than twenty miles (as the eagle flies) away. Whereas the rain forest has a personal, intimate feel, up here the sense of expanse is overwhelming. Fifteen-mile-long Hurricane Ridge Road ends at a large day lodge that doubles as a warming hut for skiers in the winter. Gentle trails lead out onto the meadows and up toward lingering snowbanks. Atop one hill you have a 360-degree view, with the craggy Barnes Range on the west, Mt. Olympus on the south, the volcano Mt. Baker on the east, and the brooding hulk of Vancouver Island lurking above the expanse of Juan de Fuca Strait to the north.

Even on an overcast day the drive is worthwhile, simply because you pass through so many life zones as you climb a mile into the sky. Almost immediately upon leaving the city limits of Port Angeles (a city we'll visit in the next chapter), you find yourself in a lowland forest where Sitka spruce has given way to western hemlock, grand fir, and a few red cedar. Flowering plants include Oregon grape, salmonberry, salal, vine maple, buttercup, trillium, and wild strawberries. Within a mile or two you climb over 1,500 feet and enter the montane forest (also called the Canadian zone), where silver fir is a prominent species. Lupine and the brushlike bear grass paint the understory a luscious blue, white, and green. At four thousand feet you pass into the Hudsonian or subalpine zone, where the trees become smaller and are spaced farther apart. Mountain hemlock and silver fir compete with Alaska cedar and alpine spruce for the scarce resources. Snow forces branches down on the ground, where they sometimes take root. When the parent tree dies, the offspring surround the stump in a cluster called a timber atoll. At higher elevations some stub trees, known as "krummholzes," are thought to be a thousand years old yet are only three to four feet high. Deer, chipmunks, and mountain goats haunt this land after the snow re-treats to higher elevations (see The Trouble with Those Goats Is They Have Too Many Kids!, below). Tiny flowers poke their heads up above small stones. You don't quite get to timberline on this road, but you do see where it occurs on nearby mountains.

I had the good fortune to be here on a sparkling clear day in late June, and though I admit to a partiality to high altitudes—the air doesn't weigh so much—my conclusion is, given the right weather, this is the grandest spot on our entire trek.

THE TROUBLE WITH THOSE GOATS IS THEY HAVE TOO MANY KIDS!

Crotchety old James J. Hill was so enamored with them, he used a likeness of a nanny for his company logo. For a century, boxcars rumbled over the nation's rails with a silhouette of the stately mountain goat encircled by the words "Great Northern Railway." Today's outdoorsmen and tourists love them, too; the Mona Lisa set of their mouth, their whimsical beard, and the pointy, banana-size prongs that seem too small to be real horns make them a pleasing sight on any backcountry trip.

Back in the late nineteenth century hunters found they made a fine game animal, and that's how the problem got started. The goats were brought here from the Rocky Mountains to serve as targets. It turned out, however, that goat meat proved to be less tasty than elk or deer, so the hunters decided to opt for a better meal. The goats liked that fine. And furthermore, they found their adopted home a delightful place to live. The cool damp forests of the Olympic Peninsula nurtured a gourmet diet that the goats couldn't resist; mosses and lichens tasted better than aspen and hemlock. They grew fat, fell in love, and made babies—so many that today more than 1,200 goats live in the park. They eat the same food as the endangered Olympic marmot, causing rangers to fear for the little rodent's continued existence. Marmots are fun to look at, too. The goats have another bad habit: they like to roll in the dirt to rid themselves of vermin and insects, and the billies, during rutting season, make wallowing part of their nuptial dance. As a result there is now so much soil erosion from goat wallows that the streams, and the trout and salmon that live in them, are becoming threatened.

The National Park Service knew just what to do: they would study the problem. They experimented with capturing the goats by means of nets dropped from helicopters; they tried herding them into pens and shooting them from the air with tranquilizing darts. A hunting season was proposed. "We may lose half a dozen hunt-ers," a cynical park ranger told me, "but at least we'll rid the park of a nuisance." But hunting is not allowed in any national park. Yet every other scheme cost too much money. So they decided to study the problem some more. That's where things stand right now. Everybody knows there are too many goats. But nobody has any idea what to do about it.

· 15 ·

SEATTLE'S PLAYGROUND

Lt. Peter Puget's Sound

The young midshipman apparently never saw the opening to the most important harbor on the Pacific Northwest Coast when he was here in 1788. Neither did anyone else on HMS *Discovery*, including his boss, Captain James Cook. But now, fourteen years later, not only did George Vancouver know that there was an intriguing waterway here, but he felt that it was unjustly called the Strait of Juan de Fuca (see Beware of Greeks Telling Stories, page 226). This time he was determined not to miss a thing, and furthermore, he would see that other landmarks got proper English names. Captain Vancouver was in a new *Discovery*, a 340-ton, copper-sheathed sloop; his mission was to make peace with the Spaniards and to determine once and for all if there really was a Northwest Passage.

Vancouver was not of the nobility like most sea captains of that day, but he was a superb navigator. Cautiously working his way along the south shore of the Strait of Juan de Fuca, he sailed into a fjordlike bay, which he named after his ship. Then, after rounding a point, he dropped anchor in a harbor that he named for the Marquis of Townshend (nobody seems to know why the "h" was dropped from the modern name). From there he sent out crews in longboats to have a look around. They brought back hand-drawn charts to which the captain, exercising the pre-rogatives that eighteenth-century explorers felt was their due, affixed his chosen names. Admiralty Inlet, of course, honored his sponsor. Curiously, he named another inlet after the English admiral who, earlier, had been rebuked for failing to relieve

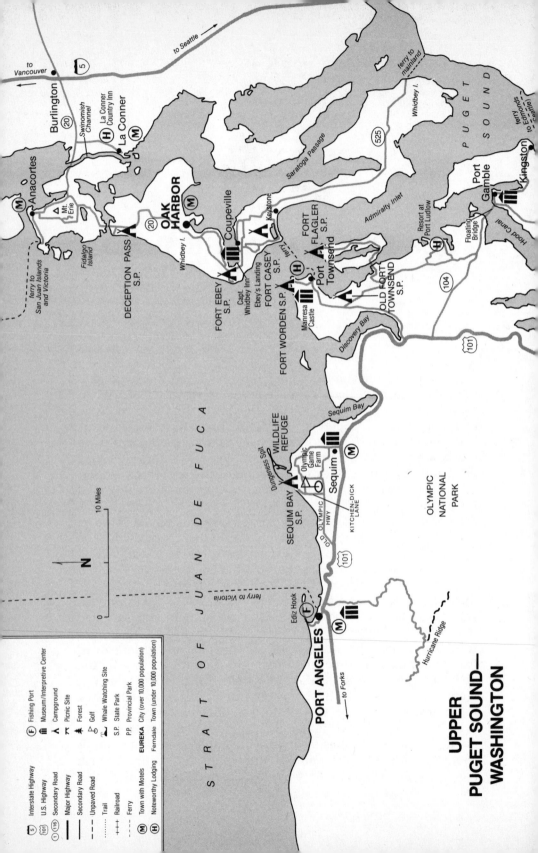

UPPER
PUGET SOUND—
WASHINGTON

Legend

Symbol	Description
5	Interstate Highway
101	U.S. Highway
1 / 11A	Secondary Road
—	Major Highway
—	Secondary Road
- - -	Unpaved Road
····	Trail
+++	Railroad
- - -	Ferry
M	Town with Motels
H	Noteworthy Lodging

Symbol	Description
F	Fishing Port
🏛	Museum/Interpretive Center
A	Campground
⊼	Picnic Site
♣	Forest
⛳	Golf
⚓	Whale Watching Site
S.P.	State Park
P.P.	Provincial Park
EUREKA	City (over 10,000 population)
Ferndale	Town (under 10,000 population)

to Vancouver

to Seattle

Burlington

Anacortes

La Conner Country Inn
La Conner

Swinomish Channel

Mt. Erie

Fidalgo Island

ferry to San Juan Islands and Victoria

DECEPTION PASS S.P.

OAK HARBOR

Whidbey I.

20

Coupeville

Keystone

Capt. Whidbey Inn

Ebey's Landing

FORT EBEY S.P.

FORT CASEY S.P.

FORT WORDEN S.P.

Manresa Castle

Port Townsend

FORT FLAGLER S.P.

OLD FORT TOWNSEND S.P.

Admiralty Inlet

Saratoga Passage

525

Whidbey I.

ferry to mainland

PUGET SOUND

ferry to Edmonds / Seattle

Kingston

Port Gamble

Hood Canal

Resort at Port Ludlow

Floating Bridge

104

101

Discovery Bay

Sequim Bay

WILDLIFE REFUGE

Dungeness Spit

Olympic Game Farm

Sequim

SEQUIM BAY S.P.

OLD OLYMPIC HWY

KITCHEN-DICK LANE

101

OLYMPIC NATIONAL PARK

Hurricane Ridge

Ediz Hook

PORT ANGELES

ferry to Victoria

STRAIT OF JUAN DE FUCA

to Forks

10 Miles

N

0

Cornwall at Yorktown (an honor repeated when his aide, Lieutenant Broughton, named the stunning Mt. Hood near Portland). He called it a channel in his log but appended the word "canal" on his map, and Hood Canal is what it has been called ever since, even though the passageway terminates abruptly sixty miles south of its entrance. But as fate would have it, he named what subsequently became the most important body of water on this coast after a fellow whose only claim to fame was that he was one of Vancouver's junior officers. So while the great city of Vancouver abuts a body of water honored by the name of a king (the Strait of Georgia), Seattle must make do with a sound named after an obscure lieutenant, one Peter Puget.

Seattleites love their sound, however. They have built their vacation houses along its furcated shore, and they have bought boats aplenty so they can poke into its thousand nooks and crannies. Puget Sound is to the Northwest what Chesapeake Bay or Long Island Sound is to the East: a popular vacationland adjacent to a major population center. We'll explore the northern reaches of this playground to get a sense of why so many tourists and vacationers come to enjoy its quiet beauty.

Shortcut Access to Northern Puget Sound

We left Highway 101 near Port Angeles, at the foot of the Olympic National Park's Hurricane Ridge. The highway swings east here and then south, so for the first part of this chapter we will be heading back toward Seattle. If you are coming from there, meet us in Port Townsend. Most people drive north on Interstate 5 to Edmonds and then take the half-hour ferry to Kingston. From there it is less than an hour's drive to Port Townsend. Along the way you pass a couple of interesting spots. **Port Gamble,** like Scotia, California, is a company town, owned lock, stock, and firehouse by the great timber firm Pope and Talbot. The company has restored more than thirty Victorian buildings, including many homes still used by their employees. The old general store with its oiled-wood floors and balustraded mezzanine is quite out of the past, and a nearby museum, owned by Pope and Talbot, houses artifacts from early sawmill days. Both the town square and the hilltop cemetery provide vistas of the sound with Mt. Baker as a backdrop. A few miles past the unique Hood Canal Bridge (it floats on pontoons), a side road leads to Port Ludlow, a huge waterfront condo-resort that includes rooms and apartments, tennis courts, one of the country's finest golf courses, several swimming pools, and a three-hundred-slip marina.

FOOD AND LODGING   Port Ludlow, Washington 98365

✔✔✔ **The Resort at Port Ludlow**   197 rooms and apartments, restaurant, bar, pool. 781 Walker Way. (206) 437-2222.

Port Angeles • Population: 17,300

Only a year before Vancouver's trip, an explorer for the viceroy of Mexico, one Captain Francisco de Eliza, poked around de Fuca's strait and named the cove behind a narrow spit of sand "Port of Our Lady of the Angels." A hundred years later it became a thriving lumber town, and so it has been ever since, with ITT Rayoner's mill on one side of the harbor and Crown Zellerbach's on the other. Port Angeles is by no means a resort city, but it does have a nice downtown area looking out over the port. The original first floor of many of the older buildings is now the basement because in 1914 merchants got tired of coping with the high tides that frequently inundated their stores. They simply raised the level of the streets by sluicing dirt down from a nearby hill. Much of this history is illustrated at the Georgian-style 1914 Clallam County Court House, which is now a museum. City Pier, with its gaggle of shops, juts out into the bay. The adjacent **Feiro Marine Laboratory** has exhibits of special interest to children. A drive out to the end of Ediz Hook provides a terrific view of the strait and a close-up look at ships being loaded with lumber, pulp, and sawdust, many of which have the appendage *Maru* painted on their transom. Port Angeles is a major overnight stopover for tourists heading either to the Olympic National Park or to Victoria, B.C., and so has numerous places to stay.

FOOD AND LODGING   Port Angeles, Washington 98362

✔✔ **Aggie's Inn**   114-unit motel. 602 East Front Street. (206) 457-0471.

✔✔ **Aircrest Motel**   25-unit motel. P.O. Box 755. (206) 452-9255.

✔✔ **Chinook Motel**   53-unit motel. 1414 East 1st Street. (206) 452-2336.

✔✔ **Red Lion Bayshore Inn**   187-unit motel, restaurant, bar, near city pier. 221 North Lincoln. (206) 452-9215.

✔✔ **Uptown Motel**   51-unit motel. 101 East 2nd. (206) 457-9434.

✔✔ **The Tudor Inn** 5-room B&B. 1108 South Oak Street. (206) 452-3138.

✔✔ **Kennedy's** 5-room B&B. 332 East 5th. (206) 457-3628.

✔✔ **Harbour House** 4-room B&B. 139 West 24th. (206) 457-3424.

●●● **C'est Si Bon** Roadside French restaurant and bar. (206) 452-8888.

●● **The Greenery Restaurant** Downtown eatery. (206) 457-4122.

Shortcut Escape to Vancouver Island

M.V. *Coho*, launched in 1959 and owned by the Black Ball Transport Company, makes two 1½-hour crossings to Victoria in the winter and four in the summer. This five-thousand-ton vessel holds one hundred vehicles, a perfect size for most of the year but much too small for the summer traffic. Advance reservations are not accepted, so during the height of the season, the ticket agents advise you to arrive several hours before sailing time. (Many RVers use the parking lot for an overnight campground.) Walk-on passengers are always welcome, so many people park at a nearby lot (modest fee) and tour Victoria sans automobile. The ship has comfortable chairs, a cafeteria and lounge, but, curiously, no duty-free shop. It's a lovely crossing, and the Canadian dock is in Victoria's Inner Harbour, directly across from the Empress Hotel; your arrival is one of spectacular beauty.

Sequim • Population: 3,180

It seems a bit hard to believe, given the nature of the country we have been touring, but guarding the western entrance to Sequim is a grain elevator. Though no longer used for its intended purpose, its very existence tells you that you're not in the rain forest anymore. The first thing a native will let you know about the town is that you pronounce it "skwim." Then he will start talking about how nice the weather is. Sequim is in the Dungeness River Valley that lies in the lee of the Olympics. Rainstorms often don't get this far inland, so Sequim boasts only seventeen inches—less than what falls on San Francisco in a typical year. The result is that the broad, almost flat plains surrounding the town were once productive farms. But now they are fast becoming homesteads; Sequim calls itself the "Retirement Paradise of the Pacific Northwest." The area boasts two other things retirees want, an eighteen-hole golf course and a large marina, this one named after the fellow who owned the land, actor John Wayne.

The drive through town on 101 is somewhat depressing—five or six miles of strip development—so it's best to get off the main road as soon as possible. Turn north on Old Olympic Highway and then left on Kitchen-Dick Lane, which leads to the **Dungeness Spit National Wildlife Refuge.** The locals maintain this is the longest natural sand spit in the country. The Dungeness crab, which *New Yorker* writer Calvin Trillin rhapsodizes about, is named for this stretch of sand. The **Olympic Game Farm,** a sort of drive-through zoo, is located near here. Portions of an unused high school now house a natural history museum, and nearby is the antique-laden **Sequim Museum.**

FOOD AND LODGING   Sequim, Washington 98382

✔✔ **Greathouse Motel**   20 units. P.O. Box 85. (206) 683-7272.

✔✔ **Red Ranch Inn**   31-unit motel. 830 West Washington. (206) 683-4195.

✔✔ **Sequim West Motel**   21 units. 740 West Washington. (206) 683-4144.

✔ **Sequim Bay State Park**   86 campsites.

●● **Three Crabs Restaurant**   Famous eatery on Dungeness Bay. (206) 683-4264.

Port Townsend • Population: 6,067

Sequim may have the weather, but it doesn't have the charm. That attribute belongs to Port Townsend, which bills itself as "Washington's Victorian Seaport." At one time, this lovely village on the northern tip of the Quimper peninsula had dreams of becoming the principal trading center for the entire Pacific Northwest, and early on it looked like those dreams might come true. A hundred years ago things were booming. The naturalist John Muir, a man given to keen observation, wrote:

> This being the port of entry, all vessels stop here, and they make a lively show about the wharves and in the bay. The winds stir the flags of every civilized nation, while the Indians, in their long-beaked canoes, glide about from ship to ship, satisfying their curiosity or trading with the crews. . . . Curious groups of people may often be seen, English, French, Spanish, Portuguese, Scandinavians, Germans, Greeks, Moors, Japanese, and Chinese of every rank and station and style of dress and behavior.

Ten blocks along Water Street were abustle; three- and four-story buildings sprang up, and wealthy men with unbridled enthusiasm began building gingerbread mansions on the bluff above town. But the boom was short-lived. The transcontinental railroads located their terminals at tidewater ports at Tacoma and Seattle, and when gold was discovered on the Yukon in 1898, it was Seattle, not Port Townsend, that became the outfitting center for the rush that followed. Port Townsend, guarding the entrance to Puget Sound, had a couple of army forts, a few sawmills, and little else to keep it alive. But fortunately the old brick buildings and Victorian mansions survived into the 1960s, a time when people looked for different reasons to settle in a particular area. Retirees wanted livability and reasonable prices, both of which Port Townsend could offer.

The renaissance was slow to begin but gained momentum in 1972 when the army turned over Fort Warden to the state for a park and people's interest in things old began to flower. The entire downtown and the mansion-dotted bluffs above were designated a Historical District. Victorian homes were made into B&Bs, and brick warehouses became antique stores, artists' lofts, and trendy shops. Old boatworks were refurbished and expanded. Today Port Townsend is the premier Victorian town on the Northwestern Pacific Coast, far outdistancing such places as California's Mendocino and Ferndale. Twice transplanted Iowan Audrey Lyon told me there are two reasons the place has become so popular: "We're less than two hours from Seattle, so it's close enough for weekend travel, and everybody works hard to see that there is a lot going on all the time. We stage plays and put on jazz concerts and host the famous Wooden Boat Festival in September. Docents even provide Friday afternoon tours through our dozen or so art galleries, and a couple of times a year we take people through the Victorians."

Jefferson County has turned an old brick firehouse into what they call "a jewel of a museum." The 1868 **D.C.H. Rothschild home** has been restored by the state. The most photographed buildings are the red-brick-towered City Hall, the turreted Starrett House, and the Italianesque Manresa Castle. Brick warehouse walls still display painted signs, now fading, advertising Bull Durham Chewing Tobacco, Coca-Cola, and what must have been a grand place, Lewis' Emporium. After-dark entertainment ranges from dining in trendy fern-draped restaurants to dancing to a rock beat in a waterfront cafe. Gone, however, are the infamous dives where innocents, having been treated to laced whiskey, were hustled to a trapdoor, thrown into a waiting skiff, and summarily shanghaied to China.

Like the town of Mendocino, the main reason tourists come here is to enjoy a simple, old-fashioned life-style. Rooms in Victorian homes outnumber those in motels. Port Townsend is the undisputed B&B capital of the West. Some are large, like Manresa Castle, an 1892 monstrosity that for a time served as home for Jesuit priests. The name comes from the place in Spain where St. Ignatius founded the order. Starrett House schedules "mystery weekends"; actors commit a crime, and guests are supposed to figure out who done it. An old downtown brick hotel, once a brothel, has been refurbished with brass bedsteads and period wallpaper. Every turn-of-the-century architectural style seems represented: Queen Anne, Italianate, Eastlake, Georgian, carpenter-gothic, and just plain terrible.

The state of Washington has done a fine job in preserving the character of **Fort Worden**—a prototypical army post chosen for the filming of *An Officer and a Gentleman*. Construction of these coastal defenses began in 1896 (the fort was named after a navy man, the captain of the ironclad *Monitor*), and additions were built during both world wars. Now, the former commanding officer's house is a museum, and the stable has been converted into a performing arts center called **Centrum.** The Seattle Symphony is one of many groups that come here during the summer. The small **Marine Science Center** is located near the handsome lighthouse. Twenty-three former officers' homes have been redone and are now available for vacation rental.

FOOD AND LODGING   Port Townsend, Washington 98368

✔✔✔ **Manresa Castle**   39-room hotel, restaurant and bar. 7th and Sheridan. (206) 385-5750.

✔✔ **Arcadia Country Inn**   5-unit B&B out in the country. 1891 South Jacob Miller Road. (206) 385-5245.

✔✔ **Bishop Victorian**   13 units with kitchenettes. Downtown. 714 Washington Street. (206) 385-6122.

✔✔ **Hastings House Inn**   7-room B&B. 313 Water Street. (206) 385-3553.

✔✔ **Heritage House**   6-room B&B. 305 Pierce Street. (206) 385-6800.

✔✔ **James House**   12-room B&B. 1238 Washington Street. (206) 385-1238.

✔✔ **Lizzies**   7-room B&B. 731 Pierce Street. (206) 385-4168.

✔✔ **Palace Hotel** 14-room refurbished hotel. 1004 Water Street. (206) 385-0773.

✔✔ **Port Townsend Motel** 25 units. 2020 Washington Street. (206) 385-2211.

✔✔ **The Quimper Inn** 6-room B&B. 1306 Franklin Street. (206) 385-1086.

✔✔ **Starrett House Inn** 9-room B&B. 744 Clay Street. (206) 385-3205.

✔✔ **The Tides Inn** 21-unit waterfront motel. 1807 Water Street. (206) 385-0595.

✔✔ **Townsend Place** 6-room B&B. 2037 Haines. (206) 385-4551.

✔✔ **Fort Worden State Park** 23 vacation housing units (1 to 6 bedrooms) in former officers' quarters. 50-site campground. P.O. Box 574. (206) 385-4730.

✔ **Fort Flagler State Park** 116 reservable campsites. Nordland, Washington 98358. (206) 385-1259.

✔ **Old Fort Townsend State Park** 40-site campground.

●●● **Le Restaurant Manresa** Elegant dining. (206) 385-5870.

●● **The Half Shell** Continental cuisine. (206) 385-5954.

●● **Lido Inn** Restaurant and bar. 4-room B&B. 925 Water Street. (206) 385-7111.

● **Lanza's Restorante** Italian cuisine. (206) 385-6221.

WHIDBEY ISLAND • Population: 45,000

We now take leave of the Olympic Peninsula and begin the island-hopping part of our northward trek. The trip across Admiralty Inlet to Keystone takes about thirty minutes. Boats sail every hour and a half or so during the summer, less often in winter. The ride is pleasant, the vessel interesting (see The Ageless Klickitat, page 240), and the service also provides a nice excuse for a day trip out of Port Townsend. Leave your car at home, ride the ferry, and then walk to Fort Casey for a picnic.

Joseph W. Whidbey, master of *Discovery,* was perhaps the first European to set foot on this gentle land, the largest island in the western United States. George Vancouver too liked what he saw:

THE AGELESS KLICKITAT

She started out life in 1929 sailing from San Francisco to Oakland, one of six sister ships built by the Union Shipbuilding Yard for the Southern Pacific Railroad. The *Stockton* was a state-of-the-art ferry, with diesel engines driving electric motor-generator sets. But completion of the Bay and Golden Gate bridges in 1936 made the ferries surplus, so they were put on the market. Puget Sound Navigation bought the fleet for $300,001, one dollar higher than a Brazilian bidder, and put them into cross-sound service. *Stockton* was renamed *Klickitat, Mendocino* became the *Nisqually, Redwood Empire* the *Quinault,* and *Lake Tahoe* the *Illahee.* Two of the six were subsequently retired, but these four dowagers have been doing yeoman duty for over fifty years.

The state of Washington acquired the ferries in 1951 when it purchased the Black Ball fleet of sixteen ships from the failing Puget Sound Navigation Co. They formed the nucleus of the largest ferry system in the United States, now boasting twenty-two ships, the biggest of which carries over two hundred cars and two thousand passengers. *Klickitat* was assigned the international route to Sydney, B.C. The four old-timers have been extensively modified over the years: new diesels in 1957 and 1982 and wider hulls and larger car decks (built out of steel and sporting round rather than square windows) in 1958. Speed was increased by several knots. The old wooden passenger cabins and wheel-houses were modernized in 1982, so the ships hardly look at all like their former selves, but this plucky fleet is expected to last well into the next century.

The surrounding country . . . presented a delightful prospect, consisting chiefly of spacious meadows, elegantly adorned with clumps of trees, amongst which the oak bore a very considerable proportion. . . . In these beautiful pastures, bordering on an expansive sheet of water, the deer were seen playing in great numbers. Nature had here provided the well-stocked park . . . which is so much sought in other countries.

Vancouver's spotting of oak rather than conifers suggests that this country is quite different from what we have been traveling through. Whidbey Island is an almost flat prairie and quite dry.

Timetables list Keystone, though there is really no town at

the ferry landing—just a campground, popular for RVers (who can make day trips on foot to Port Townsend), and another former army post. **Fort Casey,** also a state park, was, like Fort Worden, built to guard the entrance to Puget Sound. Together with Fort Flagler on Marrowstone Island, the three formed what was called "Death's Triangle," a supposedly impregnable defense of Admiralty Inlet. The invention of the airplane signaled their uselessness. Fort Casey is unique among the coastal fortresses we have seen or will visit (Marin Headlands, Forts Stevens and Canby at the mouth of the Columbia, and Fort Rodd Hill near Victoria) because the guns themselves are on display. Two giant ten-inch disappearing rifles, similar to those used here, were discovered in the Philippines and removed to this site. One stands erect in the firing position, the other lowered for reloading. The state operates a small interpretive center in the old lighthouse at Admiralty Head.

In 1978 the National Park Service took an interest in this area, establishing **Ebey's Landing National Historical Reserve.** Though there are no visitors' facilities, a handout brochure describes in detail the historical goings-on in the lovely countryside between Keystone and Coupeville. The site was named for Colonel Isaac N. Ebey, a homesteader who was gunned down by a tribe of Nisquallys in retaliation for the whites' having killed one of their chiefs. Captain Thomas Coupe was out of town at the time, so Ebey had the misfortune of being the biggest white chief *(tyee)* the Indians could find.

Coupeville • Population: 1,000

The little town of Coupeville, which looks out over eastward-facing Penn Cove, is another delightful Victorian spot, tiny when compared with Port Townsend. Before the turn of the century, sea captains came here to retire, and a few of the houses they built still stand. A couple of cafes and some old-fashioned stores and antique shops line the two-block main street, which abuts a rickety pier. Island County operates a small museum here. The town is perfect for a getaway weekend, with a nice new downtown motel and the famous Captain Whidbey Inn, a magnificent funky lodge built in 1907 out of madrona logs. A lovely restaurant looks out over the cove, and some new rooms face a nearby stocked pond. Management rents bicycles, the perfect form of recreation for this gently rolling, bucolic countryside. A controversy is developing over an unlikely subject, however (see Salmon Farms? "Not in My Backyard!," page 242).

FOOD AND LODGING   Coupeville, Washington 98239

✔✔✔ **Captain Whidbey Inn**   33-room country inn, restaurant and bar. Boat and bicycle rentals. 2072 West Captain Whidbey Inn Road. (206) 678-4097.

✔✔ **The Coupeville Inn**   24-unit motel. P.O. Box 370. (206) 678-6668.

✔ **Fort Casey State Park**   35 campsites.

✔ **Fort Ebey State Park**   50 campsites.

Oak Harbor • Population: 12,300

Oak Harbor, by contrast, has a suburban, retirement-center feel, due mainly to the nearby naval air base. The town claims a

---

SALMON FARMS? "NOT IN MY BACKYARD!"

It seemed like the Norwegians were onto a good thing: build floating pens surrounded by nets where salmon could be reared in a climate safe from predators. Entrepreneurs argued that development of an aquaculture industry in Puget Sound would help to offset the $80 million a year we spend on imported pen-raised salmon. Only eighty acres would be required, a pinpoint on the surface of Puget Sound's three million acres. If the nets had been underwater, out of sight like oyster-bed strings, things would no doubt have gone well. But each two-acre pen projected five feet or more above the water, and they had to be located in the most sheltered spots, the very same coves where northwesterners had put their life savings into retirement homes. Many home owners became what land-use planners call "Nobys"—"not in our back-yard."

"A five-acre pen operation produces the excrement of a town of 4,000," *Wall Street Journal* reporter Ken Slocum quoted residents as having complained. "The sea cages present a possible health hazard to humans, choke out sea life below, and may spread disease to wild fish."

John Forster, of Sea Farm of Norway, countered: "We're a clean-water industry, and we'd be the first to suffer if we polluted."

Nevertheless, the Nobys are marshaling their forces and lobbying Olympia. Time will tell whether the salmon served on Seattle's white-tableclothed restaurants will be domestic or imported.

Dutch heritage and, like Sequim and Port Angeles, is a nice place but hardly a tourist spot. There are a number of large motels and one first-class restaurant.

FOOD AND LODGING   Oak Harbor, Washington 98277

✔✔ **The Auld Holland Inn**   28-unit motel. 5681 North Highway 20. (206) 675-2288.

✔✔ **Best Western Harbor Plaza**   80-unit motel. 5691 Highway 20. (206) 679-4567.

✔✔ **Coachman Inn**   70-unit motel. 5563 Highway 20. (206) 675-0727.

✔ **Deception Pass State Park**   250 campsites.

●● **Kasteel Franssen**   Continental restaurant and bar. (206) 675-0724.

DECEPTION PASS STATE PARK

There's hardly a yachtsman on Puget Sound that doesn't have a story to tell about navigating Deception Pass, one of the most treacherous waterways in the country. The channel separates the islands of Whidbey and Fidalgo (Fidalgo is technically an island but, from a maritime standpoint, more a part of the mainland). Whidbey effectively shields forty-mile-long Skagit Bay from Juan de Fuca Strait, so during spring tides an immense amount of water comes pouring through the tiny gap, creating ocean-size waves. Captain Thomas Coupe is said to have astonished his neighbors by sailing a full-rigged ship through on an ebb, the only time it has been done. A one-hundred-and-eighty-foot-high bridge, anchored in the middle by a craggy island (the view from center span is terrific), soars across the narrowest place. The park here is lovely, with a long sandy beach facing west, some nice hiking trails, and a freshwater lake full of trout. The campground is one of the most popular in the state.

La Conner • Population: 600 (Two-hour side trip)

Rather than proceeding directly to Anacortes, our jumping-off place for the San Juan Islands, go east on Highway 20 and follow the signs to La Conner, a once sleepy little fishing village on the river that separates Fidalgo Island from the mainland. Though the town still has a lot of charm, it alas has been "discovered," so the five-block main street is now awash with trendy boutiques, restaurants overlooking the yacht basin, antique shops, and half a dozen art galleries. Nevertheless, like Coupeville, it is a fine place for a getaway weekend or an overnight stop on your northward trek. For some time it has been hard to get a room here on weekends because the Heron was the only place to stay, but the recently built La Conner Country Inn has eased the situation somewhat. Other motels are located along Interstate 5 ten miles away. A number of the old Victorians have been restored, one of which, the **Gaches Mansion,** is open to the public. The harbor has grown markedly in the last few years because it is a nice stopover port for boaters sailing to the San Juans.

FOOD AND LODGING   La Conner, Washington 98257

✔✔✔ **La Conner Country Inn**   28-room downtown lodgelike motel with fireplaces in every room. Restaurant, bar, and library. P.O. Box 537. (206) 466-3101.

✔✔ **The Heron in La Conner**   11-room B&B. P.O. Box 716. (206) 466-4626.

Anacortes • Population: 9,000

Anacortes, the gateway to the San Juans, is an industrial city without much charm. However, a drive to the 1,200-foot summit of **Mount Erie** can be a rewarding experience if the weather is clear, and the **Anacortes Museum** is an interesting place. A popular bicycle excursion is to take the county-run ferry to **Guemes Island** and ride around on its almost deserted roads. Anacortes has a surprising number of motels, considering that it is not on the interstate. My guess is that people leave their cars at the ferry terminal and make day trips out to the islands.

FOOD AND LODGING   Anacortes, Washington 98221

✔✔ **Anacortes Inn**   44-unit motel. 3006 Commercial Avenue. (206) 293-3153.

✔✔ **Cap Sante Inn**   21-unit motel. 906 9th. (206) 293-0602.

✔✔ **Islands Motel**   30-unit motel, restaurant and bar. 3401 Commercial Avenue. (206) 293-4644.

✔✔ **Ship Harbor Inn**   30-unit motel at ferry terminal. 5316 Ferry Terminal Road. (206) 293-5177.

●● **Boomer's Landing**   Waterfront restaurant. (206) 293-5109.

· 16 ·

THE SAN JUANS

An Insular Way of Enjoying Life

The eternal conflict between the Continental and de Fuca tectonic plates created the jumble of rocks that formed the San Juans, but it was the constant grinding of the glacier that sculpted them more or less into the shape we know today. The Puget lobe of the Cordilleran ice sheet, seven thousand feet thick in places, scoured out the earth, digging canyons and exposing the hard granitic core material. Its great weight compressed the sands and muds, pushed them into cracks, and turned them to stone. Then, about ten thousand years ago, the ice retreated and the sea poured in through the Juan de Fuca Strait, submerging lowlands under hundreds of feet of water and turning mountaintops into islands. There are nearly five hundred of them, even at high tide, but less than two hundred have names, and a fraction of those are habitable. Only five have populations large enough to support public ferry service, and two of those (Shaw and Guemes) have virtually no tourist facilities. So when we speak of the San Juan archipelago, we usually mean Lopez, Orcas, and San Juan islands.

Strange names for a land long associated with the Russians and the British. Credit a fellow named Gonzalez López de Haro, who sailed *Princesa Real* into de Fuca's strait one April day in 1790. Naming the island chain after his patron saint, he went on to christen Quimper Peninsula and Fidalgo Island after two fellow officers. Though most think Orcas Island was named after the species of whale that cavorts in these waters, de Haro had

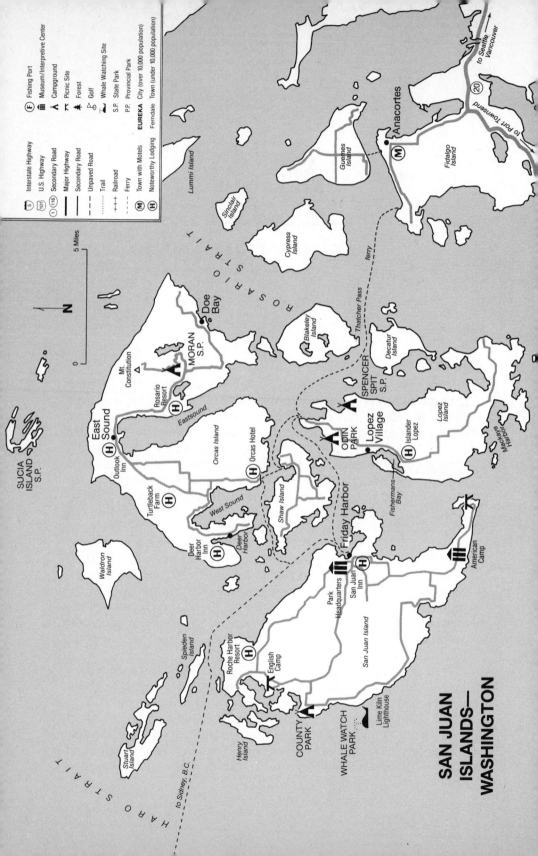

SAN JUAN
ISLANDS—
WASHINGTON

Legend

⑤	Interstate Highway
① ⑯	U.S. Highway
	Major Highway
	Secondary Road
	Secondary Road
	Unpaved Road
·····	Trail
+++	Railroad
	Ferry
Ⓜ Ⓗ	Town with Motels / Noteworthy Lodging

Ⓕ	Fishing Port
🏛	Museum/Interpretive Center
⌂	Campground
🌲	Picnic Site
🌲	Forest
⛳	Golf
	Whale Watching Site
S.P.:	State Park
P.P.:	Provincial Park

EUREKA City (over 10,000 population)
Ferndale Town (under 10,000 population)

5 Miles

0

N

ROSARIO STRAIT

HARO STRAIT

to Sidney, B.C.

to Seattle / Vancouver

to Port Townsend

②⓪ Anacortes Ⓜ

Fidalgo Island

Guemes Island

Sinclair Island

Cypress Island

Lummi Island

SUCIA ISLAND S.P.

Waldron Island

Spieden Island

Stuart Island

Henry Island

Roche Harbor Resort

English Camp 🌲

COUNTY PARK ⌂

WHALE WATCH PARK

Lime Kiln Lighthouse

San Juan Island

Park Headquarters 🏛

San Juan Inn Ⓗ

Friday Harbor

American Camp 🏛

Shaw Island

Deer Harbor Inn Ⓗ

Deer Harbor

West Sound

Turtleback Farm Ⓗ

Outlook Inn Ⓗ

East Sound Ⓗ

Eastsound

Orcas Island

Orcas Hotel Ⓗ

Rosario Resort Ⓗ

Mt. Constitution ⌂

MORAN S.P. ⌂

Doe Bay

Blakeley Island

Decatur Island

SPENCER SPIT S.P. 🌲

Lopez Village

Islander Lopez Ⓗ

ODIN PARK 🌲

Lopez Island

Fishermans Bay

Mackeye Harbor

Thatcher Pass

ferry

in fact honored the viceroy of Mexico, Don Juan Vincenté de Guemes Pacheco y Padila *Orcas*itees y Aguayo Condé de Revilla Gigedo. Lopez he presumably named after himself.

Today the archipelago is populated by vacationers, retirees, small-scale farmers, and refugees from the counterculture age who simply wanted to escape from a too crowded world and found the perfect place to do it. "We don't see down-and-outers on these islands," ranger Steve Gobat told me. "It costs a lot of money just to get out here, so those fellows going up and down Interstate 5 looking for work never come this way." He spoke the truth. The assessed valuation per capita in San Juan County is twice the state's average, and a huge percentage of the residents are college-educated. The people who visit the islands seemed to me to be about as waspish as you'll find anywhere in the United States, up-market types who have the time to find a pleasant contrast to their too hectic world of work. Island life, it seems, is insular for the simple reason that the sea presents a barrier, turning away those with either too little time or not enough money—or both.

You don't find many tourists, either, at least not those in a hurry. It's sometimes hard to get out to the San Juans in the summer (the ferries are too crowded), and there aren't a lot of places to stay, so those who come settle down for a while. "Why don't we spend a night on Lopez, a night on Orcas, and a night on San Juan before we head off to Canada" is simply a terrible idea. Islanders tell horror stories of people stranded when they couldn't get on the last ferry home and every place to stay was full. So between Memorial Day and the end of September, it is wise to book a room before you go out.

But with the difficulties come the rewards, as we shall see. The San Juans might just be the most scenic archipelago in the United States, rivaling the islands in Maine's Penobscot Bay. Washingtonians state flat out that the ferry ride through these waters is the most beautiful in the world. Maybe, but cruising Stockholm's archipelago and a Greek Islands sojourn are two contenders that come to mind, and the trip through Canada's Gulf Islands, just a bit north of here, can justly make that claim, too.

Rather than just start touring, as we have throughout these pages, I think it is best to first consider the process. How do you get there, and what's the best way to see the countryside?

Access to the San Juans

A million passengers a year ride Washington State Ferries' San Juan Islands service, nearly a quarter of them in August alone. Six sailings a day, year round, make a circuit of the islands, calling on Lopez (45-minute crossing time), Shaw (1 hour), Orcas (1¾ hours), and Friday Harbor on San Juan Island (2 hours). One boat continues on, crossing Haro Strait to Sidney, British Columbia (3¾ hours). During the summer as many as seven additional sailings are made, but most go only to Orcas or San Juan, the most popular destinations. One additional Sydney trip is offered. These are big ferries, accommodating buses and semitrucks, a hundred or more cars, and a thousand passengers. Nevertheless, a bulletin states:

> Washington State Ferries is encouraging passengers on the Anacortes-San Juan Islands-Sidney route to leave their cars in Anacortes and walk onto the ferry. Evergreen Trailways also provides service on the route with the option to board the bus on the ferry and continue on to Victoria from Sidney.

"Even the Anacortes parking lot is beginning to fill up on weekends," a fellow passenger told me. "These islands are just getting too damn popular." Increasingly, I discovered, people are turning to bicycles as the preferred mode of transportation. Island roads, save one on Orcas, are gentle and, except near the ferry docks, not too crowded—perfect cycling country. So adventuresome travelers either leave their car in Anacortes and tour by bike or drive out and then rent one to go island hopping sans auto.

The San Juans' only incorporated town, Friday Harbor, is right at the ferry terminal, so you can get along without a car if that's where you plan to stay. A minibus runs to Roche Harbor, the other popular resort on the island. Larger resorts on Orcas and Lopez provide shuttle service, given prior notice. All this is to try to alleviate the islanders' chronic annoyance: overcrowded ferries. RVers should be cautioned, too. Not only are there few overnight places to park, but interisland travel almost always requires backing onto the ferry. I watched as the driver of a Winnebago who apparently had never learned the art of using mirrors sat almost frozen as deckhands alternately coaxed, pleaded, and cajoled him into inching down the hundred-yard ramp. Apparently he was so traumatized by the experience that when we got to the next island, he drove off, made a U-turn, got right back on the boat (this time facing forward), and headed straight for the mainland.

In order to simplify fare collection, you pay for a round trip (expensive) at Anacortes. No fare, therefore, is collected on *eastbound* interisland passage or service back to Anacortes. So if you do plan to island hop, you can save some money by going to

Friday Harbor first and returning via Orcas, Shaw, and Lc
Canadians get short shrift. They have to pay a full Anac(
passage even if they are only going to one of the islands, and then
they get stuck again for a westbound fare to get home. One other
alternative is to fly. San Juan Airlines offers commuter service
from Seattle's SeaTac Airport to San Juan and Orcas islands.
Thousands of visitors, however, finesse the problem entirely by
coming over on their own boat. The San Juans, and their Canadian sister islands, the Gulfs, are the most popular sailing waters
in the Pacific Northwest.

Lopez Island • Population: 1,180

Shortly after leaving Anacortes, you'll see a wooded island
looming up on the starboard bow. Curiously, there are no cypress
on Cypress Island. George Vancouver, who named it, was a better
navigator than dendrologist. The trees are cedar. Your attention is
soon diverted to two more islands dead ahead, Blakley and Decatur, standing like sentinels guarding the secrets of the San
Juans' inner sanctum. The passage between seems much too
narrow to accommodate the huge ferry and an immense amount
of pleasure-boat traffic but is in fact half a mile wide and serves
only as a prelude to the excitement that lies ahead. Once inside,
you're surrounded by forested islands, some steep and some
gentle, but all with rocky promontories jutting out toward the
ferry, seemingly putting up a palm like a traffic cop saying "Slow
down." Place names here are decidedly English: Upright Head,
Obstruction Island, Wasp Passage, Pole Pass, and, just to give a
currency to the argument, Thatcher Pass, the one we just came
through.

Lopez is the least touristy of the three islands we will visit,
though none really deserves that label. Bucolic is the adjective
that comes to mind. The northern end is a bit rocky and forested,
but a mile south of the ferry terminal the land becomes rolling,
with hardly a house or barn to interrupt the fields and pastures.
Boaters steer clear of its shallow shore. Only two anchorages
tempt the overnighter, both so shallow skippers must check the
tide tables before attempting an entrance. The only real development surrounds Fisherman Bay, where **Lopez Village** boasts a
few stores. The nearby Islander Lopez resort complex is the only
sizable place to stay.

People here really do slow down. Though it was still early
September, I found the historical museum closed for the season.
A coffee shop seemed to be the de facto lending library—
paperbacks are passed along to anyone who needs a book to read.

While having breakfast I overheard the cook ask a middle-aged lady dressed in jeans where she had been so long. "Spent some time in jail," was her reply, delivered in a tone of voice that suggested she may have been an antiwar demonstrator. Later I learned that a number of draft resisters came here during the Vietnam War (it was a short escape to Canada). A ferry passenger told me that the population triples during summer weekends when people come out to their second homes. Many keep a clunker auto parked at the terminal so they can come across on foot and thus avoid the ferry hassles.

FOOD AND LODGING   Lopez Island, Washington 98261

✔✔ **Islander Lopez**   32-room motel, restaurant, bar. P.O. Box 197. (206) 468-2233.

✔✔ **MacKaye Harbor Inn**   B&B. P.O. Box 1940. (206) 468-2253.

✔ **Blue Fjord Cabins**   Several housekeeping cabins. Route 1, P.O. Box 1450. (206) 468-2749.

✔ **Spencer Spit State Park**   30 campsites.

✔ **Odin County Park**   20 campsites.

Orcas Island • Population: 2,560

The westbound ferries usually call on **Shaw Island** (population: 133), though few get on or off. For a long time the ferry terminal was run by a religious order; it was not unusual to see a couple of nuns doing shore duty. Since there are no tourist facilities here (save for a tiny campground) and the roads stay inland where you don't get much of a view of the water, I recommend you continue on to Orcas.

Orcas, the largest and most stunning island of the archipelago, has been described as having the shape of a horseshoe or a saddlebag. Were it not for the flat, low-lying isthmus at the north end of Eastsound, it would be two islands, one hilly and the other downright mountainy. Much of the latter is embraced by Moran State Park (Washington's largest), where those willing to walk a bit can enjoy an almost wilderness experience. Orcas is the most rugged and most indented of the San Juans, with a topography more like the Canadian Gulf Islands to the north than the relatively flat ones farther south. Three sheltered bays, one small and two large, poke inland, providing safe anchorages for pleasure boats.

Eastsound, the only real village on the island, is lovely, with a few dozen fixed-up buildings providing places to shop or eat out. Several old log cabins now house the **Orcas Historical Museum,** and a brand-new community center features a performing arts theater. The circa 1883 Outlook Inn has been refurbished with a large dining room and bar downstairs and a dozen brass-bedded guest rooms above. Eastsound Landmark Inn is a new, tastefully done condo-motel complex. What struck me most about the place was that there is not one but two bookstores, a fact that I think says a bit about who lives here (but even more about what else there is to do on the island).

Orcas's pride is the Rosario Resort, named for the strait (El Gran Canal de Nuestra Señora del Rossario la Marinera) that separates the San Juans from the mainland. A huge mansion, built in 1904 by Seattle shipbuilder Robert Moran, houses the common facilities—guests stay in outlying cottages. The place struck me as being a bit like Death Valley's Scottys Castle, an oasis of luxury in an out-of-the-way spot. Moran, who doctors said had only a few months to live (he in fact lasted another forty years), spent lavishly on his bayside hideaway, putting six tons of copper on the roof and furnishing the interior with handsome inlaid hardwoods and a parquet floor that took two years to install. The organ, still in use, has almost two thousand pipes. (One fine day I went for a hike in the mountains, rested up with a dip in the Doe Bay hot springs—suits optional—and then, just to go from the ridiculous to the sublime, listened to an afternoon concert featuring a toccata and fugue by J. S. Bach and selections of works by George Gershwin.) In the 1930s Moran sold the place to Bay Area industrialist Donald Rheem, who made his fortune in water heaters and needed a place to stash away his rather eccentric wife. She had a penchant for riding around on her Harley-Davidson dressed in a flaming-red nightgown, a habit San Francisco matrons seemed to consider a bit beyond the pale. Rosario was turned into a resort in the 1940s.

Moran donated the land for the state park that dominates Orcas's eastern lobe. Several lakes are stocked with trout and are fine places to go canoeing. A short trail leads to Cascade Falls, which is quite impressive in the spring but a disappointment in the fall when the island becomes quite dry. Thirty miles of hiking trails crisscross the parklands, and a twisty road climbs to **Mount Constitution,** at 2,300 feet the tallest thing around. The view from the summit observation tower is spectacular. Washington State Parks accepts reservations for the campground, which during the summer is almost always full.

Both Orcas and San Juan are dotted with marinas catering to

transient yachtsmen. Dockside grocery stores, laundromats, and hot showers are prevalent, and many of the very best eateries are within walking distance of a marina. An example is the Deer Harbor Inn, located in an old farmhouse in the middle of an apple orchard. "They just came with the place," was the response I got when I questioned the owner about where she assembled such an eclectic suite of furniture for the dining room. Press-backed chairs were equally at home with chrome-legged, Formica-topped tables and an ornate claw-foot buffet carved out of oak. A discussion ensued about the best way to cook salmon. "Just steam it," she said. "If the fish is really fresh, there is no way you can improve on it—no hollandaise sauce, no barbecuing with mesquite, no garlic or butter or anything like that. You know, some people claim the best way to cook a whole fish is to simply wrap it in cheesecloth and throw it into the dishwasher. A full wash-rinse cycle does the trick. Oh, it's a good idea to leave out the soap, of course!"

Sucia Island State Park, located a few miles north of Orcas, is a popular destination for Seattle yachtsmen and adventuresome travelers willing to learn the art of paddling a sea kayak. Outfitters in Eastsound and Friday Harbor run two- and three-day excursions to this wilderness retreat. You provide a sleeping bag, they take care of everything else.

FOOD AND LODGING   Orcas Island, Washington 98245

✔✔✔ **Rosario Resort**   179-unit resort/convention hotel. Restaurant, bar, spa, pool, marina, tennis, golf. (206) 376-2222.

✔✔✔ **Turtleback Farm**   7-room farmhouse B&B. Route 1, P.O. Box 650. (206) 376-4914.

✔✔ **Deer Harbor Marina and Resort**   29-unit motel-cottage complex, restaurant, bar, and cafe. P.O. Box 178, Deer Harbor 98243. (206) 376-4420.

✔✔ **Eastsound Landmark Inn**   15-unit motel kitchens near the village center. P.O. Box 101. (206) 376-2423.

✔✔ **Blue Heron**   4-room B&B. Route 1, P.O. Box 64. (206) 376-2954.

✔✔ **Captain Cook Resort**   Cabins and motel units. Route 1, P.O. Box 1040. (206) 376-2242.

✔✔ **Kangaroo House**   5-room B&B. P.O. Box 334. (206) 376-2175.

✔✔ **North Beach Inn**   Circa 1932 resort. P.C
376-2660.

✔✔ **Palmer's Chart House**   B&B. P.O. Box 51, .
98243. (206) 378-2783.

✔✔ **Orcas Hotel**   14 rooms above restaurant and bar at fei.
terminal. P.O. Box 155, Orcas 98280. (206) 376-4300.

✔✔ **Outlook Inn**   30-room restored downtown hotel/motel,
restaurant and bar. P.O. Box 210, Orcas 98280. (206)
376-2200.

✔✔ **Smugglers Villa Resort**   20 cottages. P.O. Box 79.
(206) 376-2297.

✔✔ **Woodsong B&B**   P.O. Box 32, Westsound 98280. (206)
376-2340.

✔ **Moran State Park**   136 reservable campsites. Star Route,
P.O. Box 22, Eastsound. (206) 376-2326.

●● **Deer Harbor Inn**   Restaurant. (206) 376-4110.

●● **Cafe Olga**   Natural foods restaurant. (206) 376-4408.

●● **Christina's**   Upstairs Eastsound restaurant. (206) 376-
4904.

San Juan Island • Population: 3,872

About the only thing historians agree on is that there was a
fellow named Friday. Whether he got his name appended to the
best harbor in the San Juans is open to some dispute. Some claim
that when a Spanish sea captain dropped anchor here, he hollered: "Whose harbor is this?" Others say the question was:
"What day is this?" Whichever, **Friday Harbor** with a population of 1,500 is the largest town in the San Juans and seat of
Island County—Washington's answer to Edgartown, Massachusetts.

More people visit Orcas, but this is where people live. The
biggest industry is real estate, judging by the number of agents
along Main Street. And tourism: I counted a dozen art galleries,
one T-shirt shop, half a dozen restaurants, and even a movie
theater. The town hosts a very popular Dixieland jazz festival in
July. Main Street is five blocks long with a lot of places locals use:
a large supermarket, a couple of drugstores, several saloons, and
a pool hall. The old San Juan Inn, located a block from the ferry
terminal, is the best place to stay. A lovely book-filled sitting

oom looks out over a harbor with a thousand boat masts waving with the swells.

"San Juan is a terminal moraine," I learned from a local. "In some places the gravel is several thousand feet thick, but most of our soil is clay, deposited out by the glacier. That's why the island has such a mellow feel."

Indeed it does. No place is much higher than another. Golden grain fields are framed by green forests of spruce and fir; cows graze in one pasture, sheep the next. Roads jog where section boundaries don't quite line up. I've now toured the island twice (two Septembers, spaced a dozen years apart) and have had no trouble at all succumbing to its spell. Once it was overcast and damp; the other time it was bright, with the sun so low to the sky that shadows were a quarter mile long. Each, in its way, was an enchanting experience.

The **San Juan Island National Historical Park** encompasses the sites where British and American armies stared at each other in the 1860s (see Fifty-four Forty or Fight—Over a Pig!, below). Fittingly, the American camp faces south, toward Seattle, while the English camp looks out over the former Hudson's Bay Company headquarters at Victoria. "People come to the islands because they want to get away from it all," park superintendent Steve Gobat told me. "Then they wonder what to do with themselves, so they come visit us. Most end up fascinated by what happened here.

FIFTY-FOUR FORTY OR FIGHT—OVER A PIG!

The War of 1812 seemed to end the squabbling between the Americans and British over who owned what in the north and northeast. The Treaty of Ghent established the Canadian boundary as passing through the Great Lakes and thence westward, following several rivers leading to Lake of the Woods, rivers that had been used for years by the *voyageurs* of the fur trade. Farther west, though, there were no natural boundaries, so arbitrarily the forty-ninth parallel was chosen and extended all the way to the end of the "important" world, the barrier of the Rocky Mountains. That seemed to settle things—for a while.

The sovereignty of the land west of the Rockies soon became an issue. Captain Gray and Lewis and Clark had established an American claim to what was generally called Oregon, but George Vancouver and the Canadian trappers had done their homework, too. In a Solomon-like way the two countries decided on joint ownership, an arrangement that, as time went on, became more and more unworkable. At first Hudson's Bay Company men were the only whites living here. "The Company," as everyone called it, thought the forty-ninth parallel was a fine boundary, but only as far west as the southward-flowing Columbia River. It should then follow the river all the way to the Pacific, thereby ceding to Britain most of the present state of Washington. But American missionaries, led by Methodist Jason Lee, began settling south of the Columbia, and others had covetous eyes on Puget Sound, considered to be the only possible American window on the Pacific. (At that time San Francisco's harbor was in the hands of the Mexicans, and the treacherous Columbia bar rendered that port all but unusable.) James K. Polk, the expansionist, sensed the mood of the country. He wanted not only Florida and Texas, but Oregon and a lot more. "Fifty-four Forty or Fight" was the Democrats' 1844 campaign theme, audaciously claiming the Pacific slope all the way north to Russian Alaska (at latitude 54 degrees 40 minutes)—land that few Americans had ever laid eyes on, much less colonized. No one, of course, consulted the Chinooks, Cowlitzs, Yakamas, or Bella Coolas.

Neither nation wanted to go to war over a place considered nothing more than a "pine swamp," so they compromised—sort of. The forty-ninth parallel would be the boundary all the way to tidewater on Puget Sound, but as a face-saving sop Britain was allowed to keep all of Vancouver Island. The treaty stated:

> [The boundary] shall be continued westward along the 49th parallel to the middle of the channel which separates the continent from Vancouver's Island; and thence southerly through the middle of said channel and of Fuca Straits to the Pacific Ocean. . . .

Had the treaty negotiators looked at a map, they would have seen the ambiguity of that language—it seems that there were a few islands that got in the way and that two channels were in common use. Thus the stage was set for the Pig War.

In 1859 both the Hudson's Bay Company and some Americans had established farms on San Juan Island. Lyman Cutler planted some potatoes on land that Company man Charles Griffin claimed he had no right to. Cutler got angry when Griffin's pig repeatedly raided his garden and "upon the impulse of the moment I seazed my rifle and shot the hog." The ensuing feud led both sides to mobilize. The gullible and belligerent General Harney, commander of the newly created Department of Oregon, dispatched a contingent of troops under the command of George Pickett (the fellow who was later to come a cropper while charging at Gettysburg).

The British stood offshore with a small armada sporting 167 guns and two thousand marines. Admiral Baynes, commander of the Royal Navy's Pacific Squadron, soon arrived, looked over the situation, and wisely declared: "I will not involve two great nations in a war over a squabble about a pig." Both sides backed down, but each built forts and glared at each other for twelve more years.

The soldiers had little to do—a fortunate thing, as it turned out, because one American officer, Henry Martyn Robert, amused himself by devising ways for people to behave in town meetings and the like. Much later he published his writings as *Robert's Rules of Order.*

In 1871 the dispute was finally settled in the Americans' favor, with Kaiser Wilhelm I of Germany, no less, acting as mediator.

"The locals, you know, are highly educated, so regardless of their political persuasion, they are up-to-date on what's going on. We had a big to-do about what to do with the rabbits [the American camp seems overrun with the critters]. A fellow wanted to sell licenses to hunt them, but he was shouted down by those who figured it was better to let the bald eagles keep things under control."

The only official **Whale Watching Park** in the United States is at Lime Kiln Point, located near another handsome lighthouse. Here it is the Orcas, the so-called killer whale, that draws our attention. They have never been known to attack a human but got their popular name because they feed on seals and porpoises and the salmon that cruise off San Juan Island's western shore. Before visiting the park, however, stop at Friday Harbor's **Whale Museum.** For what porpoise? Had I done so, I would have known that the three pods of Orcas I watched cavorting alongside the ferry were not that at all, but the similar-looking (but much smaller) Dall's porpoise.

In 1886 one John McMillin founded the Roche Harbor Lime and Cement Company and proceeded to build a company town that lasted well into this century. A white-balconied three-story hotel, constructed around a log bunkhouse, became a hangout for notables, including Teddy Roosevelt; VIPs still visit today. The Hotel de Haro and surrounding facilities provide one of the most splendid places to stay on our entire trip. Lovely gardens are dotted with cast-iron benches where you can read a book while basking in the sun and absorbing the salt air. McMillin's house is now a fine restaurant overlooking the large marina. Workers' homes have been turned into vacation cottages; tennis and volleyball courts and an Olympic-size pool are nearby. Desk clerk Brendon Bratt told me that most summer vacationers prefer the cottages or the newly built condos, but those who come in the winter like the coziness of the refurbished hotel. "We keep a good fire going," he said.

FOOD AND LODGING San Juan Island, Washington 98250

✔✔✔ **Roche Harbor Resort** 60-unit resort hotel, restaurant, bar, pool, marina. P.O. Box 4001. (206) 378-2155.

✔✔ **Blair House** 5-room B&B. 345 Blair Avenue. (206) 378-5907.

✔✔ **Collins House** B&B. 225 A Street. (206) 378-5834.

✔✔ **Duffy House** 4-room B&B. 460 Pear Point Road. (206) 378-5604.

✔✔ **Friday Harbor Motor Inn** 72-unit motel. P.O. Box 962. (206) 378-4351.

✔✔ **Island Lodge** Motel units. P.O. Box 1156. (206) 378-2000.

✔✔ **Moon & Sixpence** 4-room B&B. 3021 Beaverton Valley Road. (206) 378-4138.

✔✔ **Olympic Lights** 5-room farmhouse B&B. 4531 Cattle Point Road. (206) 378-4138.

✔✔ **San Juan Inn** Restored 1873 hotel; 10 rooms. P.O. Box 776. (206) 378-2070.

✔✔ **Tucker House** 3-room B&B with 3 nearby cottages. 260 B Street. (206) 378-2783.

✔ **San Juan County Park** 12 campsites.

●● **Springtree** Friday Harbor restaurant. (206) 378-4848.

Roche Harbor Resort looks out over de Haro Strait toward George Vancouver's island, the place we'll visit next.

PART FIVE

George Vancouver's Island

FOLLOW THE BIRDS
TO VICTORIA

A Bit of Olde England Along the Pacific Rim

Victoria is one of those places people either wax lyrical about or hate with a passion. "A little bit of olde England," the "world's only cemetery with a business district," and "the biggest tourist trap on the West Coast" are three phrases bandied about these days. Rudyard Kipling, that jingoistic imperialist who staunchly believed that anyone born beyond the English Channel was of a lesser breed, loved Victoria, but then he saw it in an earlier day.

To realise Victoria you must take all that the eye admires most in Bournemouth, Torquay, the Isle of Wight, the Happy Valley at Hong Kong—the Doon, Sorrento, and Champs Bay; add reminiscences of the Thousand Islands and arrange the whole around the Bay of Naples, with some Himalayas for the background.

There is still much for the eye to admire, especially if you arrive by boat from the United States. The ferries dock right downtown, adjacent to the Parliament Building and the Empress Hotel, both of which face out on the grandest waterfront esplanade in North America. Seaplanes taxi up to Wharf Street; passengers walk only a few steps to their office, shop, or hotel. Monstrous yachts, owned by visiting sheikhs and sultans, tie up nearby. Barges, loaded with trucks bound for Safeway and Eaton's, chug across the quiet water. Geraniums adorn cast-iron, tulip-topped lampposts, and flags fly from the stores along Government Street. Oddly, the Parliament Buildings are Georgian, the Empress is built in the French château style, and most

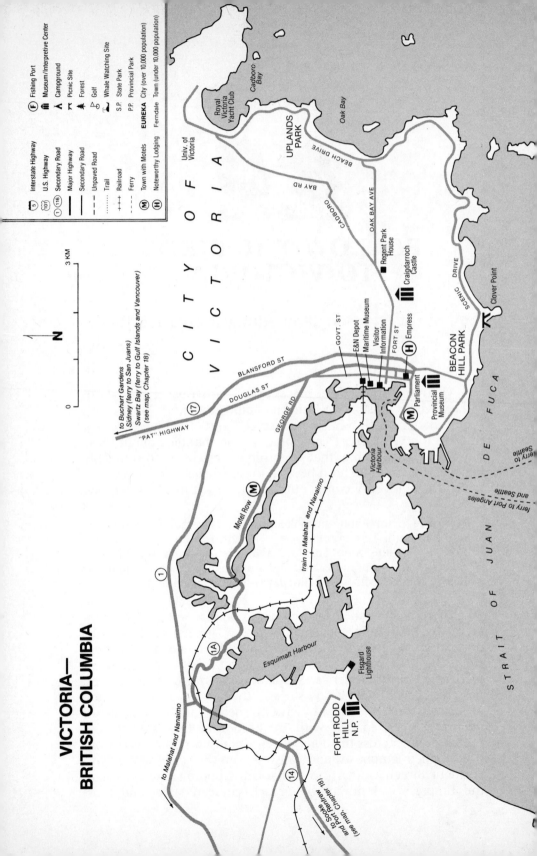

VICTORIA—
BRITISH COLUMBIA

N

0   3 KM

Legend:

5	Interstate Highway
101	U.S. Highway
1 116	Secondary Road
	Major Highway
	Secondary Road
	Unpaved Road
	Trail
+++	Railroad
--	Ferry
(M)	Town with Motels
(H)	Noteworthy Lodging

(F)	Fishing Port
🏛	Museum/Interpretive Center
▲	Campground
⅄	Picnic Site
♣	Forest
⛳	Golf
	Whale Watching Site
S.P.	State Park
P.P.	Provincial Park
EUREKA	City (over 10,000 population)
Ferndale	Town (under 10,000 population)

to Buchart Gardens
Sidney (ferry to San Juans)
Swartz Bay (ferry to Gulf Islands and Vancouver)
(see map, Chapter 18)

"PAT" HIGHWAY

17

BLANSFORD ST

DOUGLAS ST

GEORGE RD

Motel Row (M)

1

1A

to Malahat and Nanaimo

14

to Sooke
to Renfrew (B)
and Port (see map,
Chapter)

FORT RODD
HILL N.P.

Esquimalt Harbour

Fisgard
Lighthouse

train to Malahat and Nanaimo

ferry to Port Angeles
and Seattle

ferry to
Seattle

STRAIT   OF   JUAN   DE   FUCA

Victoria Harbour

CITY   OF   VICTORIA

Univ. of
Victoria

UPLANDS PARK

Cadboro Bay

Oak Bay

Royal
Victoria
Yacht Club

CADBORO BAY RD

BAY RD

OAK BAY AVE

Regent Park
House

Craigdarroch
Castle

BEACON
HILL PARK

SCENIC DRIVE

BEACH DRIVE

Clover Point

GOVT. ST

E&N Depot

Maritime Museum

Visitor
Information

FORT ST

Empress

(H)

(M)

Parliament

Provincial
Museum

of the older residences are Tudor, so from an architectural stand-point this is the least "Victorian" of all the Victorian towns we have visited on our sojourn. And it's getting less "olde England" all the time.

My wife and I sailed on *Princess Marguerite* to Victoria in the early 1960s. Though the voyage was only four hours long, we booked a stateroom on the ship—it seemed like a classy way to travel for not very much money. A porter from the Empress Hotel met us at the gangplank, loaded our baggage onto a wheelbar-row, and directed us through customs. Our room in the ivy-walled brick hotel faced directly out over the boat we had just arrived on. The lobby seemed exactly as I imagined a proper London hotel should be, a high-ceilinged room furnished with tea tables and Windsor chairs. A tiny fellow dressed in a red uniform with a shiny black pill cap scurried about, shouting: "Call for . . ." The hotel, we learned, has welcomed the rich and the famous—King Edward VIII, Winston Churchill, and Charles Lindbergh—but the guest that truly impressed the staff was the king of Siam, who arrived with fifty-six attendants and 556 pieces of luggage. The story was bandied about that in the old days everyone was so well bred that not a head turned when a masked bandit shouted, "This is a stickup!" To engage their attention, the baffled badman was obliged to fire a shot into the ceiling. It seemed to me a likely story. High tea was a rather sedate affair, attended by a few dozen guests more intent on the biscuits and crumpets than on conversation. The tinkle of spoon on plate, or the muted clank of cup on saucer, was the only break in the silence. Now the lobby chairs are gone; high tea is served in the ballroom, with three or four sittings a day. Many guests wear name tags.

Victoria's south quay is now lined with several blocks of square-sided, glass-fronted motels whose architecture and style would not likely improve the beauty of Liverpool. Twenty-story apartment buildings could have been plucked out of any North American city. The Doric-columned former Canadian Pacific Steamship Company office is now a neon-signed wax museum; a garish underwater aquarium steals the eye away from a handsome square-rigged sailboat docked alongside. Even the spanking-new, otherwise fantastic Provincial Museum is housed in a cutesy arch-columned building that reflects neither the En-glish charm of the city's past nor the native people's heritage so nicely displayed inside.

But I'm one who thinks Victoria is a terrific city to visit and embrace the tourist bureau's slogan "Follow the Birds to Victo-ria." It is one of those sit-on-a-bench-and-watch-the-people-go-by sorts of places. Conversations take place in German, Dutch, Chinese, Australian, and French; you see women dressed in saris, kimonos, and pedal pushers. Day trippers from Seattle scurry about, looking for places to shop, or pause to take in the sense of festivity that is everywhere. Tourists queue up to board a double-decker sight-seeing bus, toss coins to a bearded sidewalk musician, and snap pictures of a Royal Canadian Mounted Policeman. Hansom cabs go clopping down Bellville Street. After dark, the Parliament Building is lit with so many lights it resembles the palace at Copenhagen's Tivoli Gardens. Victoria is not olde England, but it is a foreign country where place names have peculiar spellings and you eat at licensed restaurants, buy things by the meter and liter, and discover that a twenty-degree temperature means a nice warm day.

The Honourable Gouvenors and Company of Adventurers of England Trading into Hudson's Bay removed their western headquarters to this spot in 1849 when encroachment by Americans forced them to abandon Fort Vancouver near present-day Portland, Oregon (see Two Crown Colonies: One Too Many, page 265). Victoria became the provincial capital and for years was the largest city in western Canada (it's now fourth, after Vancouver, Edmonton, and Calgary). In its early years, many of the citizens were remittance men, sons of wealthy Britishers sent out here to purge their indiscretions, living on small allowances sent from home on condition that they never return. Tennis, croquet, cricket, and "the hunt" are the preferred sports. Though its insular location inhibits rapid growth, Victoria is expanding, simply because it's a nice place to live. "The city doesn't own a snow plow," my tour guide boasted, "and we have the warmest winter weather in Canada. We don't get a lot of rain, and the growing season is 280 days. That's important because you know how we English types love our gardens." A drive through the residential area of Oak Bay confirms his statement. In spite of its isolation, Victoria has become the favored place for Canadians to retire.

Access to Victoria

The ferry from the San Juans (Chapter 16) docks at Sidney, a pleasant little town fifteen miles north of Victoria on the Saanich Peninsula. Ferries from the city of Vancouver dock at nearby Swartz Bay. The drive into town along the Pat (Patricia Bay) Highway is uninspiring. A roadside tourist office can help you find a place to stay. If you want your first view of a beautiful place to be something special, therefore, it is better to come over from Seattle or Port Angeles. As noted in Chapter 14, M. V. *Coho* makes

TWO CROWN COLONIES: ONE TOO MANY

Things were not going well for the Hudson's Bay Company at Fort Vancouver (Washington). James Douglas, the man in charge of all the Columbia Department's operations, was annoyed. His chief factor, John McLaughlin, seemed to be helping the starving pioneers struggling in from their long trek along the Oregon Trail instead of seeing to the needs of the "Honourable Company's" trappers and traders. The Willamette valley was being overrun with Americans, threatening the Crown's already contested sovereignty over Oregon Territory. In 1849, seeing the handwriting on the wall, Douglas decided to fold his tent and move north. McLaughlin resigned from the Company and retreated south to Oregon City, where he subsequently got into the history books as "the father of Oregon." Douglas moved his headquarters to a snug enclave on the southern tip of Vancouver Island, which he had founded six years before. The men had chosen the name Fort Camosun, but Douglas, hardly innocent of things political, opted for Fort Victoria. The queen promptly made the island a Crown colony. She was just in time, for there were rumors about that Brigham Young was going to bring his flock of "Saints" here. The booze-loving, backwoods trappers didn't think much of that idea.

Things did not get off to an auspicious start. Richard Blanshard, the unfortunate governor, arrived to find no welcome, no home, no salary, and no colony. Early attempts at electing a seven-man council were thwarted when only forty-seven residents could be found who owned freehold property worth £300 and were thus eligible to vote. And James Douglas wasn't about to share his power with anyone. The company had negotiated a sweetheart contract with the Crown to lease the whole of Vancouver Island—the rent: seven shillings a year. It wasn't long before Blanshard was out; Douglas ruled both Company and colony with an iron hand (Victoria's two main commercial streets bear their names).

Meanwhile, things on the mainland were going apace. Gold was discovered on the Columbia in 1855, the lower Fraser in 1857, and the fantastically rich Caraboo shortly after that. The Fraser River delta became a sea of tents and shacks and boasted a reputation rivaling that of the Barbary Coast. Simple law and order demanded a colony, and this time the queen herself got to pick what it was to be called:

> The only name which is given to the whole territory in every map the Queen has consulted is "Columbia," but as there exists also a Columbia in South America, and the citizens of the United States call their country also Columbia, at least in poetry, "British Columbia" might be, in the Queen's opinion, the best name.

Her envoys chose a mosquito-infested swamp of little charm to be the new capital, which she named New Westminster (now a Vancouver suburb). In time, of course, the gold fields played out and miners drifted away. By 1864 less than ten thousand people (four times that if you counted Indians, but nobody did) lived in the two colonies, an area larger than the original dominion of Canada. Amalgamation seemed wise, and though there were more mainlanders than islanders, the more civilized Victoria won the day and became the capital of British Columbia. An era on the Northwestern Pacific Coast ended when the newly knighted Sir James Douglas retired from the political scene, ending twenty autocratic years of rule.

---

a 1½-hour crossing from Port Angeles at the tip of the Olympic Peninsula. A nicer trip, however, is to take the well-loved *Princess Marguerite* from Seattle. The new *Marguerite* (her namesake, launched on the Clyde in 1918, was serving as a hospital ship during World War II when she was torpedoed while en route to Cyprus) went into service for the Canadian Pacific Railway Company in 1948, making a triangular route between Seattle, Victoria, and Vancouver. Low-slung (four decks) but long (368 feet), with a slightly raked bow, two canted stacks, and a cruiser stern, she is the epitome of English grace and style. Licensed to carry 1,800 passengers and fifty cars, she still has a few staterooms, a restaurant, coffee shop, bar, casino, and a duty-free store. All summer long she sails at 8:00 A.M., cruises up Puget Sound and through Admiralty Inlet, crosses Juan de Fuca Strait, and docks in Victoria a little after noon. The return voyage leaves at 5:30 P.M., so day trippers have plenty of time to shop, sightsee, or take a tour though Buchart's Gardens.

In recent years B.C. Steamship Company has put a second vessel into service, one that is more suited to carrying cars and trucks. *Vancouver Island Princess* overnights in Victoria, so you now have a choice of morning or afternoon departures each way. Though an equally fine ship, she doesn't dock in downtown Victoria, so you miss the excitement of steaming into such a beautiful harbor. The *Victoria Clipper*, a passenger-only, jet-propelled catamaran, docks nearby. Her thirty-knot speed allows her to make twice-daily 2½-hour voyages to Seattle. Otter Air, utilizing seaplanes, provides harbor-to-harbor flights from Seattle, Port Townsend, and San Juan Island. Air B.C. offers similar service from Vancouver. B.C. Transit provides bus service from Vancouver via the Tsawwassen-Swartz Bay ferry service.

Victoria • Metropolitan population: 263,180

It's easy to be put off by Victoria's blatant assault on the tourist's dollar. Brochures for Sealand of the Pacific, Royal London Wax Museum, Classic Car Museum, Undersea Gardens, Miniature World, Crystal Garden, Fable Cottage Estate, Anne Hathaway's Cottage, and Buchart's Gardens all seem to suggest that without a visit to the establishment your trip will have been wasted. Signs advertise bus tours and harbor tours, and dozens of stores push Cowichan sweaters, English woolens, Wedgwood china, and every conceivable kind of junky souvenir. So what is one to do? Answer: Enjoy the nice things Victoria has to offer and keep a blind eye to the rest.

Of the establishments listed above, **Butchart Gardens** is the most memorable. Shortly after the turn of the century, Jessie Butchart reclaimed fifty acres of her husband's limestone quarry and turned it into what some say is the finest example of the horticulturist's art this side of London's Kew Gardens. Five hundred thousand people a year visit the park, providing enough money so that even the parking lots are lavishly landscaped. Near the entrance, young lasses dressed in culottes pounce on a dropped gum wrapper with a gusto that is apparent to all. The scheme works; people are careful not to litter, and the place is as spotless as Disneyland. Spring and fall bring the azalea and rhododendron blooms, but the most popular time is in the summer when the roses are in flower and evening concerts and fireworks displays are staged. Several dining rooms encourage people to linger. The gardens, about five miles from town, are located along the Saanich Inlet—you can arrive by private boat. A million dozen daffodils a year are grown on the Saanich Peninsula. Victoria itself has numerous public gardens. Beacon Hill Park overlooks the strait, and Thunderbird Park, located in the center of town, has a lovely collection of totems.

But Victoria's pièce de résistance is the **British Columbia Provincial Museum,** a sort of cross between the American Museum of Natural History and the Smithsonian Institution, featuring reconstructions of a pioneer town, a coal mine shaft, and Captain Cook's private cabin aboard *Discovery*. Exhibits display Queen Victoria's beehive bonnet and the dagger the Hawaiians used to kill Captain Cook. Fishing, long a dominant force in the islands economy, is represented by a replica of a cannery that no doubt looks pretty much like the one Newton H. Chittenden described in his 1882 book, *Travels in British Columbia:*

> Commencing operations only five years ago, its business has assumed such proportions that it now employs a force of over 400

men, 280 Chinese, and 160 Indians, and a fishing outfit consisting in part of thirty-eight boats and nets, two seines, one steam tug and four scows.

Chinese and Indians may not have counted as "men" in those days, but exhibits of the latter's culture deserve special attention at this museum. A replica of a longhouse and numerous audiovisual displays provide a sensitive interpretation of the life and magic of the north coast tribes. The totems seem grotesque; an animated display of ceremonial masks is downright spooky. A few blocks away, the **Maritime Museum of British Columbia** has an interesting collection of ship models, including several of the Hudson's Bay Company's *Beaver,* the first steamboat to sail in these waters. One room is devoted entirely to the life of Captain Cook.

The city boasts a number of art galleries, including one devoted to a local favorite, Emily Carr. Upscale shopping is located primarily along Government Street; antique shops, said to be the best west of Quebec, line Fort Street. Eaton's is Canada's largest department store, followed closely by The Bay, the shortened name for the Hudson's Bay Company (the apostrophe disappeared from maps years ago but is still used here). Bastion Square, a refurbished warehouse district, has some interesting shops and eateries. Victoria has a substantial "Chinatown" half a dozen blocks north of City Centre. A ship chandlery called Capital Iron Works is housed in another restored warehouse.

A tour through the residential area is most rewarding. Coal baron Robert Dunsmuir's Georgian-style sandstone **Craigdarroch Castle** is open to the public, and you can visit the quaint old **Regent Park House,** one of the few "Victorians" in Victoria. Cadboro Bay, home of the Royal Victoria Yacht Club, is lovely; Oak Bay is graced with numerous fine homes. The drive along the bluffs that jut out into Juan de Fuca Strait rivals the famous forty-nine-mile drive through the streets of San Francisco.

Inner Harbour and City Centre are dotted with hotels and motels, most of which are on the expensive side. But Victoria has a "motel row," located primarily along George Road (Highway 1A), where prices are substantially lower. It is too far out to walk into town, however; fortunately B&Bs abound. The **Victoria Visitors Bureau** has an office near the Empress Hotel with a large staff ready to help you find a room. As I drove off the ferry a lady handed me a flyer advertising Ryan's Irish Style B&B. "Irish Style," I learned, is to sit around the breakfast table and yak a lot. Five days later I realized that I had learned more about life in Victoria from Frank and Sara Ryan than I could have by staying at the Empress for a month. There are so many places to stay that it seems best just to list a few highlights. Restaurants run the gamut from the expensive Chez Pierre to the trendy Spinnakers Brew Pub.

FOOD AND LODGING   Victoria, British Columbia

✔✔✔ **Empress Hotel**   420-room full-service hotel. 721 Government Street, V8W 1W5. (604) 384-8111.

✔✔✔ **Executive House Hotel**   175-room downtown full-service hotel. 777 Douglas Street, V8W 2B5. (604) 388-5111.

✔✔✔ **Huntingdon Manor Inn**   116-unit high rise near ferry terminal. 330 Quebec Street, V8V 1W3. (604) 381-3456.

✔✔✔ **Laurel Point Inn**   130-room hotel at harbor entrance. 680 Montreal Street, V8V 1Z8. (604) 386-8721.

✔✔✔ **Oak Bay Beach Hotel**   50-room hotel overlooking Oak Bay. Three miles from downtown. 1175 Beach Drive, V8S 2N2. (604) 598-4556.

✔✔✔ **Victoria Regent Hotel**   High-rise apartment hotel overlooking harbor. 1234 Wharf Street, V8W 3H9. (604) 386-2211.

●●● **Chez Pierre**   (604) 388-7711.

● **Spinnakers Brew Pub**   (604) 384-2112.

Most tourists prefer to settle down in Victoria for a while and make excursions out from there, so some suggestions follow.

GULF ISLANDS CRUISE • (All-day excursion)

Bennett's Navy, it was called, when Premier W.A.C. Bennett bought a run-down collection of privately run boats and created the government-owned B.C. Ferries. New ships were built, including five of the *Queen of Coquitlam* class, which at about seven thousand tons are said to be the largest double-enders in the world. Most boats ply between the ports serving Victoria and Vancouver, cruising the lovely inland waters of the Gulf Island archipelago before heading out into the windswept Strait of Georgia. The Gulfs are as pretty as the San Juan Islands, and in many ways the voyage is even more interesting because so much is going on all the time. Boats arrive or depart Swartz Bay every ten to fifteen minutes. The southern Gulfs (with the exception of Saltspring, which we will visit in the next chapter) are less developed than the San Juans, so in general only morning and afternoon service is provided to each port. Island hopping is not easy, but since one ferry each day makes a loop, calling at three different islands, you can see this spectacular country from the comfortable deck of a ship. And since you won't have to take your car aboard, the cruise doesn't cost very much. Pack a picnic lunch (or buy it aboard) and either take a bus to the ferry or drive to Swartz Bay and leave your car at the parking lot (modest fee).

The boat I sailed on left Swartz Bay at 10:30 A.M. and, after leaving tiny Portland Island to the starboard, sailed alternatively alongside Saltspring (port), North Pender (starboard), and Prevost (port) before docking at Mayne Island's Village Bay. Passengers for the southernmost Gulf, Saturna Island, transferred to a smaller ferry here. Ten minutes out of Village Bay, a long blast on the ship's horn announced that we were about to steam through one of the most spectacular (and most feared) stretches of water imaginable (see An Active Pass, below), one rivaling the fabled "Inland Passage" pass that Captain Cook named after his ship *Discovery*. At first it seemed as though we were entering a blind bay, but as the ship came abeam of Helen Point the captain put the helm over, and we found ourselves threading through a narrow passageway that hooked again almost immediately, this time going 90 degrees the other way. In only a few minutes we sailed first northwest, then due east, due north, and then west toward the dock at Sturdies Bay. Trees, so close we could almost touch them, supported half a dozen aeries. Passengers have seen as many as forty bald eagles on this run.

AN ACTIVE PASS

In 1855 Commander James Allen, U.S.N., while on a reconnaissance mission for the U.S. government, named the waterway after his 750-ton paddle steamer *Active.* The name proved prophetic. The pass separating Galiano and Mayne islands is a tortuous, S-shaped raceway of water, 3½ miles long and, at its narrowest point, only a third of a mile wide. On an ebb enough water pours through this gap to fill the Empire State Building every *second.* Ferry boat captains steaming at eighteen knots can find themselves going half again that speed, carried along through a blind passageway lined with dangerous shoals and crammed with a flotilla of small boats. When the wind and tide are at odds, waves, seemingly standing in place, form dangerous rips. Skippers of deep-drafted sailboats are baffled when they find the hull being pulled one way, the keel another. This is exactly the kind of water herring enjoy. Salmon enjoy herring, and boat fishermen enjoy salmon, so the stage is set for trouble.

Five million people a year go through the pass on their voyage between Victoria and Vancouver, half of them during the summer when the salmon are also here. Commercial traffic uses Active Pass, too. So it was probably inevitable that an accident would happen, and indeed one did in 1970 when the Russian freighter *Sergey Yesenin* came out of nowhere and sliced into the ferry *Queen of Victoria.* Three passengers on the ferry lost their lives. The dramatic photo of the freighter's bow, riding high on the ferry's portside rail, made news-picture-of-the-year honors. Nine years later the captain of *Queen of Alberni,* trying to avoid a lot of traffic including a ferry coming the other way, steered too far to starboard and suddenly heard the sickening crunch of hull against rock. Cars and trucks were tossed about and $1 million-plus damage was done to her hull, but no lives were lost. People were quick to blame the fishermen. Horror stories were told of skippers, fearful of losing the big one on the line, refusing to get out of the way. Ferry schedules were subsequently altered so only one boat would be in the pass at a given time, and fishermen promised to be more watchful.

As if this weren't active enough, seven thousand Brandt cormorants and five thousand arctic loons pass through each year, and ten thousand Bonaparte gulls hang around most of the time.

My ferry docked at Galiano's Sturdies Bay at noon. This lovely island is shaped like a bottle—a bottle of, well, Galliano, actually—but I learned it was named after Donisio Alcala Galiano, captain of *Sutil.* He was a Spaniard who, with Cayetano Valdés, explored these waters in 1792 but lost his life when fortune found him on the wrong side at Trafalgar in 1805. After ten minutes of swapping passengers and cars, we turned back and repeated the adventure. On the return voyage we called again at Village Bay and then sailed to Pender Island's Otter Bay terminal before returning to Swartz Bay, docking at 1:30 P.M.

These southern Gulf Islands have a few places where adventuresome travelers can spend the night. Of the three, Pender is the most scenic, with a shoreline pierced by a hundred rocky coves. Around the turn of the century, the government blasted away the isthmus separating North Pender from South Pender, so you cross the rocky-shored waterway on a bridge.

FOOD AND LODGING

Pender Island   Population: 1,020 (V0N 2M0)

✔✔✔ **Bedwell Harbour Resort**   17 lovely motel units set in an English garden at the head of South Pender's best harbor. First port of call for American yachtsmen cruising Canadian waters. Restaurant, bar, marina, pool, and customs house. Route 1, South Pender. (604) 629-3212.

✔✔ **Cliffside Inn-on-the Sea**   4-unit B&B with solarium restaurant. General Delivery, Pender. (604) 629-6691.

✔ **Prior Centennial Provincial Park**   17 campsites.

Mayne Island   Population: 531 (V0N 2J0)

✔✔ **Fernhill Lodge and Herb Farm**   6-unit B&B. P.O. Box 140. (604) 539-2544.

Galiano Island   Population: 721 (V0N 1P0)

✔✔ **Bodega Resort**   Cabins, B&B, and dining. Horse rentals. P.O. Box 115. (604) 539-2677.

✔✔ **Galiano Lodge**   Motel, restaurant, and bar within walking distance of ferry dock. Sturdies Bay. (604) 539-5252.

✔ **Montague Harbour Provincial Park**   32 shoreside campsites.

•• **La Berengerie**   3-room B&B above noted French restaurant. Montague Harbour Road. (604) 539-5392.

THE MALAHAT: E&N RAIL EXCURSION •
(All-day side trip)

Islanders mistakenly thought that as a prize for confederation, Victoria would be chosen to be the western terminus of the transcontinental railway. Rather than following the Fraser River, the route was supposed to head west from Kamloops, finding tidewater on Bute Inlet near Campbell River. A bridge spanning Discovery Pass would take trains onto Vancouver Island and thence south to Victoria. It was a pipe dream, of course; today not even a dirt road follows the route on the mainland. But a 140-mile railway did get built on the island, primarily because coal was found in abundance in the 1880s, and getting it to market became a pressing need. It wasn't easy. Victoria is separated from the rest of Vancouver Island by steep mountains on the west and by the fjordlike Saanich Inlet on the east, where the cliffs along the shore were too steep for a right-of-way. So the Esquimalt and

Nanaimo Railway had to go over the top of a ridge, the celebrated Malahat.

The E&N Railway was later absorbed by Canadian Pacific. Passenger operations are part of Via, Canada's equivalent of Amtrak. A one- or two-unit, self-propelled railcar makes a daily run to Courtenay, stopping at Duncan, Nanaimo, and Qualicum Beach along the way. We'll visit those towns in the next chapter, so suffice it here to say that you can make a pleasant day trip up and back on the train that leaves from a station at the foot of the Johnson Street Bridge, six blocks from the Empress Hotel. The view out the train window from several spots along the Malahat route is okay, but to get a better sense of the countryside, you have to drive. Several turnouts on Highway 1 offer vistas of the Saanich Inlet, the Gulf Islands, and Mt. Baker on the U.S. mainland. The Malahat Highway was completed in 1911, but for another ten years Canadians, reflecting their British origins, drove on the wrong side of the road.

JUAN de FUCA STRAIT • (All-day side trip)

It would be nice if we could continue our northward trek along the seashore, but the western coast of Vancouver Island is just too rugged to do that, at least by automobile. It is, however, possible to drive most of the way out along the north shore of Juan de Fuca Strait to tiny Port Renfrew. The first stop is the great naval base at Esquimalt.

Esquimalt • Population: 15,053

The name, some etymologists believe, is derived from the Indian *is-whoy-malth*, meaning "a place gradually shoaling"—a curious anomaly, because ever since the white man came here, the harbor has been doing the opposite. As a sop for Vancouver Island's having lost the transcontinental railway, the federal government selected Esquimalt (pronounced ess-QUY-malt) as the home of the Royal Navy's Pacific Squadron. The harbor was deepened, a massive graving dock was constructed in 1887, and in the 1890s a fort was built to guard the entrance to the bay. **Fort Rodd Hill** and **Fisgard Lighthouse** are now national historic sites. Like the Death's Triangle, which we visited in Chapter 15, huge gun emplacements were built to repulse whatever enemy might be foolish enough to try to force the strait. Like the others, no shot was ever fired in anger. The large disappearing rifles here are fake, but a smaller battery still has its weapons in at least aimable condition. The fortress, now a park, is a lovely place for a picnic, and the view from the lighthouse is fantastic. But across the harbor, the sight of dozens of idle ships of every size and description, new ones and those with barnacled hulls, offers a glaring dichotomy. Freighters and trawlers, ferries and coastal packets, rest at peace here, awaiting a better day. Many used to trade along Vancouver Island's outer shore, but new roads hastened their demise. Above the waterline, at least, Esquimalt is the real graveyard of the Pacific.

Sooke • Population: 8,800

The little village of Sooke (the "e" is silent), located twenty miles from Victoria, abuts one of the prettiest bays on the Island. A lovely little museum has many old-time artifacts, including a steam donkey engine that still gets her boiler fired up every once in a while. The lovely **Sooke Harbour House,** set in an English garden, looks out over both the bay and the strait.

Beyond Sooke the road becomes quite rural, snaking its way through recently logged-over lands. Few cars come this way. I was astounded to see a bald eagle, intent on a piece of carrion, fly almost straight into my windshield. By the time I recovered enough to stop and get out, the magnificent bird was gone. Western Forest Products Ltd. (whose motto is "Trees for Tomorrow") has worked this land for some years in partnership with the provincial government. Signs along the road explain when each tract was replanted (mostly with western hemlock), when it was thinned, when herbicides were used to control the broadleafs, and even when the trees were fertilized. Five-year-olds were the size of modest Christmas trees; most ten-year-olds had grown to fifteen feet in height.

Short trails wind down to lovely strands at **French Beach** and **China Beach** provincial parks. Since we are still well inside the strait, the water is calm, but the driftwood piles up in abundance. A cafe at the three-building village of River Jordan looks out over the Olympic Peninsula.

FOOD AND LODGING   Sooke, British Columbia V0S 1N0

✔✔ **Sooke Harbour House**   15-room country inn with restaurant. 1528 Whiffen Spit Road. (604) 642-3421.

✔ **French Beach Provincial Park**   69 campsites.

Port Renfrew • Population: 94

The road along the strait turns to gravel and more or less ends at the village of Port Renfrew. I was surprised at the neatness of the town's residential area, which overlooks a small bay. People here either fish for a living or work in the woods. They socialize in the community hall or meet in the pub at the old hotel next to the government wharf. The bartender told me that the nine upstairs rooms are mostly filled during the summer with hikers who are either starting or ending a week-long trek along the West Coast (Lifesaving) Trail. This is the southern edge of the beautiful and remote **Pacific Rim National Park,** a place we'll explore in Chapter 19. A jeep road (very bad) continues on a couple of miles to a place called **Botanic Harbour,** noted for its tide pools.

The countryside north and inland from Port Renfrew is laced with logging roads, one of which wends its way to Lake Cowichan, where it connects with a paved road to the north part of the island. The forty-mile drive, I learned, takes about an hour and a half. Though a nice shortcut to the shoreline towns in the next chapter, I was a bit reluctant to drive the route because signs announced that the road was private and subject to closure. On returning to Victoria, I queried Ernie Christmas at the British Columbia Bureau of Tourism, who, after several phone calls, found someone at the logging company who could elaborate on the rules. The road, although unpaved, is wide and well graded. The only restrictions are that you drive with your headlights on, keep a wary eye out for logging trucks, and pull over if you see one.

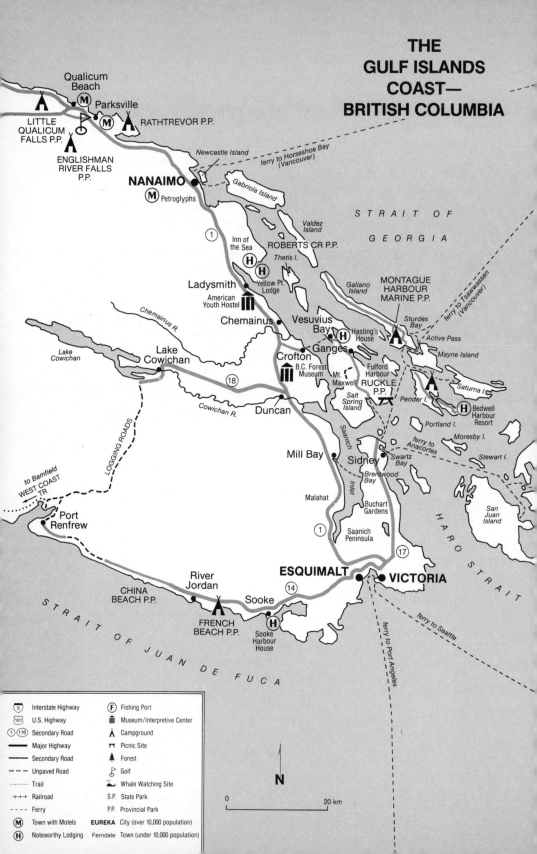

THE
GULF ISLANDS
COAST—
BRITISH COLUMBIA

Qualicum
Beach

(M) Parksville

(M)

LITTLE
QUALICUM
FALLS P.P.

RATHTREVOR P.P.

ENGLISHMAN
RIVER FALLS
P.P.

Newcastle Island

*ferry to Horseshoe Bay
(Vancouver)*

NANAIMO

(M) Petroglyphs

Gabriola Island

①

Inn of
the Sea

*Valdez
Island*

ROBERTS CR P.P.

S T R A I T   O F

G E O R G I A

Thetis I.

(H)

(H) Yellow Pt.
Lodge

Ladysmith

American
Youth Hostel

*Galiano
Island*

MONTAGUE
HARBOUR
MARINE P.P.

*Sturdes
Bay*

*ferry to Tsawwassen
(Vancouver)*

Chemainus

Chemainus R.

Vesuvius
Bay

(H) Hasting's
House

A

Active Pass

*Lake
Cowichan*

Lake
Cowichan

Ganges

Crofton

B.C. Forest
Museum

Mayne Island

Mt.
Maxwell

Fulford
Harbour

RUCKLE
P.P.

A

Pender I.

Saturna I.

Cowichan R.

Duncan

*Salt
Spring
Island*

Portland I.

(H) Bedwell
Harbour
Resort

Moresby I.

LOGGING ROADS

Saanich

Mill Bay

Sidney

*Swartz
Bay*

*ferry to
Anacortes*

Stewart I.

to Bamfield
WEST COAST
TR

*Brentwood
Bay*

Port
Renfrew

Malahat

Buchart
Gardens

*Saanich
Peninsula*

Saanich Inlet

*San
Juan
Island*

①

H A R O

①⑦

River
Jordan

ESQUIMALT

⑭

VICTORIA

CHINA
BEACH P.P.

Sooke

ferry to Seattle

FRENCH
BEACH P.P.

(H) Sooke
Harbour
House

S T R A I T   O F   J U A N   D E   F U C A

S T R A I T

ferry to Port Angeles

N

0   20 km

🛣 5	Interstate Highway	(F)	Fishing Port
🛣 101	U.S. Highway	🏛	Museum/Interpretive Center
① 116	Secondary Road	A	Campground
▬▬	Major Highway	⊼	Picnic Site
▬▬	Secondary Road	♣	Forest
– – –	Unpaved Road	⛳	Golf
········	Trail	🐋	Whale Watching Site
+++	Railroad	S.P.	State Park
– · –	Ferry	P.P.	Provincial Park
(M)	Town with Motels	**EUREKA**	City (over 10,000 population)
(H)	Noteworthy Lodging	Ferndale	Town (under 10,000 population)

18

VANCOUVER'S SUNNY INSIDE COAST

Up-Island Adventures

The Trans-Canada Highway, a five-thousand-mile, nearly continuous stretch of concrete and asphalt that eventually reaches St. John's, Newfoundland, officially begins at the southern end of Douglas Street on the shore of Juan de Fuca Strait. Canadians, considering it to be their national sinew, are quick to boast that it is almost two thousand miles longer than any U.S. counterpart. Purists, however, argue that the western terminus should not be in Victoria, but in Tofino, B.C., because that little town is actually on the Pacific Ocean and is one hundred miles farther from St. John's. Our objective is to wend our way to Tofino so you can decide for yourself. But first we'll go "up-island," as they say, exploring Vancouver's "inside," the sunny shoreline along the Strait of Georgia. The obvious way to begin is to drive north from Victoria on Highway 1, crossing the Malahat on the high-speed road, but we'll take a more interesting route by going via Saltspring Island instead.

Saltspring Island • Population: 5,450

Nestled in the lee of Vancouver Island, Saltspring is the largest and dryest of the Gulf Islands and boasts the greatest population. Many work in Victoria, I learned one weekday morning when I found myself sharing the six-thirty ferry with a hundred well-dressed passengers. Ten boats a day in each direction make the half-hour crossing between Swartz Bay and Fulford Harbour (John Fulford was captain of HMS *Ganges*). A couple of boats a day also sail from the mainland port of Tsawwassen to Saltspring's Long Harbour.

Insular life seems to foster a neighborliness and hospitality that makes a traveler feel welcome. I met Don Starlin while waiting in line for the ferry out to the island. It's common for residents to hitch a ride—that way they don't have to pay to take a car aboard the ferry—and by the end of the short voyage he had offered to show me around his modest bungalow. It became apparent that if one is frugal and willing to work, one can live out here for almost nothing. A post–World War II emigré from England, he had little respect for politicians with their government handouts ("twits," he called them), preferring instead to do things on his own. He showed me a wheelbarrow he'd built out of scrap lumber to haul apples and pears in from the orchard and explained how he had reroofed his house with hand-split shakes and had constructed a cistern to trap rainwater so he wouldn't have to use the hydro (electricity) for his deep-well pump. Before long he had me crawling under his house so he could show me how the foundations were simply cedar logs, charred to bring out the creosote, laid on the ground.

Saltspring has the same beauty and charm as San Juan and Orcas islands but without so many tourists. The only real town on the island was named not for the river in India, but after HMS *Ganges,* an eighty-four-gun frigate that in the late 1850s was flagship of the Pacific squadron. Retired in 1930, she was the Royal Navy's last sail-powered ship of the line to operate in foreign service. Like Friday Harbor, Ganges has several good restaurants, a modest shopping center (Et Cetera Books, Sunshine Farm Health Foods, and Lickitey Sip Ice Cream), an old-time general store called Mouat's, several arts and crafts shops, and a few places to stay. A small park abuts the boat basin, where the Government Wharf (run by the "warfinger") provides mooring for visiting yachtsmen.

Nestled in a nearby cove is a first-class hideaway that has all the charm of an English country inn or a French château. The main building at Hastings House is a three-story, half-timbered Tudor-style manor with a pleasant ivy-encrusted front porch, a sunny dining room, and a cozy fireplace set in a low, beam-ceilinged room furnished with antique sofas and wing-backed chairs. Guests stay in well-appointed cottages set in a garden and spend their days strolling along country lanes or rowing dinghies out in the sound. With typical British understatement, innkeeper Louise Harker told me, "Our cuisine is consistent with the setting." Hastings House is a member of a select group of inns called Relais & Chateaux, which promotes what they call the five C's: *Caractère, Courtoisie, Calme, Confort, Cuisine.*

A family farm, said to be the oldest in British Columbia, is now **Ruckle Provincial Park,** located on the eastern tip of the island. Around the turn of the century Henry Ruckle wrote:

> A man who understands farming, and has a little capital, will do as well here as anywhere in North America. We hold a very central position as to markets. The chief trouble is the clearing.

For his trouble clearing, we are fortunate to have about as pretty a place for a picnic as I have ever seen. Tables are set out on the grass near a grove of what Canadians call the arbutus tree (Pacific madrone). Some crackers, a hunk of Camembert, and a bottle of Chardonnay, enjoyed on a sunny afternoon, seems pretty close to paradise. Bicyclists encamp nearby. One told me that it is even more magical after sunset when the ferries, which pass only a few hundred yards from your tent, lend a festive mood to the night, puncturing the darkness with a thousand twinkling lights.

Saltspring lacks beaches but boasts a mountaintop belvedere as pretty as that on Orcas Island. A road, gravel in spots, leads to the two-thousand-foot summit of Baynes Peak, set in the midst of **Mt. Maxwell Provincial Park.** The view out over Fulford Harbour, Vancouver Island, and the mainland is grand indeed, much better than that from the celebrated Malahat, which we visited in the last chapter.

FOOD AND LODGING

✔✔✔ **Hastings House**   Country inn and dining room. P.O. Box 1110, Ganges V0S 1E0. (604) 537-2362.

✔✔ **Fulford Inn**   8-unit hotel, restaurant and pub near ferry terminal. P.O. Box 27, Fulford Harbour V0S 1C0. (604) 653-4432.

✔✔ **Harbour House**   20-unit motel, restaurant and bar. P.O. Box 99, Ganges V0S 1E0. (604) 537-5571.

✔✔ **Seabreze Motel**   30-unit motel. R2, Ganges V0S 1E0. (604) 537-4145.

✔ **Rita's Inn**   Modest hotel (bath down the hall) and restaurant. P.O. Box 272, Ganges V0S 1E0. (604) 537-5338.

✔ **Ruckle Provincial Park**   40 walk-in campsites.

VANCOUVER ISLAND

George Vancouver wanted to show his affection for Juan Francisco de la Bodega y Quadra by naming this island Vancouver and Quadra, but the English who settled here scotched the idea. (An American, Captain Gray, who discovered the Columbia River, also held the Spaniard in high esteem; he named his son Robert Don Quadra Gray.) By the time Vancouver had circumnavigated the island, he knew he had found the largest offshore landmass on the Pacific Coast. Canada is immense (second only to the U.S.S.R.), and British Columbia by itself is larger than California, Oregon, and Washington combined. A small-scale map is required to get it all in, so on our maps Vancouver Island looks no larger than, say, New York's Long Island but in fact has six times the area. The island's spine is a three-hundred-mile series of mountains, four to six thousand feet high, stretching from Victoria to Port Hardy. The land to the west of the mountains is pierced by a thousand bays and inlets with hardly a level piece of ground anywhere. East of the ridge, though, the countryside is more to man's liking, with broad valleys and level plains stretching inland for ten or more miles. The Indians named this country Cowichan, meaning "land warmed by the sun." It's apple orchard and pasture country, much drier and less windy than the west side, and since the shoreline faces protected water, the seas are calmer. The natives boast that this area has the warmest salt water north of San Francisco. Little wonder then that mainlanders find it an ideal place for a summer vacation.

Half a dozen ferries a day make the fifteen-minute crossing between Vesuvius on Saltspring and Crofton, a port a few miles from the Trans-Canada Highway.

Crofton/Chemainus • Population: 5,000

Before we proceed up-island, however, there is reason to detour a few miles south to visit the **British Columbia Forest Museum.** A narrow-gauge railway sets the scene for this family playground cum historical museum. A 1911 Shay locomotive or a curious little tank engine hauls cars around a park graced with paraphernalia from the timber industry. Visitors get off at displays of steam donkeys, blacksmith shops, and relocated logging camp buildings. Among other things, you learn how logs are milled, shakes split, and wood turned into paper. Giant murals, a gift of the Truck Loggers Association, depict scenes from the woods. I found myself intrigued by the loggers' jargon (see Don't Call Him a Lumberjack, page 281).

DON'T CALL HIM A LUMBERJACK

Lumberjacks may work in the puny white pine forests around the Great Lakes, but out here, where trees grow to be man-size, the fellows who cut them down and get them snaked out of the woods are loggers. They have to cope with the likes of skookums, big standing dead trees; schoolmarms, giant conifers that have split and grown into double trees; and barber chairs, trunks that splinter as they fall. The butts of these monsters are so large that fallers can't just stand on the ground and whale away with their double-bladed axes. In the old days they worked ten feet in the air, standing on six-inch-wide springboards that were wedged into notches cut in the stump. I'm told that, contrary to popular belief, loggers never did yell "Timberrr!" when the tree fell but simply shouted out whatever they thought would get their crewmates' attention.

Two buckers, one on each end, worked the sweedish fiddle, also called the misery whip, and the choke setters and chain tenders manhandled the lines set by the head rigger and operated by a donkey puncher, who responded to signals from a whistle punk. All the while the gang had to keep a wary eye out for widow makers, falling dead branches. Before the days of the donkey engine, bull punchers drove oxen over skid roads, the so-called corduroy roads built of logs laid sideways on the ground that were lubricated by a skid greaser. The whole operation was run by a side rod, the foreman, but the glamorous job belonged to the high climber.

A 1924 magazine article about the Pacific Spruce Company described a typical forest crew:

> The following is a list of men employed at each side: One windfall bucker, twelve fallers and buckers, one head bucker, four choker setters, one hook tender, three chasers, three engineers, one fireman, one whistle punk, two loaders, one foreman, and one powder monkey.

The article goes on to describe the operation:

> A head spar tree is first chosen, as close to the [railroad] track as possible and the head rigger equips it with the necessary guy lines and blocks for a 12×14 compound-geared two-speed Willamette for the high-lead system. This spar tree is also rigged for a double-boom loader operated by an 11×13 three-drum Willamette loading donkey assisted by a "monkey chunk" [log counterweight].

Where there was a nearby river, lake, or fjord, logs were hauled to dumping waters and floated to a rafting pocket, where they were dogged into storage booms and taken to the booming grounds. After a hard day's work, presumably everyone headed for the smokehouse for a bite to eat.

During the early part of this century, woodsmen were recruited from the ranks of the brindlestiffs (migrant workers), but today much of the felling and hauling is done by gyppos, independent contractors. The word is in no way demeaning.

Chemainus, located a few miles north of the Crofton ferry terminal, is a town of special interest, not only because it is a nice place to be, but because its very existence says a bit about the people who live on this island (see "The Little Town That Did," page 283). The area boasts a fine golf course.

FOOD AND LODGING

✔✔ **Twin Gables Resort**   14 cottages near Crofton ferry terminal. P.O. Box 39, Crofton V0R 1R0. (604) 246-3112.

✔ **Horsehoe Bay Inn**   11 rooms in a 100-year-old roadside tavern. Restaurant. (604) 246-4535.

Ladysmith • Population: 4,500

South Africa's town of Ladysmith was named after the wife of Harry Smith, first governor of Cape Colony. During the Boer War British troops lifted a siege of the town, an event that inspired coal baron James Dunsmuir to rename this modest village. Ladysmithers like to point out that they live directly atop the forty-ninth parallel and so this the first truly Canadian city you visit on the island. The modest downtown is close to the waterfront, so it has become a favorite resupply point for visiting yachtsmen. There is a nice beach nearby, and the Crown Zellerbach Company has a small museum and arboretum, open to the public. Various species of forest trees have been planted here, including several hardly native to the island, a dawn redwood, English yew, and a cedar of Lebanon.

Two fine resorts are located on nearby Yellow Point, both very nice yet quite different. Yellow Point Lodge, the older of the two, is set up for guests to share common facilities. They stay in modest cottages but mingle in the magnificent log-style main building, its large lounge graced with an immense fireplace. Meals are served at large tables at a single sitting (the resort operates on the American plan); people read after dinner, chat, or work on a jigsaw puzzle. By contrast, the Inn of the Sea has larger and much fancier accommodations—many have kitchens—so

"THE LITTLE TOWN THAT DID"

The deep water at Horseshoe Bay made a fine port, and the sunny reaches of the Cowichan and Chemainus rivers seemed perfect for growing fruits and grains. So people began to settle here in the 1850s, and the farms and ranches they built supplied the tables of Victoria. Then in 1862 a small water-wheel-powered sawmill was built, setting the stage for the dramatic events of the 1980s: the town of Chemainus's near death and then miraculous rebirth.

The mill grew into the Victoria Lumber & Manufacturing Company (now part of the giant MacMillan & Bloedel operation), and Chemainus became a one-industry town without much charm. The few who had ever heard about the place knew it for being the tidewater terminus of the first, the last, and longest-enduring steam rail logging operation in British Columbia, the Copper Canyon Railway. Willow Street was lined with nondescript, plaster-walled, aluminum window–framed storefronts that hardly encouraged anyone to shop here. "We used to say we came from Vancouver Island, not Chemainus," resident Alan Wylie told me. "Labor unrest and high wages became so worrisome that the company closed the mill. Chemainus was about to die."

But it didn't. A dreamer, Karl Schutz, decided to marshal the citizenry's pride in self and their interest in the past. Borrowing an idea from a village in Moldavia, he set out on a project to literally change the face of the town. Taking the history of the area as his motif, he organized the Chemainus Festival of Murals. Artists were brought in to paint whatever surface was available—a wall, the side of a building, a fire tower—with pictures of the past. The heroic faces of a band of Chemainus Indians face one street, a picture of a gang of Chinese hauling lumber another. Sailing ships lie at anchor, an iron horse chugs across a crude bridge spanning a swollen river. There are twenty murals now and a couple of statues that continue the theme. The project spurred merchants to spruce up their stores and lured others to locate here. Volunteers with a knowledge of history staff a booth where souvenirs are sold. Filmmakers came with their cameras and crews, which resulted in a half-hour television show that was aired nationwide. Chemainus became a modest tourist destination. The festival organizers even copyrighted their slogan: "The Little Town That Did."

And what of the mill that closed? "It turned out to be a ruse," a fellow told me. "As soon as they got the labor contract they wanted, the company opened it right back up again."

although there is a very nice restaurant and bar, guests tend to spend more time in their rooms. Both resorts offer swimming, tennis, and boating. The nearby **Roberts Memorial Park,** which faces out on the Strait of Georgia, is a pleasant place for a picnic.

FOOD AND LODGING Ladysmith, British Columbia V0R 2E0

✔✔✔ **Inn of the Sea Resort** 60 condo units, restaurant, bar. R.R. 3. (604) 245-2211.

✔✔✔ **Yellow Point Lodge** Lodge and cabins, restaurant, bar. R.R. 3. (604) 245-7422.

✔ **Travelers Youth Hostel** 59-bed hostel in an old brick hotel. P.O. Box 1409. (604) 245-2441.

●● **Mañana Lodge** 3-room B&B, restaurant. R.R. 1. (604) 245-2312.

Nanaimo • Population: 50,500

The Hudson's Bay Company built a fort here in 1852 when good-quality coal seams were discovered in the area. The **Bastion,** a blockhouse located on the bluff above the harbor, is the only surviving structure from that era. The coal mines gave out in 1952, and now the city serves primarily as a transportation hub (a dozen ferries a day sail to the mainland near Vancouver) and regional shopping center. As in many American cities, Nanaimo's downtown is disappointing; most of the merchants moved to giant suburban shopping centers (Rutherford Village, anchored by The Bay and Woodgrove, whose principal tenant is Eaton's). Nevertheless, the best up-island hotel is here, the Coast Bastion Inn, which has a dozen floors of guest rooms that look out on the harbor. Out front is a handsome three-story seaplane terminal built to resemble a Victorian lighthouse. A restaurant and bar occupy the upper two floors. The city, in preparation for a visit by the royal family, spruced up its waterfront and built the lovely Queen Elizabeth II promenade.

The **Centennial Museum** near the town center has a huge seashell collection, some relics depicting the large Chinese settlement here and a replica of the inside of a coal mine. An exhibit reflects on the mine explosion of 1887 when one hundred whites and fifty Chinese lost their lives. **Malispina College,** named after a Spanish sea captain, serves the educational needs of a territory the size of South Carolina.

Highlight of a visit to Nanaimo is to (figuratively, at least) haul coal to Newcastle. **Newcastle Island,** named for the Tyneside city in northern England, is the former playground for mainlanders looking for a pleasant country outing. In the 1920s, the Canadian Pacific Railway operated several ships that sailed over from Vancouver with a manifest of straw-hatted gentlemen and their parasol-attired ladies. Nowadays a passenger launch sails every hour or so from a downtown pier. Ten miles of gentle trails crisscross the island, one of which leads to Giovando Lookout, where you can watch the ferries sailing to Vancouver. It's a great place to spend an afternoon.

FOOD AND LODGING   Nanaimo, British Columbia

✔✔✔ **Coast Bastion Inn**   180-unit full-service hotel. 11 Bastion Street, V9R 2Z9. (604) 753-6601.

✔✔ **Best Western Harbourview Inn**   78-unit motel, restaurant and bar. 809 Island Highway, V9R 5K1. (604) 754-8171.

✔✔ **Highlander Motor Inn**   78-unit motel. 96 Terminal Avenue N, V9S 4J2. (604) 754-6355.

✔✔ **Moby Dick Boatel**   45-unit motel. 1000 Stewart Avenue, V9S 4C9. (604) 753-7111.

✔✔ **Westward Ho Motel**   250 Terminal Avenue N, V9S 4J5. (604) 754-4202.

✔ **Bluebird Motel**   995 Terminal Avenue N, V9S 4K3. (604) 753-4151.

Gabriola Island • Population: 1,630

Bicyclists and escapists enjoy this, the northernmost of the Gulf Islands, located a few miles from Nanaimo. Hourly ferries leave from the old C.P. docks south of the downtown area.

FOOD AND LODGING   Gabriola Island, British Columbia V0R 1X0

✔✔ **Haven by the Sea**   30-cabin resort, restaurant and bar. (604) 247-9211.

✔✔ **Surf Lodge**   20-unit resort, restaurant and bar. (604) 247-9231.

Parksville/Qualicum Beach • Population: 9,100

The Trans-Canada Highway officially becomes the car deck of a B.C. ferry at Nanaimo. In its place, the Island Highway

(Route 19) continues north, meeting the shore of the Strait of Georgia at lovely Nanoose Bay. For the next fifty miles, the road hardly leaves the coast; motorists are rewarded with one lovely viewpoint after another. This is the heart of the resort country. Motels line the highway and face out toward the water. Parksville has the principal shopping district, but Qualicum Beach is the prettiest spot. A three-mile-long promenade stretches along a sandy beach—if there were palm trees, you would think you were in Santa Barbara. Hidden in the shore pines between the two towns is a first-class golf course, and believe it or not, the croquet championship of the world is held in Parksville in August. The beaches here are unusually gentle, but the tides are often extreme (fifteen feet), so at low tide waders can walk several hundred yards out into the strait. There is virtually no surf, but the water is warm and the clamming is terrific.

Three lovely parks are nearby. **Rathtrevor Provincial Park** faces the strait and has a fine beach. The other two, **Little Qualicum Falls** and **Englishman River Falls Provincial Park,** are located inland. The Little Qualicum River is famous for its salmon and steelhead fishing.

FOOD AND LODGING

✔✔ **The Bayside Inn**   60-unit full-service bayside resort. P.O. Box 3000, Parksville V0R 2S0. (604) 248-8333.

✔✔ **Best Western College Inn**   70-unit full-service resort in the former Qualicum College buildings. P.O. Box 99, Qualicum Beach V0R 2T0. (604) 752-9262.

✔✔ **Old Dutch Inn**   35-unit motel, restaurant, bar. P.O. Box 1240, Qualicum Beach V0R 2T0. (604) 752-6914.

✔✔ **Schooner Cove Resort and Marina**   44-unit full-service resort cum yacht harbor. P.O. Box 12, Nanoose Bay V0R 2R0. (604) 468-7691.

✔✔ **The Shorewater**   24-unit oceanfront motel. 3295 West Island Highway, Qualicum Beach V0R 2T0. (604) 752-6901.

✔✔ **Tigh-Na-Mara**   42 bayside cottages. Resort. R.R. 1, Parksville V0R 2S0. (604) 248-2072.

✔ **Englishman River Falls Provincial Park**   105 campsites.

✔ **Little Qualicum Falls Provincial Park**   91 campsites.

✔ **Rathtrevor Provincial Park**   173 campsites.

●●● **Ma Maison**   French restaurant. (604) 248-5859.

More resort country, though not as intense, continues on almost to Courtenay. We'll explore that area in a while, but first there are some special reasons to travel westward to explore part of Vancouver Island's outside coast.

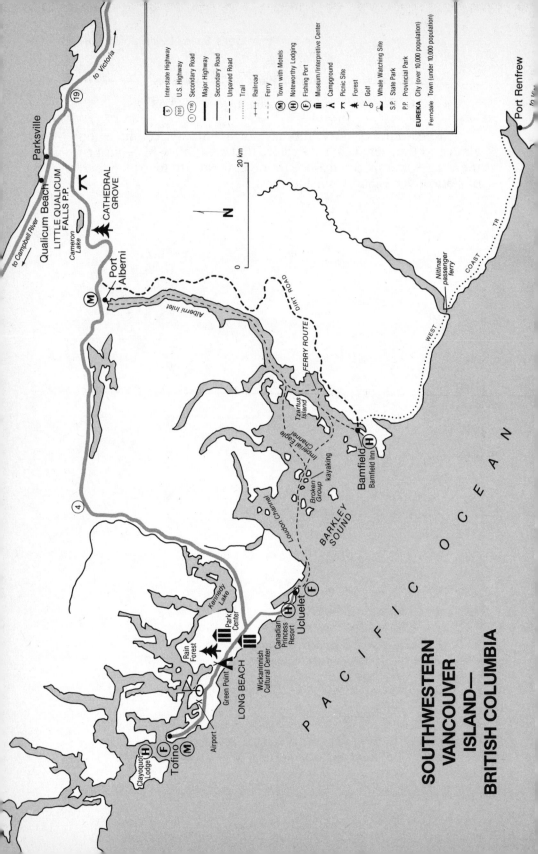

SOUTHWESTERN VANCOUVER ISLAND— BRITISH COLUMBIA

Legend

5	Interstate Highway
1 116	U.S. Highway
—	Major Highway
—	Secondary Road
— —	Secondary Road
- - -	Unpaved Road
.....	Trail
+++	Railroad
– – –	Ferry
Ⓜ	Town with Motels
Ⓗ	Noteworthy Lodging
Ⓕ	Fishing Port
🏛	Museum/Interpretive Center
⋀	Campground
🌲	Picnic Site
♠	Forest
⛳	Golf
🐋	Whale Watching Site
S.P.	State Park
P.P.	Provincial Park
EUREKA	City (over 10,000 population)
Ferndale	Town (under 10,000 population)

N

0   20 km

PACIFIC OCEAN

to Victoria
19
Parksville
Qualicum Beach
to Campbell River
LITTLE QUALICUM FALLS P.P.
CATHEDRAL GROVE
Cameron Lake
Ⓜ Port Alberni
4
Alberni Inlet
Kennedy Lake
Rain Forest
Park Center
Green Point
LONG BEACH
Wickaninnish Cultural Center
Airport
Ⓗ Clayoquot Lodge
Ⓕ
Ⓜ Tofino
Canadian Princess Resort
Ⓗ Ucluelet
Ⓕ
Loudon Channel
Broken Group
kayaking
Imperial Eagle Channel
Tzartus Island
BARKLEY SOUND
FERRY ROUTE
DIRT ROAD
Bamfield Ⓗ
Bamfield Inn
WEST COAST TR.
Nitinat passenger ferry
Port Renfrew

PACIFIC RIM NATIONAL PARK

Outside Adventures Around
Captain Barkley's Sound

> We came to another very large sound, to which Captain Barkley gave his own name. Several coves and bays and also islands in this sound we named. There was Frances Island, after myself; Hornby peak, also after myself; Cape Beal after our purser.

The seventeen-year-old bride of the English explorer penned these words in her diary one June day in 1787 when *Imperial Eagle* lay at anchor in Vancouver Island's largest inland waterway. Captain Charles Barkley's ship was flying an Austrian flag because he had neglected to get a trading license as required by the British East India Company. But his hold was already bulging with nine hundred sea otter pelts, and he wanted to trade for more before sailing off to China and, as the crew of Captain Cook's ship proved, a sure profit. Frances Barkley appreciated the naming gesture, but her husband was interested in furs, not exploration. Another five years would pass before George Vancouver proved that the sound was not part of the North American mainland.

Shortcut Access to the Pacific Rim National Park

B.C. Ferries offers nearly hourly cross-sound service from Horseshoe Bay near the city of Vancouver to Nanaimo, a twenty-minute drive to our Barkley Sound turnoff. Crossing time is an hour and a half.

Port Alberni • Population: 19,500

Highway 4, which leads over the island's spine, was originally called the Alberni Colonization Road; the government was
encouraging settlers into the more out-of-the-way places. It
didn't work; few wanted to live on the west side because the
weather was too bad. But industry did what government
couldn't, and now there is a sizable community of people living
on what islanders call the "outside." What brought them were
logs—principally hemlock logs, which tend to sink and thus can't
be rafted great distances. Timber companies concluded that it was
better to locate their mills near the forests, and of course the mills
brought the people.

Any semblance of farmland disappears as you climb toward
the 1,200-foot summit of Highway 4. A side road leads to **Little
Qualicum Falls,** a series of very impressive cataracts. The highway then skirts around tarnlike Camaroon Lake, where there is a
nice little swimming beach. **MacMillan Provincial Park,** located at the far end of the lake, is famous for its **Cathedral
Grove** of giant Douglas fir. Three hundred years ago a fire destroyed many of the trees, but there are a few monsters left, and a
walk through the forest is pleasant, Canada's answer to California's redwoods. A plaque pays tribute to David Douglas, the
Scottish-born botanist for whom the tree (which is not a true fir)
was named. Douglas, a brilliant man, investigated these woods a
few years before he was killed while cataloging the botany of
Hawaii.

Don Pedro Alberni, a Spanish sea captain, was the first really
to explore this area (thus the name of the city). Though we are
only a third of the way across Vancouver Island, it is a major port
of call for oceangoing ships. Barkley Sound and the long, fjordlike Alberni Inlet provide a forty-mile deep-water link to the
Pacific. The E&N Railway comes over the hill from Nanaimo,
bringing goods for transshipment by sea, but the giant forest
products firm MacMillan Bloedel Ltd. generates most of the cargo. Bert Simpson took a group of us on a tour of the pulp mill
where they make kraft, pulp, and newsprint. We toured the
wood room, where we watched the debarking operation, then
visited the groundwood department, where twelve giant grinders,
each with four-foot-diameter Carborundum stones, grind the logs
into a stringy mush, and finally watched in awe as a block-long,
four-story-high machine transformed a soupy puree that looked
like a watery Boston clam chowder into a marketable product.
What came out the other end was a fine-quality paper, ready
to become the phone company's Yellow Pages. This is the

clean part of the mill—Bert didn't take us through the department that takes wood chips and cooks them into a foul-smelling liquor—but we did see the hogger, a machine that makes fuel for the steam plant out of otherwise unusable wood, bark, scraps, knots, and whatever.

For its size and remote location, Port Alberni has a large number of restaurants and motels, primarily because the fishing here is so good. Natives for the most part go over the hill to Nanaimo to do their major shopping, but there is a new area called **Harbour Quay** that has some nice stores. The *Lady Rose* docks here. An outdoor farmer's market was attempted, but according to Yvonne Waveryn, it wasn't too successful because the wind blows too hard. An old Shay locomotive called "the 2-Spot" makes summer excursions along the waterfront.

FOOD AND LODGING   Port Alberni, British Columbia

✔✔ **Hospitality Inn**   50-unit motel, restaurant and bar. 3835 Redford Street, V9Y 3S2. (604) 723-8111.

✔✔ **Timber Lodge Motor Inn**   22-unit motel, restaurant and bar, pool. R.R. 2, V9Y 7L6. (604) 723-9415.

✔ **Harbour Way Motel**   24-unit motel. 3805 Redford Street, V9Y 3S2. (604) 723-9405.

✔ **Tyee Village Motel**   51-unit motel. 4151 Redford Street, V9Y 3R6.

●● **Little Villa Restaurant**   European cuisine. (604) 724-3612.

BARKLEY SOUND'S M.V. *LADY ROSE*

Thanks to a hatchery that releases ten million juveniles a year, Port Alberni boasts being "the salmon capital of the world." It might be; first prize in the salmon derby is $10,000, and on the one day I was here, there must have been five hundred small boats trolling Alberni Inlet. For tourists, however, *Lady Rose* is the reason for coming here. This well-loved old-timer (see M.V. *Lady Rose*, page 292) makes voyages out into Barkley Sound all year long, delivering groceries, mail, tools, or whatever people at isolated fishing villages might need. On alternate days she sails to Bamfield at the south entrance to the sound and to Ucluelet on the north. Ucluelet is best visited by car, so I chose to take the ferry to Bamfield.

The country is so spectacular that the boat ride invariably

M.V. *LADY ROSE*

She started out life as *Lady Sylvia,* a plucky two-hundred-ton coastal packet designed for service in these sheltered waters. She's an odd-looking craft because her owners, the Union Steamships Limited, of Vancouver, wanted a vessel low to the water so that both passengers and cargo could be transferred from hold to dock with ease and dispatch at any stage of the tide. Oversize doors were fitted into the hull, extending almost down to the waterline, and when they are open the hole is so large it looks as though the forward third of the boat might suddenly fall off. The ship has only one enclosed deck; cargo is stored forward, passengers occupy the aft section. The crew quarters are in between. If you want some fresh air, you have to go topside where the wheelhouse is located. For economic reasons, she was fitted with a single 220-horsepower diesel engine, built by a firm in England at a town with the delightful (and so British) name of Ashton-Under-Lyne.

All well and good, but there remained the problem of how to get a ship of this design from Glasgow, where she was built, to Vancouver. In 1937 no single-engine ship that didn't also have sails had ever dared an Atlantic crossing. A mechanical failure would doom both ship and crew, and for a while that is exactly what it seemed would happen. A couple of days out of the Clyde, historian A. M. Kinnersley Saul reported:

> a falling glass and a fast rising swell met them on arrival in "The Bay" and it was soon apparent that *Lady Sylvia* was a lively ship with a movement which made it difficult and often impossible to do more than hold grimly on.

She made it, of course, the voyage took sixty-four days, and she has been doing yeoman duty ever since, fortunately in more calm waters.

Renamed *Lady Rose,* she has been the year-round lifeblood of Barkley Sound since 1961. The ship is licensed to carry one hundred passengers, boasts a small kitchen that somehow keeps them well fed, and still cruises with that single engine. Her rudder system has been modified, however. Air pistons were added to assist in docking; the captain can go quickly from hard starboard to hard of port with a pull on a lever. Those low-to-the-water doors in her side perform a function never dreamed of by her designers. They are perfect for the loading and unloading of kayaks and canoes, which, during the summer, are perhaps her most lucrative cargo.

draws a host of curious travelers who spend an entire day taking in the scenery and in the process making new friends. Passengers stood about on the deck, binoculars at the ready, hoping some- one would spot a bald eagle (some did). Conversation came easily. By afternoon I had learned something about the lives of half a dozen Canadians who were out for the ride. *Lady Rose*, chugging along at eleven knots, didn't seem in a hurry. We stopped at several logging camps to deliver groceries, and once a launch came alongside and a fellow, duffel in hand, jumped aboard. At the ten-building village of Kildonan, passengers watched attentively as deckhands unloaded a crate of lettuce, and at a nearby commercial fish farm we offloaded some kitchen cabinets for a new building. These steep, narrow waterways are densely wooded, with hardly a level place for a house; so many fishermen who have mounted mobile homes on barges towed them to some secluded cove and tied them to a tree. A small craft serves to fetch fresh water and bring in a supply of cordwood. Alberni Inlet seemed to me to be as spectacular as Norway's Sognefjorden.

For information, write or call M.V. LADY ROSE: Alberni Marine Transportation Inc. P.O. Box 188, Port Alberni V9Y 7M7. (604) 723-8313.

PACIFIC RIM NATIONAL PARK'S BROKEN GROUP UNIT

When *Lady Rose* turned away from Imperial Eagle Channel and sailed into a mélange of tiny islands, some of my shipmates became eager to get to our next stop, which turned out to be a raft in the middle of nowhere. We hadn't seen a shack in half an hour, and here there was nothing but trees. The reason for our stop became apparent when a dozen kayaks and a mound of dunnage was passed out onto the float, followed by a gaggle of adventuresome souls. "See you on Wednesday," the captain shouted as we steamed away (this was Thursday). The Broken Group, it turns out, is one of North America's premier kayaking spots with over one hundred islands scattered about the mouth of Barkley Sound. Anthropologists speculate that before the white man came several thousand Indians lived here, but now they are gone. When the federal government created the Pacific Rim National Park, this was declared a wilderness area; primitive campsites were established on the six islands that have reliable potable water. Kayakers explore tide pools, walk ancient trails, fish for salmon, and scuba dive in what looks to me to be awfully cold water. The ones I met, however, had a week of perfect weather.

Bamfield • Population: 206

Lady Rose makes two stops in Bamfield, one on the western side of the inlet where most of the people live and again on the eastern shore where the dirt road from Port Alberni comes in. People living in Bamfield East take a boat to go shopping; those in Bamfield West do the same to get to their car if they want to drive into town. A marine biology laboratory, sponsored by several universities, occupies the former terminal building of the trans-Pacific cable that goes to Australia. Fishing has traditionally been the primary business in summer and shrimping in the winter. I had a nice chat with Bob Barker, who said he got 90¢ a pound for shrimp and over $2.00 a pound for salmon, but that was not really enough to make the payments on his $100,000 boat. But he seemed happy, and as soon as the craft left the dock he gave the helm over to his ten-year-old son.

Lately, tourism has taken a strong foothold here. Several outfitters take sportfishermen out in skiffs, and since this is the northern end of the West Coast Trail, a few places cater to hikers eager for a hot shower and a dry bed. A short trail from West Bamfield leads to the pretty little Brady's Beach, an excellent spot to look for whales. A fine all-day excursion is to take a small boat to the head of Bamfield Inlet and walk to Cape Beale. The lighthouse can be visited only at low tide.

FOOD AND LODGING   Bamfield, British Columbia V0R 1B0

✔✔✔ **Bamfield Inn**   First-class fishing resort near *Lady Rose* dock. Dining room and lounge. Mail address: 6151 Sheridan Road, Richmond, British Columbia V7A 1L3. (604) 728-3354.

✔✔ **Aguilar House**   7 cottages near the ocean. Home-cooked meals. (604) 728-3323.

✔✔ **Bamfield Trails Motel**   31-unit eastside motel. P.O. Box 7. (604) 728-3231.

PACIFIC RIM NATIONAL PARK'S WEST COAST TRAIL UNIT

Surely the most adventuresome walk on our entire sojourn is along the West Coast, or Lifesaving, Trail, which traverses the roadless forty-five-mile length of southwestern Vancouver Island, one of the world's most treacherous shores (see What's "Pacific" About This Ocean?, page 295). Most hikers take five days to walk from Bamfield to Port Renfrew (Chapter 18) or vice versa. The trail had its beginnings in tragedy when *Valencia* went on the beach in 1906 and there was no way for rescue parties to get to the hulk. Only 38 of the 164 aboard survived, resulting in a public clamor for better access. In his informative book *The Pacific Rim Explorer,* Bruce Obee suggests that you're walking through a graveyard:

- The engine block of *Apache Hunter* . . . sits on the beach.
- There are few remains from *Lizzy Marshall,* a three-masted bark.
- The anchor is all that remains of *Skagit,* a three-masted barquentine.
- Look for timbers from the wreck of the *Raita.*
- You may find an anchor . . . from the three-masted schooner *Vesta.*

WHAT'S "PACIFIC" ABOUT THIS OCEAN?

This area has often been called the "storm watching capital of the world," a surprising boast, perhaps, considering the name of the ocean we're looking out over. Give credit to Vasco Núñez de Balboa for that blunder. The waters must have been calm that September day in 1513 when, while standing on a hill in present-day Panama, Balboa became the first European to lay eyes on the long-sought "other sea." Explorers have mused over the name ever since. William Clark of the Lewis and Clark expedition expressed his thoughts about the misnomer as well as anyone. On December 1, 1805, while camped near the mouth of the Columbia, he wrote:

> The sea which is imedeately in front roars like a repeated rolling thunder and have roared in that way ever since our arrival in its borders which is now 24 days since we arrived in sight of the Great Western Ocian, I cant say Pasific as since I have seen it, it has been the reverse.

What Balboa didn't know was that the "other sea" was immense. You're looking at the longest unbroken stretch of water in the world. The prevailing westerlies have had a long time to build up some impressive waves; there are no peninsulas or islands to slow them down, so by the time they reach these shores they're moving at a good clip. It's little wonder, then, why this coast earned its reputation as "the graveyard of ships."

Over the years, fifty ships have met their doom on this rocky coast, and captains are still uneasy when sailing toward the inland ports. I once had the pleasure of being on the bridge of *Santa Mercedes* while entering Juan de Fuca Strait. The set-faced captain paced about nervously, alternately looking out the window and peering into a radar scope. Then his demeanor changed abruptly; he muttered, "Well, we're inside now," and promptly retired to his quarters.

In spite of the wreckage, the hikers I talked to said they had a marvelous time. The highlight of the trek is a walk along the beach where the massive Tsusiat Falls drops directly into the surf. Roland Smith of the *Lady Rose* told me that over five thousand people a year walk at least part of the trail. Some only go from Bamfield to Tsusiat Falls and then return, but over half make the entire trek. Most of those start at the southern end near Port Renfrew so they can get the hardest part over with first.

The scenery is only part of the adventure. Occasionally ladders have to be climbed and you have to cross two rivers on scary cable cars suspended a hundred feet above the water. Your partners pull on a rope to haul you and your dunnage over. A park brochure states:

> You are required to cross deep gullies on fallen trees, negotiate very steep slopes, and follow an irregular, slippery, and muddy trail.

Rangers suggest carrying a fifty-foot climbing rope to serve as a lifeline while fording streams.

Just getting to the trailhead and back to where you started is an ordeal that requires careful planning. Many do it the easy way by taking a float plane (surprisingly inexpensive) to the far trailhead and then walking back. Port Alberni has frequent bus service to the "inside" cities, and once a day a tiny bus goes to Bamfield, stopping at the northern trailhead; but there is no public transportation to Port Renfrew. So some take an extra day and leave a shuttle car there. Others enlist the help of friends making the same trip. One group starts at the south, the other the north. They exchange car keys when they meet. If this isn't enough to discourage you from making the walk, consider that at the midpoint you have to rely on being ferried across an inlet by a band of Nitinats. Daily shuttle service is offered during the primary hiking season, but at other times you have to call ahead. How? A national park brochure says: "Dial 0-711 for Campbell River radio telephone operator—ask for Nitinat Raven." Just where you find a telephone along this wilderness trail, they don't say.

Ucluelet • Population: 1,600

Nancy Panton, who works at the interpretive center near Ucluelet, told me she was sure happy when they built the road out here in 1973. "Before that all we had was *Lady Rose*, and she came only three times a week. If I had a dentist appointment, I had to stay overnight in Port Alberni. The boat brought out the groceries and such, but if we wanted booze, we had to make a special deal with the captain. Quite a change; now a half a million people a year come here." The road is twisty but paved all the way, and it is very pretty. Waterfalls cascade down from thousand-foot-high cliffs, and you skirt along the rockbound shore of Kennedy Lake.

Ucluelet lies on the south end of a twenty-five-mile peninsula that separates Barkley Sound from the intricately shaped Clayoquot Sound. Everybody admits it should be pronounced "You-clue-let," but most people drop the first "1" and just say "Ewe-klet." The word means "safe harbor." The coming of the highway turned a once sleepy little fishing village into a bustling sports center. A large firm in Victoria purchased an old hydrographic research vessel, the *William J. Stewart*, towed her to Ucluelet's sheltered harbor, renamed her *Canadian Princess*, and made her into a resort for fishermen. She has a sense of charm, with two oak-paneled salons, a mess seating sixty or more, and a couple of dozen staterooms, each with one to six berths, a porthole, and a washbasin. Unless you are fishing, though, it's best to stay at one of their handsome new lodge units ashore, because everybody gets up at 4:00 A.M. and the boat is steel—all that bustling around makes a terrible racket. The desk clerk told me they consider themselves "the McDonald's of the fishing business." For a few hundred dollars including airfare (commuter planes land near Tofino), sportsmen get two nights' lodging, tackle, and a place on a fifteen-person party boat. "The average is two fish per rod, and less than 10 percent get skunked," she said. "Our season lasts from March to September, but most spring bookings are for whale watchers."

But the town is not just for sportfishermen. A lovely lighthouse guards the northern entrance to Barkley Sound, where the tide pooling is terrific. River otter frolic in a dozen tiny coves. And just north of town is the national park with all kinds of interesting things to do.

FOOD AND LODGING   Ucluelet, British Columbia V0R 3A0

✔✔✔ **Canadian Princess Resort**   60-unit motel and staterooms, restaurant and bar. P.O. Box 939. (604) 726-7771.

✔✔ **Burley's Lodge**   Waterfront B&B. P.O. Box 550. (604) 726-4444.

✔✔ **Pacific Rim Motel** 40 units. P.O. Box 172. (604) 726-7728.

✔✔ **Sea Side Motel** 15 units. P.O. Box 164. (604) 726-4624.

✔✔ **Thornton Motel** 19 units, restaurant, bar. P.O. Box 490. (604) 726-7725.

PACIFIC RIM NATIONAL PARK'S LONG BEACH UNIT

Of all of its umpteen thousand miles of shoreline, this twelve-mile strand is Canada's only beach on the Pacific Ocean that can be driven to, and it is a beauty. In a few spots, rocky, spruce-covered minicapes jut out into the sea, but mostly the almost continuous stretch of sand is backed by low-lying bogs. A couple of offshore rocks provide a place for Stellar's and California sea lions to haul out and bask in the sun. Parking is available adjacent to the sand at three places, and four short trails lead to more isolated spots. The sea here is big enough to attract surfers, and as on the coast of Washington, the back of the beach is a pile of drift logs.

Hope for a sunny day so you can watch the sunset. I tried, and it didn't work, but locals insist that, given an unobstructed horizon, if you watch carefully just as the last trace of the sun's ball disappears, you'll see the celebrated "green flash," the Pacific Rim's answer to Switzerland's *alpenglühen,* the fiery-pink alpine glow that graces the highest peaks at sunset.

I found the rain forest here even more enchanting than at the Hoh, because the hanging gardens of moss and licorice fern seem to ooze and drip no matter what the weather. Other mosses dangle in gossamer streamers, dividing the forest into intimate green chambers. The amamabalis fir is a tree we haven't seen before, and there are specimens of the Nootka cypress, first identified by Menzies of the Vancouver expedition. Two short, self-guided trails lead into the woods.

A careful walk along the self-guided **Shorpine Bog Trail** provides some fascinating insights into this country. The retreating glacier left a clayey hardpan bowl that collects some of the twelve feet of rain that falls here each year. About four hundred years ago, sphagnum (pronounced "s-FAG-num") invaded the area, and although spongy at the surface, when compacted by its own weight it creates an acidic peat. Tannic acid, released by the sphagnum, kills bacteria and prevents decay—so it builds up, drawing water like a wick. Whereas most lakes gradually silt up, becoming marshes, then meadows, and finally forests, this bog goes the other way. The water level keeps rising, drowning all trees but the hardy shore pine. Slow to grow and slow to die, some trees live three hundred years yet gain only ten or so feet in height—a true "pygmy forest." Part of the boardwalk trail leads through a slightly higher area where water runs off, allowing bacteria to flourish. The result is an explosion of ferns, shrubs, and trees that make up the tangled, almost impassable thicket of the muskeg forest. A sizable portion of northern Canada is muskeg, and it is easy to see why early explorers hated it so.

The park is not all wilderness. An interpretive center is located along the highway, there is a golf course on the northern end, and a lovely restaurant overlooks the surf at Wickaninnish Bay. Included in that complex is a well-done display of native art and artifacts. Wickaninnish, according to Captain Barkley, was as powerful and wealthy a chief as Maquinna, a fellow we'll meet in the next chapter.

FOOD AND LODGING   Pacific Rim National Park, Long Beach Unit

✔ **Green Point Campground**   92 campsites.

✔ **Schooner Cove**   Walk-in campground.

●● **Wickaninnish Restaurant**   First-class dining overlooking the Pacific, bar.

Tofino • Population: 700

Little Tofino, guarding the entrance to Clayoquot Sound, is about as pretty a fishing village as I have ever seen. Green-and-brown cone-shaped peaks loom up across narrow inlets, making the place look like a cold-water Na Pali coast. Explorers Galiano and Valdés, who came here in 1792, named the bay after the Spanish hydrographer Vincenté Clayoquot. Civic boosters say there is a growing artists' colony here, though I suspect most clear out in the winter. The town is a bit upscale with an old-fashioned hotel and several restaurants, some art galleries, and a few tackle shops. Most places to stay are a few miles south along the beach. The smallish **Westcoast Maritime Museum** is here.

Clayoquot Sound is said to teem with Dungeness crab. Robert Gray wintered here in 1791 while he built a small sloop. All trace of his Fort Defiance is gone, but archaeologists did find a few relics, so they know its exact location. **Tonquin Park,** located at the end of a short trail, is an especially nice place for a picnic, where you can reflect on the fate of Captain Jonathan Thorn and the crew of *Tonquin* (see The Star-Crossed Astorians, Chapter 13). Adventuresome types might take the daily float plane to **Hot Springs Cove,** where you can lounge in a steaming pool or stand under a natural hot shower while watching the fishing boats go by. It is located on the Pacific shore of a roadless island twenty miles north of here.

FOOD AND LODGING   Tofino, British Columbia V0R 2Z0

✔✔✔ **Clayoquot Lodge**   9-unit fishing lodge on a private island. P.O. Box 188. (604) 725-3998.

✔✔ **MacKenzie Beach Resort**   12 cottages. P.O. Box 12. (604) 725-3439.

✔✔ **Ocean Village Resort**   48-unit cottages along beach. P.O. Box 237. (604) 725-3322.

✔✔ **Pacific Sands Beach Resort**   40 apartments. P.O. Box 237. (604) 725-3322.

●● **The Loft**   Restaurant and bar. (604) 725-4241.

A sign, near the wharf, states quite correctly that this is the true end of the Trans-Canada Highway and is, in a sense, the end of the continent. This is both the northernmost and westernmost place you can drive to in North America that looks directly out onto the Pacific. It is the logical place to end our long journey save for one fact: much of the early history of the Northwestern Pacific Coast took place at a cove just inside the mouth of the next sound north. Since it's such a mellow place, and getting there is so much fun, we'll visit Nootka next.

20

NOOTKA SOUND

A Friendly Harbor

As you proceed northward from Qualicum Beach (Chapter 18), the countryside begins to change. Vancouver Island's spine moves closer to the inside coast, there is less farmland, towns are spaced farther apart. The Strait of Georgia seems narrower, though it is giant Texada Island you are looking out at, not the mainland. Finally, at Campbell River, any semblance of gentleness disappears; mountains hug the shore. Georgia Strait simply merges into a series of island-dotted channels; Vancouver Island, for all intents and purposes, becomes part of the mainland—only here the mainland is virtually uninhabitable. For the next 250 miles north, not a single road penetrates the interior, and then what you find is one so little used it wasn't worth paving. On the island, some tiny towns are growing because of the "Inland Passage" trade, but for the most part we're at the end of the peopled part of our journey.

Early explorers found themselves cruising through a maze of waterways, sailing up what they thought were passes, only to find themselves thwarted at the head of a bay. Apparently they were somewhat at a loss as to how to name what they were seeing; our modern maps describe these waterways as bays, coves, arms, passes, canals, channels, straits, inlets, harbors (and harbours), sounds, and passages. When George Vancouver in *Discovery* lay off of present-day Campbell River, he knew he was about to enter a channel or passage and not an arm or bay, simply because he paid attention to the tidal currents. They were coming from the north, not the south.

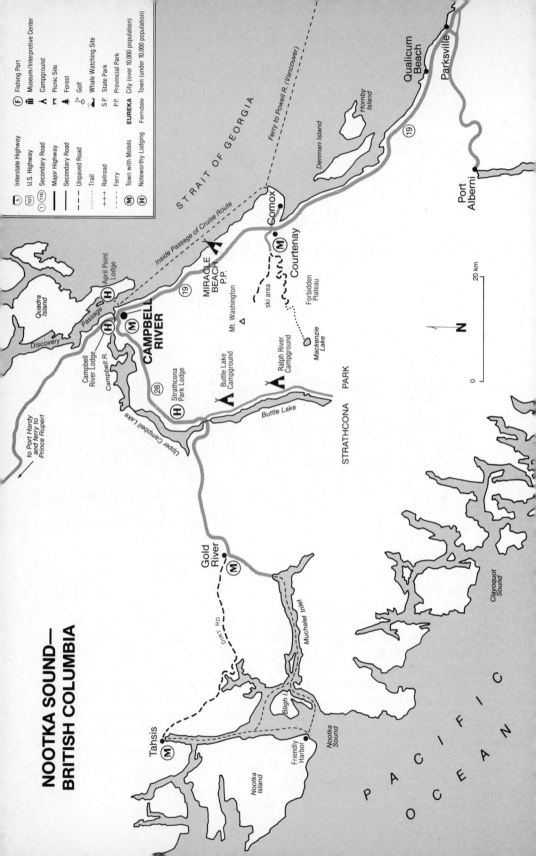

NOOTKA SOUND—
BRITISH COLUMBIA

Legend:

Symbol	Description	Symbol	Description
5	Interstate Highway	F	Fishing Port
101	U.S. Highway	🏛	Museum/Interpretive Center
1 116	Secondary Road	⚑	Campground
—	Major Highway	🏕	Picnic Site
—	Secondary Road	🌲	Forest
---	Unpaved Road	⛳	Golf
····	Trail	🐋	Whale Watching Site
+++	Railroad	S.P.	State Park
	Ferry	P.P.	Provincial Park
M	Town with Motels	EUREKA	City (over 10,000 population)
H	Noteworthy Lodging	Ferndale	Town (under 10,000 population)

STRAIT OF GEORGIA

Ferry to Powell R. (Vancouver)

Inside Passage of Cruise Route

Qualicum Beach

Parksville

⑲

Hornby Island

Denman Island

Comox

M Courtenay

ski area

Forbidden Plateau

Port Alberni

April Point Lodge

Quadra Island

H

Discovery Passage

H Campbell River Lodge

M CAMPBELL RIVER

Campbell R.

⑲ MIRACLE BEACH P.P.

Mt. Washington △

Mackenzie Lake

Ralph River Campground

28

H Strathcona Park Lodge

Upper Campbell Lake

Buttle Lake Campground

Buttle Lake

STRATHCONA PARK

STRATHCONA PARK

to Port Hardy and ferry to Prince Rupert

Gold River M

DIRT RD.

Muchalet Inlet

Bligh

Tahsis M

Friendly Harbor

Nootka Sound

Nootka Island

PACIFIC OCEAN

Clayoquot Sound

N

0   20 km

Of British Columbia's vast area, only 5 percent is used for agricultural or grazing purposes; urban use adds perhaps another 5 percent. Forests cover 55 percent of the land, and the rest is muskeg, alpine scrub, ice fields, and freshwater lakes. Much of that forestland is on northern Vancouver Island, and it is this rich timber harvest that justifies the existence of any roads or villages at all. We can visit Nootka Sound today, simply because its surrounding hillsides are a mother lode of timber.

Shortcut Access to Nootka Sound

As noted in Chapter 19, B.C. Ferries' boats sail from Horseshoe Bay near Vancouver to Nanaimo, an hour and a half drive south of Courtenay. A more scenic alternative is to drive the so-called Sunshine Coast, the eastern shore of Georgia Strait. Two ferry crossings are required to get to Powell River, where you catch a cross-sound ferry to Comox. Four boats a day make that 1¼-hour crossing.

Courtenay/Comox • Population: 16,900

Courtenay is the principal trading area for up-islanders, with a pleasant downtown fringing Comox Harbour. Its twin city, Comox (don't try and make a French name out of it), has a small fishing fleet anchored near the town center. A number of motels have sprung up along the Island Highway, thanks in part to the excellent skiing on nearby Mt. Washington.

**FOOD AND LODGING   Courtenay/Comox,
British Columbia**

✔✔ **Collingwood Inn**   60-unit downtown motel. 1590 Cliffe Avenue, V9N 2K6. (604) 338-1454.

✔✔ **The Kingfisher Inn**   30-unit motel five miles south of town. Restaurant and bar, pool. 4330 South Island Highway, V9N 5M8. (604) 338-1323.

✔✔ **The Westerly**   110-unit motel overlooking Courtenay River. Restaurant, bar, pool. 1590 Cliffe Avenue, V9N 2K4. (604) 338-7741.

✔ **Miracle Beach Provincial Park**   193 campsites.

FORBIDDEN PLATEAU

How can a curious traveler resist going to a place called Forbidden Plateau? Stories vary, but it seems that when the men were out hunting, all the Komox women and children were snatched out of their longhouses by some sort of evil thing (take your pick) and hauled into the nearby mountains, never to be seen again. After that, no Indian ever dared go there. The plateau is a portion of Strathcona Provincial Park, named after a fellow who helped get the railroad built (see Lord Strathcona, below). Some old logging roads lead into the lush interior from the Forbidden Plateau ski area. MacKenzie Lake, said to have good trout fishing, makes a nice day-hike destination. During the summer, a chair lift takes the drudgery out of the first part of the walk.

LORD STRATHCONA

I guess if I had been in Queen Victoria's shoes, I would have done the same thing—make Donald A. Smith a lord of the realm, that is. He got the railroad finished, and that was reason enough. If he hadn't, British Columbia would certainly have gone the same way as some other English colonies in North America a century earlier. The French Canadians of Quebec couldn't have cared less if that had happened, but the four other provinces, Nova Scotia, New Brunswick, Ontario, and Manitoba, thought otherwise. They dearly wanted British Columbia in the federation, and as it turned out, it would cost them dearly. As an inducement to become part of the dominion, Premier John Macdonald had promised that in ten years they would have a railway.

It's hard for Americans, looking at modern, bustling Canada, our biggest trading partner, to realize that on the eve of dominion in 1867 (the word "kingdom" was rejected), the country had less than three million people living in an area second only to Russia in size. That's about the present population of British Columbia. The cost to build a railroad to the West didn't seem worth it; "insane" was the word the opposition leader, Alexander Mackenzie, had used.

But some Americans had different ideas. After the dust of the Civil War had settled, politicians looked west; in 1869 a U.S. Senate committee report declared:

The opening by us first of a Northern Pacific railroad seals the destiny of the British possessions west of the ninety-first meridian. They will become so Americanized in interests and feelings that they will be in effect severed from the new Dominion, and the question of their annexation will be but a question of time.

It didn't happen, of course, but several times the Canadian Pacific Railroad was on the verge of bankruptcy. But by hook or by crook (plenty of the latter), the Canadians got here in time. One of those most responsible was a dour Scotsman, an ex–Hudson's Bay Company man who had gotten rich off the spoils of Manitoba. As Pierre Berton described him in his book *The National Dream/ The Last Spike:*

> There was something a little frightening about Donald A. Smith. Perhaps it was the eyebrows—those bristling, tangled tufts that jutted out to mask the cold, uncommunicative gray eyes and provide their owner with a perpetual frown. At fifty-eight, Smith had the stern look of a Biblical patriarch.

Smith had become partners in a railroad venture with James J. Hill, the Canadian expatriate who got his own title, "the Empire Builder," for having finished the Great Northern Railway across North Dakota, Montana, Idaho, and Washington. With profits from the shipment of the grain harvests of the valley of the Red River of the North, the future lord became enormously wealthy and with his cousin, George Stephen, bankrolled the Canadian Pacific venture, even after the government refused more aid. For that bit of self-sacrifice, Queen Victoria not only bestowed upon him a knighthood, but later elevated him to the peerage with the rather grand title of duke of Strathcona and Mount Royal. The railway was completed, not in ten years as promised, but completed. On November 6, 1885, at Craigellachie, British Columbia (which he named after a symbolic rock in his native Scotland), Donald A. Smith got the honor of driving the last spike. On the first blow, he missed.

Campbell River • Population: 17,000 (double that in salmon season)

If you believe the Chamber of Commerce's literature, Campbell River, not Port Alberni, is the salmon capital of the world. At the risk of offending Alberniites, I think the folks in Campbell River are right, certainly from a historical standpoint. Ever since 1923, when Edward Painter established a fishing camp on Tyee Spit, the fame of Campbell River has spread, drawing rich and famous people from all over the world. The spawning grounds of Campbell River and the currents and tides of Discovery Passage combine to make this a truly remarkable fishery. Traditionally it has been a rich man's sport; you need a boat, and unless you know the waters, you have to hire a guide (two hundred here are licensed). But the city recently constructed a pier that juts out into the pass and then parallels the flow of the water. Now anyone with a rod and a license can have a shot at the big one.

True sportsmen, however, look down on those with big tackle and heavy weights who barge up the pass in overpowered boats "looking for meat." Sixty years ago they formed the **Tyee Club,** exclusive only in the sense that it is difficult to join. Officially, a *tyee* (an Indian word meaning "chief") is any mature chinook weighing more than thirty pounds. To become a member you have to catch one, but only under supervised conditions. You must fish from a rowboat, use a rod of a maximum size with tackle of less than twenty-pound test, and the lure must conform to certain specifications, including the lack of a barb. No "jigging," either. I talked to a member who related the now widespread story of the fellow who did things just right and caught an incredible fifty-eight-pounder. The trouble was, he had broken his rod that spring, and the fellow who fixed it made it half an inch too long.

The newly built Tyee Plaza provides a nice focus for the downtown shopping area. A statue of a high climber, his axe dangling from a rope around his middle, boldly stands lashed to the top of a sixty-foot-high tree. In *The Last Wilderness*, Murray Morgan described this knight of the forest:

> No sight in the woods is more thrilling than that of the high climber working on a great spar—the tiny man against the giant. The climactic moment came when the top finally went crashing to the ground and sent the spar into a sudden, violent motion. Then, while the spar jerks and vibrates, the . . . high rider as often as not waves his free hand like a bronc rider or climbs the last few feet to the still-quivering bole and stands on his head.

Campbell River has a bit of an old-world flavor, the best eating being at the Bavarian Dining Room, curiously located in the Austrian Chalet Motel. One would have thought they'd have picked an Austrian rather than German state name—the Tyrolean Dining Room, perhaps. Nevertheless, the food is great and the rathskeller cozy.

FOOD AND LODGING   Campbell River, British Columbia

✔✔✔ **April Point Lodge**   28-room deluxe fishing resort on Quadra Island. Restaurant and bar. P.O. Box 1, V9W 4Z9. (604) 285-3329.

✔✔✔ **Campbell River Lodge**   30-room river's-edge fishing resort. Restaurant and bar. 1760 Island Highway, V9W 2E7. (604) 287-7446.

✔✔✔ **Coast Discovery Inn**   100-room, six-story, full-service downtown hotel overlooking yacht basin. 975 Tyee Plaza, V9W 2C5. (604) 287-7155.

✔✔ **Anchor Inn**   78-room motel overlooking Discovery Passage. Restaurant and bar. 261 Island Highway, V9W 2B3. (604) 286-1131.

✔✔ **Austrian Chalet Village**   51-unit motel, restaurant and bar. 462 South Island Highway, V9W 1A5. (604) 923-4231.

✔✔ **Marina Inn**   56-unit motel, restaurant and bar. 1430 South Island Highway, V9W 1B7. (604) 923-7255.

✔ **Elk Falls Provincial Park**   121 campsites.

●● **Bavarian Dining Room**   (604) 923-4202.

INSIDE PASSAGE • (The final escape!)

Most tourists who visit Campbell River continue on up-island another 140 miles to **Port Hardy,** where they catch B.C. Ferries' boat to Prince Rupert. The ship used to sail from Kelsey Bay, only fifty miles from here, on a voyage that took twenty hours. During the summer they couldn't satisfy the demand for staterooms, so when the Island Highway was extended, *Queen of Prince Rupert* was moved to the Queen Charolete Islands run, and the new and larger *Queen of the North* was put on the "Inside Passage" route. She sails northbound one day, southbound the next, making the trip in fifteen (mostly daylight) hours. She arrives about 10:00 P.M., and those sailing north have to be at the dock at 6:30 A.M., so Port Hardy's innkeepers find themselves full to the brim one night with both arriving and departing passengers and empty the next.

FOOD AND LODGING   Port Hardy, British Columbia V0N 2P0

✔✔ **Best Western Port Hardy Inn**   84-unit motel. P.O. Box 1798. (604) 949-8525.

✔✔ **Glen Lyon Inn**   28-unit motel. P.O. Box 103. (604) 949-7115.

✔✔ **Seagate Hotel**   84-unit motor hotel. P.O. Box 28. (604) 949-6348.

STRATHCONA PROVINCIAL PARK

You bid adieu to the tourist world when you leave the Island Highway at Campbell River and go west on Highway 28. The road to Gold River is first class and paved all the way. An hour and a half is ample time to get to the dock on the Muchalat Inlet, where you catch the boat to Nootka. But allow time to explore the northern end of Strathcona Provincial Park. A paved road skirts along the bank of skinny, eighteen-mile-long Buttle Lake, which, if the water were salt, we would call a fjord. Two campgrounds hug the shore, and there are easy nature trails to Lupin Falls, Karst Creek, and Myra Falls.

In the late 1950s Jim and Myrna Bouldings started a summer youth camp along the shores of Upper Campbell Lake. They specialized in outdoor education, and their clientele grew both in numbers and in age, so that now activities range from youth leadership programs to Elderhostel courses in local ecology. People of all ages come to develop skills in canoeing, kayaking, sailing, rock climbing, ski touring, backpacking, winter camping, and animal tracking. Strathcona Park Lodge developed out of these programs. It's hardly a children's camp anymore. Guests stay in lodge rooms or in cottages overlooking the lake, meals are prix fixe, and there is a bar for the grown-ups.

FOOD AND LODGING

✔✔ **Strathcona Park Lodge**   47 rooms and cottages, restaurant and bar. P.O. Box 2160, Campbell River V9W 5C9. (604) 286-2008.

✔ **Buttle Lake**   85 campsites.

✔ **Ralph River**   76 campsites.

Gold River • Population: 2,300

It took barely six months for Gold River to go from nothing to a respectable town. In 1956 this site was chosen to house the workers employed in the new mill eight miles farther down the road at the head of Muchalet Inlet. For tourists, the primary attraction is that Gold River is a nice place to spend the night before boarding *Uchuck III*, and a ride on this stalwart vessel is simply a dandy way to end this expedition of discovery.

FOOD AND LODGING   Gold River, British Columbia V0P 1G0

✔✔ **Coast Gold River Chalet**   91-unit motel, restaurant. P.O. Box 10. (604) 283-2244.

NOOTKA SOUND'S *UCHUCK III*

Strangely, the very fact that there are so few roads on Vancouver's outside means you can actually get a closer view of what's going on than you otherwise might. You have an amazing opportunity to peer into the past, because what happened a hundred years ago along the Mendocino coast is happening here right now. For the people who work in the woods, a "coastal packet" provides the only link to the outside world. The commerce of the island is happening right before your eyes, because virtually all of a lumber camp's supplies are brought out in *Uchuck III*'s hold. While waiting for the ship to sail, I watched in amazement as deckhands worked the ship's crane, hoisting aboard crates of lettuce and tomatoes, bakery products, unpackaged sheet metal ducts, a repaired set of jaws for a giant logging machine, spools of wire rope, bottles of propane, and dozens of huge tires. A tiny forklift truck belowdeck shuttled the merchandise around in a hold that ran the length of the ship. Deckhands then covered the hatch and set about loading two fair-size trucks aboard. *Uchuck III* is half again as big as *Lady Rose*, but I couldn't imagine where they were going to put those trucks. They had done it before, obviously, because each crewman knew just what to do. Stools, made out of steel pipes, were set on the deck. Cradles were placed under each truck's wheels and connected to cables running to the ship's davits. A fellow standing near the bow operated the machinery that swung the vehicles aboard. The truck's inside wheels fitted nicely on the stools while the outside wheels simply dangled out over the water.

Another show was being staged at the nearby mill. Log trucks lined up under a giant A-frame called a "Bohemian boom," and in a matter of minutes a rope was slung around their loads and the logs lifted off and summarily dropped into the water. That's when the show really began. A tiny ten-foot-long boat, with a hull shaped like a walnut shell, started riding herd on the logs. Called "boom boats" or "log broncs," their powerful engine drives a propeller that can be steered in any direction, giving the craft an amazing agility. The operator swung the craft around, put the bow up on a log and nudged it ahead, swung back for a different angle of attack, and repeated the process over and over, bobbing, weaving, rocking, and twirling as though he were doing a pirouette on a ballet stage (though I'm sure he would rather have been compared with a range rider rounding up a stray dogie). A fleet of these aquatic acrobats performed at Vancouver's Expo in 1986.

Fewer tourists ride *Uchuck III* than *Lady Rose*, so Master (not

Captain—that title is not proper for a ship of this type) David Young felt comfortable inviting me onto the bridge. The ship's five-foot-diameter oak wheel was as well polished as the twin-handled brass engine-room telegraph nearby. Two diesels power this relic from World War II. "She's the only wooden-hulled ship still licensed to carry passengers," Dave told me. "The old gal was built in Portland, Oregon, to be a mine sweeper. That's why the three-inch-thick fir planking, but she is still a good ship, and we have kept her well maintained and up to date."

Of that, I had no question—nor of his seamanship. Even though it was a clear day, every turn of the wheel brought a new entry into the log. "It's a good habit," Dave said. "Some days are foggy, and even though we have radar, it's helpful to know what the proper heading is."

What puzzled me was how they got paid for what they were doing. Unpackaged goods, no bills of lading, nobody signing for anything. It didn't seem like a modern way of running a freight business. "Oh, they trust me," Dave replied. "My ship provides the only way these camps get their supplies, so if I don't get paid, they don't get to eat."

Our destination that day was Tahsis, another instant town like Gold River, this one with a past. Tahsis was the winter home of the great chief Maquinna, who, leading a procession of thirty-two canoes, paddled out to greet Captain Cook. The warm reception the navigator received prompted him to name the cove "Friendly Harbor." Cook soon sailed off to the Sandwich Islands, where, of course, he met his death at the hands of some warring Hawaiians. History has its strange intertwinings, however. An obscure corporal named John Ledyard from Connecticut, who was aboard *Discovery*, published an account of Cook's third voyage a full year before the official admiralty report came out. Thomas Jefferson, then ambassador to France, met Ledyard, listened to his stories about this remote country, and promptly made two attempts to smuggle him through Catherine the Great's Russia so that he could have another look around. The venture failed, Ledyard died in Cairo on his way back to America, but the episode is credited with having ignited Jefferson's interest in the West and his subsequent decision to send out Lewis and Clark.

For twenty years, meanwhile, Maquinna traded with the white man, dined on his ships, imitated his table manners, and even learned to speak his language. Robert Haswell, who spent the winter here aboard *Columbia*, wrote:

Fue incidents marked the time. The natives visited us allmost every day with fish and deer and oil and a fue skins. Our chief amusements were fouling and hunting. In both we had tolerable success. The weather was general rainey and very disagreeable.

But Maquinna felt he had been taken advantage of and, by 1803, decided he had had enough of the white man's ways. When Captain John Salter in *Boston* made an unfriendly gesture, the chief made his move. Feigning innocence, a crewman who was belowdeck during the resulting melee was allowed topside. The sight that greeted him was the heads of the captain and the rest of the crew lined up neatly along the thwart. Two years later, the suviving crewman was rescued from the Indians by one Samuel Hill in *Lydia* out of New York, a fellow who missed his chance for a prominent place in the history books. In 1805 Hill sailed into the Columbia but somehow missed a rendezvous with Lewis and Clark, who were then building Fort Clatsop barely ten miles away.

Nootka Sound is every bit as pretty as Barkley Sound and even wilder. Jack McCullough, a log truck driver from Gabriola Island, told me they don't bother to cut above three thousand feet. "At this latitude, the trees are too small," he explained. *Uchuck III*, I learned, is not big enough to haul the really heavy equipment, so the timber companies barge out a bulldozer to clear a staging area and then build some crude roads up into the woods. Then they barge out the "steel tree" (the modern equivalent of the spar tree) and the big rigs they use to get the logs down to the water. The houses are floated out, too, so presto— you have a logging camp. We called on half a dozen that day— some twice, because we picked up propane bottles, offloaded them at Tahsis for refilling, and then carried them back on the return voyage.

We tourists ate in the lounge or paced the deck looking for eagles. John Lloyd from Saltspring Island said he once saw sixty-seven on a single voyage. "They must have come in from out of state," he chortled. We steamed past Gore Island, honoring the lieutenant who brought Cook's ships home to England, and by Bligh Island, named for Cook's navigator. Near Friendly Harbor, a couple got on proudly carrying a box full of iced salmon.

For information, write or call M.V. UCHUCK III: Nootka Sound Service Ltd.: P.O. Box 57, Gold River, British Columbia V0P 1G0. (604) 283-2515.

Tahsis • Population: 1,739

Tahsis was a surprise, quite modern, with an oceangoing steamship docked at the sawmill wharf. The barmaid, Jacquie, told me she usually drives to town rather than take the boat, even though you have to cope with an hour and a half of potholes before getting to a paved road. This road, built in the 1970s, severely cut into *Uchuck III's* revenues, so she is now subsidized by the government.

FOOD AND LODGING TAHSIS, BRITISH COLUMBIA V0P 1X0

✔✔✔ **Nootka Island Fishing Camp**   14-room American plan resort. P.O. Box 820, Gold River V0P 1G0. Radio phone: Estavan 23 Tyee Warrior Channel N10420.

✔✔ **Coast Tahsis Chalet**   21-unit motel, restaurant and bar near boat dock. P.O. Box 400. (604) 934-6301.

~~~~~~~~~~~~~~~~~~~~~~~~~~~~~~~~~~~~~

THE NOOTKA CONVENTION

It was an irate Estivan José Martínez who, one July day in 1788, stepped aboard *Princess Royal,* ordered Captain Thomas Hudson off, and took possession of the ship for the Spanish Crown. The British captain had no right to be in Nootka Sound; it was time to show the flag. Martínez also had his men seize *Argonaut* and summarily dispatched the two vessels to Mexico. The English were outraged; after all, it was no less a person than Captain James Cook who had sailed into this harbor ten years earlier, dropped anchor, and spent a month repairing *Resolution* and *Discovery.* By right of discovery, this land belonged to King George.

Both claims had some foundation, it turned out. Fifteen years earlier Martínez had been a pilot aboard John Pérez's ship when, while trying to escape from a storm, he had sailed into Nootka Sound. Indians had come aboard and stolen a silver spoon, the same spoon Cook later reported as having seen being used as a neck ornament. Two years later, Bruno Heceta in His Catholic Majesty's Ship *Santiago* sailed by. Though the Spanish never published their discoveries and none had even gone ashore, Alexander VI's papal bull of 1493 had given Spain rights to everything that lay more than 3,700 leagues west of the Cape Verde Islands—in other words, the entire Pacific Ocean.

The British, however, had been here in force: James Hanna in 1785 and again in 1786. James Strange in *Experiment* left an officer, Dr. John Mackey, who spent a miserable year living with the Indians. Captain Barkley rescued the poor fellow a year later. John Meares, who owned the two seized vessels, had arrived with a crew of twenty Chinese laborers who promptly set to work building *Northwest America,* the first ship ever to be launched on this coast. A further clouding of the issue arose when Captain Gray and his boss, John Kendrick, arrived in *Washington* and *Columbia* and holed up for the winter at this now popular spot. (Gray sailed on to China and then to Boston, thereby becoming the first American to circumnavigate the globe.)

But it was power politics, not the niceties of the rules of possession, that decided the matter. John Meares raised a ruckus in the English press; the monarchy got belligerent and threatened war. Spain turned to France for help, but Louis XVI, burdened with his own revolution, declined. On October 28, 1790, Spain, knowing it was hopelessly outgunned, agreed to the "Nootka Convention," in which she essentially ceded any right to the Pacific Coast north of San Francisco. Meares got his two ships back and $200,000 in damages. The following year the British Crown sent George Vancouver to Nootka to iron out the details with Bodega y Quadra, and although the two didn't agree on everything, they subsequently became fast friends.

Nootka (Friendly Harbor) • Population: 4

Several days a week during the summer, *Uchuck III* makes an all-day voyage to nearby Friendly Harbor. History buffs have a couple of hours to browse around, to visit the now abandoned church, admire its stained-glass windows depicting the signing of the Nootka Convention (a gift of the Spanish government), and reflect on some of the things that went on here. In my view, it's the perfect place to end this adventure. Historically, everything comes together at Nootka. Most of the characters we have met on this sojourn (with the notable exception of Juan de Fuca), the explorers who left their names on the landscape, came here: the Englishmen, John Meares, Charles Barkley, Joseph Whidbey, Peter Puget, George Vancouver (who wins the prize for the most places named after him), and Captain Cook; two Americans, John Gray and Jonathan Thorn; and, of course, the Spaniards—Bodega y Quadra (whose name surfaced barely fifty miles north of San Francisco), Lopez de Haro, Alcala Galiano, Alejandro Malaspina, Cayetano Valdés, Don Pedro de Alberni. They all rendezvoused at Nootka, to learn the latest scuttlebutt, to trade with the Indians, to repair their ships and build new ones, to talk things over, and to bicker about who owned what (see The Nootka Convention, page 312). From 1778 on, everybody knew about San Francisco, and they knew about Nootka, but it took a long time for them to learn about what lay in between.

So how is Nootka doing today? Ray and Terry Williams are the Indian couple who live here. The people I talked to didn't know if they had any children. They also couldn't recall Ed and Pat's last name. Ed and Pat keep the lamp in the lighthouse going.

Bibliography

Alt, David D., and Donald W. Hyndman. *Roadside Geology of Northern California.* Missoula, Mont.: Mountain Press, 1975.

―――. *Roadside Geology of Oregon.* Missoula, Mont.: Mountain Press, 1978.

Berton, Pierre. *The National Dream/The Last Spike.* Toronto: McClelland and Stewart Ltd., 1974.

Chittenden, Newton. *Travels in British Columbia.* 1882. Reprint. Vancouver, B.C.: Gordon Soules Book Publishers, 1984.

Douthit, Nathan. *A Guide to Oregon South Coast History.* Coos Bay, Ore.: River West Books, 1986.

Federal Writers Project—WPA. *California: A Guide to the Golden Gate.* New York: Hastings House, 1939; Pantheon Books, 1984.

―――. *Washington: A Guide to the Evergreen State.* Portland, Ore.: Binfords & Mort, 1941.

Hart, John. *San Francisco's Wilderness Next Door.* San Rafael & London: Presidio Press, 1917.

Hayden, Mike. *A Guidebook to the Northern California Coast.* Los Angeles: Ward Ritchie, 1970.

Johnson, Bolling Arthur, ed. *Pacific Spruce Corporation.* 1926. Reprint. Newport, Ore.: Lincoln County Historical Society.

Kent, William Eugene. *The Siletz Indian Reservation 1855–1900.* Newport, Ore.: Lincoln County Historical Society, 1973.

Kesey, Ken. *Sometimes a Great Notion.* New York: Viking Press, 1964.

Lavender, David. *Land of Giants: The Drive to the Pacific Northwest, 1750–1950.* Garden City, N.J.: Doubleday & Co., 1950.

Lewis, Oscar and MacMullen, Jerry. *Bonanza Inn.* New York: A. A. Knopf, 1939.

Lillard, Charles. *Seven Shillings a Year: The History of Vancouver Island.* Ganges, B.C.: Horsdal & Schubart, 1986.

McFeely, William S. *Grant: a Biography.* New York: Norton, 1981.

McKelvie, B. A. *Pagent of B.C.* Scarborough, Ontario: Nelson Canada, 1953.

McNairn, Jack. *Ships of the Redwood Coast.* Stanford: Stanford University Press, 1945.

Makah Cultural and Research Center and Washington State Historical Society. *Portrait in Time: Photographs of the Makah by Samuel G. Morse, 1896–1903.* Seattle, 1987.

Morgan, Murray. *The Last Wilderness.* New York: Viking Press, 1955.

Mueller, Marge. *The San Juan Islands Afoot & Afloat.* Seattle: The Mountaineers, 1979.

Mullen, Barbara Dorr. *The Mendocino Coast.* Mendocino: Mendocino Community Land Trust, Inc., 1981.

Murray, Keith. *The Pig War.* Tacoma, Wash.: Washington State Historical Society, 1968.

Obee, Bruce. *The Gulf Islands.* North Vancouver, B.C.: Whitecap Books, 1985.

————. *The Pacific Rim Explorer.* North Vancouver, B.C.: Whitecap Books, 1986.

Perry, John, and Jane Greverus Perry. *The Sierra Club Guide to the Natural Areas of California.* San Francisco: Sierra Club Books, 1983.

————. *The Sierra Club Guide to the Natural Areas of Oregon and Washington.* San Francisco: Sierra Club Books, 1983.

Powers, Alfred. *Redwood Country: The Lava Region and the Redwoods.* New York: Duell, Sloan and Pearce, 1949.

Weaver, Harriett E. *Adventures in the Redwoods.* San Francisco: Chronicle Books, 1975.

Williams, Paul M. *Oregon Coast Hikes.* Seattle: The Mountaineers, 1975.

Wood, Robert L. *Across the Olympic Mountains: The Press Expedition, 1889–90.* Seattle: The Mountaineers, 1967.

INDEX

317